Windows Terminal Services

Windows® Terminal Services

Christa Anderson

San Francisco   London

Associate Publisher: Neil Edde
Acquisitions Editor: Chris Denny
Developmental Editor: Brianne Agatep
Editor: Kathy Grider-Carlyle
Production Editor: Liz Burke
Technical Editor: Scott Warmbrand
Book Designer: Bill Gibson
Electronic Publishing Specialist: Judy Fung
Proofreaders: Laurie O'Connell, Nancy Riddiough, Nelson Kim, Amey Garber
Indexer: Ted Laux
Cover Designer: Ingalls & Associates
Cover Illustrator: Ingalls & Associates

Copyright © 2003 SYBEX Inc., 1151 Marina Village Parkway, Alameda, CA 94501. World rights reserved. No part of this publication may be stored in a retrieval system, transmitted, or reproduced in any way, including but not limited to photocopy, photograph, magnetic, or other record, without the prior agreement and written permission of the publisher.

Library of Congress Card Number: 2002109627

ISBN: 0-7821-2895-5

SYBEX and the SYBEX logo are either registered trademarks or trademarks of SYBEX Inc. in the United States and/or other countries.

Screen reproductions produced with FullShot 99. FullShot 99 © 1991-1999 Inbit Incorporated. All rights reserved. FullShot is a trademark of Inbit Incorporated.

Internet screen shot(s) using Microsoft Internet Explorer 5 reprinted by permission from Microsoft Corporation.

TRADEMARKS: SYBEX has attempted throughout this book to distinguish proprietary trademarks from descriptive terms by following the capitalization style used by the manufacturer.

The author and publisher have made their best efforts to prepare this book, and the content is based upon final release software whenever possible. Portions of the manuscript may be based upon pre-release versions supplied by software manufacturer(s). The author and the publisher make no representation or warranties of any kind with regard to the completeness or accuracy of the contents herein and accept no liability of any kind including but not limited to performance, merchantability, fitness for any particular purpose, or any losses or damages of any kind caused or alleged to be caused directly or indirectly from this book.

Manufactured in the United States of America

10 9 8 7 6 5 4 3 2 1

This book is dedicated to everyone who ever read Windows and .NET Magazine *(and its previous incarnations), or the* UPDATE *newsletters in which I covered server-based computing, and wrote to tell me an article was great—but when was I writing the book? Here it is, and thank you for the encouragement. This book is for you.*

Acknowledgments

This book was a long time in conception. I've been writing about Terminal Services and server-based computing in general for several years now, but this is the first time I have put all that information together into a single book. Figuring out how to tell the story as a whole was quite a job, and I'm deeply grateful to everyone who helped me do it.

That "everyone" makes a long list. Chris Denny got the project going and shepherded it along until he was promoted (Congratulations, Chris!), when Brianne Agatep took it over and continued the great work. Kathy Grider-Carlyle's excellent copy editing caught grammatical errors and generally made sure that I said what I meant. Many thanks also to technical editor Scott Warmbrand, who checked and verified everything. Once the writing and editing was finished, Liz Burke managed the production process to get the book from its electronic form to the object you're holding in your hands, and compositor, Judy Fung, created these pages with precision and expertise. Proofreaders, Laurie O'Connell, Nancy Riddiough, Nelson Kim, and Amey Garber checked each line of the copy before printing to eliminate any final copy errors. And I can't forget Mark Minasi, who asked me to write this book for his series.

Contents at a Glance

Introduction . . . . *xiv*

Chapter 1   Introducing Windows Terminal Services 1

Chapter 2   Core Parts of Windows Terminal Services 31

Chapter 3   Planning the Terminal Server Environment 77

Chapter 4   Rolling Out Terminal Services 109

Chapter 5   Preparing Client Connections 175

Chapter 6   Managing Terminal Sessions 239

Chapter 7   Installing and Tuning Applications on an Application Server 265

Chapter 8   Supporting Printing in a Multiuser Environment 341

Chapter 9   Ongoing Server Management 375

Appendix A   Additional Reading and Resources 425

Index *437*

Contents

Introduction . . . . *xiv*

Chapter 1 **Introducing Windows Terminal Services** 1
    Origins of Windows Terminal Services 2
        Citrix and Multi-Win Emerge 3
        Microsoft Gets into the Act 4
        Comparing Windows Terminal Services and MetaFrame . 18
    Applying Windows Terminal Services 22
        Lower Maintenance 23
        Supporting Multiple Offices 23
        Simplifying the User Interface 24
        Support for Windows Terminals 25
        Why Terminal Services Are Not a Universal Fix 27
    Summary 30

Chapter 2 **Core Parts of Windows Terminal Services** 31
    The Server-Based Computing Processing Model 31
        Processor Allocating Basics 32
        Memory in a Multiuser Environment 34
    Running Sessions on an Application Server 37
        The RDP Display Protocol 37
        The ICA Display Protocol 38
        How Sessions Are Initialized 38
        Connecting to a Session 39
        Disconnecting from and Reconnecting to a Session . . . 40
    MetaFrame-Specific Concepts: IMA Architecture 41
        Background: Why MetaFrame XP Has a New Organizational
            Model 42
        How MetaFrame XP Servers Communicate 43
        Accessing Farm Information: Understanding Direct and
            Indirect Mode and the Local Host Cache 45

	The Terminal Server ToolKit	46
	Windows 2000–Specific Application server Management Tools	46
	MetaFrame XP–Specific Tools	55
	Supported Client Types	65
	Personal Computers	65
	Windows Terminals	66
	Handheld PCs	66
	Licensing Terminal Services	66
	Windows 2000 Server Access Licensing	66
	Application Licensing	75
	Summary	75
Chapter 3	**Planning the Terminal Server Environment**	**77**
	Planning the Server Side	77
	Choosing Server Roles	77
	Terminal Server Sizing	78
	How Many Servers Do You Need?	93
	Adding MetaFrame XP	94
	Planning for the Citrix Management Console	98
	Reducing Bandwidth Requirements	99
	Choosing Client Types	99
	User Training	106
	Summary	107
Chapter 4	**Rolling Out Terminal Services**	**109**
	Installing Terminal Services	109
	Installing Terminal Services on an Existing Windows 2000 Server	110
	Automatically Deploying Terminal Servers	119
	Remote Installation Services	136
	Customizing Menus to Make Terminal Services Optional	146
	Installing MetaFrame XP	155
	Setting Up The Data Store	155

	Setting up Network Connections and Shadowing	157
	Configuring Drive Letter Mappings	159
	Configuring Web Services	159
	Final Touches: ICA Files and Licensing	160
	Applying Updates to MetaFrame XP	160
	Rolling Out the ICA Client	161
	Unattended Installations	161
	Preparing a MetaFrame Server for Cloning	169
	Upgrading to MetaFrame XP	170
	Summary	174
Chapter 5	**Preparing Client Connections**	**175**
	Creating Client Connections	175
	Setting Up PC Support	176
	Setting Up and Creating Connections on a Windows Terminal	212
	Setting Up a Handheld PC	215
	Updating Client Display Protocols	217
	Editing Server-Side Session Settings	217
	Configuring RDP Settings	218
	Editing ICA Settings	231
	Summary	237
Chapter 6	**Managing Terminal Sessions**	**239**
	Using Standard Management Tools	240
	Permitting People to Manage Servers	240
	Gathering User and Process Information	244
	Sending Messages	248
	Terminating Applications	251
	Taking Control of User Sessions	252
	Ending—or Preventing—User Sessions	259
	Shutting Down the Server	261
	Controlling User Connections	262
	Summary	264

Chapter	7	**Installing and Tuning Applications on an Application Server . . 265**

How Applications Work in a Shared Environment 265
    Choosing Applications 266
    How Application Installation Works 269
    Installing Multiuser-Enabled Applications 272
Tuning Installed Applications. 272
    Why Do We Need to Tune Applications? 273
    Editing Application Settings Manually 277
    Application Compatibility Scripts 278
    Registry Settings for Application Tuning 283
Publishing Applications with MetaFrame XP. 290
    Publishing Applications to Program Neighborhood . . . 291
    Publishing Desktops 299
    Publishing Content 299
Load Balancing Application Servers 300
    How Load Manager Determines Where to Start an ICA
        Session 300
    Understanding the Built-In Load Balancing Evaluators . . 302
    Applying Load Evaluators 303
    Creating Custom Load Evaluators. 305
    Renaming and Deleting Load Evaluators 314
Installing Applications with Installation Manager 314
    Installing Installation Manager. 316
    Packaging Applications and Hotfixes for Installation . . 319
    Using Citrix Packager to Build or Edit Project Files . . 328
    Restoring the Packaging Server 330
    Publishing Packages 331
    Creating Server Groups for Application Deployment . . 333
    Scheduling Installation Jobs 335
    Troubleshooting Installation Jobs. 337
Summary 339

Chapter 8		**Supporting Printing in a Multiuser Environment**	**341**
		How Windows 2000 Printing Works	341
		Printing Pieces	342
		The Printing Process (and Why Printing Can Be Problematic)	345
		Controlling Driver Distribution	348
		The Universal Printer Driver	348
		Using MetaFrame XP's Printer Driver Distribution System	351
		Authorizing Driver Installation	355
		Uninstalling Old Drivers	356
		Correcting Driver Name Mismatches	357
		Windows 2000 Terminal Servers	357
		MetaFrame XP Servers	358
		Controlling Bandwidth Requirements	360
		Controlling Client Printer Usage	362
		Printer Settings for RDP and ICA Users	362
		Assigning Printers to User Accounts	369
		Manually Mapping Printers to Terminal Sessions	371
		Summary	373
Chapter 9		**Ongoing Server Management**	**375**
		Securing Application Servers	375
		Server Security	376
		Network Security	392
		Client Security	396
		Checking Resource Usage	398
		Windows 2000 System Monitor	398
		Resource Manager (MetaFrame XPe)	412
		Summary	423
Appendix A		**Additional Reading and Resources**	**425**
		Basic Administrative Scripting Concepts	425
		Scripting Hosts and Script Engines	426
		Statements and Comments	427

VBScript Data Types 427
Operators. 428
Procedures 428
Objects, Properties, and Methods. 428
Useful VBScript Statements for MetaFrame Scripting . . . 429
MetaFrame Scripting 431
Preparing to Develop (and Run) MetaFrame Scripts. . . . 431
MetaFrame Management Object Architecture. 432

Index *437*

Introduction

A while ago, I saw an interview with a comedian who'd just starred in a very successful movie. When the interviewer described him as an overnight success, the comedian objected, pointing out that he'd been working as a comedian for quite a while and had just become known. His overnight success had taken him about fifteen years.

Adoption of Windows Terminal Services hasn't taken fifteen years, but the parallel works. Multi-user Windows has been around in various forms since the early 1990s, almost as long as NT itself. However, only recently has it begun to come into its own, because only recently has it become easy for people to experiment with it. Come to think of it, many people may not have known that multi-user Windows *existed* until Windows 2000 came out. Before then, Terminal Services was available only as a separate entity from the Windows server operating system.

This book is a guide to building a working server-based computing environment, with or without the assistance of MetaFrame XP. In it, I explain what Windows 2000 Terminal Services is, tell you what's coming in .NET Server, and describe the capabilities that MetaFrame XP, the latest version of Citrix's MetaFrame helper software for Windows Terminal Services, can add to your server-based computing environment. Although you can buy a ton of additional tools to support this application's servers, I've stuck with the tools available to you in the box. Believe me when I tell you that they should keep you busy for a while.

What's in This Book

Here's a quick breakdown of topics as they come up in this book.

Chapter 1, "Introducing Windows Terminal Services," introduces Windows Terminal Services in general and goes into a little of the history of the products that support it—and which we will cover. This chapter also talks about the features of each of the products we'll discuss in this book.

After Chapter 1 discusses the separate products, Chapter 2, "Core Parts of Windows Terminal Services," discusses the general architecture of Windows Terminal Services. In this chapter, you'll learn how multiuser Windows divides processing time and memory among the processes competing for them, see how MetaFrame XP application servers communicate, see the tools available for application server administration, and learn how the licensing system works. (Here's a hint: it's complex.)

Chapter 3, "Planning the Terminal Server Environment," looks at the planning process, discussing server sizing, bandwidth needs, the costs and benefits of the various types of terminal clients, and the training that users may need.

After you've done your prep work, Chapter 4, "Rolling Out Terminal Services," explains how to enable Windows Terminal Services on a Windows 2000 computer, how to install MetaFrame XP and feature releases, and how to automate any of these tasks for a faster rollout.

When the servers are ready to go, you'll still need to get terminal clients onto the client computers, so we'll cover that in Chapter 5, "Preparing Client Connections."

Once clients can use the application servers, you'll need to keep an eye on their sessions to ensur that they can get to the resources they need. Chapter 6, "Managing Terminal Sessions," discusses session management and the ways that you can restrict user resources.

Chapter 7, "Installing and Tuning Applications on an Application Server," explains how to install applications onto application servers and make those applications available to people.

Chapter 8, "Supporting Printing in a Multiuser Environment," discusses printing in a shared computing environment.

Finally, Chapter 9, "Ongoing Server Management," discusses some server administration you may not need to do to get the application servers available, and the Appendix introduces the MetaFrame XP scripting interface for server administration independent of the Citrix Management Console or command-line tools.

Conventions Used in This Book

Any discussion of computer technology can become complex very quickly. Because this book talks about an operating system, a service on an operating system, *and* a separate third-party product that depends on that service (and sometimes gets into different versions of the service), I think we'd better sort out the terminology before we get any further.

In this context, an *application server* is a server with Terminal Services enabled in Application Server mode and intended for use by more than one person. An application server may be running any Windows server operating system that supports Terminal Services. Therefore, even though they support a form of Terminal Services that allows you to display a remote Desktop for your workstation on another computer, Windows XP computers with Remote Desktop enabled are *not* application servers because only one person can use them at a time.

Generally speaking, I'm talking about Windows 2000 Terminal Services in this book. I've explained some differences found in .NET Server (especially when it comes to the new client display capabilities). Because recent (NT 4 and later) Windows server operating systems are pretty similar in terms of base architecture, any reference to "NT-based operating systems" refers to any Windows server operating system from NT 4 on. If I refer to Windows Terminal Services on its own, I'm talking about the service, not an operating system attached to it.

The MetaFrame discussions can be interesting, because we've got three flavors of MetaFrame XP and two feature releases to deal with. When I'm referring to a feature enabled only through the addition of a feature release, I'll say so explicitly. Chapter 1 explains which features are associated with which version and feature release of MetaFrame XP.

Keeping Up-to-Date

As some of you know, I was the columnist and news editor for *Windows 2000 Magazine*'s server-based computing "UPDATE" newsletter until the advertising downturn in the tech recession ended its publication late last year. (This, sadly, can be the fate of advertising-dependent newsletters with no paid subscription base.) The loss of the newsletter bugged me (and about 40,000 other people) then and it still bugs me now; I have all this great information and little place to share it in a timely manner. The lead time for print magazines is fairly long, and the lead time for books is even longer.

There's also the matter of publishing updates to the book. Now that RC1 for .NET Server is out and (according to Microsoft) is largely feature-complete, I'd like to tell you what I learn about it. More feature releases for MetaFrame XP will also come out as we go. It'd be nice if I didn't have to wait for the next edition to tell you about the new stuff or correct errata, and it'd be nice to have a place to mention the tools that don't really fit into this book but that could be worth investigating. I also appreciate reader input. If you have a question, it's likely that someone else has the same one, so it'd be great to answer everyone's questions all at once instead of in individual e-mails. (By the way, questions are always welcome, but I can't guarantee that I will always know the answer to a very specific question with circumstances I can't duplicate, and specific, brief questions are *always* appreciated.) In my years as a writer, I've gotten a lot of helpful tips from readers who have run across a specific problem that I've never seen. I'd like to share that insight with other people who could use it—credited to you, of course, unless you specifically ask me to leave your name out of it.

Then there's stuff that doesn't actually fit in the book but is still relevant to server-based computing. I avoided talking about specific third-party products here because there are too many and I wanted to focus the discussion on what you can do with the tools in the box. However, some third-party tools fill in gaps in the core product features. I may or may not use these tools myself, but I figure that someone might want to know about them.

To address all these issues, I've decided to start a personal server-based computing newsletter, to be published as I have something to add. (Probably about once a month.) Just you and me—no advertising (although if a product comes out that sounds like it might be interesting, I'll mention it). If you want to subscribe to the newsletter, sign up at my Web site at www.isinglassconsulting.com and I'll put you on the list.

Thanks for reading!

Introducing Windows Terminal Services

Server-based computing (sometimes called *thin client computing*) refers to a computing model in which the lion's share of all application processing takes place on a centralized server, and the client is only responsible for displaying output. The alternative moniker *thin client computing* sometimes confuses the issue. What makes thin client networking and computing "thin" is not the size of the operating system nor the complexity of the apps run on the client, but how processing is distributed. In the Windows world, server-based computing depends on one—or many—*terminal servers*. These terminal servers run the same kind of operating system used by other Windows servers, with the addition of a somewhat different computing model and the addition of a service called *Terminal Services*.

In this book, I'll be talking about *Windows Terminal Services*, meaning the terminal services capability present in modern Windows NT-based operating systems. However, the multiuser capability is not unique to Windows. In fact, as you'll see here, multiuser capability was first a Unix thing, albeit one that worked a little differently from Windows Terminal Services. The function was similar, but the technology to produce it and the end result differed.

> **NOTE** In this book, I'll have occasion to refer to more than one version of multi-user Windows operating systems. Where applicable, I'll identify them by name (Windows NT, Terminal Server Edition (TSE), Windows 2000, and .NET Server), but because they're all based on the core NT architecture I'll refer to the operating system *generically* as NT.

Origins of Windows Terminal Services

As you probably know, computing started out server-based. A computer was too expensive and too unwieldy to put on an individual's desk (or even in an individual's office), so the computer had its private room and people accessed it through punch cards and, later, terminals. The terminals had no processing power locally; their sole function was to display the applications that the people using the terminals were running on the big computer in the server room.

Fast forward to the advent of the personal computer and the popularization of stand-alone computers. Windows was one of the operating systems that popularized a stand-alone environment where applications could run locally—new applications designed for a single-user environment meant that you could do things in DOS and Windows that were simply not possible on a mainframe. However, in Win2K the server OS included support for Terminal Services, and now in Windows XP even the client OS supports remote access. How did Windows move from stand-alone standard-bearer to multiuser operating system?

The process wasn't short; it took Microsoft a while to embrace the server-based model even to the extent that it has today. Originally and for many years, Microsoft operating systems were desktop-centric. Early versions of Microsoft operating systems (DOS and Windows) did not even include network support, although this became part of the core OS with Windows for Workgroups. Even after network support became part of the core OS and Microsoft introduced NT, its server operating system, Microsoft still viewed the server as a sort of central storage area but the desktop as the place where you ran applications. Unix was the multiuser OS, and Windows (and DOS, and Macintosh, and so on) was the stand-alone OS—backed by a server. Because desktop computers were very expensive in the early and mid 1990s, it took a while for computers to become considered an intrinsic part of the work—and often home—environment (at least in part because of the expense involved in purchasing and maintaining them). By the time computers became both more powerful and less expensive, the stand-alone model had already taken hold. Because Microsoft owned so much of the desktop, the fact that Microsoft was a single-user OS effectively meant that most people used the single-user model. Even with the advent of a class of service providers called *application service providers* (ASPs) who run applications on large servers that people can access using the public data networks, most people still run their home and work applications from the computer they're sitting in front of. In the late 1990s, a few consumer ASPs hit the stands, but most failed due to lack of interest. (Business ASPs have done better, but have still mostly prospered in specialized markets.)

For all the popularity of the single-user OS, other options have existed as long as the stand-alone desktop has. One, the X Window system, was developed at the Massachusetts Institute of Technology in the mid-1980s. The X protocol allows two computers to work together: one running an application and storing data and one producing the graphical output from that application. X.11 makes the machine connecting to the application host into a graphical server that processes graphical primitives for execution on the "client" machine—the one where the application's graphical output is displayed. Although X.11 provides a very rich operating environment, this richness has a couple of drawbacks. The protocol is very bandwidth-intensive, so that X in its native form does not run well over low-speed connections. X also works only with Unix clients—other types of clients cannot use it. (Several companies have tweaked the protocol to address these problems, but using these solutions requires using their software—they're not available with HP-UX or Solaris out of the box.) X Window sessions are entirely independent of each other, so that one person cannot view another's session to offer help or provide training. Some applications require a great deal of tuning to make them work properly from an X session—it's not always just a matter of finding the server with the application you want and plugging it in. And finally, you can't disconnect from one X session and reconnect to it from another computer—the sessions are negotiated between a specific client and server, so you can't put your work "away" from one client machine and then reconnect to it from another one. In short, using X sessions allows people to run applications on very powerful Unix servers as though that powerful server were their desktop machine, but otherwise looks much like working at your desktop.

Citrix and Multi-Win Emerge

Another option, and the basis to the technology we're going to cover in this book, is Multi-Win. In the late 1980s, Ed Iacobucci, then the head of the joint Microsoft/IBM design team working on OS/2, suggested to the two companies that OS/2 be enhanced to become multiuser instead of a stand-alone OS. Neither company was interested, so Iacobucci formed Citrix Systems in 1989 to develop his idea of an operating system that could support multiple users.

Citrix most often calls multiuser computing server-based computing (a term that I believe the company coined and one I like). *Server-based computing* signifies the same thing as *thin client computing* but puts the emphasis on the server—where it belongs—and does not mislead people into believing that the model requires thin client devices to work. The operating system is multiuser; the computing model is server-based computing.

The first version of Multi-Win was actually a series of extensions to OS/2—not Windows—that made the OS multiuser. Later, Citrix developed a remote protocol to allow people to use the operating system across IPX/SPX and TCP/IP networks. OS/2, as you may recall, was a good operating system, but it didn't really take off for the mass market—in no small part due to the limited number of applications available. Therefore, the next logical step for Citrix was to add the multiuser ability to a popular operating system that *did* have applications available. On that principle, they approached Microsoft again to license NT to add multiuser extensions to the operating system. Microsoft agreed. Really, the decision was a no-brainer for Microsoft. If Citrix was correct that there was a market for multiuser Windows, then Microsoft could sell applications to the people running those Windows terminal servers. If Citrix was mistaken about the potential market, then Microsoft didn't lose anything. The first version of Multi-Win for NT was based on NT 3.51.

Citrix didn't keep Multi-Win all to itself, but licensed it to several companies who used it as the basis for their own multiuser operating systems such as NCD's WinCenter.

Microsoft Gets into the Act

WinFrame had one drawback: it supported only the boxy UI used in NT 3.51. Microsoft saw the success of WinFrame and, in 1997, licensed the Multi-Win technology back from Citrix to use as the basis of the first Microsoft multiuser operating system. Released in July 1998, Windows NT, Terminal Server Edition (TSE) was based on Windows NT 4, Service Pack 3.

TSE had its following (and even halfway into 2002 still does), but it also had many drawbacks that limited its usefulness. One was support for the product. TSE and NT 4 used different service packs, because the two operating systems were different enough at the kernel level that Microsoft had to develop the fixes and patches for the multiuser operating system separately from those developed for the single-user operating system. The TSE service packs frequently trailed the NT 4 service packs by months, frustrating and confusing many customers. The confusion got even worse around the time of SP6 for TSE and NT. Problems with SP6 for NT (released many months ahead of SP6 for TSE) led Microsoft to re-release the service pack at SP6a. However, the TSE service pack (which contained the fixes in SP6a) was identified as SP6. This led to no end of confusion from people who thought that Microsoft had released only a broken service pack for the multiuser operating system.

> **NOTE** In April 2002, Microsoft released a post-SP6 hotfix rollup for TSE. If you need it (and you have already installed SP6) then you can see the list of fixes and get the rollup at http://www.microsoft.com/technet/security/news/nt4tsesr.asp.

The newness of TSE also meant that it was harder to get support from Microsoft for TSE than for NT 4. Thankfully, Microsoft has become much more committed to supporting Terminal Services and seems finally to have "gotten it."

A second problem with TSE was related to the first: NT 4 was built before TSE, so the single-user operating system was unaware of the possibility of a multiuser environment. This made editing domain-wide user account settings for terminal services difficult. User account information for terminal server accounts, for example, was limited to the account information available to ordinary accounts, so that you couldn't easily provide an alternative profile for use with terminal sessions. It might seem that the answer to this dilemma was simple: store user accounts on the operating system that was aware of multiuser capabilities. Sadly, it wasn't that easy. Although TSE had its own User Manager tool to match that of NT 4, and this tool was terminal services-aware, TSE servers were not good candidates for domain controllers. Both roles are demanding and the way that an application server prioritizes processes is more like a workstation than a server. You must also edit client permissions to allow them to log onto the TSE server, since ordinary users are not normally permitted to log on locally to an NT Server and, effectively, that's what people connecting to an application server are doing. All things considered, it's much easier to use Terminal Services in a Windows 2000 domain than in an NT 4 domain.

TSE's functionality was also extremely limited. Even in Windows 2000 and (in the betas) .NET Server, Windows Terminal Services is *still* more limited than the current version of MetaFrame, the companion offerings from Citrix (more on this in a minute), which is why Citrix has a market for MetaFrame. But at this writing, it's possible to run Windows Terminal Services on its own, in a completely RDP-only environment with no helper software, and have it work quite well. This was possible only in a very limited way with TSE; in February 2000 when Windows 2000 was released, most people (70 percent by Microsoft's count, 90 percent by the count of the Gartner Group) used MetaFrame to supplement TSE. On the other hand, TSE was the first multiuser operating system based on NT 4 instead of 3.51, so it developed a following pretty quickly among those who understood the power of terminal services but needed the NT 4 UI.

Windows 2000 Server

With the coming of Win2K, Terminal Services became part of the core Windows server operating environment for the first time. Having Terminal Services as part of the core operating system helped encourage people to experiment with server-based computing. First, the risk involved in trying out Terminal Services was minimal. Formerly, you had to purchase an entirely separate operating system if you wanted to experiment with Terminal Services. Because Win2K supports Terminal Services on its own, experimenting with this service means only enabling the service from the Control Panel and rebooting the machine, and then installing the client component onto a test computer.

Win2K Terminal Services was also an improvement on TSE. RDP 5, the display protocol that came with Win2K, was faster than RDP 4. People running a terminal session from a PC could cut and paste data between local and remote sessions. (They couldn't cut and paste *files*, but a Resource Kit tool supports this to some degree.) Win2K Terminal Services supports client printer mapping, so that anyone running a terminal session from a computer with a printer attached doesn't have to share the printer with the network to make the printer available to the terminal session. Because Win2K Terminal Services was just one more part of the core operating system, managing terminal server accounts from a Windows 2000 domain controller was much easier than it was with an NT 4 domain controller. These improvements made Win2K Terminal Services an attractive proposition for a lot of people who hadn't experimented with TSE.

Finally, Win2K supported Terminal Services in two modes. Application Server mode, the mode found in TSE and the one that I'm focusing on in this book, made it possible for many people to use the same computer. Remote Administration mode, in which up to two people with administrative accounts can access a single server, does not change the way that the server executes but instead provides remote access to the server from any machine supporting RDP, and without using up a license. Table 1.1 summarizes the differences between the two modes of Windows Terminal Services.

Table 1.1 Application Server Mode versus Remote Administration Mode in Windows 2000

Feature	Application Server Mode	Remote Administration Mode
Licensing	Per-seat	Per-connection
Number of Simultaneous Connections	Unlimited (according to licensing and load balancing)	Up to two
Effect on Server	Changes processing mode to be more like a workstation	None
License Server Required?	Yes	No

Terminal Services in the form we're discussing in this book doesn't really use Remote Administration mode. I mention the addition of Remote Administration mode as an advantage mainly because it gave potential adopters of Terminal Services a useful way of experimenting with the technology without first creating an application server. Once you get used to using it, Remote Administration mode spoils you for anything else: it's an incredibly handy way of being able to access multiple servers from the same console. It's even better than having a keyboard/video/mouse switch. Remote Administration mode allows you to share a Clipboard between the local computer and the remote computer, and only very expensive KVM switches can function across an IP network. Remote Administration allows you to manage computers even from another building or state, so long as the computer is still functioning.

Remote Administration mode is so useful that it's enabled by default in .NET Server—you don't need to install Terminal Services to get it. In the next generation of Windows NT, Terminal Services refers only to Application Server mode.

In mid-2000, Win2K Terminal Services got another boost in the form of the Terminal Server Advanced Client (TSAC) package. This package had three parts: an MSI package of the RDP client for publishing with Win2K group policy objects, a helper component that you could use to publish RDP sessions to users connecting from within a browser, and a Microsoft Management Console snap-in that you could add to Win2K Professional and Server computers to connect to terminal servers from the MMC. The MMC tool is very useful for remote administration, because it allows you to monitor multiple remote server Desktops from a single window.

Windows .NET Server

The latest version of Windows Terminal Services comes with Windows .NET Server. Like Win2K Terminal Services, this version of the product will be a serious improvement on its predecessor in terms of client feature set. At this point, the product is still in beta, but from what I've seen, it's got some good additions to its client-side feature set: true color support, sound, and local drive mapping to terminal sessions.

For those new to Terminal Services, until the summer of 2000 all Windows Terminal Services—RDP or ICA—had a maximum color depth of 256 colors. For many applications, this was acceptable, but the reduced color depth had its failings. For those running both local and remote applications from a PC, the reduced color visually distinguished the remote applications from the local ones, not only destroying any illusion that the remote applications were really running on the local computer, but making the remote applications look less attractive. (This may sound trivial, but I've seen more than a few comments on Terminal Services bulletin boards to the effect that the lower color depth was a problem for people.) Second, some applications need full color depth to work properly—you can't run a CAD design tool in 256 colors and get everything out of it. Citrix made greater color depth possible with the Feature Release 1 (FR1) patch for MetaFrame 1.8 that it released in the summer of 2000, but that didn't help people running native Windows Terminal Services. Not until the most recent version of RDP did True Color support become possible without MetaFrame.

At first, the addition of sound seems relatively minor. The sound quality isn't good enough to make people want to play music from an application server, and this wouldn't be very practical in any case. However, sound *is* good for applications such as training videos. For example, the chip manufacturing plants for Motorola's Tempe-area plants use server-based training videos to teach new employees their jobs. The training videos have a streaming text component to supplement the voice-over—when you're watching something, it's easier to listen to instructions than to read them. The sound benefit won't be as obvious or as frequently used as the greater color depth, but it will come in handy for those in similar situations.

The addition of local drive mapping should help a lot. TSE didn't support any local device mapping or interaction with remote sessions. You had local computer resources and remote computer resources, and they were completely separate—you couldn't even cut and paste *text* between the two unless you were using MetaFrame. In Windows 2000, the situation improved. Not only was there a shared Clipboard between local and remote sessions, the new RDP client supported client printer mapping, which meant that if your local computer had a printer attached to it and you wanted to use that printer with remote applications, you could do so without sharing the printer with the network and connection from within the remote session. However, local drive mapping was not available, making it difficult to share *files* between local and remote sessions. The newest version of RDP automatically maps client-side drives to terminal sessions. This presents a bit of a security hole—if you don't want people to be able to copy files to a floppy disk, then you might want to disable this feature. It's also demanding of bandwidth, since copying files takes the same amount of bandwidth whether you're doing it from Explorer or from a terminal session. However, it's a helpful addition and does improve interaction between local and remote applications.

Terminal Services functionality in the next version of Windows isn't limited to the server side. Windows XP Professional includes a limited RDP server function that you can use to connect remotely to the XP Pro machine from another computer. The catch—and you knew there was one—is that XP Pro supports exactly one live connection. Not only does XP Pro support only one remote connection, you can't even use it from a remote connection and the console simultaneously. Connect from the console, and the remote connection gets disconnected. Connect from the remote session, and the console session has a blank screen with a dialog box telling you that the console is locked while the other session is active. Terminal Service Lite, this isn't—it's more like a way of remotely accessing your own computer.

In RC1, the server-side tools have also improved. One of the headaches of managing Windows 2000 application servers is that you have to manage the servers individually. Although the Windows 2000 tools allow you to connect to more than one server from the same UI, you can't create configuration settings that you can then apply to all servers at once. .NET Server's RC1 adds some group policies that *do* control some configuration settings, which means that you can now apply all these settings to multiple application servers at a time.

Understanding MetaFrame

Licensing Multi-Win back to Microsoft didn't shove Citrix off the Windows terminal services gravy train. In fact, for a time it secured its position, because TSE really needed helper software to make it work well. Citrix provided that helper software in the form of MetaFrame.

The first version of MetaFrame didn't do a great deal more than return TSE to the capabilities that WinFrame already had, albeit one using the NT 4 shell. MetaFrame 1.0, released in 1998, supported just about any existing client type (instead of the Win32 clients that native RDP is effectively limited to) and ran on any Windows-supported network protocol, instead of just TCP/IP. MetaFrame 1 also supported seamless windows, making remote applications appear to be running on the local machine, and a Clipboard shared between local and remote applications. Clients could also use local Desktop resources such as files and printers. In addition to its client-side features, MetaFrame 1 also provided server-side management tools that TSE didn't have, such as session shadowing and application deployment and management tools.

MetaFrame 1.8 had all these features and added several more. Remote applications became easier for users to access with the addition of the Program Neighborhood (which provided links to individually published applications in the same server farm) and Application Launching and Embedding, which allowed MetaFrame server administrators to put application icons inside web pages. The new version of MetaFrame supported SpeedScreen2, which made remote applications appear more responsive by echoing user input to the screen before it would have been there in an ordinary remote session. Server management was also improved with some optional components of load balancing, automated application installation, and resource management and monitoring tools. In the summer of 2000, Citrix released Feature Release 1 (FR1) for MetaFrame 1.8, adding some additional features to the product—including the next version of SpeedScreen, support for True Color in terminal sessions, and NFuse, the basis of a web-based Program Neighborhood that extended single-logon access to published access beyond Win32 clients.

The most recent version of MetaFrame, MetaFrame XP (no relation to Windows XP) includes the client-side improvements found in FR1 and adds some server-side features. It's packaged differently, too. Citrix sold MetaFrame 1.8 as a basic package with add-ons: you bought MetaFrame, and then you added load balancing and/or resource management services and/or installation management services, all as separate products. MetaFrame XP is packaged differently: rather than being sold as a single product with add-ons, there are three different kinds of XP: XPs, XPa, and XPe. XPS, the base product, supports the following:

- Application publishing
- XP's new printer driver and print bandwidth management capabilities
- Read access to the Active Directory
- Centralized license management
- Publishing applications from web pages with NFuse 1.5
- Advanced session shadowing
- Client time zones so that user clocks depend on their location, not the location of the terminal server

XPa includes all these features and adds load balancing.

XPe, the enterprise edition of MetaFrame XP, supports all the previously named features and adds the following:

- System monitoring
- Remote installation services
- Application installation management services
- Interaction with network management tools Tivoli and HP OpenView

All versions of MetaFrame XP support high color (new with Feature Release 1 for MetaFrame 1.8), sound, a shared clipboard between local and remote sessions, and automatic printer mapping and printer bandwidth and driver management. To help you sort out the differences between MetaFrame XPs, XPa, and XPe, see Table 1.2.

Table 1.2 Features of MetaFrame XP and Version Availability

Feature	Description	MetaFrame XP Version
Installation Management Services	Allows you to package applications for automatically installing on other MetaFrame servers.	MetaFrame 1.8 with the IMS add-on, MetaFrame XPe

Table 1.2 Features of MetaFrame XP and Version Availability *(continued)*

Feature	Description	MetaFrame XP Version
Load Balancing	Permits the administrator to create rules determining which terminal server a user will connect to, thereby spreading the load of supporting users without overloading a single server.	MetaFrame XPa and XPe
Web-based Program Neighborhood	Lets you publish applications from a web page using the application's icon.	All versions of MetaFrame XP, if you install NFuse support (included with all versions)
Resource Management Service	Support for auditing, system monitoring, billing.	MetaFrame XPe
Session Shadowing	Allows an administrator or Helpdesk person connect to a user's terminal session (with that user's permission) from another ICA session. The person shadowing can either give themselves observation-only capabilities or can actually interact with the shadowed session.	MetaFrame 1.x, MetaFrame XP
Network-Management Tools	Makes a MetaFrame server cooperate with external resource-management tools for network and system monitoring.	MetaFrame XPe

Just in case you didn't find all the versions of MetaFrame XP confusing, Citrix released Feature Release 1 (FR1) for MetaFrame XP in October 2001, and then FR2 in the spring of 2002. When you add these optional upgrades, you'll add a number of new features to MetaFrame, listed in Tables 1.3 and 1.4.

Table 1.3 New Features in FR1 for MetaFrame XP

Feature	Description	Application	Version Limitations
Auto Client Reconnect	Automatically attempts to reconnect a user accidentally disconnected from their session (perhaps because of a line failure).	Enable for people using slow or unreliable connections, so that if they're disconnected from the MetaFrame server it will attempt to reconnect them without their help.	None
CA Unicenter TNG Plug-In	Plug-in for using TNG for system monitoring, like IBM's Tivoli and HP Openview.	Gather information about your network with additional tools.	MetaFrame XPe only; requires installation of Network Manager add-on
Citrix Universal Print Driver	A new print driver that is not printer-specific.	Allows you to support numerous client-side printers without having to install drivers for each printer.	None
Citrix Web Console	MetaFrame XP management from a web interface instead of the Citrix management Console.	Provides one more way to manage MetaFrame XP servers.	None

Table 1.3 New Features in FR1 for MetaFrame XP *(continued)*

Feature	Description	Application	Version Limitations
Connection Control	Limits the number of concurrent connections for a given user or application.	Use to make applications available to users without letting those applications or users crowd out other people needing to use the MetaFrame server.	MetaFrame XPa and XPe only
Content Publishing	Permits you to push actual content to the user desktop, not just application links. Works like publishing an application.	Add video, memos, etc to the user desktop, updating from a central location. Content is presented in an application on the client computer, not in an application published from the MetaFrame server.	None
CPU Prioritization for Applications	Give high-priority applications more CPU time.	Ensures that the most important applications aren't robbed of the CPU cycles they need by lesser applications.	MetaFrame XPa and XPe only
Enhanced Application Packaging and Delivery	Group servers by operating system or server function and distribute applications accordingly.	Apply service packs and applications to servers according to their function, using pre-created groups.	MetaFrame XPe only; requires installation of Installation Manager add-on

Table 1.3 New Features in FR1 for MetaFrame XP *(continued)*

Feature	Description	Application	Version Limitations
Enhanced Citrix Management Console	Licensing and Server sections of the Citrix Management Console now have more sections. (Additionally, some dialog boxes have more or different sections so as to accommodate new features added with FR.)	Works just like the previous Citrix Management Console, but with the addition of new tools and capabilities. Online Help color-codes features included only in FR1 so you won't be confused about available options if not all servers have FR1 applied.	None
ICA Session Monitoring	Monitors ICA network traffic.	Gather network usage data to make sure that you've got enough bandwidth for all the tasks MetaFrame users are trying to perform.	MetaFrame XPe only
Improved Printing Performance	ICA performance has been streamlined to reduce print time by up to 50% over slow links.	Reduces printing time for connections over the WAN for any printers not already using PCL.	None

Table 1.3 New Features in FR1 for MetaFrame XP *(continued)*

Feature	Description	Application	Version Limitations
Novell NDS Support	Allows you to publish applications and content to Novell Network Directory Services (NDS) users and groups, as you currently can with Active Directory.	Use MetaFrame servers with Novell networks instead of just Windows networks.	None
Program Neighborhood Agent	Enables you to push applications to the desktop of computers from NFuse servers.	Allows you to prevent users from reconfiguring the ICA client.	None
SSL Encryption	Passes ICA traffic through a firewall using secure HTTP.	Make MetaFrame servers available via the Internet without compromising server security.	None
Support for NFuse 1.6	Next generation of MetaFrame's web-based Program Neighborhood.	Nfuse makes it possible to display applications from many MetaFrame servers—Windows and Unix—in a single browser window in a customized Web page.	None

Table 1.3 New Features in FR1 for MetaFrame XP *(continued)*

Feature	Description	Application	Version Limitations
ThinWire Performance Enhancements	Reduces per-connection bandwidth requirements for connections using 24-bit color over slow connections.	Allows people connecting to the MetaFrame server over a dial-up connection to more easily use color-rich displays.	None

Table 1.4 New Features in FR2 for MetaFrame XP

Feature	Description	Application	Version Limitations
Content Redirection	Simplifies the process of using file associations with published content.	Allows you to use server-based applications to display published content.	None
Delegated Administration	Rather than giving Citrix Administrators all-or-nothing control over the server farm, allows you to delegate control of parts of the farm to certain accounts, while still locking them out of other parts.	Makes it possible to expand the circle of Citrix Administrators without giving people with specific jobs more control over the server farm than they need—or should have. You can set the degree of control at a very low level. For example, it's possible to permit a Citrix Administrator to disconnect sessions but not reset them.	None

Table 1.4 New Features in FR2 for MetaFrame XP *(continued)*

Feature	Description	Application	Version Limitations
Enhanced System Monitoring and Analysis	New Summary Database tab of Resource Manager allows you to track user history on a server, and the Billing tab to create billing reports.	System Monitoring with MetaFrame XP and FR1 allows you to get historical data, but doesn't support trend data. The new Billing tab allows you to create billing reports by cost center (user-defined group) or domain. This is most useful for an ASP or university, but potentially applicable for corporate in-house use.	MetaFrame XPe
Support for NFuse 1.7	More detailed control over client-side settings from the Web interface. Control authentication method, load balancing, firewall settings, and method of ICA Client deployment.	This is the next generation of the Web-based Program Neighborhood.	None
User Collaboration	Permits users to shadow other user sessions.	Allows users to share the same session and thus easily cooperate on documents or provide troubleshooting for each other.	None

Table 1.4 New Features in FR2 for MetaFrame XP *(continued)*

Feature	Description	Application	Version Limitations
User Policies	Allow you to configure MetaFrame server settings for groups of users instead of for all users of a server.	Not everyone using the same server necessarily needs the same settings (such as time zone settings). Creating user policies allows you to apply different settings to people based on what group they're in.	None

Because FR1 and FR2 are optional add-ons and licensed separately from MetaFrame XP, I'd rather not assume that everyone reading this has already installed the feature releases. Therefore, although I'll explain how to use these new features, I'll also make it clear when those features depend on a specific feature release (or a specific version of MetaFrame XP).

Comparing Windows Terminal Services and MetaFrame

Windows Terminal Services has continued to evolve (in Windows 2000, it's roughly where MetaFrame was with version 1), but so has MetaFrame, particularly on the server/administration side. Let's take a look at what MetaFrame has to offer that native Windows Terminal Services does not.

Support for Non-Windows Clients

Strictly speaking, even Terminal Services in Win2K does not support all Windows clients—it works only with Win32 operating systems and Windows for Workgroups. If you have Windows 3.*x* or DOS clients, or some brand of Unix (including Linux) or Macintosh clients that you'd like to run Windows applications in a native Win2K environment, you'll need a third-party solution. The newest version of the RDP client, the Remote Desktop client, works only with Win32 operating systems. MetaFrame's ICA protocol works with just about any operating system out there.

> **TIP** If the only reason you're considering MetaFrame is to get support for non-Windows clients, there are other options. A (free!) native Linux RDP client is available for download from http://www.rdesktop.org/. Hob, Inc has developed HOBLink JWT, a Java client for DOS, Linux, Macintosh, Unix, OS/2, handheld PCs, and of course Windows operating systems. (HobLink is not free.) You can get this client from http://www.hobsoft.com/.

Multiprotocol Support

Windows Terminal Services uses RDP to pass user input and terminal output between client and server. RDP depends on TCP/IP, whereas ICA can use TCP/IP, IPX/SPX, or NetBEUI. Frankly, RDP's dependence on TCP/IP isn't much of a problem, since the ubiquity of the Internet makes TCP/IP the transport protocol of choice on most networks anyway. However, Terminal Services does lock you into one network protocol, making it impossible to use network protocols to isolate parts of the network. ICA, in contrast, supports both IPX/SPX and NetBEUI.

Seamless Client Sessions

Seamless client sessions sound as though they are only an interface thing, but there's actually a bit more to them than that. For a couple of reasons, RDP sessions are not really meant to display a bunch of individual applications to a PC interface.

First, there's the matter of how individual applications look to the person using them. When you're setting up an RDP connection on a PC (I'll discuss the mechanics of doing this in Chapter 5, "Preparing Client Connections"), you can pick the size of window that you want the remote Desktop to display: 640×480, 800×600, or 1024×768, or 1280×1024. Pick a window size smaller than your current Desktop, and you'll be fine—the window just won't take up as much room as other applications on your Desktop. (The window won't display in the reduced resolution; it will just be a smaller window with the same resolution as the rest of your display.) Pick a size the same size as your current Desktop, however, and there is a problem: a 1280×1024-sized window on a 1280×1024 local Desktop doesn't fit, because the Taskbar at the bottom of the local screen uses up some of the screen real estate. The terminal window will have horizontal scroll bars, and it will be impossible to see the entire terminal session Desktop or application window unless you go into full-screen mode, thereby concealing any locally running applications. Microsoft did this on purpose to provide more screen real estate, but I think it's a mistake. Making people scroll to see the entire Desktop is a help-desk call waiting to happen. Seamless client sessions, in contrast, fit neatly into the available Desktop area on the client. Even when they're maximized, you can see the entire session window without scrolling.

> **TIP** You can use the Ctrl+Alt+Break sequence to toggle between a Windows Terminal Services full-screen session and the same session in a window on the local Desktop.

Then there's the matter of how remote sessions are identified. Even if they're running only single applications, RDP terminal sessions are also identified in the Windows Taskbar with a Terminal Services icon, not the icon of the application being run. For those running multiple individual applications from the terminal server, this can make finding applications difficult—it's easier to just run all applications from a single window.

Client experience isn't all that counts. Seamless Windows are also an improvement from the application server administrator's perspective, because of the way that Terminal Services uses memory. I'll talk more about how memory works in Chapter 2, "Core Parts of Windows Terminal Services," but for now just understand that, while some files can be shared between terminal sessions, some files are unique to each session. The more individual sessions, the more memory space these session-specific files are taking up. Therefore, every time a user connects to an application server via RDP, that user is initiating a new session—even if it's the same user and the same server. MetaFrame's Seamless Windows avoid this memory problem. All seamless windows running from the same application server are running in the same session and thus sharing those same core files. Rather than running one instance of (for example) WinLogon for each application, they're running only a single session and, therefore, need only a single instance of all the session-specific processes such as the ones supporting the Win32 subsystem and network authentication (so long as the user is running all applications from the same server).

> **NOTE** There is one exception to this rule: published desktops. Published desktops need their own system environment (obviously), so they'll need their own copies of the same environment processes that applications with no desktop could share.

The only catch to seamless windows is that the MetaFrame server publishing them must be able to support the same video resolution or greater than the client. Otherwise, the seamless window will use the greatest resolution available on the server.

Server Farming

With Win2K, you can create client connections that supply only applications, but the user must know which server is running the application and make an explicit connection to it. With MetaFrame, you can create general client connections to a set of servers running a certain application, without the client having to know or care which server is providing the application. These are called *published applications*, and I'll explain how to set them up in Chapter 7, "Installing and Tuning Applications on an Application Server."

A related benefit of server farming is support for what Citrix calls the Program Neighborhood. The Program Neighborhood is a collection of links to applications, links that can be backed by one or more servers in a server farm so that users only have to know which application to connect to (and you can tune the apps available according to who's logged in) and click on the link. NFuse, MetaFrame's web-based Program Neighborhood, works the same way. Because there are versions of MetaFrame for both Windows and Unix (Solaris, HP-UX, and AIX), using either version of the Program Neighborhood means that it's possible to access both Windows and Unix applications from the same place.

Load Balancing

As we'll discuss in Chapter 3, "Planning the Terminal Server Environment," an application server can support only a finite number of connections, with the maximum number depending on the server's oomph (to use the technical term) and the degree to which the applications running on the server tax that oomph. Therefore, many organizations using Terminal Services have more than one terminal server. But how do you keep one terminal server from getting overloaded when another one is underutilized? The answer to that question depends on load balancing.

A need for load balancing is not unique to multiuser Windows; it's the ability of multiple servers to work in tandem so that the least-busy server processes client requests. Windows 2000 Server does not support load balancing. Win2K *Advanced* Server and Windows 2000 DataCenter support Network Load Balancing for user logons (see sidebar). To get application load balancing for Windows 2000 Server, you'll need a third-party product such as Citrix's Load Balancing Services (separate from but dependent on MetaFrame 1.8) or use the load balancing component in MetaFrame XPa and XPe.

Windows Load Balancing

Network Load Balancing (NLB) is designed to spread out user connections among servers by allocating servers to client requests according to client IP address. (MetaFrame load balancing spreads out user connections according to server stress at the time the user is attempting to connect. In theory, this should keep the load on the servers distributed fairly evenly. In practice, it doesn't always work this way because the client is assigned a server based on the server's stress level *at the moment the client is trying to connect*, not on any kind of long-term pattern of stress level. However, some load balancing is better than none.)

The sessions remain on the server they started from; sessions do not move to another server should one become available. When a user disconnects from a terminal session on a server that's part of an NLB cluster, if the user's IP address changes before she reconnects (perhaps because she's logging in from a different computer or because the client machine's DHCP lease ended), she may reconnect to a different server when trying to reestablish a disconnected session. If you want disconnected clients to connect to the same terminal server when reconnecting, the client computers need to use static IP addresses and you must configure NLB to use Single Affinity. I'll talk more about load balancing terminal servers in Chapter 4, "Rolling Out Terminal Services."

Table 1.5 shows you the capabilities in each version of Windows Terminal Services and these versions of MetaFrame, so that you can see which features are available in each tool.

Table 1.5 Comparing Client-Side Features of Windows Terminal Services and MetaFrame

Feature	TSE	Win2K TS	Windows XP TS	MetaFrame XP
Load Balancing	No	Limited	No (and not relevant)	In MetaFrame XPA
Client-side printer mapping	No	Yes	Yes	Yes
Client-side drive mapping	No	No	Yes	Yes
Support for sessions in browser		Yes (with TSAC add-on—IE only)	Yes (IE only)	Yes
Native support for non-Windows clients	No	No		Yes
Supported color depth	256	256	High-color	High-color
Seamless windows	No	No	No	Yes
Sound	No	No	Yes	Yes

Applying Windows Terminal Services

So that's where Windows Terminal Services came from and how it compares with MetaFrame XP. Why is either one useful?

- Server-based computing requires less maintenance than desktop-centric computing
- Server-based computing makes it easier to support outlying offices and people working from remote locations
- Server-based computing makes it possible to really streamline the desktop environment

- Server-based computing allows you to use Windows terminals, making it possible to bring computing to:
  - Low-security computing locations
  - Places with no room for a computer
  - Environments that are bad for a computer or that computers could hurt

Let's take a look at these in more detail.

Lower Maintenance

If you always install applications once and never touch them again, then server-based computing may not have much to offer you from a lower-maintenance perspective. More likely, however, you'll upgrade applications or apply patches regularly. If you're working in an all-Windows 2000 or later environment, then you could use group policies to deploy applications, but doing so requires a fair amount of setup and creating distribution files for applications that don't come with automated installation files. It also doesn't work with client operating systems other than Windows 2000 or Windows XP. Distributing applications with group policies is also not something that you want to do over low-bandwidth or heavily used networks—it can take a lot of network bandwidth.

In contrast, installing all applications onto a single terminal server (or on only a few terminal servers) means that you don't have to install or upgrade the application on dozens or hundreds of client computers, but can do it once. The changes will take effect as soon as the client logs onto the terminal server, without requiring any changes on the client's part.

Supporting Multiple Offices

Being spread over multiple locations isn't unique to large companies. Some smaller companies may experience the same thing: the main company is located in one office and, as the company outgrows its original space, it gets branches rather than moving to an entirely new building. The trouble with spreading out like that is that someone needs to keep an eye on the servers at each of the offices. Hiring all these maintenance people can get expensive, and sometimes isn't possible—you may not be *able* to hire the people you need to keep the computers up at all locations. To keep the main IT staff from having to make house calls to the outlying offices, you could maintain an application server in the main office, and then let the people in the outlying offices connect to that terminal server to run the applications and get to the data on the main servers. Working from a server-based environment has several advantages. You could potentially use low-maintenance Windows terminals at the outlying offices. You don't have to worry about synchronizing data between multiple offices, and the people in charge of keeping the servers up and running only have to worry about maintaining servers at one site. Although the satellite offices won't be completely management-free, it'll be much easier to keep them running if you only have to maintain the network and the client machines, not servers, data, and applications.

While you're thinking about supporting remote offices, think about supporting remote users. Server-based computing makes it practical to give users remote access to applications in a way that's really not feasible using dial-up connections. For example, I know a travel company with a sales force that brings new meaning to the concept of being on the road. They're not just out of the office, or out of town, or even out of the country; they sometimes work from a separate continent altogether—and sometimes a continent without a high-speed or very reliable wired infrastructure. Inconveniently, the sales folk still need access to the files and customer information located back in the main office in the United States, so that they can be sure that they're getting the most recent information available. At one point, the sales staff were dialing up to a remote access connection to download the most recent data to their laptops. However, this solution got expensive quickly, because downloading database changes isn't the fastest job in the world and some telephone lines are capable of supporting only a very slow connection. Also, if the connection dropped during the download, then the person in Morocco had to start over. Using a Terminal Services connection allowed the company to keep all the important files on the servers in the main office and allowed the remote sales staff to edit the database and see current information—all without worrying about the connection dropping because the person reviewing the data could reconnect right back to where she was if the connection dropped.

Simplifying the User Interface

I'm not buying this idea. I get a lot of reader mail that gives the lie to this statement, and even outside work time I'm the favorite source of free tech support for my parents (and some of my friends and *their* parents). Experienced users may find it easier to customize their interface, but those who are less experienced find all sorts of pitfalls when it comes to using their computers: so many options that they get confused, and too many ways to break something. (Frankly, even the experienced can run into this problem. Every time that Microsoft releases a new operating system, I have to find everything all over again.) There are still people who get great joy out of successfully configuring their computers, but far more people view the configuring as a means to an end, not the final goal.

Thin client computing, in combination with group policies and/or published applications, can make the interface more task oriented for users. If people only use single applications, you don't even have to display a desktop for them—this doesn't even require group policies. This is particularly true with Windows-based terminals, which are little more than a monitor, a box, a keyboard, and a mouse. There's nothing local to break and no way to break it. Set up user rights and system policies thoughtfully, and users can't configure the Win2K terminal environment either.

Support for Windows Terminals

I keep bringing up the use of Windows terminals in a server-based environment. Why?

One of the big advantages to Windows Terminal Services is that they allow you to get the capabilities of a PC on devices other than a PC. The dream of "a PC on every desktop" will remain a dream, if for no other reason than that in some environments the conditions are bad for the PC or the PC is bad for the environments. You can't—and shouldn't—run a PC everywhere.

Some work areas are bad for PCs. PCs do not like dust, excessive heat, or vibration... and *you* will not like maintaining the PCs if you try to use them in an environment that has any of these characteristics. Warehouses, especially those with heavy machinery and lots of shaking, are not good places to run PCs. The reverse may also be true—PCs can be bad for the work area. Clean rooms where chips and boards are made are good candidates here. First, you can't have dust in a clean room, and the fans in a PC kick up dust. Second, becoming sanitized to enter a clean room is neither simple nor inexpensive—you don't want to put devices that need care and feeding from the IT staff in there. Third, any place where space is at a premium is a good candidate for Windows terminals. For all these reasons, Windows terminals have been becoming a popular choice for the factory floor.

Finally, PCs are a commodity item—if you leave them unattended and unguarded in some place that just anyone can get to them, they will disappear. For this reason, Windows terminals are becoming a popular choice in environments that are PC-unfriendly but need access to Windows applications. Shipping areas and unattended trucker kiosks (where the truckers can log in to display and print their shipping orders from a terminal) are two good examples of how to use Windows terminals like that. Terminals are also good for locations where you can't use a PC for security reasons—specifically, because you don't want the PC to grow legs and walk off.

> **NOTE** Legend has it that a truckload of new Windows terminals was stolen from a large company—and then the terminals were returned anonymously a few days later once the thieves realized that their booty was useless. I can't vouch for the truth of this story, but it makes the point pretty well—Windows terminals aren't a real prize for thieves.

This isn't to sell you on the idea of Windows terminals, but to point out that sometimes they're useful—and you can't use them for much without an application server.

A Low-Power Solution

If you're weighing the benefits of Windows terminals and PCs, think about how much it will cost to run each type of device. You've probably heard of the concept of Total Cost of Ownership (TCO), which reflects the cost of owning each kind of device—not just its sticker cost, but how much it will cost you to run the thing. TCO can be hard to calculate because much of it depends on how much IT time you have to spend on keeping a device running, but there is one element to TCO that you can figure out for yourself without too much hassle: how much it costs to power the devices.

For the past couple of summers, power costs in California have been high and the state's been experiencing rolling blackouts. Elsewhere in the United States (I'm sorry, I don't know about other countries) power cost has also been rising, although not always to the same extent. It's natural for companies faced with rising power bills to wonder how they could reduce those power bills. Sadly, rated power usage for a device does not tell you how much power a device uses, it tells you how much that device is *rated* to use. A 300-watt power supply does not necessarily pull 300 watts; it is rated to handle it if it has to. In order to determine the degree of the power differential between Windows terminals and PCs, a couple of colleagues and I performed two studies of thin client devices both at a customer site and in the lab, comparing their relative power requirements. The full studies are online (for free!) at NCD's and Wyse's websites at http://www.ncd.com and http://www.wyse.com, respectively, but here's the gist.

We found that as a proportion, thin client devices use significantly less power than their PC compatriots when both are in use. NCD ThinStar 200 devices used about 10 watts of power pretty steadily all the time they were turned on, regardless of whether they were being used. PCs, in contrast, used an average of 66 watts of power (the rate fluctuated a bit more than the thin clients did, but not hugely). Interestingly, both a 200MHz PC and a 1GHz PC use about the same amount of power when the more powerful machine is running line-of-business applications. Not until we started playing Diablo II (in the name of science, really!) did the more powerful PC use more power—about 85 watts.

You can't calculate power usage for terminals without taking the terminal servers into account, of course. The terminal server support in our case study was two terminal servers and eight modems, and the total drew about 300 watts of power. Thus, if there were 30 Windows terminals, we'd have to allocate an additional 10 watts of power to each of them (for the servers), bringing them to a total of about 20 watts. The more Windows terminals you have in proportion to the terminals, of course, the better the power savings.

> **A Low-Power Solution** *(continued)*
>
> I don't expect anyone to choose Windows terminals over PCs *solely* to save on the power bills. However, if power costs are an issue for you and you have a large network, then exchanging PCs for thin client devices could save you some money. If you're interested in more details about how this could work, look at those studies.

Why Terminal Services Are Not a Universal Fix

I just discussed some good reasons to use Terminal Services. However, Terminal Services won't work for everyone. Why won't Terminal Services completely replace desktop-centric computing? There are two main reasons:

- Demanding applications or users
- Not all applications work well from terminal sessions

Although similar, these explanations are not quite the same thing.

Demanding Clients

Terminal Services will not provide a full-scale 2GHz computer to all the people using it. The point of Terminal Services, after all, is that much of the power of that 2GHz machine is going to waste when used by a single person or application. If it's not going to waste, if an application demands much or all of the computing power of that high-scale computer, then the application may not be a good candidate for a server-based computing environment. This doesn't mean that it's impossible to run high-end applications from an application server. Online training companies can and do offer biotech modeling and engineering applications for their customers. However, running high-end applications from an application server does mean that you'll need to make sure that any terminal server running those applications is powerful enough to serve the needs of all the people who will be running those applications simultaneously. If you are using PCs as terminal clients and have the option of running some applications from the terminal server and some locally, that may be the best solution for the applications that don't play well with others.

16-Bit Applications

Terminal Services works best for Win32 applications. The reason for this has to do with how Win2K itself runs Win32 and Win16 applications. Win32 applications running within the same session can share any files found in common between the applications so long as no application is modifying those files—at the first change, the Win2K process manager will create a new instance of the file so that the applications don't overwrite each other's work (and, more likely, crash). This technique is called *copy on write*. But Win2K is a 32-bit operating system and can't run Win16 applications on its own. Instead, it creates a Virtual DOS Machine (VDM), which is a 32-bit application, and runs the Win16 application within the context of that VDM. The VDMs can share any files that they have in common, but the 16-bit applications running within the context of those VDMs cannot—even if, say, you're running two identical copies of the same application. Combined with the fact that translating 16-bit calls to the operating system into 32-bit calls takes some overhead, in practical terms this means that, all else being equal, Win16 applications don't perform as well in an application server environment as Win32 applications. These 16-bit applications will work—a good thing, since you may not have a choice about running them if your company uses these applications and 32-bit versions are not available—but, proportionate to their relative memory requirements, they'll use more memory than Win32 apps will.

> **NOTE** Depending on the applications you're talking about, lack of support for copy-on-write with Win16 applications may or may not make a lot of difference. Memory was rarer and more expensive when most 16-bit applications were under development. 16-bit applications developed for low-memory PCs tend to be more streamlined than 32-bit applications developed when 256MB of RAM in a single desktop computer were the norm.

In addition to the extra memory that all 16-bit applications demand, DOS applications present another problem. DOS applications were written for a single-user, single-tasking environment. To be as responsive as possible, DOS applications constantly poll the keyboard buffer, looking for input—think of a six-year-old repeating, "Are we there yet? Are we there yet? Are we there yet?" This constant polling means that a DOS application in the foreground, even when not doing anything, is using up an astounding amount of processor time. This is acceptable and even helpful in a single-user, single-application environment, because (in the slower machines these applications were originally designed for) it could make an application more responsive. It's death when that processor time has to be shared with a couple of dozen people.

Taming DOS Applications

Windows NT, Terminal Server Edition (TSE), includes a utility called DOSKBD that modifies a program's keyboard polling to improve system performance when you run DOS-based programs. Essentially, DOSKBD puts a program to sleep when it polls the keyboard buffer too often and negatively affects server performance. Win2K doesn't include a copy of DOSKBD, and the TSE version doesn't work with Win2K Server Terminal Services.

> **Taming DOS Applications** *(continued)*
>
> When Windows 2000 came out, we were told that the Windows 2000 Resource Kit would eventually include a Win2K-compatible version of DOSKBD, but the plan changed. There won't be an equivalent tool for Windows 2000 or for .NET Server. (And this means that new users of Terminal Services are out of luck, as Microsoft stopped making TSE in August 2000 and the only copies for sale are those made before that time.) However, there's another option. Go to http://www.mindspring.com/~dgthomas/tame.htm and check out Tame, a tool for tuning DOS applications in a Win2K environment. That's the advice you'll get from Microsoft Support if you ask about tuning DOS applications.

You're also limited to running DOS applications in a window—you can't run them in full-screen mode. (This can actually lead to a problem wherein it appears that an application won't run at all. DOS applications are set by default to run in full-screen mode, but full-screen mode doesn't work on an application server because it would be too memory-intensive to load DOS font sets. You can fix this by setting the application to run in a window instead of full-screen mode.)

Badly Designed Applications

This is probably self-evident, but it's worth noting: Applications with memory leaks are a problem in a single-user environment, but this problem is exacerbated when dozens of people are running the application on the same computer. Just as DOS applications can't constantly poll to see if they've gotten any new data without impacting everyone else using the server, applications compatible with a multiuser environment cannot have memory leaks. Similarly, some applications identify people by IP address, not username. Because all applications running on an application server will have the same IP address, these applications won't be able to communicate properly. Over the past year or so, I've seen many manufacturers make their applications compatible with a multiuser environment, but this is far from universal. Always find out whether the applications you're using will work from an application server before committing yourself to working that way.

The bottom line is this: Server-based computing is best suited for people who run Win32 applications that don't require a powerful computer devoted to their needs. People who don't fit this profile may continue to need personal computers for their more compute-intensive or memory-intensive tasks.

Summary

That's the story of where Windows Terminal Services came from, what you can do with it, how it works, and when it will and will not suit you. As you can see, Terminal Services isn't likely to completely replace every desktop-centric computing environment, but it's an awfully useful adjunct to more traditional environments. In Chapter 2, I'll move on to some key concepts of server-based computing, including how the server works, how sessions work, the types of supported clients, and the licensing model. I'll also introduce you to the tools you'll be using to support Terminal Services.

Core Parts of Windows Terminal Services

In Chapter 1, "Introducing Windows Terminal Services," I explained how Windows Terminal Services developed and compared its features with MetaFrame. In this chapter, I'd like to take a look at how Windows Terminal Services *works*, from the server through the display protocol to the client, and how it's licensed. I'll also discuss the tools you'll be using in the course of this book.

The Server-Based Computing Processing Model

All individual connections to an application server—all *sessions*—use the same resources: CPU cycles, memory, and disk and network card access. To show you how this works, I'll need to briefly explain the low-level operating system processing model.

An application server is different from other Windows servers in one key way: it's set up to act like a workstation, not a server. The difference lies in the relative importance of the applications running on the server. A file or e-mail server assigns equal importance to all current tasks whether they are running in the foreground or in the background, because it's responsible for ensuring that everyone using the server has equal access to the resources that the server is managing. An application server is different. Like a workstation, it assumes that the task in the foreground is the one that the user is interacting with, and thus the most important. Of course, a terminal server will have more than one task in the foreground, but the basic model holds true: to a Windows terminal server, the important applications—the ones with the highest priority—are the ones with which people are actively interacting. This is key because the CPU is allocated to applications based on the priority given those applications.

Because in Windows 2000 the core operating system supports Terminal Services, the operating system works differently depending on whether or not the Terminal Services service is running on the computer. For this reason, you can't stop the process that supports this service (TERMSRV.EXE). If you want to disable RDP sessions temporarily, you'll need to disable the protocol rather than pausing or stopping the core service—Windows 2000 won't let you do it.

Processor Allocating Basics

You run applications, or programs, but all NT server operating systems (NT, Windows 2000, and now .NET Server) divide their time into *processes*. Programs are a set of instructions for the computer to execute; processes represent a set of resources allocated to executable *threads* created within the context of the process, including virtual memory, a Program ID, a priority indicating that process's importance, and system resources. Processes roughly (but not exactly) correspond to programs, so it's common to say that a process is running.

To the operating system, however, applications do not run: threads do. Threads are the executable part of a process, so every process contains at least one thread and threads exist only within the context of a process. Therefore, the operating system identifies every thread according to the process to which it belongs. Thread priority is based on process priority (a thread can have a priority lower than that of its process, but never higher), and a thread can only use the virtual memory and other system resources allocated to its process. If a process is terminated, then all the threads running in that process are also terminated. Similarly, when the last thread in a process finishes executing, then the process ends.

> **NOTE** To ensure that all threads eventually get a chance to execute, the process scheduler gradually increases the priority of low-priority threads until they're scheduled CPU time.

Every time the NT process scheduler allocates the processor to a thread in a different process, it performs a *context switch* wherein it unloads the process-specific information used for that thread and loads the process-specific info for the other thread.

So far, the key points are these:

- NT operating systems run the highest-priority thread available.
- CPU time is divided into quantums. Threads get to run until the end of their quantum (unless interrupted by a higher-priority thread) when the scheduler will determine whether another thread of the same priority is available.
- Every time a thread from a new process begins executing, NT operating systems unload the resources used by the first thread and load the ones used by the second thread.

Getting back to Windows Terminal Services... When more than one person is using an application server, each person has a self-contained view of the server called a *session*. On a single-user computer, all the processes running can be jumbled together, organized by their process ID and spawning process (since the job of one thread within a process may be to start another process) but not otherwise. On a multiuser machine, of course, many instances of the same process may be running, but they must be maintained independently of each other. Therefore, on a multiuser server running processes are identified not only by their process ID, but also by the session ID of the session that initiated them, and threads are identified by their name and an internal session identifier. For example, several people could be running Acrobat Reader on the application server. The first thread begun that manages Acrobat reader would be AcroRd32/0, the second would be AcroRd32/1, and so on.

Every session runs the processes shown in Table 2.1.

Table 2.1 Processes Common to Terminal Services Sessions

Component	Function
Win32 Subsystem	Win32 subsystem required for running Win32 applications (including the Win2K GUI).
User Authentication Module	Logon process responsible for capturing username and password information and passing it to the security subsystem for authentication.
Executable Environment for Applications	All Win32 user applications and virtual DOS machines run in the context of the user shell.

The other processes in the session will depend on the applications that the user is running. The really crucial points to be learned from this are that every session has its own copy of the Win32 subsystem (so it has a unique Desktop and unique instances of the processes that support the Desktop) and its own copy of the Winlogon application that authenticates user identity. Session processes are not spawned by the Terminal Server process, but are created by the Session Manager.

Each session has a high-priority thread reserved for keyboard and mouse input and display output. Because all session threads have the same priority, the scheduler processes user input in round-robin format, with each session's input thread having a certain amount of time to process data before control of the processor passes to another user thread. Therefore, the more active sessions that are in place, the more competition there is for CPU time. Application-related threads have the same priorities that they would have if running on a single-user operating system.

That's how the processor allocating part works. How about memory management?

Memory in a Multiuser Environment

There are two types of memory: *physical memory*, represented by the amount of RAM installed in a computer, and *virtual memory*, the amount of memory that a computer can *address*. NT operating systems use both of these approaches in the form of the Virtual Memory Manager (VMM), the part of the operating system that handles the interaction of virtual and physical memory. Briefly, every process running on an NT operating system has 4GB of virtual memory addresses available to it: 2GB for user-mode functions, which is all separated from the others, and 2GB for kernel-mode processes, which is all shared. (Retrieving data from kernel-mode memory is faster, but the shared space makes the data more vulnerable to overwriting by another process, which will cause both processes to crash. If one of the processes is CSRSS.EXE, the Win32 subsystem on which NT operating systems depend, you don't want it to crash.) User-mode processes can share data with each other through a function called *copy-on-write* sharing. Many applications share files that they use, such as common DLLs. Copy-on-write allows processes using the same files to reference the same ones unless and until one process needs to write to the file. At that point, the process will make a copy of the file and write to that copy, leaving the original intact for the other process.

> **NOTE** Eventually, a 64-bit version of .NET Server will make these memory limitations obsolete. However, for now commercially available operating systems are 32-bit, so we'll stick with that scenario.

The alert reader has noticed that most computers running NT operating systems do not have 4GB of RAM installed and certainly do not have enough RAM installed to dedicate 4GB of it to each process running on the computer. This is correct, and the reason why I said that every process has 4GB of *virtual* memory addresses. The processes don't need 4GB of memory to run; they're just designed (almost certainly) for a single-user environment, so they need to feel like they've got 4GB of memory all to themselves. The VMM's jobs are to make sure that there's a unique place in physical memory for each process to store its data and to map the relationship between physical and virtual memory for each process.

> **NOTE** The fact that most Windows applications are written for a single-user environment can make it difficult to execute some of these applications, either because they can hog resources or are used to identify the person running them according to computer name or IP address, not username. Chapter 7, "Installing and Tuning Applications on an Application Server," discusses some of the ways you can edit application settings to make them work better in a multiuser environment.

The VMM makes memory available to processes in two steps. First, when the OS creates a process, part of that process's resources are the virtual memory addresses available to that process. Earmarking addresses for a process is known as *reserving* memory for that process—those addresses are marked as belonging to WordCruncher or Solitaire or whatever the application supported by the process is, but this reserved memory consists of addresses only, not actual storage space. When the VMM allocates some disk storage space in the paging file, called the *backing store*, then that memory is *committed*. Committed memory is private to a process. (Why reserve and then commit? The reasons are complicated and interesting mainly if you're a developer, but in a nutshell it's because doing it this way is less resource-intensive than gradually increasing the amount of committed memory, and if reserved memory never gets used before the process is deleted then it's very easy to un-reserve it and release it for use by another process.)

The second part of VMM's job is to know where the data stored in physical memory is located. When a process is using data (files or user data), that data is originally stored in RAM to the extent possible and stored in holding areas called *pages*. Those pages are listed in a directory called the *page table*. If the process doesn't use some data for a while, and physical memory is getting crowded, then the VMM evaluates the data that the process is holding in memory to see which data was least recently used. That data gets paged to the hard disk, where it's still available, but takes a little longer to retrieve. Getting to data stored in RAM is faster, but there's a lot more room in a paging file. The data that the virtual memory manager maintains in RAM for a process is called that process's *working set*. Because the process is storing data in virtual memory without regard to whether the data is in RAM or in the paging file, the VMM has to know where the data is. It does this with a set of structures in the page table called *page table entries* (PTEs). Hence, the VMM can always find data stored in physical memory by checking the PTE for that virtual address. Because PTEs are not process-specific, there's a chunk of kernel-mode memory reserved for the storage of PTEs.

> **NOTE** An application server needs more PTEs than a single-user server or workstation does, because of the larger number of applications and drivers in memory. It would be theoretically possible for a server to run out of PTEs if stressed enough, thereby limiting the maximum number of concurrent sessions. Therefore, in addition to the core space set aside for system PTEs, application servers can draw on an extended area of memory reserved for them. TSE had 384MB of extended space for PTEs, and Windows 2000 Server has 400MB. .NET Server allocates a maximum of 1.3GB of PTEs, of which 1GB is contiguous.

That's (very briefly) how virtual memory works in a single-user operating system. A multiuser operating system makes things a little more difficult, but the basic functionality is the same: shared space for important and stable processes like those supporting the operating system, and separate space for memory processes that need to coexist but cannot be trusted not to overwrite each other. Multiuser NT also uses copy-on-write and gets a good deal of use out of it, because, in a multiuser environment meant to provide a group of users with a common set of applications, there are apt to be many instances of the same application in memory simultaneously. To add multiuser functionality to the mix, multiuser NT uses an additional area in memory: a separate chunk of kernel-mode memory called SessionSpace.

In a single-user operating system, it's okay for the core parts of the OS to share kernel-mode memory, but some of this information is not compatible with a shared environment. You certainly don't want different sessions reading each other's working set lists, and you don't need to load printer drivers for all of them. Therefore, while *most* kernel-space memory is shared, on multiuser NT there's an area of memory called SessionSpace. SessionSpace allows each session to maintain a unique copy of the Windows subsystem and GDI (video and printer) device-driver processes. All processes identified with the same Session ID get to share the SessionSpace for that ID. Processes begun in a different session (or from the console) will have a different SessionSpace.

In TSE, this SessionSpace was in a different area from that of the single-user version of the operating system. However, in Win2K SessionSpace virtual addresses are always in the same space, regardless of whether the processes using it were created from a terminal session or from the console (or created on a Win2K server without Terminal Services enabled). In Windows 2000, 60MB of virtual memory addresses are allocated to SessionSpace.

Running Sessions on an Application Server

You can run all the sessions you like on the application server, but that won't do you any good unless you can view the session output from a remote computer and send input to the application server for processing. The mechanism that allows you to do both is called the *display protocol*. A display protocol downloads instructions for rendering graphical images from the application server to the client, and uploads keyboard and mouse input from the client to the server. Which display protocol you use depends on the kind of application serving you're set up for. Those using Windows 2000 Terminal Services alone will use RDP, while those with MetaFrame XP installed will use the ICA display protocol. Chapter 1 describes the capabilities of the types and versions of the display protocols, but here's a little more information about how they work.

The RDP Display Protocol

Win2K natively supports the Remote Desktop Protocol (RDP) version 5, based on the T.120 protocol used for NetMeeting. The RDP client that comes with Win2K Server provides a point-to-point connection that runs with TCP/IP to display the Windows 2000 Server Desktop on the desktop of a client running any Win32 operating system (including Windows CE) or Windows for Workgroups 3.11. The Remote Desktop that comes with Windows XP and is available for download from the Microsoft web site works only with Win32 operating systems.

> **NOTE** You can run multiple sessions from a single client, and even multiple sessions for a single user (although for reasons of profile maintenance and memory usage, this may not be the best plan). However, each session is still a point-to-point connection.

RDP5 and later also supports optional bitmap and glyph (character) caching, which allows the client device to store commonly used bitmaps and characters used in terminal sessions so that it doesn't have to wait for them to be downloaded from the terminal session. For example, if the icon for Microsoft Word has already been downloaded to the client, there's no need for it to be downloaded again as the image of the Desktop is updated. Cached data is stored in the cache on the hard disk for a limited amount of time and then eventually discarded using the Least Recently Used (LRU) algorithm. When the cache gets full, the data that has been unused the longest is discarded in favor of new data.

In Win2K, the image on the screen is updated about 20 times per second when the session is active. If the person logged in to the session stops sending mouse clicks and keystrokes to the server, then the application server notes the inactivity and reduces the refresh rate to 10 times per second until client activity picks up again.

The ICA Display Protocol

Application servers with MetaFrame XP installed can use either RDP or ICA, MetaFrame's display protocol, but you'll almost certainly use ICA for terminal sessions. In effect, ICA is similar to RDP, but it works a little differently. Rather than relying on the underlying operating system on the client to help it create graphical output, ICA is more of a screen-scraping technology, using one virtual channel in the display protocol to send the initial image of the terminal session and then updating that image on the client where it changes. Being independent of the client operating system makes ICA able to run well on a wider variety of platforms than RDP can; although there are Java and Linux-based RDP clients, these run a little more slowly than the native Windows RDP client because the client itself must contain the graphical rendering logic instead of being able to call on capabilities already present.

Unlike RDP, ICA supports a many-to-one session architecture, where a client may be running more than one session on their desktop, but all those sessions are in fact tied into a single session on the server. Seamless Windows uses this many-to-one connection, but ICA sessions running in a window do not.

How Sessions Are Initialized

A Windows 2000 application server starts in the same way that a Windows 2000 server does: it loads the NT kernel, begins services, and prepares for the initial user logon. Running sessions, however, is a little different.

The very first session initialized on the application server is the console session, which uses Session ID 0. No one has to log onto the application server's console for this session to be created—the Session Manager handles it by creating the SessionSpace area in memory and loading Win32K.SYS, the Windows subsystem device driver, even before WinLogon begins. The Windows subsystem loads and configured mouse, keyboard, and display drivers are made ready. When the WinLogon process is initialized, Windows 2000 starts the TermServ service, which reads the Registry to see which display protocols are supported on the local server. Again, this service cannot be stopped or paused from the GUI or the command line. If you need to disable connections to the application server, you'll need to disable RDP and/or ICA from the command line with `change logon` or by disabling the protocols from the Terminal Services Configuration tool.

When the Terminal Services service starts, it creates two user sessions right away. These sessions aren't active; they're just waiting for users to connect to them—having idle connections waiting reduces the time required for users to connect to the application server. To create each idle session, the Session Manager generates a unique Session ID for the idle session (these Session IDs may or may not be numbered consecutively) and passes it to the VMM to create the new session's SessionSpace private area in kernel-mode memory. The Memory Manager also loads the Window Manager and the GDI kernel component into memory. Next, NT checks to see whether Win32K.SYS has been previously loaded into memory (which it has, since the console session is using it) and connects to that instance of the Windows subsystem driver. The *data* portion of Win32K.SYS is private to the session, but the code is not. When the Windows subsystem is ready, the Session Manager maps itself into the SessionSpace for the new session, so that all processes it spawns use the memory in SessionSpace and inherit the session's Session ID. The Session Manager then loads the Win32 subsystem (CSRSS.EXE) and WinLogon processes for that session, then disconnects itself from that session's SessionSpace. To finish the process of creating the idle session, the Terminal Services service creates a protocol listening thread that waits on the protocol listening port (3389, for RDP) and loads the RDP device keyboard and mouse drivers. (It does not load the RDP display driver until someone connects to the idle session.) The idle sessions are displayed in the Terminal Services Manager with a session state of Idle.

> **NOTE** The number of idle sessions waiting for users is determined by the IdelWinStationPoolCount key in HKLM\System\CurrentControlSet\Control\Terminal Server. The default value of this key is 2, making two sessions, but you can increase it. Doing so uses up system resources, however. Remember that the application server must maintain a copy of the Windows environment even for idle sessions. Only increase this value if enough people are logging on quickly enough that the application server seems to be bogged down creating new sessions.

Connecting to a Session

When someone attempts to connect to an application server via RDP, the listening thread picks up on the request and connects you to the WinLogon service running in one of the waiting idle sessions. When WinLogon detects the request, it queries the Terminal Services service for the client's display driver, and then (assuming that the connection is through RDP) loads the RDP display driver, RDPDD. The next step is creating WindowStation and desktop objects to provide the user with a Desktop on the application server. There's actually three desktop objects: one displaying what you normally think of as the user Desktop, one for logging on, and one for the screen saver (if you should be so foolish as to permit application server users to run screen savers).

> **NOTE** When you attempt to disconnect from an application server session, then the WinLogon service creates a fourth view of the Desktop: the disconnect Desktop.

Once the Desktop objects are ready, WinLogon negotiates the encryption level used for that RDP session, then calls the Local Security Authority (LSA) process on the application server so that it can load the authentication package to use. Normally, this will be the default Windows authentication package; one of the settings for RDP and for individual users allows the application server administrator to tell the LSA to use another authentication package if one is loaded.

At this point, the person trying to connect to the application server sees the familiar Windows Logon screen prompting them for their username, password, and (if they're logging onto the domain instead of to a user account stored on the application server) domain. When the person connecting has provided this information, the WinLogon service passes it to the security system for checking against the user account database on the server or domain controller. The authentication package makes sure that the user is allowed to log on, and has no account restrictions, then, if all goes well, passes the user information back to the LSA to creates an access token for the user. The LSA creates the access token that will identify everything the user does (and includes the user's Session ID), and gives the WinLogon process a thumbs-up for letting the user log on and a handle to the user's access token and user profile information. When the person has logged on, their application Desktop object is marked with their SID so that no one else can write to it. WinLogon loads the shell used to display the user Desktop, runs any logon scripts, and otherwise prepares the user and the application server to interact with that user session.

> **NOTE** The number of sessions that an application server can run depends on how many sessions the hardware (especially memory) can support and how many licenses are available. When a client logs off her session, the virtual channel to that client machine is closed and the resources allocated to that session are released. If an application server client disconnects from an active session without logging off, that session remains active on the Terminal Services server. Active sessions get processor time even if they don't have data to process. Although it's handy to disconnect from a session and find yourself back in exactly the same place, if a session will be unused for a while, it's a good idea to end it altogether and log back on later.

Disconnecting from and Reconnecting to a Session

A person running a terminal session can get out of it in one of two ways: terminating the session or disconnecting from it. If they log off the session from the Shut Down Windows menu, then they're terminating the session. The Terminal Services service tells WinLogon, and WinLogon terminates the network stack for the session. All processes associated with the session are deleted and its SessionSpace memory is released. If the person *disconnects* from the session by closing the session window or choosing to disconnect from the Shut

Down Windows menu, then all the data and applications that they're using remain in memory, so that if they reconnect to the session they can start working again from where they left off.

> **TIP** Because disconnected sessions continue to use resources and can confuse users who thought they'd logged off, it's a good idea to educate users about the difference between terminating a session and disconnecting from it. I'll talk about other user training issues in Chapter 3, "Planning the Terminal Server Environment."

When a user attempts to disconnect from their session, the Terminal Services service cleans up the user environment and halts all further drawing actions—the user display will no longer be updated. Win32K.SYS changes the current Desktop object to the Disconnect object, which prevents the screen from being updated. All processes in the session remain active and may be scheduled for CPU time by the process scheduler. The Terminal Services service changes the state of the session (visible from the Terminal Services Manager) from Active to Disconnected.

MetaFrame-Specific Concepts: IMA Architecture

So far as session creation and resource allocation goes, it doesn't matter much whether you're talking about MetaFrame or Windows 2000 Terminal Services; the two types of application server work in pretty much the same way. However, once you move beyond the single server model, MetaFrame adds another organizational level: the server farm. Windows 2000 application servers really don't share much information—they share a license server, and they can communicate with a domain controller to tell them whether a user is allowed to log on and what kind of access he or she gets to the server. .NET Servers share a little more, or at least can draw some common information in the form of Group Policies applied to application servers. MetaFrame XP application servers, in contrast, have a whole network architecture that allows servers in the same farm to communicate for load balancing, license pooling, printer driver sharing, and more.

Why the additional network organization? If your network has only a single application server, understanding how clients find applications to use is easy: the clients connect to the application server and use the applications installed on that server. If the server doesn't have enough connection licenses for all the clients, the clients can't connect to the server. The server must have drivers installed for any client-side printers that will be used in terminal sessions. MetaFrame servers don't just support per-server connections, though—they also use published applications that people can use without having to know which server they're installed on. To support published applications, you have to hide the individual servers while still keeping them accessible. The server farm abstracts the interface to the individual application servers. People *can* connect specifically to a particular MetaFrame application server, but they don't have to.

As you'll see, MetaFrame XP has *farms*, the logical groupings of servers used in previous versions of MetaFrame, but now these farms work a little differently from the way they did in MetaFrame 1.8. MetaFrame XP also introduces the concept of *zones*, physical groupings of MetaFrame servers.

Background: Why MetaFrame XP Has a New Organizational Model

The reorganization of farms and the introduction of zones in MetaFrame XP aren't just cosmetic. The point is to make MetaFrame servers communicate a bit more efficiently.

MetaFrame 1.8 used the ICA Browser service to maintain data about MetaFrame servers and published applications in a farm. This service has three parts: a master browser, member browsers, and the client systems. All MetaFrame servers run the ICA Browser service; the browser uses directed packets (UDP, for networks running TCP/IP) to communicate with the ICA Browser service running on other MetaFrame servers. The master browser maintains the browse list, the central information store for the farm. If you're familiar with browse lists in NT and Windows 2000, this will sound familiar.

So long as all the servers that need to communicate are on the same subnet, this setup works fine. The difficulty occurs when MetaFrame servers need to communicate with MetaFrame servers that lie on another subnet. As noted earlier, MetaFrame 1.8 member and master browsers communicate through UDP, a connectionless broadcast protocol. UDP is fast and uses little bandwidth because one packet is audible to all hosts on the network and the hosts don't have to reply. However, it will not work in large networks if the network administrator in charge of the network routers turns off UDP forwarding. No UDP forwarding means that communication is cut off. (To make it work at all, you have to either set up an ICA gateway or open port 1604 on the router to make the ICA Browser service available, with port 1494 providing the ICA connection to the application running on the MetaFrame server.)

> **NOTE** This functionality isn't limited to MetaFrame XP. With the introduction of Feature Release 1 for MetaFrame 1.8 and NFuse, you no longer have to leave port 1604 open between two subnets connected with a router.

One possible hack for making MetaFrame servers able to communicate across a router is to direct users to a specific MetaFrame server, but then we're back to the individual-connections-to-individual-servers scenario. Besides, even if you do this, then each subnet of the network has to be its own farm—no browsing, license sharing, or printer driver sharing across subnets.

How MetaFrame XP Servers Communicate

MetaFrame XP doesn't use UDP for inter-server communication, but instead uses the Independent Management Architechture (IMA) service, supported with TCP/IP. This means that UDP forwarding isn't necessary to communicate across subnets. To minimize traffic (because TCP/IP uses more bandwidth than UDP), MetaFrame XP server farms are organized into *zones* that normally have some relation to the physical layout of the server farm and will often be subnet-specific. However, cross-subnet traffic can still be kept to a minimum by designating one *data collector* for each zone. The data collector keeps a database of all the farm's resources, collects information about the resources available in its own zone, and updates the other data collectors in the other zones to let them know what resources are available in its zone. Any time any of the following events (collectively known as *session data*) takes place, the member server informs its data collector:

- ICA client logons and logoffs
- ICA session disconnects and reconnects
- Server and application load changes
- License acquisition and release
- Server brought online or goes offline (either reboots or restarts the IMA service)
- Changes to published applications
- IP and media access control (MAC—the hardwired network card address) address changes

Using this information, the data collector can provide a clear picture of the MetaFrame server farm (the servers available, the clients using those servers, the load on each server, the licenses in use, the applications available in the farm, and the network address of each server) at any given time. For faster access, the data collector keeps all session data in RAM. If the data collector doesn't hear from a member server within the preset interval (by default, 60 seconds), the data collector will ping the member server through IMA to make sure that the server is still online.

> **TIP** Because a data collector must maintain session data in RAM, this MetaFrame server will require more memory than other servers that do not have this load. The more member servers that are in the zone, the more memory the data collector will need to store session data.

Where did this data collector come from, anyway? The first server in a zone to come online is the zone's data collector; this server is marked as being the Most Preferred. If the current data collector goes offline, a member server loses contact with the data collector, a new server joins the farm, the zone configuration (name, membership) changes, or you force an election, the zone will hold an election to create a new date collector. Of the available MetaFrame XP servers, the server considered Most Preferred will always win the election, and if more than one server has the lowest master ranking, the one with the highest Host ID will become the data collector.

> **TIP** If you're planning to take the current data collector server offline, you can make sure that the best server for the job becomes data collector by making another server Most Preferred before shutting down the current data collector.

After the election, the member servers contact the new data collector to see if it is available. If servers that were available prior to the election recognize that the data collector has not changed, those servers *do not* resend their information. Only the servers that lost contact send a complete update to the data collector. A complete update contains information about connected sessions, disconnected sessions, load management, and other dynamic data. Only the information that isn't already on the data collector is sent in order to cut down on the network traffic. Obviously, if the election produces a new data collector, all of the member servers must perform a complete update, so the election of a new data collector on a busy MetaFrame network can produce quite a bit of traffic. If a remote data collector loses an election, it notifies all data collectors of the change. If a remote data collector goes offline, all data collectors eventually reestablish a connection to the new remote data collector.

Because of the introduction of zones and their site-specific data collectors, MetaFrame farms can now span multiple subnets and even different networks, greatly simplifying server management and user access to applications. A farm may have only a single zone, but you can split it into as many zones as needed to cut down on traffic over slow links while still sharing management information among all the zone locations.

> **NOTE** You can have multiple farms, too, but doing so limits you because MetaFrame XP farms don't talk to each other. The only reason to maintain separate farms is to keep the servers absolutely separate; perhaps, for example, if you were an application service provider (ASP) maintaining one farm of MetaFrame servers for in-house use and one farm for customers. Chapter 3 discusses the ramifications of single-farm and multiple-farm configurations.

Accessing Farm Information: Understanding Direct and Indirect Mode and the Local Host Cache

The information that each zone's data collectors share is kept in a repository of persistent farm-wide information called a *data store*. Member servers use the IMA service to read the content of the data store to gain information about what's on the network. The servers will attempt to connect to the data store when starting up, and they will query it at 10-minute intervals to see if any changes have been made and request those changes, if any. When you start the Citrix Management Console or refresh it, it's connecting to the IMA service to access the data store for the farm.

The way that these servers get to the data store depends on how you set up data collection when installing MetaFrame. I'll discuss the logic behind the different ways of setting up data collection in Chapter 3 and the mechanics of installing MetaFrame XP in Chapter 4, "Rolling Out Terminal Services." For now, just understand this: when installing the software on the first server in the zone, you'll be prompted for the location of the data store's backing database. If you choose the default option of backing the database with Access, that server will be the only one with direct access to the data store—all other servers in the zone will need to ask the IMA service on that first server to pull data for them. (The first server in a zone is always the preferred data collector unless you explicitly engineer things to make another server the preferred data collector. Therefore, this server is the logical location for the data store.) This data-request process is called accessing the server in *indirect mode*. However, if you back the data store with Microsoft SQL Server or Oracle, the member servers will be able to access the data store without the help of a server that has a direct connection. This latter method of accessing the data store is called *direct mode*. At least one server will always access the data store directly.

The practical implications of these descriptions of indirect mode and direct mode are probably clear. Small farms with few servers can use indirect mode without significantly impacting network speed, but larger farms should back the data store with a database that supports direct mode to reduce the load on the data collector and speed up member server queries. Citrix recommends that you use direct mode for data store access as often as possible. Direct mode reduces the load on the data collector and allows the server to get its information more quickly because the server won't have to wait for the data collector to read or write to the data store. Also, direct mode is a more reliable method of making the data store available. If a member server relies on another server (not necessarily the one hosting the data store) to provide access to the data store, and the server with direct-mode access to the data store goes offline, the member servers relying on that server won't be able to get to the data store. The only catch to using direct mode is that doing so requires setting up and configuring SQL Server or Oracle on a separate data store server; therefore, to use direct mode you'll need to know how to use those products ahead of time.

If one data *collector* goes offline, the zone holds an election to create a successor—again, like Windows 2000 browsing. If the data *store* becomes unavailable because the server that the data store is on is being rebooted or goes offline for a longer period, this is more problematic. The server farm doesn't instantly quit working, however. While a server farm doesn't fully function without its data store, without one the farm will continue working for 48 hours, although configuration changes to the farm won't take effect until the data store comes back online. During that 48 hours, the server can rely on its local host cache, an Access database on each MetaFrame XP server that servers use to minimize network traffic. Rather than constantly pinging the data store, they can just read and write to their local host cache. When starting the IMA service and every few minutes thereafter, they can report or gather any changes. Because the local host cache only stores information useful to an individual server, if the data store is unavailable for 48 hours straight, the server won't work anymore because it can't read licensing information from the data store. The local host cache reduces network traffic and keeps MetaFrame servers working if the data store is unavailable for a short time, but you'll need to be sure that member servers have a reliable connection to the data store to work properly.

That's how server-based computing works from the inside. Let's take a look at some of the tools you'll use to manage it from the outside.

The Terminal Server ToolKit

This book is task-oriented; rather than running through a list of available tools and then discussing how to use them, I'll introduce management tasks that you'll need to fulfill and explain how to accomplish them using the tools available to you. To make that work, however, you'll need to know where the tools controlling the settings are located, and it'll be easier if you have an idea of which tool you'll use to accomplish a particular task beforehand. Therefore, in this section I'll introduce the available tools. This chapter isn't a complete how-to, just a road map to the tools you'll use to manage Windows 2000 Terminal Services and/or MetaFrame XP.

Windows 2000–Specific Application server Management Tools

When you install Terminal Services on a Windows 2000 server, you'll also install a bunch of tools for managing terminal sessions and servers. Additionally, because Windows 2000 is built to support terminal sessions, you'll find that some of the mainstream tools in the OS also have Terminal Services–aware features.

> **NOTE** Even if you're using MetaFrame XP, don't skip over this section. As you'll see in later chapters, MetaFrame administrators will use the Windows 2000 tools to supplement the Citrix Management Console and other MetaFrame management tools.

Terminal Services Client Configuration

Windows XP Pro is the first operating system to have the RDP client pre-installed. If you're not using Windows XP, then you'll need to install RDP support on the client somewhere. The Client Creator tool (called Client Configuration if you're looking at the contents of the Administrative Tools menu) is intended to help you do that. Run this tool, and you'll see a dialog box like the one in Figure 2.1, listing the types of supported clients and telling you how many floppy disks you'll need to install each client type.

Figure 2.1 The Terminal Services Client Configuration tool is used for making RDP installation disks.

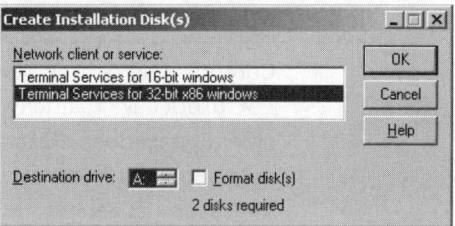

An updated and improved RDP client called the Remote Desktop comes installed on Windows XP and will be available for distribution with .NET Server, but is also available for download from the Microsoft website. (Chapter 5 discusses where to get the client and how to install it.) Even though Remote Desktop won't give you the full experience of RDP with .NET Server, I still prefer it even with Windows 2000—it's faster than the older RDP client and I like the UI. The bottom line is this: Forget the Client Creator.

Terminal Services Configuration

Unlike the Client Configuration tool, the Terminal Services Configuration tool has a useful purpose. It's got two sections: Server Settings and Connections. The Server Settings folder displays all of the current server settings shown in Table 2.2.

Table 2.2 Server Settings Displayed in Terminal Services Configuration

Setting	Description
Terminal Server Mode	Remote Administration or Application Server. Cannot be changed without reinstalling Terminal Services.
Delete Temporary Folders on Exit	Deletes the contents of temporary folders when a user quits his/her terminal session (Yes, by default).
Use Temporary Folders Per Session	Specifies whether all terminal sessions use the same temporary folder or each one gets its own (separate folders by default).
Internet Connector Licensing	Enables ICL licensing if these licenses are installed.
Active Desktop	Toggles the Active Directory on and off (on by default).
Permission Compatibility	Controls whether the permission set used is for TSE users (less restrictive, but works with most older applications that may need broader access to the application server) or Windows 2000 access (more restrictive, but may keep some applications from running).

Most of these settings may be changed from the Terminal Services Configuration tool, with the exception of Terminal Server mode. To change this setting, you must reinstall Terminal Services and reboot the server. The two modes differ pretty significantly in the way that they make the server set application priority.

> **NOTE** In .NET Server, you'll be able to configure all these settings through Group Policy Objects, rather than having to tune them on a per-server basis. Computer Configuration\Administrative Settings\Windows Components\Terminal Services contains all settings except the mode in which Terminal Services is installed.

The Connections section of this tool lists the display protocol settings for the installed network adapters (you can either have one set of settings for all installed adapters or, in servers with more than one, create different settings). To get to these settings, pick a connection from the list and double-click it to open the dialog box in Figure 2.2. From here, you can tune per-connection RDP settings, adjusting the settings for such items as remote control settings, automatic device mapping, and the like. These settings are available on a per-user basis from the user account properties, visible from Active Directory Users and Computers on domain controllers or, if you're running the application server outside a domain, in Local Users and Computers.

NOTE Not all the settings available with this tool will work with RDP. The Audio Mapping settings on the Client Settings tab only apply to servers running MetaFrame.

Figure 2.2 Edit per-connection settings from the Terminal Services Configuration tool.

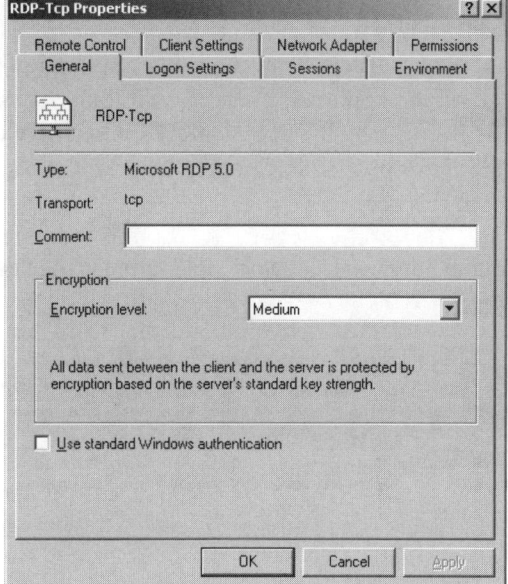

Terminal Services Manager

The Terminal Services Manager allows you to keep tabs on what's happening on the application server. From the window shown in Figure 2.3, you can initiate remote control of user sessions, see a list of processes for each session (or running on the entire application server), view session status, end processes in sessions, or even end a user's session.

Figure 2.3 Control terminal sessions from the Terminal Services Manager.

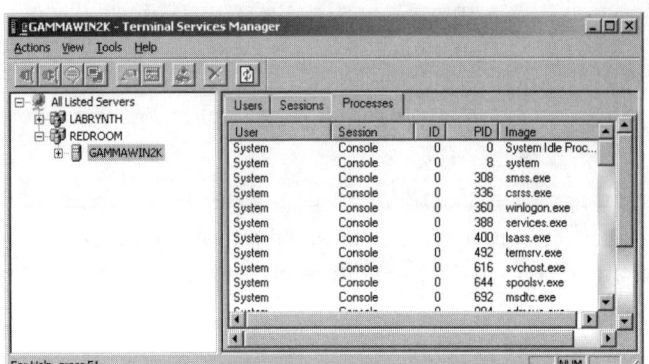

Terminal Services Licensing

Terminal Services Licensing differs from the other application server tools in that it doesn't necessarily go on the application server itself, but works with it. You'll use this tool (shown in Figure 2.4) to install and activate Terminal Services License Packs. We'll discuss the mechanics of this process in Chapter 4, and I'll explain the Terminal Services licensing model later in this chapter.

Figure 2.4 The Terminal Services Licensing tool manages the licensing for the domain or workgroup.

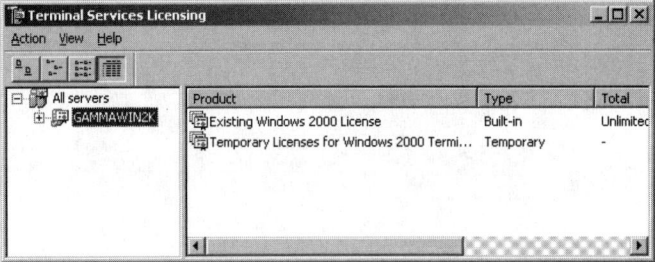

Command-Line Utilities

In addition to the graphical tools I've introduced, Windows 2000 Terminal Services also supports a number of command-line utilities. I'll show you how to *use* these tools in context, but Table 2.3 contains a quick list of what they *are*.

Table 2.3 Command-Line Terminal Services Tools

Command	Function
change logon	Temporarily disables logons to an application server. Useful when you're tuning or adding applications to the application server and don't want people using it.
change port	Changes or displays COM port mappings for MS-DOS program compatibility. For example, you could use this utility to map one port to another one, so that data sent to the first would actually go to the second.
change user	Flips between Execute mode and Install mode. Used when installing applications on the application server. (Add/Remove Applications runs this tool automatically; you'll only use Change User when you're installing an application without invoking Add/Remove Applications.)
cprofile	Removes unnecessary files from a user profile. You can only run this tool on profiles not currently being used.
dbgtrace	Enables or disables debug tracing.
flattemp	Enables or disables redirected temporary directories, which you can use to send .tmp files to a location other than the default.
logoff	Ends a client session specified by session name or session ID, either on the local application server or on one specified.
msg	Sends a message to one or more clients.
query process	Displays information about processes.
query session	Displays information about an application server session.
query termserver	Lists the available application servers on the network.
query user	Displays information about users logged on to the system.
register	Registers applications to execute in a system or user global context on the computer.

Table 2.3 Command-Line Terminal Services Tools *(continued)*

Command	Function
reset	Resets (ends) the specified terminal session.
shadow	Monitors another user's session with Windows Terminal Services remote control feature. Cannot be executed from the console, and cannot shadow the console. You can only shadow one RDP session from another one.
tscon	Connects to another existing application server session.
tsdiscon	Disconnects from an application server session.
tskill	Terminates a process, identified by name or by process ID.
tsprof	Copies the user configuration and changes the profile path.
tsshutdn	Shuts down an application server.

Windows 2000 Tools with Terminal Services Enhancements

In addition to the Terminal Services–specific tools, other Windows 2000 Server tools have some enhancements that show up when you install Terminal Services.

The System Monitor (Windows 2000's answer to the NT Performance Monitor) picks up some additional counters when Terminal Services is installed: Terminal Services and Terminal Services Session. The Terminal Services object has counters for keeping track of the number of disconnected sessions, idle sessions, or the total number of sessions. Terminal Services Session's counters keep track of all session information, including:

- The percentages of time the session spent in privileged (kernel) mode or user mode
- The percentage of processor time the session is using
- The luck the terminal session is having in using the client-side cache to display bitmaps or glyphs (characters) in the terminal session, thus improving session performance
- The handle count for all processes running in the session (thus pointing to the amount of system resources the session is using)
- Session input and output performance, compression, and error information
- Memory use as reflected in page faults, use of the paged pool, bytes of memory used that cannot be shared with other sessions, and total bytes of memory used

- The thread count for the session
- The amount of virtual memory addresses used by the session
- The amount of data that the session is holding in memory

> **NOTE** Some of the Microsoft Windows 2000 documentation asserts that adding Terminal Services adds User and Session objects to the System Monitor, but this is incorrect.

The Windows Task Manager also has some additional options when Terminal Services is installed. You won't see these options unless you explicitly enable them, but if you edit the columns shown on the Processes tab, you'll see a dialog box like the one in Figure 2.5, permitting you to add Session IDs to the list of available columns.

Figure 2.5 You can monitor system processes according to the session that initiated them.

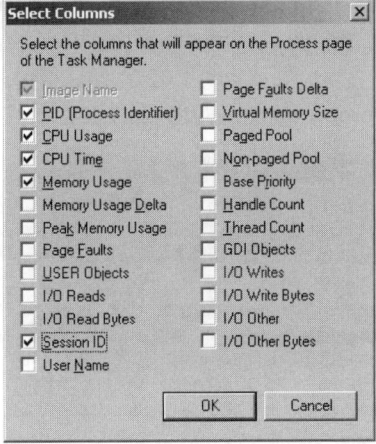

Finally, the Windows 2000 user account information is Terminal Services–aware. You can configure the session information as you can with Terminal Services Configuration, but on a per-user basis. For example, you can disable remote control for a particular user or only enable client printer mapping for people accessing the application server across a high-speed network. As you can see in Figure 2.6, the client information properties contain three tabs specific to Terminal Services:

- Terminal Services Profile specifies the profile to use within terminal sessions, if different from the user's main profile.

- **Sessions** tells the application server what to do if an account gets disconnected or is left idle.
- **Remote Control** tells the application server what kind of remote control is possible for this user's terminal sessions.
- **Environment** configures the user's terminal session environment, overriding any client connection settings created on the client end. You could use this setting to, say, make sure that a user could only run a single application from the application server, not a Desktop, even if they'd created a connection to the application server's Desktop. This tab also controls the mapping of client-side devices to terminal sessions.

NOTE Not all options on these tabs are available to RDP clients. For example, RDP 5 clients (those using Windows 2000 Terminal Services) cannot use client drive mapping—that version of RDP does not support it. In Windows 2000, you can check the box on the Environment tab that supports client drive mapping, but that setting won't actually do anything unless MetaFrame is installed on that application server and the user connects with ICA.

Figure 2.6 User account properties in Windows 2000 are Terminal Services–aware.

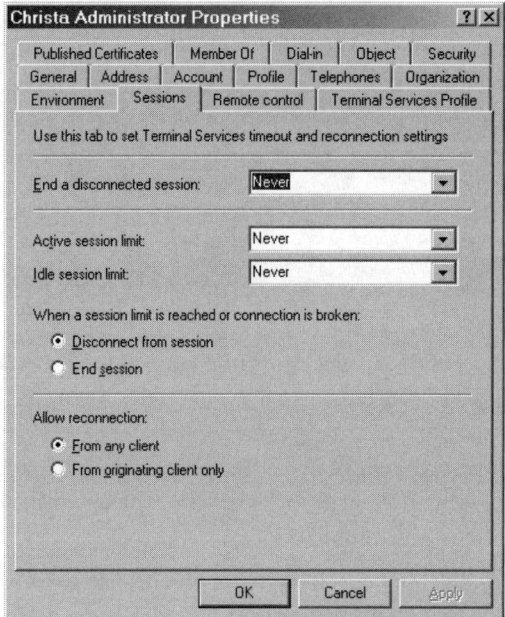

You don't have to enable Terminal Services on a computer to get this additional information; it's always there. (In other words, you don't need to enable Terminal Services on the domain controllers where you're maintaining user accounts.) Normally, the per-user settings override the per-connection ones, but you can override individual settings from Terminal Services Configuration.

> **NOTE** In .NET Server, you'll be able to configure user settings with Group Policy Objects, rather than having to tune them for either all people using the same connection or on an individual basis. These settings are located in User Configuration\Administrative Templates\Windows Components\Terminal Services.

MetaFrame XP–Specific Tools

There are two main groupings of MetaFrame settings. ICA client configuration settings are found on the ICA toolbar and in the MetaFrame subfolder of the Citrix program group, and most server-related settings are available from the Citrix Management Console.

The ICA Toolbar

MetaFrame has had a Citrix program group containing links to its management tools since version 1. These tools were also available from a taskbar normally located along the right-hand side of the screen, containing icons for some management tasks. (You can also drag this toolbar to another border of the screen or drag it to the middle to make it a freestanding toolbar.) You can get to the icons quickly from this toolbar, but doing so requires that you be pretty familiar with the tool icons, as the icons themselves are no more intuitive than Windows icons generally are. I've identified each in Figure 2.7.

Figure 2.7 The ICA Administrator toolbar

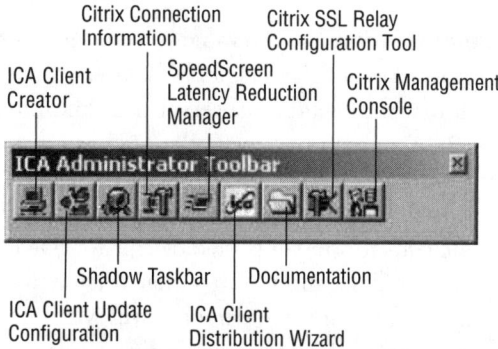

In the following sections, we'll look at what each of these tools *does*.

> **NOTE** The tools found in the ICA Administrator toolbar are also available from the Citrix program group. Although the program group appears to contain a couple of tools not available from the ICA Administrator toolbar (like the Published Application Manager), this is misleading. Those tools don't work with MetaFrame XP; they are just there to provide backward compatibility for MetaFrame XP servers working in Interoperability Mode with MetaFrame 1.8 servers before you upgrade them to MetaFrame XP.

ICA Client Creator Like its Windows 2000 relative, the ICA Client Creator in Figure 2.8 is a not-very-useful tool you can use to create Setup installation disks for the ICA client used to connect to MetaFrame servers. Again, I'd use this tool only if I had no other way to get the ICA client files to client computers. After you install MetaFrame XP onto a Win2K server, the ICA client installation files are located in %*systemroot*%\system32\clients\ICA folder, and MetaFrame has a number of ingenious ways for distributing and updating those clients, as we'll discuss in Chapter 5.

Figure 2.8 The ICA Client Creator is normally the tool of last resort for installing the ICA Client.

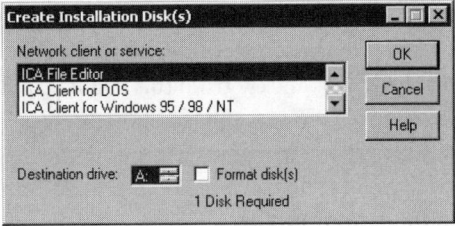

ICA Client Update Configuration MetaFrame servers can maintain a client database, checking the version information of ICA clients when users connect to them, and updating client files if it turns out that the MetaFrame server has a more recent version of the client files. (Sadly, Windows 2000 doesn't have a similar feature for updating RDP client files—I wish it did.) You can configure the client update settings with the ICA Client Update Configuration tool. When you first open this tool, it appears to present you with nothing more than a list of all the ICA clients for the supported platforms, but as you can see in Figure 2.9 it's a bit more than that. You'll use this tab to gather version and description information for a particular client, the circumstances under which the MetaFrame will (or won't) update client files, and the event logging settings for recording client updates. I'll talk about how to use this tool in Chapter 5.

Figure 2.9 The ICA Client Update Configuration tool

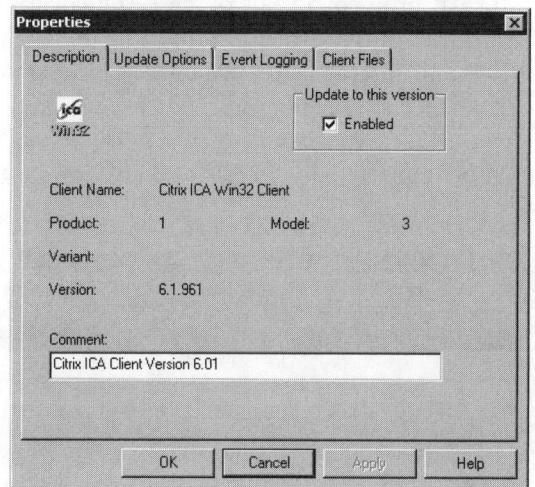

Shadow Taskbar Shadowing—remote control, to Windows 2000—is the act of connecting one session to another session so that the activity in one session is visible from another, allowing the person doing the shadowing to watch or even interact with the shadowed session's activity. As you'll see in Chapter 6, "Managing Terminal Sessions," you can shadow sessions from the Citrix Management Console; however, if you don't need the Citrix Management Console at the moment, consider using the Shadow Taskbar instead. Once you've logged onto this tool (to provide your shadowing credentials—only administrators are allowed to shadow sessions) then you'll see the dialog box in Figure 2.10. Using this dialog box, you can find the session you want to shadow according to the username, the name of the published application that person is using, or the server they're logged onto.

Figure 2.10 The Shadow Taskbar makes it easy to find the user session that you want to shadow.

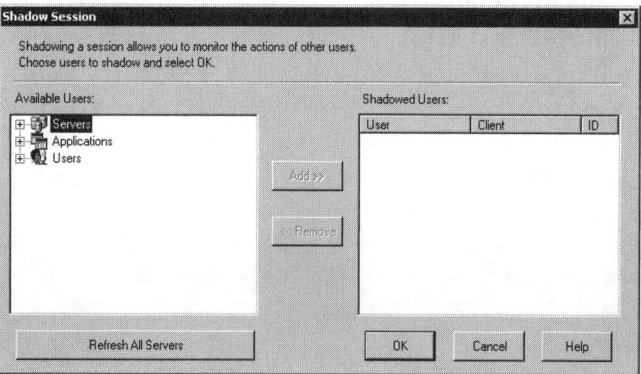

Citrix Connection Information   The Citrix Connection Information tool in Figure 2.11 is very similar to the display protocol portion of the Terminal Services Configuration tool found in the Administrative Tools program group. Using this tool, you can view and edit connection properties for all currently installed display protocols and the network protocols and NICs with which the display protocols are associated.

Figure 2.11   Use the Citrix Connection Information tool to view and edit display protocol settings.

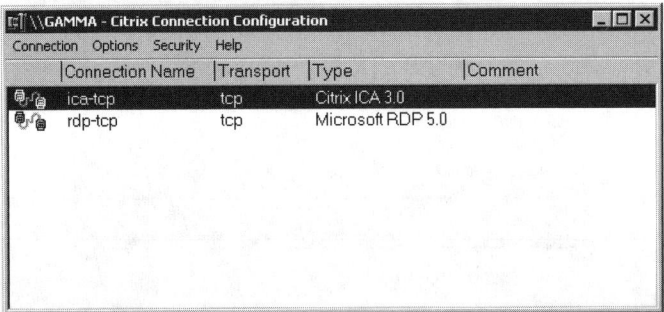

Right-click on the entry for each display protocol, and you'll open a Properties sheet to view or edit the display settings. Most of what you'll do here is determine the channels that are available to the people using the display protocol, thereby determining which features of the display protocol are available.

SpeedScreen Latency Reduction Manager   SpeedScreen Latency Reduction (SLR) is a way of making applications running from a MetaFrame server appear more responsive. As I explain a little later in this chapter, user input goes to an application server via one of the channels in the display protocol. The results of that user input—characters typed into a word processor, for example—are displayed in the client's session via another channel of the display protocol. A long delay—latency—between the time the user provides the input and the results of that input appear on the screen can be disturbing and can lead the user to believe that the application isn't working properly. SLR helps sidestep any latency problems by caching user input and showing it—or showing a "Hey, I'm getting to this" mouse pointer—on the screen before that input has had the time to make the round trip from user to application server and back again. You can change the SLR settings for applications from the SpeedScreen Latency Reduction Manager. As shown in

Figure 2.12, all published applications and MetaFrame servers are listed, so you can be selective about how you're applying SLR.

Figure 2.12 Use the SpeedScreen Latency Reduction Manager to configure SLR settings.

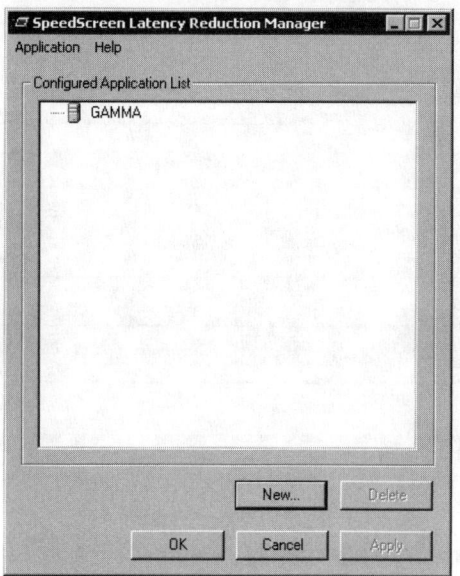

ICA Client Distribution Wizard The ICA Client Distribution Wizard is pretty much what it sounds like: a tool for updating the current database of ICA client files so that you can make sure that you've got the right ones available for use with ICA Client Update. You can install ICA Client files while installing MetaFrame, using the CD-ROM of client files that comes with MetaFrame XP, or you can download more recent versions of the client files from the Citrix website and install them with this wizard. Chapter 5 explains how to use this wizard to update the ICA Client files.

Citrix SSL Relay Configuration Tool Applications published with MetaFrame to a web browser support the Secure Sockets Layer (SSL). Use the SSL Relay Configuration tool shown in Figure 2.13 to configure the current SSL settings, such as the supported encryption types.

Figure 2.13 You'll use the SSL Relay Configuration tool to secure applications published with NFuse.

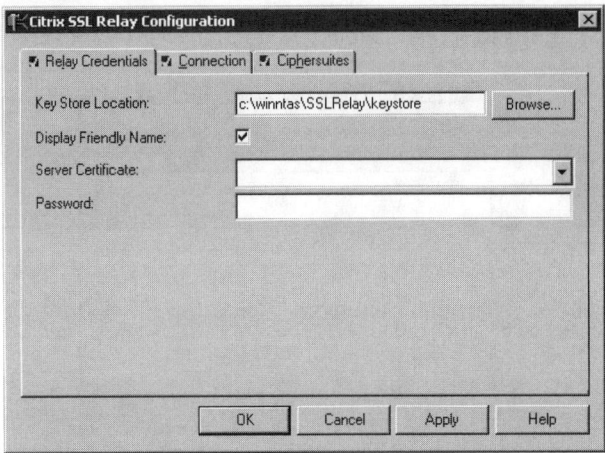

That's it for the ICA Administrator Toolbar. Now, let's take a look at the second set of MetaFrame management tools contained in the Citrix Management Console.

Navigating the Citrix Management Console

Although they'll still need Terminal Services Manager and Configuration for some purposes, MetaFrame XP administrators will spend a lot of time with the Citrix Management Console. One of the major improvements in MetaFrame XP is its consolidation of many management tools into the Citrix Management Console. Rather than having one tool for licensing, one tool for server administration, and so forth, you can manage everything—servers, users, applications, and printers—from a single Java-based console, shown in Figure 2.14.

Figure 2.14 The Citrix Management Console

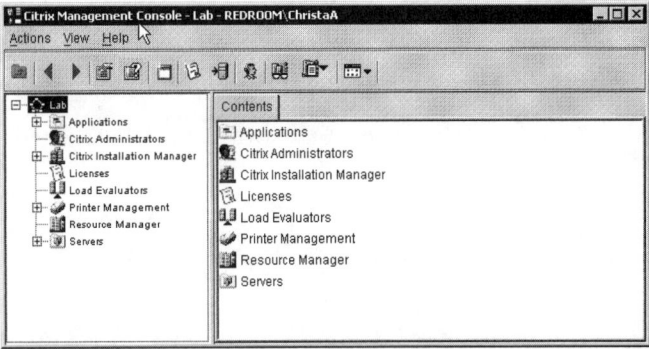

> **NOTE** According to Citrix, the Citrix Management Console is Java-based rather than an MMC snap-in so that MetaFrame for Unix servers could use the same console. The tradeoff, unfortunately, is that the Java-based console is a memory hog. An MMC-compatible snap-in for the Citrix Management Console is included in FR2, so you can make MetaFrame management part of a customized MMC tool instead of having to run a separate tool to support it.

The Citrix Management Console is more comprehensive than the Terminal Services Manager. You'll use it to do all of the following:

- Gather session information (mainly identifiers and running applications) from the perspective of usernames, session IDs, or processes
- Publish applications and application packages you've created with Installation Manager (an option with MetaFrame XPe)
- Set load balancing rules for servers and applications (MetaFrame XPa and XPe only)
- Add licenses to the MetaFrame XP server farm or activate the ones you've already installed
- Manage client printer drivers and limit printer channel bandwidth
- View current per-server information
- Add and remove user accounts in the list of Citrix administrators
- Monitor system performance and create usage reports, if you've installed the Resource Manager that comes with MetaFrame XPe

Not only does the Citrix Management Console provide a unified interface for most server-management tools, you can also use it from a Windows computer that isn't an application server—even from a workstation. If you browse the setup CD-ROM, you'll see that you can choose to either install MetaFrame XP or install the console. If you install the console onto a computer, you can manage application servers from that computer *without* using an ICA license or Terminal Services client access license (TSCAL), even if you're running the console from a Windows operating system (OS) that doesn't come with a TSCAL. (Although the Citrix documentation states that the console will work on NT and Win2K machines but doesn't mention Windows *9x*, I've successfully installed and used the console from a Windows 98 computer.) In practical terms, this means that you can manage a MetaFrame XP server farm without sitting at the console, without running a memory-hungry application on a MetaFrame server, and *without* using up an ICA connection license or TSCAL to do it.

Only certified Citrix administrators can use the Citrix Management Console, and those administrators must supply their username, password, and domain each time they try to open the console—no pass-through authentication allowed. Even domain administrators are forbidden access to the tools unless you specifically add them to the list of Citrix administrators. When you installed MetaFrame XP, you named one Citrix Administrator. Until you add more accounts to the list using the steps in Chapter 6, only that account will be able to use the tool.

MetaFrame XP Command-Line Utilities

So far in this chapter, we've focused on MetaFrame's graphical tools, but you can do quite a lot from the command line as well. I'll talk about these tools in context throughout the book. Just for reference, Table 2.4 lists the tools that come with MetaFrame XP.

Table 2.4 Command-Line Utilities in MetaFrame XP

Command	Function
altaddr	Specify server alternative IP address, as when providing a single IP address for an entire server farm.
app	Runs an application and a batch file, so that you can automatically copy files to new directories or clean up files created while the application was running.
auditlog	Can be used to extract and format security information from the server's event log. To use this command, you must first enable security logging.
change client	Displays, updates, or changes ICA Client device mapping for client-side drives, printers, and ports.
chfarm	Moves a MetaFrame XP server from its current farm to a different (IMA-based) farm or an entirely new farm.
clicense	Add, remove, or view Citrix licenses for the selected farm.
cltprint	Set the number of ICA Client printer pipes, which represent the number of print jobs that can be sent to the printer at one time (the default is 10). Use to provide wider access to a printer or (more likely) to limit that access over low-bandwidth connections.

Table 2.4 Command-Line Utilities in MetaFrame XP *(continued)*

Command	Function
ctxxmlss	Change the XML service port number (80, by default). The original setting is configured during MetaFrame installation.
dsmaint	Configure the IMA data store, or create a backup copy of an Access-based data store.
icaport	Configure TCP/IP port number used for ICA sessions (1494 by default) or restores it to its default setting.
query farm	View information about servers in the farm and the applications published there.
twconfig	Tune ICA display settings for the current server (not for an entire farm; to do that, you'll need to use the Citrix Management Console).

Extras for MetaFrame XPe

MetaFrame XPe administrators have a couple of additional tools in their belts: Installation Management Services for application packaging and delivery to multiple servers, and Resource Management Server for real-time resource usage and reporting.

Installation Management Services MetaFrame 1.8 administrators will recall the Installation Manager as an add-on, but in MetaFrame XP it's been repackaged to be included with MetaFrame XPe. It's not automatically installed with the enterprise version of MetaFrame XP, but the installation CD is part of the package.

For those who aren't familiar with the concept of Installation Manager, you may be wondering why you'd bother with it. It's really an enterprise tool, meant for those who have a lot of servers to manage. Setting up and maintaining a couple of MetaFrame servers—installing MetaFrame XP, installing and tuning the applications to publish, and applying service packs, feature releases, and hotfixes to those servers—is no big deal. Make that couple of MetaFrame servers 20, however, and installing applications and hotfixes on all those servers becomes a larger task. Make those 20 MetaFrame servers 200, and you have a lot of work on your hands.

Installation Manager allows you to streamline the process of deploying applications and hotfixes to MetaFrame servers. After creating packages in MetaFrame's native ADF format or acquiring MSI files from the manufacturer (or making them yourself with Windows 2000's version of WinInstaller), you can deploy those packages for automatic installation to MetaFrame XP servers with the Installation Manager service installed, managing the whole process from a central console. Using a packaged installation, you can perform all of the following tasks from a centralized console:

- Install an application without using the product CD.
- Repair a damaged application.
- Remove or uninstall an application.
- Describe the application and its requirements.
- Tell the Installer service how to access the application files.

In other words, the reason for using Installation Manager is the same reason that you'd use Windows 2000's Remote Installation Services to install servers or IntelliMirror to install applications—simplicity. Using Installation Manager or any other automated installation tool requires some up-front time, but when it comes to repetitive tasks that you'll need to perform many times and in exactly the same way, that initial setup time saves steps in the long run.

Using Installation Manager isn't just a matter of installing the service on one MetaFrame server and letting it rip. To use the service, your network will need four types of servers. A file server stores the ADF and MSI packages used to distribute applications and hotfixes. A server with the Citrix Management Console installed manages the packages. A packager machine—preferably one not used for anything else, for reasons that I'll explain when we talk about packaging—wraps applications into Windows Installer MSI files or Citrix Installation Manager ADF files. The MetaFrame servers receiving those packaged files for automated installation need the Citrix Installer service on them, and must all have a network protocol in common. Once you have all that in place, the process of distributing applications with the Installation Manager looks like this:

1. Create installation packages (ADF and/or MSI files) and store them on a file server.
2. From the CMC, a Citrix administrator assigns applications to MetaFrame servers with the Installation Manager service installed.
3. When you initiate the installation, the MetaFrame servers connect to the file server and install the assigned applications.

In other words, to use Installation Manager, you'll need all the following:

- Administrative rights to manage farm servers
- A management console to assign packages to MetaFrame servers

- A packager computer running Windows 2000 and preferably also running MetaFrame XP, used to create installation packages
- A file server with enough room to store all the installation packages
- The Installer service installed on every MetaFrame XP server that you want to be able to receive packaged installations

I'll talk about how to install and use Installation Manager in Chapter 7.

Resource Manager Server   The Resource Manager allows you to collect server and/or application data from a variety of sources and display it either in real time or in reports, rather like the Windows 2000 System Monitor and Task Manager. You'll need to install support for the Resource Manager on any server for which you want to gather metrics. To install it, just get the CD from the MetaFrame XPe kit, choose to install the product, and let it copy the files—that's it. Once you've done so, you'll see a new entry in the Citrix Management Console called Resource Manager, from which you'll create reports in HTML or comma-delimited files and edit settings to make Resource Manager send you alerts through SNMP or e-mail. Adding support for the Resource Manager also adds new resource management sections to the sections for servers and published applications.

Supported Client Types

Any device that can use RDP (or ICA if the application server is running MetaFrame) can connect to a Windows application server if it's got the appropriate client software installed.

Personal Computers

The most popular Terminal Services client these days is the PC. This is due to a couple of factors. First, unless they're starting afresh, people already have the PCs. Even though WBTs are a little less expensive than low-end PCs—not much, though—they're still an added cost. Second, because not all applications work well in an application server environment, it's often best to run some applications from the terminal server and some locally. Unless you're buying new hardware and don't anticipate any need to run applications locally, you're more likely to have to work with PCs for at least some of your terminal clients.

Windows 2000 and .NET Server come with client software for adding RDP support to PCs running Windows, but you can also get third-party RDP clients written in Linux, or running in Java and thus platform-independent. I'll explain where to get those clients and how to install them in Chapter 5. Citrix maintains a large library of ICA clients for almost any operating system.

Windows Terminals

A Windows terminal is any terminal device designed to connect to a Windows application server. A Windows-*based* terminal (WBT) is such a device that's running a Windows operating system locally—CE or (less frequently) Embedded NT or even Linux. A Windows terminal includes a processor, some amount of memory, network and video support, and input devices: a keyboard (or equivalent) and mouse (or equivalent). The case is generally sealed, and a monitor is not included. The operating system (Windows CE, NT Embedded, Linux, or a proprietary operating system) is stored in local memory. Because it doesn't run applications locally, a Windows terminal doesn't need much memory or CPU power. That said, a Windows terminal's "thin" profile would put many older PCs to shame. A typical WBT might have a 200MHz CPU and 16MB of memory installed; as recently as when Windows 95 hit the market, a reasonably well-equipped PC had a 486DX CPU and 8MB of RAM. Windows terminals are thin, but they're not going to replace the wraith du jour on the modeling circuit.

Choosing a Windows terminal can be more of a chore than it immediately appears—although the devices are pretty similar, they've got subtle differences that can really make a difference in the real world. In Chapter 3, I'll explain more about these differences and give you some tips about how to choose a model that you like.

Handheld PCs

A handheld PC or Pocket PC can look like anything from a laptop's younger sibling to a Palm Pilot. Normally, handheld PCs run WinCE and, therefore, run only WinCE-compatible applications such as Pocket Office. But by downloading and installing the Terminal Services client, you can run Win32 applications or manage a server via RDP when connected to an application server over wired, wireless LAN, or dial-up connections. A handheld PC that runs WinCE can support an RDP PocketPC client available for download from the Microsoft website.

Licensing Terminal Services

So far, we've covered servers, the display protocol, and client types. The last core issue I'd like to talk about in this chapter concerns licensing, because this can be a complicated topic.

Windows 2000 Server Access Licensing

To use an application server, you need the Client Access License required to use any Windows 2000 server *and* a license to run terminal sessions from a Windows 2000 server. Windows 2000 Terminal Services uses two kinds of licenses. Terminal Server Client Access Licenses (TSCALs) and Internet Connector Licenses (ICLs).

TSCALs are issued on a per-seat basis. Anyone in a company who's using the application server must have a TSCAL, regardless of whether they're connecting via RDP or ICA. TSCALs are sold for the retail trade in 5-packs and 20-packs; a 5-pack costs $749 retail and an upgrade from a TSE 5-pack costs $349. (For those not mathematically minded, the retail price comes to just under $150/head retail, which is about what TSE TSCALs cost. The upgrade is about $70/seat.) You will need to *activate*—register with Microsoft—all TSCALs before a trial period of 90 days has expired.

> **NOTE** Those using MetaFrame with Windows 2000 may assume that they only need to license MetaFrame access, because people are getting to the application server via ICA, not RDP. *This is not the case.* Application server licensing is independent of the display protocol used to get to the application server; each computer used to access the application server needs a TSCAL whether terminal sessions use ICA or RDP.

The way that you buy TSCALs determines how you pay for them and how much flexibility you have in the purchase. Most people who buy small volumes of Microsoft products will buy their TSCALs as part of a 5-CAL or 20-CAL Microsoft License Pack (MLP). Physically, an MLP is a thin cardboard envelope that contains the end-user license agreement (EULA) denoting the number of CALs purchased. The MLP for TSCALs in Win2K also includes a license code, a 25-character alphanumeric code that indicates what the license is for and how many TSCALs it purchases (so that you can't fudge the entries and say that you bought 20 TSCALs when you really only bought 5). You can only install an MLP once. Small to medium customers will get their licenses through a program called Microsoft Open License, which allows you to purchase a user-specified quantity of licenses, after which Microsoft issues you an Open License Authorization and license numbers for the licenses, which you can install as many times as you need. Select and Enterprise Agreements for large customers work like open licenses, except that the customer provides their Enrollment Agreement number instead of the Open License numbers.

If you mistakenly issue a per-seat license to a computer that isn't going to be using the application server, then how do you get it back? Sadly, this isn't as easy as it ought to be. Historically, licensing for Win2K application server in Application Server Mode has worked like this: Microsoft licenses access to a Windows application server on a per-seat basis. When you access an application server from a client device, the server checks to see if that client device has a TSCAL granting it access. If it already has one (either by having a TSCAL previously assigned or by being a Win2K Pro machine that has built-in license), then the client logs on. If it doesn't, then the terminal server contacts the license server and gets a TSCAL assigned to that client device. That TSCAL is then stored on the client's hard disk and never leaves. The license server associates that TSCAL with the client, removing it from the "available" pool to the "assigned" pool.

This licensing method is, shall we say, less than perfect. If you reformat or retire a client computer, then its TSCAL is gone and the license server is none the wiser—the TSCAL doesn't go back to the license server. Additionally, a machine that logs onto the terminal server once and never again will eat a TSCAL. Buggy clients can also eat TSCALs if they're not able to "remember" that they have licenses—some Windows terminals have had this problem. Linux isn't consistent in how it uses TSCALs, either. Some versions of Linux draw licenses from the unlimited pool, as though they were Windows 2000 Professional workstations. Some, however, are issued two licenses for each machine: one for the machine's name in uppercase, and one for the machine's name in lowercase. Even apart from the problem of clients taking extra licenses, the per-seat model has problems, particularly *that there is no warning that this is how licenses are used.* Yes, it's per-seat licensing, and we really should know how a product is licensed before we use it. However, the real world doesn't always work that way, and irreversibly issuing licenses to machines that perhaps shouldn't have them but won't give them up doesn't leave a whole lot of room for error. I have talked to more than a few people who were experimenting with their new terminal server from client machines, only to discover later that after their testing and experimenting they had no licenses left. The only way to get those lost licenses back was to call the Microsoft clearinghouse and tell them how many licenses you'd lost to get a new license key. While the waiting time to talk to a clearinghouse agent isn't long and the people at the clearinghouse are pretty responsive (and did not require any kind of proof from me; as one agent I spoke to observed, they're operating on the honor system), placing a telephone call to recite a license number is not something you want to do very often.

Until April 2001, that was the way license reclamation worked, and it was a real sticking point for Terminal Services adoption. However, Microsoft has issued a hotfix for Win2K Terminal Services that helps resolve the problem. (SP3 includes this fix.) Although it won't fix *all* licensing woes, it helps with the ones associated with one-time users inadvertently walking off with TSCALs. Rather than permanently assigning TSCALs to clients, after you apply the hotfix to all application servers and license servers the license server will give first-time requesters a TSCAL with a timeout period (a randomly assigned interval between 52 and 89 days). When the user logs onto the application server, the application server tells the license server that the license has been validated—i.e., used by someone with permission to log onto the application server. The TSCAL is then assigned to that machine. Every time someone connects to the application server from that machine, the application server will check the expiration date on the TSCAL. When the expiration date is under 7 days, it will renew the TSCAL assignment to that machine for another 52 to 89 days. Should the client machine not log into the application server before its TSCAL expires, its TSCAL will return to the pool of available licenses.

This fix applies only to TSCALs assigned after you apply the hotfix or service pack to all application servers and license servers. If you lose the license database to a dead hard disk or other catastrophe, you'll still need to call the clearinghouse to get your licenses back. This method still assigns licenses to machines, not to users—you can still run out of TSCALs if Joe User logs onto the application server from every device he can think of. However, it appears that the licensing model should now allow unused licenses to eventually return to the pool of available licenses, and that's a start.

> **Can Windows Terminal Services Be Licensed Per Connection?**
>
> The necessity to license Windows Terminal Services on a per-seat basis for in-house use is a source of frustration to some. Although it allows you to get double duty out of shared computers, it does penalize companies with users who want to log on from more than one location. Because one of the advantages of using Terminal Services is that it allows you to get to the same application set no matter what client type you're logging on from (Windows 2000 computer, Windows 95 desktop, Windows terminal, or even a handheld computer), this can be a little tough on the customer who'd like to provide that location independence to their user base. Windows 2000 application servers are often MetaFrame servers, and MetaFrame is licensed on a per-connection basis, so the per-seat licensing is even more aggravating because it requires you to keep track of two different licensing models to access the same server. Although it isn't yet finalized, it appears that Microsoft may be offering per-connection licensing in .NET Server.
>
> It might occur to you that a middleware product licensed on a per-connection basis—one that allowed a computer to act as a launching point for a number of Windows terminal sessions—might be way of accessing an application server on a per-connection basis. (Tarantella and ThinAnywhere are two examples of like products.) The idea would be that you'd use only one TSCAL: the one issued to the middleware server accessing the Windows terminal server, and then you could use the per-connection licensing to the middleware server to your heart's content. This would allow as many people as needed the connection to use the terminal server. Nice idea, but it doesn't work. Although the Windows terminal server would only issue a single license to the middleware server, you'd be breaking the licensing agreement, which specifies that each person *using* the terminal server needs a license, if you did this. The end result is that there is no legal way to circumvent the in-house per-seat licensing.

Windows 2000 Professional comes with its own TSCAL for Windows 2000 Terminal Services, so any Windows 2000 Pro machine connecting to a Windows 2000 terminal server will not use up licenses from the installed license packs. However, you still need a license server to use the Windows 2000 TSCALs. Because .NET Server is still in beta, its licensing is not yet finalized. However, given the current licensing model it seems likely that Windows XP Professional clients will have built-in TSCALs for using .NET Server Terminal Services, while Windows 2000 Pro and other client types will need TSCALs to access a .NET Server terminal server.

What if you don't have a license server set up or the application server can't get to it for some reason? Does that prevent anyone from using the application server? Not quite—in that case, they can get a temporary license. If a client machine with no TSCAL (or a TSCAL from the Unlimited pool that has not yet been listed in the licensing database) attempts to connect to an application server and the license server isn't available or has no license packs installed, then the terminal server will issue that client machine a temporary license. That temporary license will expire after 90 days and the machine will no longer be able to connect to the application server.

Internet Connector Licenses

The Windows 2000 Terminal Services Internet Connector License (TSICL) allows a maximum of 200 concurrent users to connect anonymously to an application server via the Internet. That's right—you can't use a TSICL to dial into the network from home but will instead need a TSCAL for your home computer. The TSICLs are solely for the purpose of demonstrating web-enabled applications to Internet users. Not only that, but according to Microsoft, you can't install the TSICL pack on a Win2K application server that's for employees. The server will only allow client access to Terminal Services through the Internet—anyone who logs onto that server will use one of the TSICLs and will connect as an anonymous user. A 200-pack ICL for Win2K costs $9,999, and these ICL packs are only available to Microsoft Select volume customers.

Frankly, the TSICLs aren't good for much, since you can't legally use them to give employees home access to Terminal Services. Although it might sound as though the TSICLs are useful for application service providers (ASPs, which are companies that lease applications to people via a dial-up connection), they're really not—ASPs have a different licensing model. As noted earlier, the only use I can see for these licenses is for people offering samples of their software via a website.

Figuring out which license gets used when can be tricky, so Table 2.5 sums up the licensing requirements for different kinds of client and connection scenarios.

Table 2.5 Terminal Services Client Access License Types

Situation	Terminal Services License Type Used	Cost
Users connecting from Win2K Professional desktops	Built-in license	N/A
Users connecting from any desktop not using Win2K Professional	Terminal Server Client Access License (TSCAL)	A 5-pack of TSCALs costs $749 retail, and an upgrade from a TSE 5-pack costs $349.
Anonymous users connecting to the application server via the Internet	Terminal Services Internet Connector License (TSICL)	200 simultaneous anonymous connections cost $9,999. Must be purchased separately.
Users connecting when a Terminal Services licensing server is absent or has no license packs installed	Temporary 90-day license issued by Terminal Server	N/A, but license will cease working after 90 days and you will not be able to renew it. For those machines to connect again, you'll need to set up a license server with TSCALs.

MetaFrame XP Licensing

After you've sorted out Windows Terminal Services licensing, MetaFrame XP licensing is relatively simple. MetaFrame XP is licensed solely on a per-connection basis. You can install any version of MetaFrame XP on as many servers as you want, but you must pay for each concurrent connection to the server.

MetaFrame XP uses two types of licenses: product licenses and connection licenses; a licensing serial number can include either or both. A *product license* is a license to run a particular kind of MetaFrame XP product on a server: XPs, XPa, or XPe. A server farm must have a product license with one license count to run Citrix server software on each server in the server farm. When you add a Citrix license to your server farm, the product license provided by the license number appears on the Product tab in Citrix Management Console. Only one product license appears on the tab, even if the product license—such as a MetaFrame XPa product license—enables more than one Citrix product. A server only actively uses a product license when the IMA service that allows it to communicate with the other MetaFrame XP servers in the farm is running. With a MetaFrame XPa or

MetaFrame XPe product license, which enables multiple products on your servers, you cannot divide the product license to enable one product on one server and other products on other servers.

A *connection license* enables ICA Client connections to MetaFrame XP servers. A server farm must have a connection license with one license count for each concurrent ICA connection to the MetaFrame XP servers in the farm. Each MetaFrame XP product license provides one grace license for the administrator to connect to the server console. The grace license prevents the server from reporting a licensing error if you install no connection licenses and log onto the server before putting it into service for ICA Clients. License serial numbers that you receive with MetaFrame XP can provide connection licenses alone or in combination with a MetaFrame XP product license. If you add more users, you can get additional connection licenses with the license count you require.

> **NOTE** Product and connection licenses are normally *pooled*, or general to the entire MetaFrame XP farm. Pooling licenses makes them available to any server or client that needs them without reference to which server they're trying to connect to. You can, however, assign some subset of connection licenses to a particular server if you want to guarantee that a certain number of licenses will always be available to that server.

Feature releases get license numbers, too. You'll need to provide licensing information for every feature release that you want farm servers to be able to use.

MetaFrame XP Licensing Numbers

When you install MetaFrame XP and set it up, you'll spend some time typing in long strings of numbers. Each string of numbers has a different purpose. To help you ensure that you've got your server set up properly, read on to understand what all the strings of numbers are for. You've got to worry about the following:

- Product codes
- Serial numbers
- License numbers
- License activation codes

Each Citrix software package includes a *product code*, a number that looks like 0E11-0923, located under the sealed flap of the product package. (By opening the seal, you're agreeing to the end-user license agreement.) This number identifies the type of MetaFrame XP installed; distinguishes from among retail, evaluation, and not-for-resale product versions; and specifies the product license a server needs to get from the license pool to function. Identifying a server with a product code limits the server to accepting only the license types available to that product type. For example, a MetaFrame XPa server can't draw from the pool of available MetaFrame XPe licenses, and an evaluation copy of MetaFrame XP must draw from the pool of evaluation connection licenses.

> **NOTE** The use of product codes to identify valid license types means that you're not guaranteed a connection just because you have connection licenses available in the server farm. To connect to a server, you must have a connection license that works with that server's product code.

The product's *serial number* is under the same sealed flap as the product code. The serial number represents the licenses you bought, as opposed to the product code's representation of the types of licenses available to that server product. The server's serial number is a 25-character (five groups of 5, separated by dashes) group of alphanumeric and symbol characters identifying the software package you purchased. For licensing of MetaFrame XP and other IMA-based Citrix products, you use a *license number* that is derived from each serial number you enter in a server farm. The Citrix Management Console displays each license number, which consists of the original serial number plus additional characters; these additional characters are referred to as the machine code.

The *license numbers* do the actual work of providing licenses, whether server or connection, or both. You'll need to install license numbers on a MetaFrame XP server before it will accept connections. License numbers appear on the License Number tab of the Licensing tool. Just as you'll need to activate TSCALs, you'll also need to activate ICA Client connection licenses.

To start using MetaFrame XP, you need a MetaFrame Starter System consisting of the server media and 20 user licenses. The retail price for the Starter System depends on whether you get Subscription Advantage (SA), which gives you free Feature Releases and product upgrades. Table 2.6 outlines the pricing scheme for MetaFrame XP.

Table 2.6 MetaFrame XP Pricing Structure

Version	Retail Price (with SA)	Retail Price (without SA)
MetaFrame XPs Starter System	$5800	$5000
MetaFrame XPa Starter System	$6900	$6000
MetaFrame XPe Starter System	$8000	$7000

If you need more licenses beyond the 20 that come with the Starter System, you can purchase them separately in groups of 5, 10, 20, or 50 and add them to the central server. The price for the packs depends on how many licenses are in it, but the pricing structure works more or less like this: the retail price for MetaFrame XPs connection license is $290 with SA and $250 without; for XPa it's $345 with SA and $300 without, and for XPe it's $400 with SA and $350 without. Complete pricing information and tools for helping you find a Citrix reseller are on the Citrix website (http://www.citrix.com).

> **NOTE** If you already use MetaFrame 1.8 and you bought SA, migration to the closest-available MetaFrame XP package is free. The match isn't perfect (say, for someone who bought RMS but not load balancing—unlikely, but possible), but Citrix tells me that it'll do its best to make people happy when it comes to upgrades.

Remote Administration Mode Licensing

Although this book focuses on Terminal Services in Application Server mode, not Remote Administration mode, the licensing difference between the two is worth pointing out. Remote Administration mode does not use the same licensing model that Application Server mode does. You don't need a TSCAL to access a server for remote administration. Rather, the server will accept only up to two simultaneous connections (disconnected sessions count toward the two even though they're not currently in use), and only from accounts with administrative privileges. Because Remote Administration mode licensing is done on a concurrent-user basis, not per-seat, it doesn't matter which computer a person connects from.

The way that Remote Administration mode licensing works offers a nice back door into using Terminal Services. If only a couple of people need to use an application server at a time, then you can set up Terminal Services in Remote Administration mode and give people Administrator-level accounts to log on with. This will, of course, give those people complete access to the application server—this isn't something you'd want to do casually. And the server will not be optimized for running applications, but for running server processes. But developing on a server running in Remote Administration mode is one way to provide access to an application server for a limited number of trusted people, say developers wanting to test their applications. Even better, it allows those developers to test their applications in a multiuser environment.

Application Licensing

Application licensing for Terminal Services works according to the licensing model for the application. When Windows Terminal Services first became available, this fact offered some potential loopholes for applications licensed according to where the application *ran*, not where it was *displayed*. Since the application ran only on the application server, obeying the letter (if not the spirit) of the licensing agreement might have permitted you to get away with having only one license for each application server running the application.

As Windows Terminal Services has increased in popularity, more application vendors are supporting their applications in a multiuser environment, which is helpful. The vendors that haven't yet made this move are working to do so—I've talked with some who are trying to sort out why their customers are having problems running their products from an application server instead of from a single-user workstation. With this improved support, however, comes a catch: those application vendors are going to license their products in a way that makes sense in a multiuser environment. I can't tell you how a particular product will be licensed sight unseen, but always check the license agreement and get enough licenses before running applications from a terminal server. If you're using MetaFrame XP, then Load Balancing or Resource Management Server may be able to help you monitor your application usage.

Summary

In this chapter, I've explained some of the key fundamentals of how Windows Terminal Services works, from the server-side functioning through the display protocol to the client. At this point, you should also understand how Terminal Services licensing works. In Chapter 3, we'll take a look at how to apply this information when it comes to server sizing and planning the Terminal Services rollout, before completing the installation in Chapter 4.

3

Planning the Terminal Server Environment

Chapter 1, "Introducing Windows Terminal Services," explained the origins of Windows Terminal Services and explained how you can use them—and where you can't. Chapter 2, "Core Parts of Windows Terminal Services," examined some key concepts of Windows Terminal Services you should be aware of before starting (for example, the tools you'll use to manage servers and user connections, and the licensing structure). You're probably eager to start *using* the terminal servers, or at least installing them, but first we need to cover one more topic: planning the structure of the server-based computing network.

Planning the Server Side

As the server goes, so goes the terminal server experience. Obviously, the hardware you supply the server with will affect server performance. Perhaps less obviously, the role you assign the server in the network will also affect terminal server performance.

Choosing Server Roles

A Windows 2000 server may be either a member server or a domain controller. Most of the time, an application server should not be a domain controller. First, and most important, the stress of authenticating user access to the domain isn't good for terminal server performance. Second, the permissions attached to the domain controller don't normally allow people to interactively log on to a domain controller, which is what people are doing when they log on to a terminal server.

> **NOTE** It *is* okay to install Terminal Services in Remote Administration mode on a domain controller. It is also a good idea, giving you an easy and inexpensive way of remotely controlling servers. Just don't try to make a domain controller an application server.

When it comes to licensing, however, the story changes. Whether you're using just Windows Terminal Services or adding MetaFrame XP, you'll need a Terminal Services licensing server. If you're using Windows 2000 domains, this licensing server must be a domain controller. If you're using NT domains or workgroups, then the licensing server will be a member server.

Terminal Server Sizing

When it comes to creating a terminal server, the first things many people think of are processor speed and memory. They're important—and that's why I put them at the top of the list—but they're not the only pieces of a terminal server you need to consider, and you'll ignore the others to your peril. When choosing hardware for a terminal server, consider the entire package:

- Processor
- Memory
- Hard disk, including file system and RAID for data protection and performance
- System bus type
- Network card
- Video capability
- Number of servers you'll use

Choosing a Processor

Processor speed is basic to everything a computer does. When you're sizing a terminal server, consider both how that processor works and how many processors you'll need.

Balancing Cache and Calculating Speed   When choosing a processor for a terminal server, don't be blinded by the speed rating, its measurement in megahertz (MHz). A processor's speed measures only one aspect of that processor's abilities: how fast it can process data. Although this is important, being able to crunch numbers quickly doesn't help if the numbers in need of crunching aren't available to the processor. Therefore, data may be stored in the processor's *cache*, a location on board the processor where it (the processor) can store information that it's likely to need again in the near future. Older processors only had an cache internal to the processor called the L1 cache, but modern processors have both the L1 cache and a larger external cache made of static RAM (SRAM) called the L2 cache. SRAM remembers everything from the time the data goes into memory until the time the data is either removed or the machine is turned off. Unlike dynamic RAM (DRAM), the component of main system memory, SRAM does not need to be refreshed every four milliseconds, so it's much faster than DRAM. It's also a lot more expensive.

> **NOTE** Just to confuse things, some processors have begun incorporating L2 cache into the processor to speed things up and now have an external *L3* cache. However, the basic principle remains the same: some cache is inside the processor and some is outside. The cache that's inside the processor can spit out data as fast as the processor can use it; cache outside the processor is a little slower, but it's larger than the internal cache and still has lower retrieval times than main memory.

There is no relationship between processor speed and cache size—faster chips do not necessarily have larger caches. These days, I'd almost certainly go for the larger cache, unless we were talking about a *serious* speed disparity. If you're weighing a 700MHz processor with a lot of cache against a 1.4GHz chip with a little cache, go for the 700MHz processor. Terminal servers can be computer-bound, but they are more likely to be memory-bound, and the difference between 700MHz and 1.5GHz isn't enough to justify deliberately choosing less cache space.

How Many Processors Does a Terminal Server Need? At this writing, most applications and many functions of the operating system that a terminal server will need to support are *single-threaded*. Single-threaded programs are written to execute instructions linearly on a single processor, as in this very simplified example:

First do A

Then do B

Then do C

Then do D

Because the program is designed for the instructions to be executed linearly, double-teaming the code won't improve performance even if the instructions happen to execute on more than one processor. A *multithreaded* application or operating system, in contrast, is designed to execute on more than one processor at once, thereby reducing the required execution time. Because the server can do A and B at the same time, it gets to C more quickly, but program design is more complicated.

Windows servers, and especially shared application servers, are always doing more than one thing at a time. Having more than one processor in a computer reduces the waiting time for any single processor. Processor speed is not the main bottleneck of a terminal server. However, if you're buying a new system, I'd suggest that you at least plan for a multiprocessor system, so that you can add more processing power without having to replace the server's motherboard. That said, given Windows server operating systems Win32 architecture, I'd probably top servers out at two-way (that is, two processors) instead of four-way. A 32-bit operating system can only address 4GB of RAM, so a four-way server could potentially increase the likelihood of a RAM bottleneck by concentrating too much processor power in one place, without having room for the memory to back that processing power. If you need more processing power than one two-way server can give you, then you probably need more memory and I/O power, too, and will benefit from another server. When Windows operating systems are normally 64-bit, then more processors in a single terminal server will make more sense.

I'll talk more about how many servers you'll need a little later in this chapter. For now, we'll look at the other big issue in building a terminal server: main memory.

Main Memory

You really can't put too much RAM in an application server. Here's why.

32-bit operating systems can address up to 4GB of memory storage—that is, they can recognize 4GB of addresses for storing data. This 4GB may not be (and usually isn't) backed by 4GB of RAM. Rather, this *virtual storage area* is backed partially by RAM, and partially by an area on a hard disk called the *paging file*. So far as it can, the server will store data that it is currently using in RAM. Although, as we've seen, RAM is slower than processor cache, it's a heck of a lot faster than a hard disk. It takes nanoseconds to pull data from RAM and microseconds to pull data from the paging file on disk. However, when RAM gets full, the excess will go into the paging file—*paged out*, to use the jargon, to be retrieved to RAM and *paged in* when an application or the operating system requests it. Most data can be paged to disk without harm; any data that must remain in RAM (because retrieving it would take too long) is stored in the non-paged pool set of addresses in virtual memory so that the data can't be paged out to the hard disk. All the data that an application has stored in RAM at any given moment is called that process's *working set*. A process's working set can be only so big; when it extends its bounds, the Memory Manager sends the data that the process isn't currently using to the paging file. In Windows 2000, the least recently used data goes to the paging file first.

Keeping track of the location of data—is it in RAM or in the paging file?—is vital. Applications are not designed to know the physical location of their data; they're designed to request the data stored at a particular virtual address. When an application requests some data, the Memory Manager looks in its records to see to what physical location—RAM or paging file—the requested virtual address maps. If the information requested is in RAM, then the Memory Manager retrieves it. If the information is in the paging file, the Memory Manager pages it back into RAM and *then* gets it as though the data had been stored in RAM all along. Although paging sounds time-consuming and slow (and, if you overuse paging, it is), realistically, you'll always have some data paged to disk. Modern operating systems are designed to work this way to permit more data to be loaded into memory than would fit if RAM were the only possible storage space. You just want to limit its use, because reading data from the paging file on the hard disk takes more time than reading it from RAM. To do that, you need more memory. Most terminal servers these days will have 1GB or more of RAM.

However, just throwing more RAM at the server isn't a guarantee of good performance. When choosing memory for a terminal server, you have to consider memory speed and reliability.

Memory Speed Considerations   When looking at memory types, you may see *dynamic RAM (DRAM)* or *synchronous DRAM (SDRAM)*. Both kinds of dynamic RAM can only hold data for up to four milliseconds before that data must be refreshed. The difference between the two comes in cost and performance: DRAM is cheaper, but slower.

> **NOTE**   Don't confuse SDRAM with the SRAM used to back the processor's external cache. SDRAM isn't static RAM, it's faster dynamic RAM.

Conventional DRAM is *asynchronous*, meaning that it is not attuned to the system clock. Wildly oversimplified, accessing data stored in DRAM works like this:

1. An application requests some data that is stored in memory, referencing a particular virtual address location.
2. The Memory Manager looks in its records to see what physical location maps to that virtual memory address. If the requested information is in the paging file, it pages that information back into RAM.
3. The Memory Manager passes this information to the memory controller, which finds the chips corresponding to the Memory Manager's physical address.
4. Having found the data, the memory controller makes the chips feed the requested information onto the data bus, where the processor or another device that needs the data can get to it.

The time required to complete this process is the memory's *access time* (similar to a hard disk's access time). Asynchronous DRAM has access time that is counted in nanoseconds (ns), or billionths of a second. Most DRAM you'll see these days has access times of 50–70ns. The lower the access time, the better—but even 60ns RAM is operating at less than 33MHz while server motherboards will operate at upward of 100MHz. Why so slow? Not only does DRAM have to take some time to find the right piece of physical memory to start from, it has to sling the contents of memory into the memory bus one block at a time and then go back and find the next piece of data to send to the bus rather than finding the data and retrieving it in a single action. A type of DRAM called Extended Data Output (EDO) speeds things up by giving conventional DRAM help finding the next piece of data to send to the bus so that it's ready to go when the DRAM can send it, but even EDO memory is much slower than the motherboard. Slow memory that can't remotely keep up with the processor's demands for information leads to cycles called *wait states* when the processor isn't doing anything but waiting for data. Ideally, the server will experience as few wait states as possible—that's downtime to a processor. You're going to have wait states, because a server's motherboard operates at a minimum of 100MHz and a processor may be 10 times faster than that, but the idea is to minimize them as much as possible.

SDRAM can be faster than asynchronous DRAM for two reasons. First, it uses a bursty technology to look at a whole bunch of data at once. Second, it's synchronized with the system clock—in other words, it can work as fast as the motherboard can (up to 100MHz, at this point).

NOTE When purchasing SDRAM, make sure that it can keep up with your motherboard. Some SDRAM is rated for 100MHz, but some is slower than that.

SDRAM takes as long as DRAM to get oriented. However, once it finds the initial starting point for the memory it needs to pull data from, SDRAM can read entire blocks of that memory all at once, instead of finding one piece of data, sending it to the memory bus, finding the next piece of data and sending that to the bus, and so on. This significantly reduces memory access times. SDRAM is often rated at 12, 10, or even 7 nanoseconds. However, these numbers don't tell the whole story. They don't necessarily refer to actual access times, but to the maximum speed at which the SDRAM module can burst data onto the bus. This does not include the time required to find the first block of memory to read from, the way asynchronous DRAM speed ratings do, which is why SDRAM access times are much lower than DRAM access times. SDRAM with a rated speed of 7ns is not 10 times faster than DRAM with a rated speed of 70ns, it's only faster once it finds its starting point. However, the way that SDRAM finds and retrieves data should make it faster than DRAM.

> **NOTE** There are several different kinds of SDRAM. Check with your hardware supplier to find out which will work best for your terminal servers.

Memory Reliability: Understanding Error Checking and Correcting The accuracy of your terminal server's memory is even more important than its speed. Why would it be inaccurate? Recall that DRAM/SDRAM won't remember anything for longer than 4 milliseconds and must be continually reminded of what it knows. (I'm sure that you've met some people like this.) Data is stored as electrical charges that are on (1) or off (0), and "on" is registered as an electrical impulse of, say, 5 volts. If the charge is 5 volts, then it's a 1; if it's 0 volts, then it's a 0. The trouble is that voltage is not an all-or-nothing proposition: it's not like a light with a conventional switch that flips on or off, but more like a light with a dimmer switch that has a range between "all on" and "off." If you turn a dimmer switch down low enough, it can be hard to tell if the light is on or off, so it is with memory voltages. If the sensor reading the memory value detects 4.9 volts, it's going to assume that that counts as a 1. But if the sensor detects lower voltage of, say, 1 volt, then even though the bit really should be a 1, the sensor may read it as 0 because its voltage is so low. In a binary system, exchanging a 0 for a 1 makes a lot of difference. *Bit-flipping* can take place because of *hard errors* or *soft errors*. Hard errors mean that you've got damaged hardware and will be consistent until you replace the hardware. Soft errors may be caused by any number of problems: minor damage, static shocks, heat, timing problems, wandering poltergeists in the motherboard...you get the idea. A soft error might repeat, or it might not, which means that it's easy to mistake soft errors for buggy software. Buggy software causes problems, obviously, but buggy *hardware* can, too. Just for one example, I've got one older server that routinely blue-screens every time the server room gets too warm. Keep the room cool, and it's fine.

To avoid problems caused by sensor errors, you can get error-checking or error-correcting memory. There are three main classes of memory. *Non-parity* memory has enough storage space to hold its data, nothing more. Eight bits hold 1 byte of data. *Parity* memory adds an extra bit for parity information, so that holding 1 byte of data takes 9 bits. When DRAM sends memory to the memory bus, having the parity information acts as a sort of reality check—is that really what I meant? If the results don't correspond to the parity information, then the memory controller can try reading it again. Parity checking provides single-bit error detection for the system memory, but does not handle multibit errors and can't correct memory errors. Therefore, for those times when you need to know that you've made a mistake and would like to correct it, there is an alternative. An advanced class of parity memory called *error correcting code (ECC)* memory can not only detect memory errors but fix them on computers with a chipset supporting ECC (you'll need to check to see if this is true of your hardware). ECC can detect both single-bit and multibit errors and can fix single-bit errors. Parity memory is more expensive than non-parity, because it has overhead for the parity information. ECC is even more expensive because of the additional redundancy required to support its greater error-handling skills, using 7 bits to protect 32 bits, or 8 bits to protect 64 bits. Special ECC memory modules are designed specifically for use in ECC mode, but most modern motherboards that support ECC will work in that mode using standard parity memory modules as well. You will need to enable ECC support in the BIOS. While ECC represents a slight slowdown in memory speed, its ability to handle errors is well worth it on a terminal server. The application server is not the place to scrimp on hardware.

How Much Memory Do I Need?   As I said earlier, memory is the most likely bottleneck on a terminal server. Not only do you have to maintain applications and the operating system in memory, you have to maintain the data that those applications are using. The amount of memory you need depends on how people are using the terminal server. Microsoft and Citrix both suggest certain guidelines for calculating how much memory "task-based" and "knowledge users" will need, but a better idea is to run a pilot with a few typical users and see how much memory they need, scaling the requirements based on the results. (The memory requirements scale pretty linearly once you take into account the needs of the base operating system and of MetaFrame if you're using it.) More memory is *never* a bad idea. Be sure to plan your memory placement to make it easy to add more if you need it. In other words, don't fill in all the slots with small memory modules; get large modules and leave some slots open.

When calculating the memory requirements of a MetaFrame server, don't forget to take the CMC into account if you'll ever run it directly on the application server. The Java-based CMC goes through memory like it hasn't had a decent meal in weeks, and the more servers and applications that you have in your farm, the more memory it will need. Citrix recommends that you have a *minimum* of 64MB of RAM in a computer just to support the CMC, let alone anything else you might be doing. The idea of using Java was to make it possible to manage MetaFrame XP for Windows and MetaFrame XP for Unix servers from the same console, since both Unix and Windows computers can run Java. In practice, this hasn't gone so well.

> **NOTE**   Because the Java-based tool is so memory-hungry, FR2 for MetaFrame XP has a MMC-based Citrix Management Console. Those not using FR2 should seriously consider managing the servers remotely from a workstation with the console installed to avoid stressing the server unnecessarily.

Server Disks

Another key element of a fast and reliable server is a fast and reliable disk drive. Although today's marketplace offers two alternatives—IDE and SCSI—the choice for MetaFrame servers will almost certainly be SCSI.

IDE versus SCSI A hard disk has two important parts: the disk itself and its controller card. To avoid the noise problems inherent in a disk design wherein the drive controller and the hard disk are connected by floppy cables, in 1988, Western Digital and others developed a standard called the *Integrated Drive Interface (IDE)*. An IDE drive's host adapter is for handling communication between the motherboard and the drive controller, not for doing any kind of data manipulation. The host adapter identifies each device linked to it according to whether it's a "master" or "slave" (or sometimes "secondary slave") device. The original IDE technology had a couple of limitations. First, you could only plug up to two devices into the controller card. Multiple drives (or other IDE devices, such as tape drives) required additional controller cards. Second, the drives weren't very big. The maximum size of an IDE drive is 528MB, which isn't remotely large enough to be useful on any kind of modern computer. An enhancement of IDE called EIDE (Extended/Enhanced Integrated Drive Electronics) helped alleviate these problems. EIDE controllers can accommodate up to four devices and can be *huge*—I've seen them at 120GB, and I'll bet that by the time you read this even larger sizes are available. EIDE drives are quite inexpensive, too. But since the amount of disk space and the cost of providing it may not be the most important thing about a terminal server's disks, I must recommend another disk technology: SCSI.

SCSI (Small Computer Systems Interface) was originally developed by Apple Computer. As in EIDE, SCSI puts the drive controller and the hard disk in a single unit connected to the motherboard with a host adapter. The difference lies in the way that the drive controller communicates with the host adapter. SCSI host adapters can accommodate any kind of SCSI-compatible device. The devices connect to each other in a daisy chain that may extend outside the body of the computer and, in basic SCSI, can include up to seven devices in addition to the host adapter. Although each device is connected to another device, not to the host adapter, all can communicate with the host adapter. The host adapter tells which device in the chain is "talking" to it by the SCSI ID assigned to each device. ID 7 is reserved for the host adapter, IDs 0 and 1 are for hard drives (with 0 reserved for the boot drive), but IDs 2–6 may be used by any other device in the SCSI chain. The IDs don't have to go in order of where the devices are in the SCSI chain, nor do they all have to be used (that is, you don't necessarily have to have seven devices in the chain). The only vital points are that the reserved IDs must be used for their purpose and must terminate the SCSI chain on both ends. Table 3.1 describes the several different kinds of SCSI that Citrix recommends for using with MetaFrame. As you would guess, faster is better.

> **NOTE** SCSI-1, the predecessor to SCSI-2, used a 25-pin connector and did not support SCSI chains. When people refer to "SCSI" without elaborating, they're probably referring to SCSI-2, not SCSI-1.

Table 3.1 Types of SCSI Interfaces

SCSI Type	Description
SCSI-2	8-bit bus; supports data rates of 4Mbps
Fast and Wide SCSI	16-bit bus; supports data transfer rates of 20Mbps
Ultra SCSI	8-bit bus; supports data transfer rates of 20Mbps
Ultra Wide SCSI/SCSI-3	16-bit bus; supports data transfer speeds of 40Mbps
Ultra2 SCSI	8-bit bus; supports data transfer rates of 40Mbps
Ultra2 SCSI Wide	16-bit bus; supports data transfer rates of 80Mbps

Even more important than data transfer rates is the difference in the way that EIDE and SCSI get data on and off the data bus. EIDE and SCSI host adapters may each have several devices attached to them. However, EIDE can listen to only one device at a time, which means that a fast hard disk could be held up waiting for the host adapter to finish reading from a slow CD-ROM drive. It also means that the single device that the EIDE host adapter is listening to is taking up all the cable bandwidth, crowding out any other devices with waiting read or write instructions. SCSI, in contrast, can handle communicating with more than one device at a time: the host adapter can multitask and the devices in the SCSI chain can share bandwidth. While the CD-ROM drive is turning to find the requested data, the host adapter can write data to a hard disk. The bottom line is this: When picking a device interface for terminal servers, get SCSI.

Reducing Downtime with RAID Subsystems   Disk type is related to data protection. Data protection isn't just about backups. You need to back up terminal servers, particularly if you're using MetaFrame, since you'll need to preserve the data store recording the server farm information, but backups have one major failing: you have to restore them. If the system disk on a terminal server fails, then that server is unavailable until you fix the problem or restore the backups to another server—not an instantaneous process. Considering that a single terminal server may be supplying applications for dozens of people, downtime is less than ideal.

One way to reduce server downtime in the event of disk failures is to arrange data on a redundant array of independent disks (RAID). I've discussed RAID in significantly more detail in *Mastering Windows 2000 Server, Fourth Edition* (Sybex, 2002), but here's the gist as it relates to terminal servers.

RAID is designed to protect data from single disk or controller failures through a combination of distribution and redundancy—in short, by treating multiple disks as a single unit and writing either original data or a means of re-creating it on all disks in the array. For example, disk mirroring is one kind of RAID. When you mirror data, you are maintaining a copy of the mirrored partition on a separate disk. If the original disk fails, then you have—and can use—the copy. Some forms of RAID use the redundant data for reducing disk read times, too. The more alike the disks in an array are, the better they will perform in tandem.

Types of RAID Broadly speaking, there are two approaches to fault-tolerant RAID: complete duplication and the creation of parity information for regeneration. RAID 1, *disk mirroring*, is the most common type of data duplication and the simplest form of RAID. When two disks are mirrored, they're treated as a single entity called a *mirror set* with a single drive letter. All changes applied to the storage area represented by this drive letter apply to both disks in the mirror set. If one disk fails, then the data in the mirror set remains available because the duplicate disk is still running. The mirror set won't be fault tolerant until you replace the dead disk and regenerate the mirror information onto it, but the data will be available.

> **NOTE** Of course, if the two disks in the mirror set are controlled by a single controller card and the controller card fails, you're in trouble. Mirroring disks controlled by different controller cards is called *disk duplexing*. Apart from the use of two controllers instead of one, disk duplexing is identical to disk mirroring.

RAID 1 works pretty well even in software. It has low processor overheard because all the drive controller must do is write data to two disks, rather than one, and read times are actually *reduced* over ordinary disk reads because the drive controller can draw data from two sources. Disk mirroring's low overhead makes RAID 1 the only type of data-protection RAID that you're likely to use in software—the software version of RAID 5, as we'll see in a minute, is *not* a good idea on terminal servers (or any other kind of server, for that matter). RAID 1 is also relatively inexpensive, because you need only two disks to use it—all other forms of fault-tolerant RAID require at least three physical disks. However, disk mirroring uses disk space very inefficiently, because there's a 1:1 ratio of original data and redundant information. It's also impossible to scale. You can't make a mirror set bigger if you run out of room; all you can do is make a new, and larger, mirror set. Therefore, another kind of RAID, although having some disadvantages of its own, addresses some of the shortcomings of disk mirroring.

The best-known form of parity-based RAID is RAID 5, *disk striping with parity*. In RAID 5, three or more physical disks are grouped together in a *stripe set* with a single drive letter treated by the file system as though it were located on a single physical disk. When you write data to the stripe set, the data is distributed over the stripes. In addition to the data, the disk controller creates parity information for the data stored in the stripe set. The parity and data are written over the disks in the stripe set in stripes so that no single disk contains both original data and the parity information required to regenerate that data. Therefore, if one disk in the stripe set fails, a RAID 5 volume can continue functioning, although reads will take much longer than they will when the stripe set is complete—the original data on the dead disk will have to be regenerated from parity information. If a second disk in the stripe set fails before you replace the first one, the entire array will become unreadable.

The number of disks that you can place in a stripe set depends on the RAID controller you're using, but it's pretty high—even Windows 2000 software RAID 5 can support up to 32 disks in an array. The more disks in the stripe set, the greater the data storage efficiency, since RAID 5 will use the equivalent of one disk in the stripe set to store its parity information. Therefore, a three-disk RAID 5 volume will use $\frac{1}{3}$ of its space for parity information, but a five-disk volume will use only $\frac{1}{5}$ of the total space. RAID 5 has low disk access times for reads, because the disk controller can read from more than one disk at a time. However, it has high disk access times for writes, because it must both generate parity information when writing data and write that data and parity information to all the disks in the array.

> **NOTE** RAID 0 works like RAID 5 in that it stripes data across multiple physical disks, but RAID 0 is purely a performance configuration and does not generate any parity information. If one disk in a RAID 0 stripe set fails, the entire array is unreadable. That's the point of RAID combinations such as RAID 10 and RAID 0+1, which combine mirror sets and RAID 0 volumes to provide both data security and improved performance. The catch to those RAID combinations, of course, is that they require a *lot* of disks to work. Additionally, RAID 0+1 is not very scalable, because it uses the mirror model as its core structure, not the stripe set model.

RAID 5's biggest disadvantage is that it must generate new parity information each time you write to the disk, and all the calculations required to do this take up a *lot* of processor power. Although Windows 2000 supports RAID 5 in software, don't use it on terminal servers—the processing required to create all that parity information will destroy performance. If you'd like to use RAID 5 for data protection, then RAID hardware will probably serve you better.

I've presented RAID as a dichotomy between redundant information and parity-backed information. Those aren't the only choices; some types of hardware RAID combine data redundancy with another kind of RAID—RAID 0. As you can see in Table 3.2, RAID 0 provides no data protection, but it does improve read and write speed, thereby combining well with RAID 1's data protection.

Table 3.2 Common Hardware and Software RAID Types

RAID Level	Description	Effect on Disk Access Times	Minimum Disks Required	Available in Windows 2000?
0	Data is broken down into blocks and written to all the disks in an array. Not fault tolerant—if one disk in the array fails, the entire array is unreadable.	Performance enhancements for both reads and writes.	2	Yes
1	Partitions on two disks are made a "mirror set" and treated as the same space for reads and writes. If one disk fails, then you can read from the other half of the mirror set. Requires 100% extra disk space for redundancy. Disk mirroring done with dual drive controllers for greater protection is called *disk duplexing*.	Same performance as a single disk for reads, faster for writes.	2 (maximum of 2)	Yes

Table 3.2 Common Hardware and Software RAID Types *(continued)*

RAID Level	Description	Effect on Disk Access Times	Minimum Disks Required	Available in Windows 2000?
5	Striped partitions are grouped in a disk array. During writes to the array, the RAID subsystem generates parity information for the data, and the data and parity information are written across the entire array. If one of the disks in the array fails, then any missing data may be reconstructed from the parity information.	Good read rates because of multiple data sources, poor write rates because of generating and writing parity information.	3	Yes
10	RAID 0 array whose segments are RAID 1, to get the reliability of RAID 1 with RAID 0 performance. Expensive and difficult to implement, because the drives must be synchronized for best performance. Difficult to scale, because the stripes are made of mirror sets (and, therefore, require two disks to add one stripe), but may be able to survive more than one disk failure.	Good I/O rates.	4	No

Table 3.2 Common Hardware and Software RAID Types *(continued)*

RAID Level	Description	Effect on Disk Access Times	Minimum Disks Required	Available in Windows 2000?
0+1	RAID 1 array whose segments are RAID 0 arrays. If one segment goes out, then RAID 0+1 is no longer fault tolerant. RAID 0+1 is *not* the same as RAID 10.	High data transfer performance and same reliability as RAID 5.	4	No

Hardware versus Software RAID I've mentioned "hardware RAID" and "software RAID" several times now without really explaining what I mean. Regardless of the form of RAID you're talking about, the way it functions remains basically the same: data is read from and written to an array of disks, not a single disk. From a computer's perspective, this is contrary to the natural order of things. Therefore, to use RAID, someone has to tell the drive controller where to write the original data, how to generate parity information (if applicable), how to read data from the array, and how to read data in case of disk failure. Who's doing the calculating depends on the kind of RAID you're using. If you're using RAID implemented in software, then the computer's processor does the calculating. If you're using RAID implemented in hardware, then the RAID hardware may have its own processor for handling RAID processing.

Windows Server products—NT, Windows 2000, and .NET—all support RAID 0, 1, and 5 in software. Purely software RAID is simple to set up and inexpensive—the only cost is that of the hard disks. However, with the possible exception of RAID 1 for protecting the system volume, a hardware solution with a dedicated processor will work better for a terminal server. Software RAID does not support some recovery functions of hardware RAID, such as hot-swapping to immediately replace failed disks, and RAID 5 in particular is very hard on a server's processor because of all the parity calculating it needs to do. About the only advantages to purely software RAID are cost and support for disk duplexing, which is not an option with all hardware RAID solutions.

Not all hardware RAID is created equal. The simplest forms of hardware RAID are similar to the purely software solutions. Simple RAID controllers are ATA/IDE adapter cards and replace a drive controller. In many ways, they *are* a drive controller—the IDE models support the two channels (for a total of four drives) that you expect from IDE drive controllers, and they use the standard bus to communicate with the computer's CPU. The difference is that part of their communication includes requests for RAID functions (generally limited to RAID 0, 1, and 0+1), so that the processor can tell the controller where to write the data. Their advantage is that they provide inexpensive data-protection RAID to operating systems that don't support RAID in software and without the availability problems of dual-boot systems, but since they rely on the processor for all their calculations, they're not ideal for protecting a stressed server. They also have all the disadvantages of IDE that we discussed earlier. They are nice for important client workstations, but not much better for terminal servers than pure software RAID. More advanced (and expensive, I'm afraid) RAID controllers have on-board intelligence that takes the load off the computer's CPU. These typically SCSI RAID controllers don't stress the CPU of the computer they're protecting and are, therefore, more likely to support the CPU-intensive RAID 5. They also support many drives. Higher-end RAID controllers may also support hot-swapping in case of drive failures, which you won't see with Windows Server's RAID. RAID hardware is usually not compatible across different brands, makes, and models—if a RAID controller fails, you must replace it with another controller of the same type. *RAID enclosures* go a step further than intelligent RAID controllers by housing the disks in a physical container with its own power supply and fans, so that the fans and power supply in the main computer case aren't strained by supporting large numbers of disk drives. Simple RAID enclosures will connect to the RAID controller on the server's motherboard. The highest-end external RAID arrays will have an internal RAID controller. Hard disks may use SCSI cabling or plug directly into the backplane. These external arrays can attach to the server either via the network or with direct SCSI cabling.

Ultimately, you may not need all the bells and whistles of the most expensive forms of hardware RAID, but some form of RAID is a good idea so that you're not dependent on backups. Find some form of RAID that protects your data without impacting server performance.

Choosing a File System (or Why You'll Use NTFS) This isn't actually much of a choice: use NTFS instead of FAT or FAT32, the other available options with Windows 2000 and .NET Server. NTFS's support for local file permissions means that it's possible to lock down the server (which, don't forget, people are directly accessing) in a manner not possible with a file system that only supports network-level permissions. Only NTFS volumes support Windows 2000 file encryption, disk quotas, volume mounting, and data compression. If you want to use any of these features in Windows 2000, you'll need NTFS. NTFS's transaction logging is designed to avoid volume corruption in case the server is interrupted in the middle of a write. Finally, NTFS is much more space-efficient than FAT or FAT32 when it comes to large volumes. You can only use FAT on volumes up to 4GB in size, which means lots of disk partitioning on modern disks. At that size the clusters, the minimum storage unit, are huge.

Because each cluster can contain only one file (or part of one file), large clusters can imply a lot of wasted space on a volume. FAT32 fares better in the space-efficiency race, but lacks the other features that make NTFS valuable.

If you're concerned about using NTFS on the system partition because you can't read it when you boot from a floppy, don't be. Windows 2000 has a NTFS-capable tool, called the Recovery Console, that administrators can use to access local volumes, start and stop services, copy and paste files, and make repairs.

Other Server Parts

Just to round off, I'd like to take a quick look at the remaining pieces of the MetaFrame server that you should consider when choosing hardware: system bus, video cards, and network interface.

System Bus Type Actually, this one isn't really a question. Even if you could use ISA (which is increasingly hard to find), you wouldn't. It's too slow to use in a server, so you'll be using PCI, no question.

Network Cards ICA and RDP (in the latest version, anyway) are highly compressed and use little bandwidth, but because the terminal server handles all network requests, you should use a high-performance network interface card (NIC). Consider dedicating one NIC to servicing RDP or ICA sessions and using a second NIC for other traffic.

Video Cards Both MetaFrame XP and .NET Server support 24-bit color in terminal sessions. A terminal session can't display a color depth greater than that available on the MetaFrame server, though—so if you plan to use 24-bit color (it's optional; you can and sometimes still should use 256 colors), then you'll need to get a decent video card on the server. Don't go overboard, however: the quality of the display on the client end will depend more on the client's video card than on the card installed on the server.

How Many Servers Do You Need?

I've alluded several times to the fact that I'm a fan of having more less-powerful terminal servers than fewer more-powerful ones. Here's why.

First, as I've explained more times than is probably necessary, Windows terminal servers—with or without MetaFrame XP—are memory bound, not processor bound. The limit of a 4GB addressable memory area per server means that you can get more memory out of a group of terminal servers if you have more servers. However, even memory isn't the only bottleneck: you have to worry about network access, disk access, and so on. You can add more disks, and you can dedicate a network card to terminal session traffic so that other network use doesn't interfere with terminal sessions, but once again, more servers mean more in-server bandwidth. More servers do not help the *network* bandwidth problem, but high-speed networks will alleviate that problem.

Second, access to terminal servers is licensed for the client, not for the server. Well, mostly. You have to buy a server license for every server on which you install Windows 2000 or .NET Server, and that's not an inconsiderable proposition. But once those servers are paid for, the terminal services license assigned to each client computer is good for any terminal server. MetaFrame XP is licensed by client connection only, too—you can install the software on as many servers as you like without changing your licensing fees.

Finally, having more servers reduces the impact of one server going offline, either by accident or by intent. If you have two terminal servers capable of supporting a total of 50 users, then if one of those servers goes to the Great Data Center in the Sky you've lost 50 percent of capacity—ouch! If those two terminal servers were four, then losing one server would reduce capacity by only 25 percent.

Adding MetaFrame XP

The previous recommendations apply to a Windows 2000 terminal server running on its own or with MetaFrame, but adding MetaFrame requires some additional planning. Not only do you need to beef up the servers a bit (especially the servers responsible for maintaining the server farm information), but you'll also need to consider the operating system requirements and server roles for MetaFrame application servers and administrative console support.

OS Requirements for MetaFrame XP

We'll start with a simple one. Considering that I'm discussing Windows 2000 Server and .NET Server in this book, this one is easy: Citrix recommends that you use one of those operating systems to support MetaFrame XP, because some features are available only with support for Active Directory. (You don't have to use Active Directory to use MetaFrame XP, however.) To run MetaFrame, you must install Terminal Services in Application Server mode. To use NFuse, Citrix's web-based Program Neighborhood tool, you'll also need Internet Information Services (IIS) 4 or later and the Java Virtual Machine (JVM) installed with IIS.

Planning the Server and Domain Structure

Installing MetaFrame XP successfully isn't just a matter of installing the software on a Win2K server, installing licenses, then pushing the ICA client out to everyone. The process is quite a bit more complicated than that, because the way that the Win2K domain structure works can impact the way that your MetaFrame XP server farm functions—or doesn't function, as the case may be.

Server Naming Pay attention to server names. A domain will never contain servers with duplicate names—you won't be permitted to duplicate machine names within a domain. However, a MetaFrame server farm could contain servers from more than one domain. If you end up with duplicates, you'll need to change the name of one of the servers in the farm before installing MetaFrame XP—servers in the same farm cannot have the same name. On a similar note, MetaFrame XP servers can have extended characters (characters not found in the ASCII character set, such as Cyrillic letters) in their names only if you're using Win2K DNS for name resolution. If you're not, you'll need to change the server names to ones that don't include extended characters before installing MetaFrame XP.

Planning the Active Directory   Planning the Active Directory for a network is a far more complicated topic than I can hope to cover in one part of one chapter on running terminal servers, but you do need to know a little bit about Active Directory to make the structure work well with MetaFrame XP server farms. The recommendations are simple: Put all servers in a single domain. If that's not possible, put them all in a single forest, and do not put the server farm's domain(s) in trust relationships with NT 4 domains. The reason why Citrix recommends this bears a bit more explanation.

You're probably aware that Windows 2000 domains are not identical to NT 4 domains. NT 4 domains are monolithic entities that can't contain any containers other than groups, and they can't themselves be contained. The only way NT 4 domains can communicate with each other is through the use of one-way, non-transitive trust relationships. Although you can manipulate the trust relationships to create a master-domain structure or a multiple-master-domain structure, doing so gets very complicated. Windows 2000 domains can be grouped in structures called *trees,* and trees can be grouped in structures called *forests.* All domains within the same forest or tree automatically trust each other. Domains in separate forests do not trust each other, but you can set up single non-transitive trust relationships between domains in separate forests to facilitate resource sharing, but only the two domains that explicitly trust each other will share information. Getting back to Citrix's recommendations about putting all the servers in a farm in a single domain or at least a single forest, you may see why this recommendation isn't a bad idea: having everybody in the same forest simplifies trust relationships among servers. If the servers in the farm trust each other, then it's easier to manage user and group access to server farm resources. Trust is all very well, but MetaFrame XP server farms are designed to work even if they're geographically distributed, and you don't want domain controllers replicating the security database over slow links. Although the domains in the same forest trust each other, they don't share a security database. Therefore, to reduce intersite traffic, you can put the various domains in separate forests or use Active Directory sites to isolate them.

There's also the matter of User Principal Name (UPN) support, if that's important to you. UPNs allow you to log onto the domain using a format that looks like *username@domainname*.com–basically, they're a shortcut, allowing you to log onto a nested domain without having to get über-precise about which domain you're connecting to. UPN works by tracking down the domain that users belong to, even if users identify themselves only by the root domain (for example, acme.com) and the domain holding their user accounts is somewhere lower in the tree (for example, `acme.development.com`). A domain in one forest cannot search a domain in another forest, because the domains don't trust each other. Therefore, if your server farm has more than one forest you can't use UPNs to log on.

If a server farm must contain domains that don't trust each other, you'll need *trust-based routing* to determine which servers are allowed to communicate with each other. In trust-based routing, a request to enumerate users for, say, application assignment or to authenticate a user, is routed to a server that has the required domain trust relationship if the originating server does not. During a *trust query cycle*, a MetaFrame XP server registers its trusted domains with the server farm's data store. This operation occurs during every service startup and approximately every six hours while the service is executing. Therefore, the data store is a central repository of all trust data for the servers in the server farm. When a server needs to perform an operation on a domain that it doesn't trust, the server determines from the data store which servers can perform the operation, then routes the request to the most accessible server.

Planning for Load Balancing in User Account Permissions   When you publish an application in a server farm, you select the servers to host the application and Citrix Management Console lists the user accounts from the trust intersection of all the servers (accounts that are trusted by all the servers). You then select the users and groups that you want to allow to use the application. After you select users, changing the list of host servers can change the trust intersection, which can make the application unavailable to users who are no longer in the servers' trust intersection. If the trust intersection changes, the console informs you and removes from the authorized users list those users who are no longer eligible to use the resource.

If you publish an application or content from a group of servers for load balancing, make sure that the people (individuals or groups) to whom you've granted access to the published material have access to all the servers publishing it. If more than one server is publishing an application or content, you can't predict which server the ICA client will connect to—that's the point of publishing applications in a farm instead of direct connections to a server. If a user doesn't have the right to log on to all the servers publishing the application or content, sometimes he or she might be able to launch the published material and sometimes not. To prevent unpredictable access, MetaFrame XP removes users from the authorized users of a published application or printer if the accounts aren't trusted by all the host servers.

Choosing a Database to Back the Data Store

Chapter 2 explains the role of the data store in a MetaFrame XP server farm. When installing MetaFrame XP, you must choose a type of database to use for the data store for your server farm. You have three options: Microsoft Access, Microsoft SQL Server 7 SP2 or SQL Server 2000, and Oracle—specifically, Oracle8*i*, version 8.1.6 (recommended); Oracle 7, version 7.3.4; or Oracle 8, version 8.0.6.

> **NOTE** Although the data store is an ODBC database, Citrix does not support its use with all ODBC-compliant databases, just the ones listed here.

Microsoft Access is fine for smaller farms (and, considering that Citrix considers 50 servers a "small" farm, you may never need anything else). If you do need to support a larger farm, consider backing the data store with SQL Server or Oracle. If you choose either, the data store will be on a dedicated server that you must set up before creating the server farm, and you'll need to have ODBC drivers on the servers in the farm so that they can access the data store. Notice that you're installing the *drivers* on the MetaFrame XP servers, not on the database engine. Do *not* attempt to put a SQL Server- or Oracle-backed data store on a MetaFrame server. The stress of supporting the database will seriously impact the application server.

If you use Access to back the data store, the data store will be present on the first server you set up in the farm, so make sure that this server has some extra resources: a minimum of 20MB of disk space for every server in the farm and an additional 32MB of RAM if the server will host connections. Because the Access database engine and ODBC drivers are part of Windows 2000 and .NET, if you use Access to back the data store, then you don't have to install any drivers or configure the database before installing MetaFrame XP. SQL Server and Oracle will require at least 20MB of disk space for every 100 servers in the farm, and in server farms with lots of published applications and printer objects, lots of RAM.

Which is the better choice? As usual, it depends. Access is much easier to use than either SQL Server or Oracle, but it is not suited for really huge server farms. Both SQL Server and Oracle support database replication, which you can use to reduce the strain on the data store. Of the two enterprise-class choices, SQL Server might be a more popular choice; because it is made by the same company that makes the base OS, using it allows you to use NT authentication for the database instead of requiring a separate Oracle logon. That said, much of the choice between SQL Server and Oracle will depend on which one you already have and are comfortable using. Working with either is not for the uninitiated; Citrix recommends that you stick with Access unless you know how to use one of the other choices.

Chapter 2 discussed some of the other ramifications of choosing each database type, particularly the path that MetaFrame servers must take to refer to the data store. I don't want to completely rehash the discussion again, but here's a quick review: If you back the database with Access, the servers in the farm will access the data store in *indirect mode*—that is, that server will be the only one with direct access to the data store and every other server in the farm will depend on that first server to get data for it.

> **TIP** The servers in the farm will connect through port 2512 to the server holding the data store. If the servers are on different subnets, make sure that this port is open.

Using SQL Server or Oracle to back the server means that member servers will be able to access the data store directly—in *direct mode*. (It doesn't *have* to be in direct mode, but when you use the larger database types, that's an option that Access does not support.) For small farms, using indirect mode is okay, but the single server with a pipeline to the data store will represent a potential bottleneck or a real bottleneck if the farm is big enough and the servers in it have to wait in line to reach the data store. The intermediary server also represents a single point of failure: If it goes down, none of the other servers will be able to read the data store. Your choice of database isn't the only factor that could slow down the farm, but it is a factor that you need to keep in mind.

If you want to give servers a direct connection to the data store, you'll need to set up the ODBC drivers on the servers so that they can talk to the SQL Server or Oracle database. Indirect mode, obviously, only requires the ODBC drivers on the server with the direct channel to the data store. SQL Server databases support a combination of direct and indirect access to the data store, so you might keep this option in mind. If you decide to do so, just install the first server into the server farm in direct mode and configure it to point to the database, then install subsequent servers by pointing them to the direct server you installed first, providing the name and password for the Citrix administrator account you created while installing the first server.

Planning for the Citrix Management Console

The Citrix Management Console is installed on all MetaFrame XP servers by default. However, you can install the Citrix Management Console on computers that aren't MetaFrame XP servers—even on computers that aren't servers at all. Seriously consider doing so. Although you'll want to have the Citrix Management Console locally available on all MetaFrame servers in a pinch, running the console on a computer other than the MetaFrame server itself will keep the console from stressing the server when the server's trying to do other work. As I mentioned earlier, the Java-based Citrix Management Console is not the world's most memory-efficient tool, and the more managed objects (servers, applications, printers) you have, the more memory it will need.

To run the console on a separate computer, you'll need an OS that supports it. According to Citrix, NT-based operating systems are the only choice, but I've run the Citrix Management Console from Windows 98. (I haven't really stress-tested it, because Win98 is not my preferred working environment. I can't really recommend doing this because I don't trust Windows 98 to not crash when you're in the middle of publishing an application, but it will install and it will work.) You'll also need the Sun Microsystems' Java Runtime Environment (JRE), but if the JRE isn't already installed when you begin to set up the console, you'll be able to install it with the Citrix Management Console.

Reducing Bandwidth Requirements

With every version, RDP and ICA become more and more capable. In .NET Server, RDP can do just about everything that the current version of ICA can do: support 24-bit color, perform client drive mapping, provide sound to terminal session, and automatically map client-side printers to the terminal session.

The catch is you may not want to provide all those capabilities, because they'll slow down the terminal session. Color is probably least harmless, and it is a nice feature to have—it's a lot more enjoyable to use applications from within a terminal session when the applications don't use fewer colors than the locally installed applications. Sound can be useful for limited applications, such as training videos. (I really don't recommend letting users stream sound if they're listening to Internet radio from a browser running in a web session, and it won't sound all that great if they try.) But, particularly for terminal sessions running over slower links such as WAN connections, don't automatically assume that you want to automatically map client printers and drives. Although mapping client drives makes it *much* easier to copy files between local and remote applications, copying those files takes up as much bandwidth as copying files across a network normally does—this is not necessarily a fast process. Printers are even more of a headache. Not only are print jobs larger than the files that spawned them, but if you support client-side printer mapping, you have to worry about supporting client-side printer drivers and client-side printers that you may have no physical access to, because the printer is two cities away. The bottom line is this: These features are cool and useful, but they're also enabled by default and they probably shouldn't be. When choosing the features of RDP or ICA that you want to enable, take into account the stress they'll put on the server or network and the stress that supporting them may put on you.

By the same token, when creating a user profile to use with terminal sessions, tune it so far as possible to reduce stress on the network and the server. Screen savers are out, wallpaper should be used at a minimum, and this is not the time to use cute little noises to signify that you've maximized a window.

Choosing Client Types

Chapter 2 briefly introduced the types of client computers you can use with a Windows terminal server. Let's take a closer look at what those client types mean and why you'd pick one over another.

Personal Computers

As I mentioned in Chapter 2, PCs are currently the most popular terminal services client. Even if PCs had no other advantages in a server-based environment, they'd be the most popular client type for one very good reason: people have them around. Using any other client type means that you have to explicitly purchase a device with the sole purpose of being a Windows terminal server client.

But simple accessibility isn't the only reason why PCs are popular thin clients. First, they're flexible. Many people find that it works best to run some applications from a terminal server while running others on the client computer. If this is true for you, you'll find it much easier to load applications on a PC than to purchase the (less common) Windows terminals that *can* run locally installed applications. If you choose the latter route, then you'll need to get the applications preinstalled. Loading applications onto a Windows terminal is also expensive. The terminals themselves cost more than PCs (relative to what you're getting) and a terminal that can run locally installed applications is more expensive yet.

A PC is a good choice for a thin client if you'll need to run applications other than the ones on the terminal server and can get away with using a PC, instead of one of the professional-model Windows-based terminals that run an embedded 32-bit operating system and can run applications locally. RDP in Win2K maintains a single Clipboard for local and remote applications, so application interaction is an option. And .NET Server's RDP client even maps client-side drives to the terminal session, so that PC clients have complete access to all client-side resources. Using terminal services allows you to run both Windows and, say, Macintosh or Linux applications on the same computer and even exchange information between those applications. So, unless you're in a position to run *everything* from the application server, a PC is probably the best choice.

The operating system you choose also enters into the PC decision. It's not a matter of compatibility, since RDP works with all Win32 operating systems and Windows for Workgroups, and there are third-party Java and Linux RDP clients that allow just about any platform to use RDP. But, as I said in Chapter 2, Win2K Professional computers come with a TSCAL—they can draw from the "unlimited" pool of licenses on the terminal services license server. Therefore, Win2K computers effectively have free access to a Windows 2000 application server, and Windows XP will probably have free access to a .NET Server application server. (I say "probably" because as of June 2002 the licensing model still isn't finalized, but that's what I expect.) NT-based operating systems, such as Windows 2000 and Windows XP, are more reliable than any Windows 9*x* platform; so if you are torn between the two platforms and thinking about using Windows Terminal Services to provide some applications, then the NT-based operating system would be the better choice if only for the licensing benefits.

To summarize, you may want to use PCs to connect to a terminal server for the following reasons:

- PCs are the most convenient hardware platform for those who need to run applications both locally and from terminal sessions.
- Using PCs allows you to extend the useful life of those PCs, because the resource strain on a PC running terminal sessions is so low.
- Using PCs means that you can use an operating system that can draw from the "unlimited" license pool for terminal services use.

Windows Terminals

Why would you *not* use a PC as a thin client, if they're so flexible and can provide you with cheaper licensing if you use an operating system that comes with a TSCAL?

There are several reasons, actually. PCs have moving parts, and those moving parts can break. Since PCs use locally installed applications and configurations, installing a new PC is not usually a fast process. Even if you've automated, it's possible to open a PC case, meaning that it's possible for unfriendly coworkers to walk off with computer memory. (I would not have believed this if I hadn't seen it. The sad truth is that it's not a bad idea to physically inventory hardware so that you can easily tell if one computer has absconded with another computer's memory.) PCs almost always have floppy drives and frequently have removable drives, providing an avenue for data to leak out of the computer and viruses to leak in. PCs blow and inhale dust, making them a bad choice for environments that are either very dusty (and, therefore, harmful to the computer) or need to be kept very clean (and, therefore, can't have a PC fan blowing dust around). The bottom line is this: PCs are the choice for low purchase cost and flexibility; Windows terminals are the choice for low administration and running costs, small footprint, and high security.

A Windows terminal is a simple computing device designed to run applications from a Windows terminal server, either using the RDP protocol native to Windows Terminal Services or the ICA protocol used with MetaFrame. I'm calling them generically Windows terminals because their prime function is to display applications running on a Windows terminal server, not because of their operating system. Although most Windows terminals run some variant of Windows (CE or NT Embedded), a few run other operating systems such as some variant of Linux—the only requirement for a Windows terminal is that it be able to support a display protocol used to connect to a Windows terminal server. Some Windows terminals also support one or several kinds of terminal access, so you can use the same client computer to connect to a Windows application server and a mainframe.

Windows terminals that run Windows locally are called *Windows-based terminals (WBTs)*. Microsoft recognizes two forms of WBTs. Standard WBTs have a keyboard, mouse, serial ports, parallel ports, and a network connection—10 or 100BaseT. Many newer terminals have one or two USB ports as well. For logical connections, Windows terminals generally support RDP, ICA, and at least one (and sometimes many more) kinds of terminal emulation, so you can use a single terminal to get to both Windows terminals and mainframes. Windows terminals have no hard disks.

> **NOTE** Support for removable media (through USB ports, usually) is available for some Windows terminals, but it's still rare and it's always optional.

Chapter 5, "Preparing Client Connections," will discuss in detail the process of setting up a Windows terminal, but here's the gist for now. Configuring a Windows terminal is simple. Windows terminals use TCP/IP to communicate with the network, so you'll need to specify whether the device is getting an IP address from a DHCP server or if it's hard-coded. You'll also need to choose display settings; most Windows terminals I've seen support resolutions of at least 1024×768 and even 1280×1024 or more, and refresh rates of 75–85Hz are usual. If you change either of these core configuration options, you'll need to restart the machine. You'll need to know what you're doing when setting up a Windows terminal (or need a good manual), as no pop-up help is available.

Those are the basics of a Windows terminal, but those basics may not help you much when it comes to choosing a particular model. When choosing a model of Windows terminal, ask yourself the following questions:

- What kind of management software does it use?
- Does it have an integrated monitor? Do you want one? (You might not. Although an integrated monitor can save space, combining the two devices complicates terminal and/or monitor upgrades.)
- What operating system does it run, and how does this affect system use and performance?
- How fast does it display screen updates?
- Does it support the resolution you need?
- What kind of security options does it support?
- How important is a low boot time when you turn it on?
- If you're using RDP or ICA's sound, does the device have speakers? How do they sound?
- Does the device's design make it easy or difficult to set up and use? Does the design fit in the environment where it needs to work?
- Does the device have all the ports you need?

Many of these questions are pretty self-explanatory, but I'd like to take a look at how operating system and terminal hardware may affect performance.

Evaluating Terminal Operating Systems The software on the Windows terminal—its operating system and the display protocol it uses to communicate with the terminal server for any given session—may have more influence on the device's performance than the hardware does. The operating system influences device design. Early in the life cycle of Windows-based terminals, many manufacturers used proprietary operating systems to support their terminals, but once Windows CE became available—the first CE-based Windows terminals appeared on the market in mid-1998—the trend started working back from specialization into standardization, using premade operating systems. Once a platform was readily available, it made less sense to build your own, especially once Linux became a practical thin client operating system and offered the flexibility of design that used to be possible only with a proprietary operating system. Besides, as one OEM I talked to put it, it's much harder to hire developers skilled in a proprietary operating system than it is to hire developers skilled in a widely used OS. These days, you've got three main choices when it comes to the operating system in a thin client device: Windows CE, Windows NT Embedded, and Linux. The operating system influences performance, since the efficiency of the network and video drivers in the device will affect how quickly it can shove data around. However, since you can't very easily pick and choose the drivers that a given OEM is going to use, it makes more sense to consider how the operating system affects terminal design.

Operating system influences how standardized the terminal is. Any Windows terminal powered with NT Embedded or Windows CE must conform to the model that Microsoft set out for Windows terminals using those operating systems: Standard Windows terminals use Windows CE and currently do not support locally installed applications, and Professional Windows terminals use NT Embedded and have a locally installed copy of Internet Explorer and Media Player. OEMs can't go outside this design, and they must follow a particular design when creating an interface for the configuration and session setup tools on the terminals. The OEMs can add to these interfaces, but the basic tool layout must always be the same. Linux terminals have neither these restrictions nor this consistency. A Linux terminal may include any device that its manufacturer deems necessary or desirable, and design its interface in any way it pleases. However, this means that Linux terminals are less predictable than their Windows-based cousins. If you can set up one Windows terminal, you can set up another one without having to think about it much. The same is not necessarily true of Linux terminals. If you know what you want to do you can figure it out, but you can't go from one Linux terminal to another and automatically know where all the tools are the way you can with a WBT.

Finally, the operating system that your terminals use may influence the types of display protocols available to you or the quality of the display protocols. As of November 1999, the restriction on RDP working with non-Windows clients ended and a Linux-compatible version of RDP became available. However, it's not installed on all Linux boxes, and frankly, at this point, it doesn't work as well as the ICA client for Linux. Although it has hopefully improved by the time you read this, right now I'd skip the Linux RDP clients and use ICA instead.

Terminal Hardware and Device Performance How do the devices compare on the inside? One of the easiest criteria to isolate is processor speed. Faster is better, right? Well, yes and no. It's not a *bad* thing to have a fast processor, and some thin client devices that do more local processing benefit from more power. However, because of the way thin client devices work—and because of what they're designed to do—processor speed simply isn't as important as some other factors. You can't evaluate a thin client device like a PC, because it's not doing the job of a PC and it operates in an environment different from that of a PC. In its simplest form, a thin client device is an extension of the terminal server with a remote display.

Whether you're using RDP or ICA with Windows Terminal Services or using the terminal emulation packages that many thin client devices come with, the method of getting graphical data from the server to the client remains roughly the same. When you connect to a terminal server, the server assigns a session to you and identifies it internally. Any applications that you run from that session are associated with that session, so that what you do with your applications doesn't affect other people in their sessions who may be using the same application. The terminal server's monitor doesn't display the application output for any session except the console session. Instead, the display drivers for remote sessions download to each session's client the commands needed to show application output, window resizing, text input, and so forth. In the other direction, each session's client uploads mouse clicks and keyboard movements up to be interpreted for its session only. As you might guess, remote sessions use different video and client I/O drivers than the console session does, because the data takes a different path.

On the client end, the hardware required to manage this is a network interface so that thin client and terminal sever can communicate, a video card and monitor so that the client can render and display the output, and a processor to do the processing of the network and video data. If the client is using some device connected to its local serial, parallel, or USB port, then the display protocol will also transport the information needed to make that client-side device work with the session running on the terminal server. The key innards to the terminal, therefore, are the network interface, the video card, the memory used to hold data, and the processor. One possible layout for these innards is that used by National Semiconductor, in which key system components are divided into two groups connected by a PCI interface that also interfaces to the network card. One group does number crunching and the other does data I/O.

Without going into the gory details of every chip on the terminal's motherboard, the basic idea is that the path from the Windows terminal to the terminal server starts with a PCI-based network card. When the network delivers data to the Windows terminal, the PCI card passes it to the PCI interface to the number-crunching half, where the CPU, memory controller, bus controller, video generator, and SDRAM are. As the video generator creates graphical output, it passes the output to the display module on the I/O side of the terminal, where the interfaces to all ports are placed. Because the terminal's primary job is to display output generated on the terminal server, the critical data paths are to the network controller and to the video display. If these paths are slow, the device will be slow. Certainly, the more information that's going between client and server, the more that the processor has to do. However, when you're talking about a 200MHz processor, rendering graphical output and interpreting rendering instructions simply isn't all that taxing. The brains of the terminal can handle information as quickly as the network interface can pass it along and can shove that data to the video output as quickly as the video can accept it.

That's not to say that processor speed is never important. When you're talking about devices that have locally installed applications, processor speed can make a serious difference just as it can in the PC world. As you'll see in the following reviews, several thin client models have locally installed web browsers. Professional-model Windows terminals include a locally installed copy of Internet Explorer and Media Player in the specifications for the boxes, and thin client devices based on Linux often have a locally installed copy of Netscape. In fact, in some cases, the concept of a "thin client" is getting decidedly chubby, edging from that lean and mean look into solid-state PC wannabes.

When it comes to thin client devices that aren't running locally installed applications, however, processor speed becomes much less important to overall performance. In these cases, the processor is rendering the graphical commands sent from the server, and the memory is supporting the locally installed operating system and any working data needed to process those commands. Yes, a faster processor will process these graphical commands more quickly than a slow one, and more efficient video and network drivers will improve client output. However, unless you're holding a stopwatch in your hand, the difference is often not enough to be noticeable. When it comes to output in a strictly thin client environment, the locally available speed simply isn't all that important. Congestion at the server level or at the network level is likely to have a far greater impact on performance on the thin client than the processor power is.

Security Securing Windows terminals can be an issue. A small number of Windows terminals require you to include logon information when setting up a connection to a terminal server. This means that anyone who can get to that connection can log onto the terminal server, and from there access any domain resources attached to that account. If you choose such a terminal, then you'll need to protect it. In general, I'd advise against including logon information in any connection setup unless you're in an extremely trusting environment or give few permissions to terminal users. Some terminals include password information or card readers as an extra layer of support.

Handheld PCs

Chapter 2 introduced handheld PCs for people who hadn't seen them already. Just to review, they're Windows CE-based devices with a little bit of memory (mine has 8MB of RAM and 8MB of ROM), a small keyboard and small screen, and a place to plug in a network card. Because they're such low-powered devices, they're both extremely light and power efficient.

However, handheld PCs are more of a secondary client than a primary work space. Their most important failing is that they can't run full-fledged Windows applications, but only their CE-based equivalents. With the lightweight CE applications, you can't do any work more serious than taking notes or doing a little e-mail without being attached to a terminal server. Even apart from that, handheld PCs are physically limited. Even the handheld PCs shaped like a small laptop instead of a Palm Pilot have small screens. (Personally, I wouldn't even *try* using one of the teeny handhelds as a terminal client if I needed to do more than glance at a file, even though it's theoretically possible.)Although you can get used to a handheld PC's smaller keyboard (even people with large hands can learn to use it with a little practice), it is a little awkward to use.

With all those drawbacks, why *would* you use a handheld PC as a thin client? One big reason: mobility. Any time that you'd need a walking-around computer, a handheld could be invaluable. A PC is an impossible computing choice for traveling or computing when you don't have a fixed desk but need to log on . A laptop, while more practical for mobile computing, is heavy and awkward on the show floor or when walking around a warehouse. Windows terminals are wired devices that in almost all cases require a separate monitor. In contrast to all these, handheld PCs weigh almost nothing and have very long battery life, making them a good choice for situations demanding real mobility. They also don't have hard disks or fans, so they will neither blow nor suck in dust like PCs. They're durable, too—I would never recommend that you *purposely* drop a handheld PC, but I've dropped mine without hurting it. So, if you need a lightweight, self-contained terminal client, a handheld PC is a good choice.

User Training

Finally, when planning the server-based network, think about user training. In my experience, there are a few key sticking points:

- Only using the terminal server from authorized computers.
- Not "losing" applications due to Desktops larger than the client-side Desktop.
- Disconnecting and terminating terminal sessions properly.
- If you're using Windows terminals, it's okay to turn them off when you're not using them.

How can you *stop* people from logging on to the terminal server from a particular computer?

It seems like it should be such a simple thing: when you're done using the terminal server, log out as though you were logging off from your computer. But, particularly when running applications in a window instead of in full-screen mode, it's not always that simple. Far too often, users end their terminal sessions by closing the session window, not by logging off the terminal server. While this has an effect on the terminal server—even an inactive session still uses some memory—the possibility of user confusion is another problem. If a user disconnects from their terminal session and then attempts to initiate another connection from another computer, they'll be asked whether they want to connect to the former session or create a new session, thereby (if they choose the latter) possibly opening many sessions at a single time. If they're creating all these sessions from the same computer, this won't affect license usage, but it will strain the server and potentially confuse the user trying to figure out why his files are open.

I think that the problem is one of user habit. In any other case, you close an application either by choosing File ➤ Close or, more frequently, by clicking the X button in the upper-right corner of the application window. You only log off when you're done working. Therefore, if you want people to completely disconnect from a terminal server when they're done with their sessions, you'll need to help them get in the mindset of logging off. It might help if you have people run their terminal sessions in full-screen mode, so that they think of the terminal session as their "second computer."

Running applications in a window has another drawback: it's easy to lose icons. You'll need to make sure that anyone using the terminal server is aware that a session running in a window may not be able to display the full Desktop at one time, thereby preparing them for scrolling up or down as the situation requires.

> **TIP** If you're publishing a complete Desktop from a terminal server, you could edit the wallpaper to display instructions for logging off terminal server sessions and for finding buttons concealed by the window margins.

Summary

In any kind of network deployment, a little planning can save a lot of time cleaning up post-deployment messes. In this chapter, we've talked about the planning involved on both the server and client sides of the equation. Based on what you've learned so far, you should now be ready to install Windows Terminal Services and MetaFrame XP using the techniques in the next chapter.

4

Rolling Out Terminal Services

Chapter 3, "Planning the Terminal Server Environment," discussed planning for a multiuser computing environment. At this point, you should have sufficient servers with the hardware you need to support the people and applications that will be using them. Your user profiles and group policies are designed for a multiuser environment, and you know whether PCs or Windows terminals—or both—are the best choice of client machine for your needs. Now it's time to stop planning and start doing, which means it's time to get a terminal server up and running. This chapter will discuss the methods you can use to set up a terminal server, whether you're installing the service onto an existing server or creating a new server from scratch. I'll also talk about how to incorporate MetaFrame into your network, if you're planning on adding that to the mix.

Installing Terminal Services

The initial version of Microsoft Terminal Services was built into Windows NT, Terminal Server Edition (TSE), a product entirely separate from the core NT OS. You could neither uninstall TSE's Terminal Services nor change the mode they operated in to Remote Administration—no matter what, the TSE server was always an application server. In Windows 2000, things are different. Terminal Services is a service like any other, loaded in the same way as services such as Remote Installation Services or Internet Information Services, and Windows 2000 uses the same service packs regardless of whether the service is enabled.

> **NOTE** In .NET Server, Terminal Services is enabled in Remote Administration mode by default.

Terminal Services is not normally enabled in Windows 2000 Server, and not enabled for Application Server mode in .NET Server. Installing the service for application servers is simple, though. Just make sure that you pay attention to the options while installing the service (hint: blindly clicking "Next" to install with the default options is not what you want to be doing here). Install Terminal Services first, and *then* install any applications that you want to publish from the terminal server, or else you may need to reinstall them for the shared environment.

The way you install the service depends on whether you're setting it up on an existing server or creating an entirely new server. As you'll see here, the wizard for installing Terminal Services is simple to follow (again—so long as you pay attention to what you're doing), and it's a good idea to go through the process by hand once so you're familiar with the steps. However, I'm also a big fan of automating terminal server rollouts, since you're likely to need more than one server. You can clone terminal servers, but I'll also show you how to use Windows 2000 unattended installation and Remote Installation Services to create them from scratch.

Installing Terminal Services on an Existing Windows 2000 Server

If you're installing Terminal Services on a server that's already set up, then go to Add/Remove Programs in the Control Panel and click Add/Remove Windows components to open the list of available services. Scroll down in the list, and you'll see both Terminal Services and Terminal Services Licensing, as shown in Figure 4.1. Check the box for Terminal Services. Do *not* check the box for Terminal Services Licensing unless, based on the information in Chapter 3, the terminal server should also be a licensing server.

Notice that the Details button is active when you select Terminal Services. If you click this button, you'll see the list of possible Terminal Services features that appears in Figure 4.2. If you want the server to be an application server, you *must* select the check box for Enable Terminal Services. The client files, however, are optional. Windows 2000 and previous operating systems don't come with RDP support pre-installed as part of the operating system, so you'll want the client files somewhere on your network so you can get the files to the client computers. However, if you have more than one terminal server you don't have to install the client files on every single one. Check the boxes for the parts of Terminal Services that you want to install, click OK to return to the Windows Components Wizard, and click Next to continue.

Figure 4.1 All Terminal Services–related functionality is provided as a service in Windows 2000.

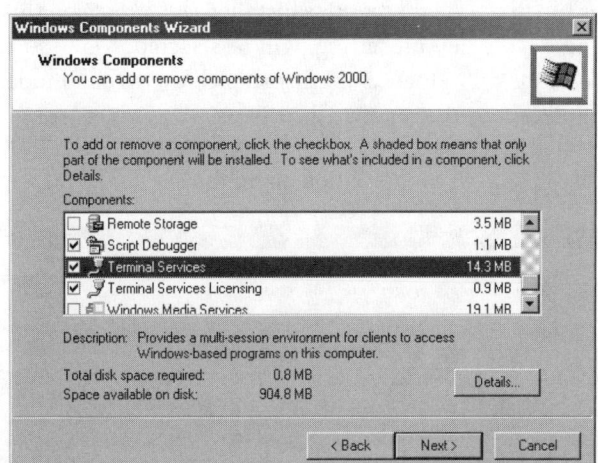

NOTE You don't necessarily need the client files. First, if all your client machines are running Windows XP, then you needn't install the client files. Windows XP comes with an RDP client (and a limited RDP server component). Second, if all clients will be using the web-based RDP client, you'll need to download the ActiveX control from the Microsoft website but you don't need the client files that come with the CD. Third, the next generation of RDP client (the Remote Desktop) is available now. As long as I didn't need to support Win16 clients, I'd probably download the Remote Desktop and put it on the server before using the client files that install with Windows 2000.

Figure 4.2 The client creator files are an optional component of Terminal Services.

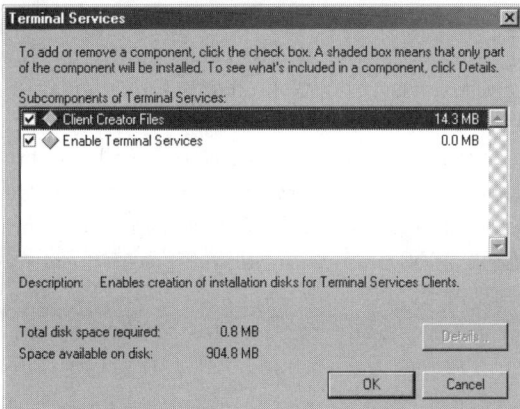

In the next screen of the wizard, you'll need to choose an operation mode for Terminal Services. If this is the first time that you've installed the service on this computer, Remote Administration mode, the default setting, will be selected. Make sure you select Application Server mode as shown in Figure 4.3. If you pick the wrong mode, you'll need to reinstall the service and reboot the server. Click Next.

Figure 4.3 Select the correct mode for installing the service.

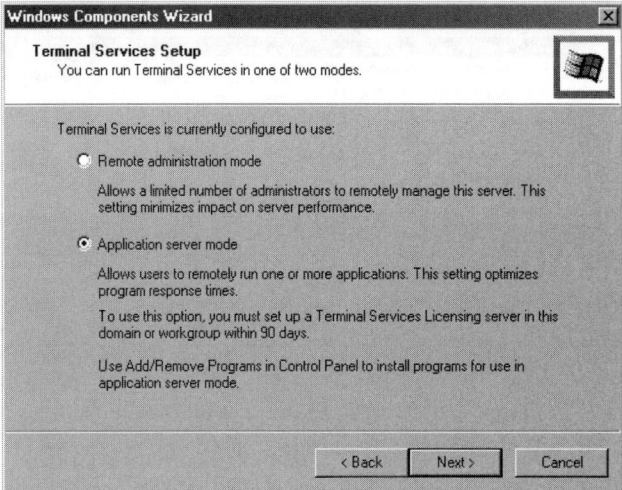

If you chose to install Terminal Services in Application Server mode, you'll next be prompted to choose the security level for the computer. The dialog box explaining this (see Figure 4.4) isn't all that helpful; you are given a choice between permitting Terminal Services users full access to the Registry (Terminal Server 4 permissions) and limited access to the Registry (Windows 2000 permissions). Your decision depends on whether the applications that people will run during their sessions will write to the Registry only while you're installing them or while people are *using* those applications. Applications generally run using the security permissions of the people who initiated them. Choosing the Terminal Server 4 permissions option creates a local group called Terminal Server User (analogous to the Interactive group) on the terminal server, and it adds anyone currently logged onto a terminal session to this group. Members of the Terminal Server User group have greater access to the Registry than do members of the Users group, so giving them this access makes it more possible for people using the terminal server to corrupt the Registry. The Windows 2000 permissions do not create this group, but they leave everybody in Interactive. If the applications only write to the Registry when you're installing them, you can pick the default, and more secure, option of Windows 2000 permissions. Otherwise, you'll need to pick the Terminal Server 4 permissions. Click Next.

Figure 4.4 Older applications that write to the Registry while executing will need TSE-compatible permissions.

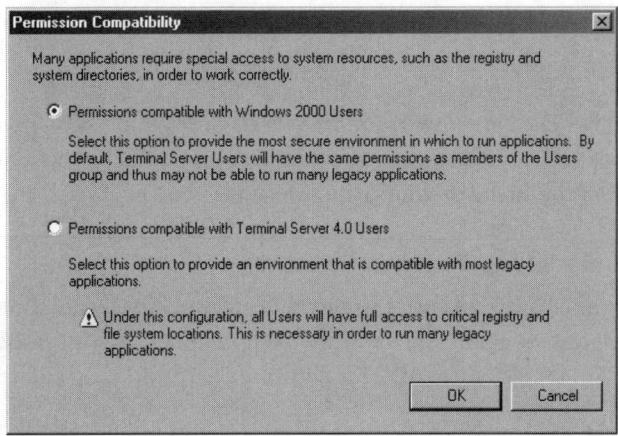

> **TIP** If you're not sure whether an application writes to the Registry while executing, you can experiment with running the application using the Windows 2000 permissions and see if it runs. If it doesn't, then you know that it needs the expanded permission set. You can revert to the TSE permissions from the Terminal Services Configuration tool without reinstalling the service.

Recall that you're not supposed to install applications on the terminal server until after you've installed the service. If you *have* previously installed applications on the terminal server (Notepad and other preinstalled Windows applications don't count toward this), then the next screen of the wizard will display a list of those applications and warn you that you may need to reinstall them. There's not a lot you can do about this from this window—just note the applications you might need to reinstall and click Next to move on.

Finally, Setup will update the Windows 2000 server and make the necessary changes to enable Terminal Services. When it's finished, you'll see a dialog box telling you so. Click the Finish button, and restart the server when prompted. At this point, the server is ready to begin accepting connections, and the Administrative Tools folder will now include several new tools: Terminal Services Configuration, Terminal Services Manager, and Terminal Services Client Creator.

> **NOTE** The process of installing Terminal Services in Application Server mode on a .NET Server is even simpler. Choose Add or Remove a Role in the Manage Your Server screen to start the Configure Your Server wizard. Choose Terminal Server from the list of server roles, then wait for Setup to finish—you don't have to do anything. The server will reboot, and the application server will be ready to take connections. To change any options from the default, you'll need to configure the server manually or with Group Policies.

Removing or Modifying Terminal Services

To remove Terminal Services entirely from a Windows 2000 server, just run Add/Remove Windows Components again and uncheck the box next to Terminal Services, completing the wizard as you would normally. You'll need to reboot after you're done.

Because Remote Administration is so useful, it's more likely that you would revert a retired application server to Remote Administration mode. To do so, reinstall the service and choose the appropriate mode. Again, you'll need to reboot when you're done.

Installing Terminal Services Licensing

Terminal Services Licensing is not part of the Terminal Services service. Depending on the logical organization of your network, this service may not reside on the same computers as terminal servers. As we discussed in Chapter 3, the placement of the license server depends on the type of domain in which your terminal servers are based. In Active Directory domains, Terminal Services licensing servers must be domain controllers so that they can share information with each other. In workgroups and NT4 domains, the licensing servers will be member servers (obviously, since Terminal Services Licensing is a Windows 2000–only service not found in TSE and the addition of a Windows 2000 domain controller would make the network into a Windows 2000 domain). Because domain controllers make lousy application servers, license servers will not be application servers in an Active Directory domain.

Installing Terminal Services Licensing is much like installing any other Windows 2000 service. From Add/Remove Programs in the Control Panel, choose Windows Setup. Scroll down the list until you find the entry for Terminal Services Licensing, and check its box. This service has no optional components. When you click Next, the Setup Wizard will ask whether the license server should be available to your entire enterprise (Windows 2000 domain controllers only) or to the domain or workgroup. The answer depends on whether you want to make the licensing database available across domains. If you choose to make the license server available to anyone in the enterprise, then people in trusted domains will be able to pull TSCALs from the license server. If only the local domain gets access to it, then only computers connecting from the local domain can draw licenses from this pool.

There are reasons to choose either option. Confining the license server to the current domain or workgroup gives you more control over who's using TSCALs. Since TSCALs are permanently assigned to computers, not to users, this may not be a bad thing if your company's domains are organized by department and TSCALs are included as part of the departmental budget. Making the TSCAL database accessible to all computers in the enterprise makes the licensing structure more flexible, since running out of licenses in one domain does not mean that people can't use licenses from a different domain.

When you've made your decision, choose a location for the licensing database—*%systemroot%*\System32\Lserver is the default. Make sure that you put the licensing database somewhere where it will get backed up. If you have to recreate the licensing server, then you will need this database. When you click Next, Setup will copy the files it needs, and you're done. The server will now have a new addition to its Administrative Tools group: Terminal Services Licensing. The license server isn't really set up—you haven't added any licenses to it, or activated the server to make it able to publish "official" licenses—but the service is installed.

To install Terminal Services Licensing onto a .NET domain controller (you'll need to do this, as .NET doesn't seem able to use Win2K Terminal Services Licensing servers even though it can "see" them), you'll follow the same process. Unlike Terminal Services, Terminal Services Licensing is not a server role. The server will not need to reboot when you finish.

Now that it's installed, let's set it up. When you first start the licensing tool, it will browse for license servers on the network and then report back with the ones it found, as shown in Figure 4.5.

Figure 4.5 Use the Terminal Services Licensing tool to manage license usage.

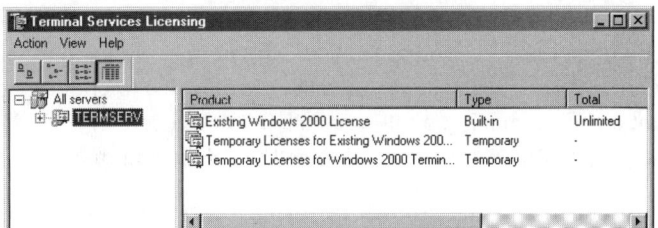

Windows 2000 Terminal Services took a cue from Citrix and set up the same kind of licensing-enabling procedure. You can't just plug in the terminal server, tell the license server how many licenses you've bought, and let people log on. Although the temporary licenses will function for a limited time (90 days), to fully enable the terminal server licenses, you'll need to activate the server and download the license key. Since Windows XP came out, most people know what activation is—and many have strong opinions about it—but for those who don't, activation associates your product key with a server. It's essentially a way of making sure that you've really paid for the licenses you're using. (According to Citrix, product activation also helps technical support keep track of you for better customer support, but I have a sneaking suspicion that the "let's make sure people are paying for what they use" issue is a little more important—not that it wouldn't be important to me, of course.) When you activate a license server, you're providing your product number to Microsoft. Microsoft then runs an encryption algorithm on it and sends you back the results as your activation code. You then give Microsoft back the activation code, they run another encrypting algorithm on it, and they send you a license code that corresponds to that activation code. This is an extra step, and that's annoying, but the procedure itself really isn't too arduous.

When you first open the Terminal Services Licensing tool, it looks like Figure 4.6. As you can see, the licensing server is present but not yet activated, so it can only issue temporary licenses that expire after 90 days. To make the license server ready to monitor license usage and to issue TSCALs, you'll need to activate the server and install the license pack assigned to that server. To do so, follow these steps:

1. Right-click the server, and choose Activate Server from the context menu. Click through the opening screen.

2. Choose a method of contacting Microsoft to get a license. You have four options for contacting Microsoft to give them your product number. The Internet, the default option, gives you a direct connection to Microsoft but requires that the license server have an Internet connection. Other options include the Web (whether from the license server or another computer with an Internet connection), the telephone, or fax. For this example, I'll choose the Web (see Figure 4.6) and click Next.

NOTE If you choose to contact the licensing people via telephone or fax, the next screen of the wizard will display a list of countries to choose from so that you've got a shot at making a toll-free call. If you're licensing TSCALs for the MSDN version of Win2K, you'll need to call the clearinghouse.

3. Now you need to take the product ID displayed in the screen (see Figure 4.7) and go to https://activate.microsoft.com. On this web page, you'll have a choice of activating a license server or installing license packs. Choose to activate the server, and choose Next.

Figure 4.6 Choose a way of contacting the Microsoft clearing house to get an activation code and valid license packs.

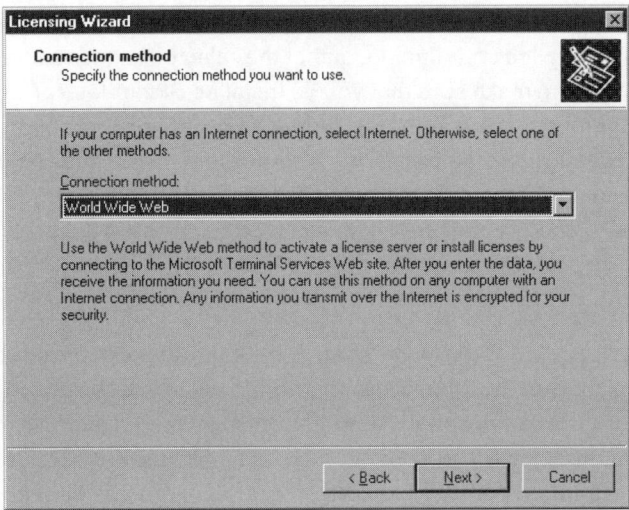

Figure 4.7 Take the product ID here, and send it to Microsoft to generate an activation code.

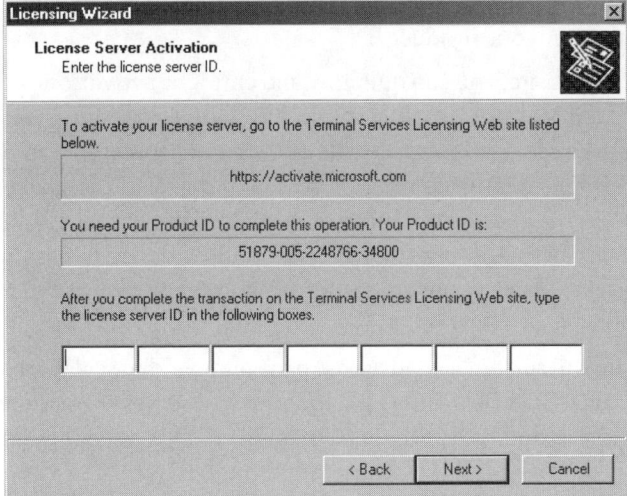

> **TIP** If you see an error message telling you that the Licensing Wizard cannot connect to the selected license server and prompting you to make sure the licensing service is installed and running, or that the selected license server's activation status is unknown, make sure that you've installed SP2 or later. This can happen if you're logged on with a roaming profile and the terminal server is set up to delete the roaming profile cache. It's also possible for this to happen if you're using a mandatory profile. The problem is that activating the server requires editing the profile, and in either case, you can't. SP2 addresses the problem if you're using roaming profiles with profile deletion enabled, but you can't activate a server when using a mandatory profile.

4. On the next screen of the Web Wizard, fill in the required product ID number, personal information, and purchase method (Select or Enterprise, Microsoft Open License, or Other to install via a retail licensing code). Click Next, review the information on the screen, and then click Next again to submit it. The website will spit out your activation code. Give it to the wizard to activate the server, which will then appear in the licensing tool with a status of Activated (green, and with a little picture of a certificate instead of the red X that unactivated servers get). Be very sure that you enter the product ID correctly, or the activation code won't work on your server. The Microsoft licensing clearinghouse generates that activation code by performing an algorithm on your product ID.

5. Back on the website, you can quit now and enter the activation code you just got into the Activation Wizard, or while still in the Web Wizard, you can get client licenses based on the code displayed. You'll need client licenses, so you might as well continue. Click Yes to move to the next screen of the Web Licensing tool, where you'll need to fill in the codes of all the license packs you have (the MLP number, or your Open License or Enrollment Agreement number, depending on what kind of customer you are). Again, confirm the information that you've entered, and click Next to submit it.

6. The website will spit out a valid license pack number that will work with the server you activated, and which you can plug into the license server. Notice that it will only work with this server, and if the license pack number is for a retail purchase, you can only install it once. To install the license pack number, return to the Terminal Services Licensing tool, right-click the activated server, and choose Install Licenses from the context menu. When prompted, fill in the license pack number as shown in Figure 4.8.

Figure 4.8 Installing the client access licenses

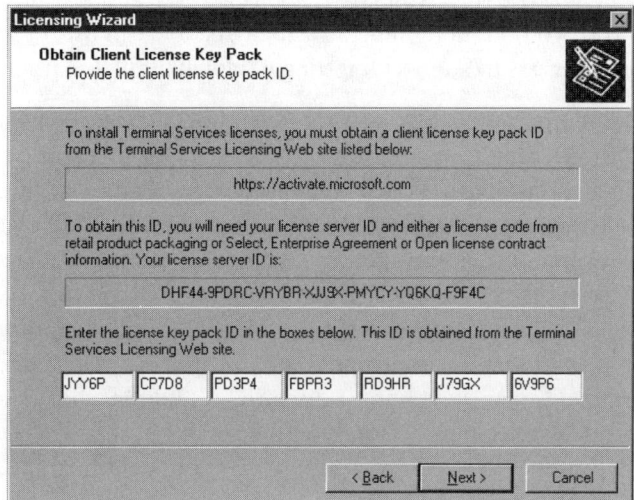

Once you install the license pack, the license server is ready to go.

> **TIP** If the license server won't accept a license pack and you're *sure* you typed it correctly, the database might be damaged. If it is, you can rebuild it by uninstalling the licensing service, reinstalling it, and then reactivating the server.

All that said, here's a warning: You have 90 days to activate a TSCAL license server. Use those 90 days to make sure that you're running the licensing service on the computer that you want to take the job. The client licenses you create will work only on the server you've activated, and the activation code is based on the product ID.

Automatically Deploying Terminal Servers

That's how you install Terminal Services on a server that's already set up and running, but what about a server that isn't installed yet? You can add Terminal Services to a server while you're installing it. Better yet, though, you would be adding Terminal Services to an automated installation of the operating system. You could really save yourself some time there.

You would automate the creation of a terminal server for the same reasons you would automate the installation of any other server: speed and consistency. When first introducing Terminal Services to your organization, you're probably—and wisely—going to be a little cautious about it. Rather than immediately replacing the local Desktop, you're going to have a few people use the terminal server, run a few applications, and see how the server performs so you can determine how many people can use a terminal server. You don't need many servers to support a testing deployment like that.

If server-based computing works well for you, though, you'll probably need to add more servers. At the very least, you'll want one more for a degree of redundancy. This is where automated installations will come in handy, because adding more servers can be more trouble than it initially appears. Installing an operating system isn't difficult, but it's time-consuming. You can spend an entire day clicking the Next button and have little to show for it other than a few installed servers. Okay, fine—you'll delegate the task to someone else, since it's such a simple job. Trouble is, installing an operating system and collection of services *is* a simple job, but it's also an exacting one. If you're building a terminal server, you want it done right, and that means installing all applicable hotfixes and service packs, installing the service in the right mode, and making sure that you've applied the security settings that you want for that server. This is not necessarily the job for the new intern.

One way to resolve the problem of duplicating servers is to clone them, and, should you decide to do so, you'll get good duplicates of the terminal servers. However, Windows 2000 does not come with cloning software. (SysPrep is not a cloning tool but a pre-cloning tool that scrubs SIDs and machine-specific information from a source operating system before you clone it.) It *does* come with a couple of automated deployment tools that you can use to save time and script an installation so that it always comes out the way you wanted it: Registry tweaks, hotfixes, security patches, and all. You don't have to rely on someone following instructions. You can create scripts and setup routines that allow you to roll out terminal servers with the right hotfixes, service packs, and applications all installed. Then, when you need to add capacity or quickly replace a server, you can pick the setup routine that creates the kind of server you need and let it go.

Over the next pages, I'll explain how you can create an unattended installation script for installing a terminal server (and how to run this installation) and how to fine-tune the Terminal Services settings with this installation script. Next, I'll show you how to take unattended installations one step further by using Remote Installation Services (RIS) to streamline the installation UI while still offering you choices that a straight unattended installation cannot. (The following explanations are specific to automated installations for creating terminal servers. In *Windows 2000 Automated Deployments and Remote Management* (Sybex), I explored scripted installations, Remote Installation Services, and packaging Registry changes in a broader sense.)

> **TIP** If you haven't used unattended installation scripts in Windows 2000, be sure to read the "Scripted Installations" section first. RIS uses scripts similar to the ones that ordinary unattended installations use, but it carries them a bit further to enhance what you can do with them.

Prep Work

Simply automating installations instead of sitting in front of a monitor displaying the progress of file copying will save you quite a bit of time, but you can save even more with a little judicious prep work. Let's take a look at how to update the installation files to automatically install Service Pack 2 and to package Registry changes and applications so that you can apply those packages during installation, or even to terminal servers that you've previously set up.

Updating the System Files To back an automated installation for a terminal server, you'll need the operating system files stored in \i386 on the installation CD. Setup can use these files just as well from a hard disk as it can from a CD, and it's almost always to your advantage to let it do so. Installing from a network location means that you don't have to get out the CD every time you want to install the operating system and, as you'll see, makes it easier to apply OEM drivers and other helper files to an installation. Installing from a network location gives you another advantage: you can apply the most recent service pack to the installation files before using them to install the operating system, so that you don't have to apply the service pack separately after installing the OS. Service packs are always important, but you're really going to want to put SP3 on your application servers because of the fix to Terminal Services Licensing that allows you to reclaim unused TSCALs. A complete list of all the fixes included in SP3 (including fixes for printing, other licensing problems, security settings associated with shadowing, and other issues) is available from http://support.microsoft.com/default.aspx?scid=kb;en-us;Q320853. In this example, I'll show you how to apply SP2 to the installation files.

The process for applying a service pack's updates to the installation—what's called *slipstreaming* the service pack into the installation—is simple. Copy the \i386 folder from the Windows 2000 Server CD to the server's hard disk. Download SP2 (currently at http://www.microsoft.com/windows2000/downloads/servicepacks/sp2/). Next, expand the service pack files onto your computer by typing **w2ksp2 -x** and, when the service pack asks where to expand itself, tell it to go into, say, *C:\Tools\SP2*. When it's done, you'll see a dialog box telling you that the extraction is complete.

Once the service pack files are installed on the server, you're ready to update the \i386 folder you copied to the hard disk. Navigate to the \Update subfolder in the folder where you stored the service pack files and run the UPDATE command to point to those files (for example, **update -s:d:\winnt**). This will update the \i386 folder stored in that location with the service pack. (Don't add \i386 into the path, or UPDATE will look for an \i386 folder subordinate to the one you named—it assumes that the folder it's updating is called \i386.)

The /i386 folder's files are now updated for SP2. You can use the updated files for backing a scripted installation or to make images for a RIS-based installation. The version information for any installations backed by the updated files will reflect the addition of SP2.

Recording Registry Changes with WinInstall When you install Terminal Services using an unattended installation, you must install the service with the default settings. If you know ahead of time what tuning you'll want to do to the terminal server, you can use WinInstall to record the changes as an MSI file and apply those changes either during an unattended installation or as a stand-alone executable. You can also use this tool to automate software installation. While WinInstall won't help you much for your first terminal server rollout, it can help a lot with your second, fourth, or tenth.

> **TIP** If you're planning to record only Registry changes, not package applications, you might think of using REG files instead. I'd stick with the MSI files. If you use an MSI file instead of a REG file to store the changes, they'll be stored in Add/Remove Programs and you can repair or update them accordingly. MSI files are an easier way of making sure that all changes get recorded. With REG files, it's easy to miss something and make an update file that doesn't accomplish its job. I've seen the REG file fail to work when the MSI file worked perfectly.

Although a detailed examination of WinInstall is a topic for another book, here are the steps you'll need to take to package changes to the operating system that you can apply during installation or afterward.

Go to another computer—*not* the one you'll be using to record changes—and put the Windows 2000 Server installation CD in the drive. Browse to \valueadd\3rdparty\mgmt\winstle on the Win2K installation CD and run SWIADMLE.MSI. You'll see a dialog box with a status bar on it; a few seconds later, WinINSTALL LE will be installed into Program Files\Veritas Software\Winstall.

> **WARNING** Do not install WinInstall on the computer where you'll be recording the changes. Otherwise, the changes could be dependent on finding WinInstall on the target computer and won't work properly. For the same reason, when recording the changes on the template computer you'll want to connect to the shared Winstall directory using its UNC name, not with a mapped drive letter. You want the template computer to be as vanilla as you can possibly manage.

Once you've installed WinINSTALL LE, you've got two new tools on your system: Discover (for creating new MSI packages) and the Software Console (for editing MSI packages). Share the Winstall directory with the network so you can use Discover from another computer.

Go to the template computer, and make sure that it's as plain vanilla as possible. Ideally, the template computer should be a freshly installed terminal server using all the default settings. Discover will record only what you *change*, not what's different from the default settings; therefore, to make a good package, the template server will need to be configured as much like the target servers as possible. This means default settings for all Terminal Services configurations.

Next, create a network connection to the Winstall directory on the other computer. Again, don't use drive letters, just use the *servername**directoryname* connection. Once you're in the directory, run Discover (DiscoZ.EXE) to begin the wizard that walks you through the process of recording the changes. The whole recording process looks like this:

1. Pick a name for the package you're creating, and choose a location where you'll store it. Make sure that this location will be network-accessible. I suggest that you store all MSI packages in a central and obviously marked folder so that you can find them easily. (You can always hide the shared folder by giving it a share name with a dollar sign at the end of it.)

2. Select a local disk where Discover can store its temporary files. This will be a temporary folder off the root of the selected drive. Make sure there's room enough to store the files. The temporary storage will have to be local, because you shouldn't use mapped drive letters on a template computer and DiscoZ will only accept a drive letter.

3. Choose the drives that Discover should scan for changes. You only need to scan any drives where changes might take place, Initially, no drives will be chosen to scan; use the Add and Remove buttons to select or deselect drives to scan.

> **TIP** If you're recording only Registry changes, the only drive you need to scan is the one containing the system files. If you're installing applications, make sure that you scan the drives where they'll be storing files.

4. Choose the directories and files to be excluded from the scan, chosen separately for each drive to be scanned (if you selected more than one drive, you'll need to choose the drive letter from the drop-down list at the top). By default, Discover will skip all machine-specific and user-specific data unless you tell it otherwise. Generally, you can stick with the defaults.

   When you click Next, Discover will back up all the files that you've chosen to scan for changes to its temporary directory. If you chose the Enhanced Registry Scan, then it will inspect all the Registry entries as well.

5. When it's done with the scan, you'll see a dialog box prompting you to run the Setup program for the application you're packaging. Run Setup, or cancel out and go to Terminal Services Configuration to make the changes that you want to record. Likely candidates are disabling Active Desktop (waste of bandwidth) and editing the application security settings. Make sure that everything is as you want it, reboot, and then begin DiscoZ again.

> **NOTE** Not sure of what changes you might want to make? Chapter 6, "Managing Terminal Sessions," explains the Terminal Services tools in more detail, and Chapter 7 covers Registry edits for application tuning. For now, go to Terminal Services Configuration and make sure that the Active Desktop and application security options are configured as you want them.

6. Restart Discover. This time, the beginning window will tell you that it's in the process of building an installation package, tell you that the Before package is complete, and ask you whether you want to perform the "After" snapshot now or abandon the "Before" snapshot and start over. If you click Cancel, you'll just exit Discover. Keep the default, and click Next to take the After snapshot.

7. Discover will scan all the directories you selected earlier again. You don't need to reselect them, nor will you have a chance to do so. If Discover can't copy any files for some reason, you'll see an error message telling which file is presenting the problem. You'll have the option of aborting, retrying, or ignoring. Aborting ends the After snapshot, Retry attempts to read the file again, and Ignore skips the file. Any files that you choose to Ignore will be logged on the `FileErr.txt` error log in the DiscoZ directory.

8. When you complete the package, you'll see a Conversion Successful dialog box listing any warnings that happened with the conversion. For example, if the application creates shortcuts when it installs, that will be noted in this folder, as will any references to absolute paths or UNCs that might not be available on the target computers. These warnings don't necessarily mean that a package won't work—they seem largely informational.

After you finish taking the "After" snapshot, you'll see a dialog box telling you that the snapshot is complete and telling you the name and path of the MSI file Discover created. If you were using DiscoZ to package applications, uninstall the application you've created and start the process over. Ideally, instead of just uninstalling the application you'll reinstall the OS to get the template as clean as possible.

Here are some things to keep in mind when creating and applying MSI packages:

- Again, keep the template computer as much like the targets as possible. Get rid of any mapped drives. The template shouldn't have any applications installed that don't normally come with Windows, lest the extra applications have the same DLLs as the applications you're installing so that the installation process might skip a needed file.

- Package information in small chunks. As you'll see in the course of this book, you can do quite a bit of Registry editing when tuning a terminal server, but not all of those changes will apply to all terminal servers. If all your terminal servers will be identically configured, it's okay to lump changes together in a single batch, and easier, too. You'll only need to apply one MSI package to apply all changes or to install an entire application suite. But if your terminal servers will be a mixed bunch, with some needing one set of tweaks and others needing another set, then record those tweaks separately. Even if you're only packaging Registry changes, consider doing them one at a time. That way, you can set up a RIS installation to pick from a menu of possible changes and tweaks to use on different servers.

- You can only apply an MSI package once—once it's installed, it won't install again. Therefore, if you need to reapply the changes packaged in an MSI file, you must either choose the Repair option or first remove the package before reapplying. Otherwise, you'll spend a lot of time banging your head against a wall trying to figure out why the package won't apply.

- Finally, test packages carefully before deploying them. Most packages should work just fine on a variety of hardware, but you should be sure of this before you depend on them.

Now that we've applied SP2 and packaged the Registry changes, let's create an automated installation, beginning with a simple script so that you can see how the process works.

Scripted Installations

Installation scripts are the simplest form of unattended installations. The script takes your place in front of the console by answering all the questions that the installation routine puts to you, using the settings that you created ahead of time. The requirements for using installation scripts are low: you don't need Active Directory, you don't need a DHCP server...you don't even need a *network*. All you need to run an automated installation from the script itself are the installation files and the script itself. This makes scripted installations a handy choice for times when you don't have a full network backing you, but you just need to roll out servers.

> **TIP** Although you don't *need* a network to support a scripted installation, using a network makes it much easier to really automate the installation process with updated OS Setup files and additional drivers and MSI files. Try to have at least a simple Windows 2000 workstation around to launch the installation process. The installation server doesn't have to be fancy; it just has to have the Setup files and installation scripts available.

Using Answer Files

At its simplest, an unattended installation requires only a single script, but it can involve up to three script-related files: an answer file containing the core elements of the installation, a uniqueness database file customizing the script for a specific purpose, and a batch file for initiating the process.

The answer file follows the structure of the INI files used with 16-bit Windows. Keys define settings that are part of Windows 2000 installation, such as the computer name, the password, and the services to install. The values for the keys determine the answers that you provide to the installation routine. For example, when you run Windows 2000 Setup manually, at some point the installation routine will prompt you for the computer name. In an answer file, ComputerName is the key, and the name you provide is the value. To make it easier to organize the keys in an answer file, Windows 2000 organizes them into sections of related keys. So that you can tell at a glance what a section is doing, Windows 2000 installation scripts support comments preceded by semicolons, which the Setup routine does not interpret. In the following example, the section is [Identification], the comments explain the purpose of this section, JoinDomain is the key, and REDROOM is the value.

```
[Identification]
;This section names the domain I want this computer to join, and
;provides the name and password of an account able to add a machine
;account to the domain.
    JoinDomain=REDROOM
```

The answer file controls the basic settings for an entire unattended installation. A terminal server's answer file will contain all the sections in Table 4.1.

Table 4.1 Required Sections for Terminal Server Answer Files

Section Name	Purpose
[Data]	Tells Setup how to partition the hard disk when installing Windows 2000.
[Unattended]	Tells Setup to perform an unattended installation and identifies the folder where the OS files will go.
[User Data]	Provides the computer's name and the full name and company name of the person doing the installing.
[GUIUnattended]	Lists the administrator's password and identifies the computer's time zone.
[Networking]	Tells Setup which network components to install.
[Identification]	Identifies the workgroup or domain the server should join, and (if joining a domain) provides administrator account information to permit it to do so.
[LicenseFilePrintData]	Identifies the client access model the server's using (since workstations must have a client access to connect to any kind of Windows server) and the licenses available. This licensing information is separate from Terminal Services Licensing.
[Components]	Lists the services and components that should be enabled or disabled. You don't have to specifically enable or disable default components, but since games are installed by default and Terminal Services is not, you'll need to add and edit this section.

> **WARNING** The password information contained in the GUIUnattended and Identification sections is in plaintext. Considering that these passwords are for a local administrator's account and a domain administrator's accounts, it is vital that you protect any unattended installation scripts. In other words, you *are* storing these files on an NTFS directory and setting permissions, aren't you?

The simplest way to get these required sections and the required keys into your unattended installation script is to use the Setup Manager tool available for download from the Microsoft website and included in the Resource Kit. After telling the Setup Manager whether you want to create an installation script for Server or Professional, and that you want to create a new answer file instead of editing an existing one or copying the current computer's configuration, follow the steps prompting you for the following:

> **NOTE** You might think that you can use the Copy The Current Computer option to clone a terminal server. Sadly, you can't. This option really doesn't copy the current computer configuration; it takes some of the settings and applies them to the installation script. The only way to clone a terminal server is with a third-party tool such as Ghost or DiskImage. Automating the installations just allows you to build terminal servers quickly and consistently.

1. The degree of automation (fully automated or permitting the person running the installation some degree of input). Plan to fully automate the installation, or you'll be stuck sitting in front of the console again.
2. Your name and company name.
3. A name for the computer, either set for all users of this answer file, one generated by the Setup program (personally, I can't see any reason to do this), or one chosen from a text list to create an easily customizable installation script.

> **NOTE** Choosing a name from a text list creates a Uniqueness Database File to accompany the answer file for the scripted installation. I'll explain how and when to use UDFs in the next section.

4. A password (blank is acceptable, but a bad idea for a terminal server) for the local Administrator account.
5. The display and network *client* settings, and the name of the workgroup or domain that the computer should join during Setup.
6. The time zone in which the computer will be located.
7. The location and (if applicable) name of the folder where the /i386 files used to install Windows 2000 will be located.

> **TIP** Storing the /i386 files on a network share is much more convenient than using the CD. Having the /i386 directory on the hard disk allows you to apply service packs to the files pre-installation, and makes it easier to add drivers and application installation files to the OS installation. If you do store the /i386 files on a network share, make sure that you assign the directory a name a bit more descriptive than the default, so that people can easily distinguish the Windows 2000 Server directory from the Windows 2000 Pro directory.

8. The name and location of any extra files that you'd like to add to the Windows 2000 installation, including:
   - OEM drivers
   - A different HAL driver (if needed)
   - Any extra routines to run after Setup
   - The location of any special bitmaps or wallpaper to display during Setup
9. The name of the answer file (the default is always unattend.txt).
10. Any additional settings, such as Internet Explorer settings or the like.

If you used (and disliked) the NT4 Setup Manager tool, you'll be glad to know that Windows 2000's Setup Manager is a big improvement over its predecessor. First, it's set up as a wizard, not like a Properties sheet. Although some parts of NT operating systems have become wizard-happy to a ridiculous degree, wizards are really good for walking you through a series of steps. It's possible to forget to fill out part of a tabbed Properties sheet, but it's difficult or impossible to forget to fill out a page of a wizard—the information is presented in such small chunks. For really crucial settings the wizard won't proceed until you *do* supply those settings.

Another advantage to the new Setup Manager is that it includes settings that you had to add by hand with the NT 4 unattended installation scripts. Among the additions that will make you happy when scripting Terminal Services installations are these:

- Automatic license agreement means that you no longer have to manually edit the answer file (or monitor an installation so you can manually agree to the licensing terms) to agree to the EULA. In fact, if you're doing a completely automated installation, you must include the setting that automatically agrees to the EULA for you.
- Support for automatic Administrator logons permits you to make Setup log on once (or more than once) after installation and carry out any additional housekeeping needed to set up the terminal server, like applying REG files to make Registry edits or installing applications.

- Good graphical support for adding third-party drivers allows you to get all those client printers set up while you're installing the operating system, rather than doing it afterward. You can also easily apply the newest drivers of any kind, so that you're not starting out with Windows 2000's two-year-old drivers... or no drivers at all, since two and a half years is plenty of time to come up with hardware that didn't exist when Windows 2000 was released.

This list doesn't include all the edits required for even a workstation setup, let alone a terminal server. To fully automate the installation of *any* class of computer, you'll need to add the Product ID key to fully automate the installation, and terminal servers (and other servers) require a bit more editing than that. However, these additions will at least reduce the amount of editing you have to do and, therefore, reduce the chances that you'll forget something important. Forgetting a key isn't destructive, but installing the OS incorrectly does slow you down, and the whole point of this exercise is to save time.

Creating a Terminal Server   Using the Setup Manager will get you a working server installation script, but it won't get you a terminal server, because Setup Manager has no UI for enabling or disabling services and components. To create a terminal server and install the client files on the server, you'll need to add a section called [Components] and make two changes to it. First, add a key called TSEnable and set its value to On. Second, if you want to make the RDP client files available to users, add a key called TSClients and set its value to On. (If you don't install these files, then although the directory path for the client installation files will still be on the server, the Disk1 and Disk2 folders that hold the Setup files will be empty. The Components section should look something like this:

```
[Components]
    TSEnable = ON
    TSClients = ON
```

In addition to system services, the [Components] section covers games and color schemes. Games are installed by default, so if you'd like to create a terminal server without games you'll need to explicitly disable them.

Adding TSEnable to the [Components] section gets you only halfway to installing Terminal Services for an application server. Enabling this key will indeed install Terminal Services—but in Remote Administration mode, the default. Once you install the service using the default settings, putting the service into Application Server mode requires completely reinstalling the service using the procedure we discussed earlier. To make an application server instead of an ordinary server with Remote Administration enabled, you'll need to add a [TerminalServices] section to the answer file or UDF, like this:

```
[TerminalServices]
ApplicationServer=1
```

> **NOTE** You cannot enable both Terminal Services in Application Server mode and the Cluster Service. This combination works in Remote Administration mode, but if you configure the script to enable both the Cluster Service and Application Server mode, then the Cluster Service will install and Terminal Services will install in Remote Administration mode.

A complete answer file for installing a Windows 2000 terminal server could look like this. I've commented the sections so that you can see how the installation is progressing.

```
;SetupMgrTag
[Data]
;Automatically partitions the hard disk and sets the stage for an
;unattended installation.
    AutoPartition=1
    MsDosInitiated="0"
    UnattendedInstall="Yes"


[Unattended]
;Tells Setup to perform an unattended installation to \WINNT and to
;skip the EULA query.
    UnattendMode=FullUnattended
    OemSkipEula=Yes
    OemPreinstall=Yes
    TargetPath=\WINNT


[GuiUnattended]
;Creates an Administrator's password of "blank", tells Setup to log on
;once after the installation is complete. The time zone for this
;computer is Eastern.
    AdminPassword=blank
    AutoLogon=Yes
    AutoLogonCount=1
    OEMSkipRegional=1
```

```
            TimeZone=35
            OemSkipWelcome=1

        [UserData]
        ;Provides the name and company name, tells Setup to pull a computer
        ;name from a list (see [SetupMgr] section), and provides the ProductID
        ;so I don't have to type it in.
            FullName="Christa Anderson"
            OrgName="Acme Corporation"
            ComputerName=*
            ProductID=XXXXX-XXXXX-XXXXX-XXXXX-XXXXX

        [LicenseFilePrintData]
        ;Sets up Server Licensing (not Terminal Server licensing)
        ;in per-seat mode.
            AutoMode=PerSeat

        [SetupMgr]
        ;Tells Setup where to find the shared installation files and lists
        ;the computer names to use.
            DistFolder=C:\win2000dist
            DistShare=win2000dist
            ComputerName0=TermServ1
            ComputerName1=TermServ2
            ComputerName2=TermServ3
            ComputerName3=TermServ4

        [Identification]
        ;Tells Setup which domain the server should join and provides the name
        ;and password of someone with the right to add computers to the domain.
```

```
    JoinDomain=REDROOM
    DomainAdmin=ChristaA
    DomainAdminPassword=blank

[Networking]
    InstallDefaultComponents=Yes

[Branding]
    BrandIEUsingUnattended=Yes

[Proxy]
    Proxy_Enable=0
    Use_Same_Proxy=0

[GuiRunOnce]
;Installs support for a printer shared from \\sandworm and applies the
;Registry edits we packed into tsreg.msi.
    Command0="rundll32 printui.dll,PrintUIEntry /in /n \\sandworm\hp41"
    Command1="msiexec /i tsreg.msi"

[Components]
;Installs Terminal Services and the client installation files, and
;prevents the installation of games.
    TSEnable = ON
    TSClients = ON
 solitaire=Off
 freecell=Off
 pinball=Off
 minesweeper=Off
```

```
[TerminalServices]
;Installs Terminal Services in Application Server mode.
    ApplicationServer=1
```

Creating a Terminal Services Licensing Server If you're working in a Windows 2000 domain, the Terminal Services licensing server will need to be a domain controller. Most likely, you'll create licensing servers by installing the service on an existing domain controller or server, using the short process I described earlier in this chapter. If you happen to be building a script for a server or domain controller from scratch, however, then you can do so by adding a line to [Components] to enable the licensing service, like this:

```
[Components]
    LicenseServer = ON
```

Using Uniqueness Database Files

If you're scripting an installation to apply to more than one server, then you have a choice about how you'd like to make the changes. One option is to edit the answer file: install the server, then edit the answer file for the next server, then install the server, then edit the answer file for the next server.... You get the idea. Another, more palatable, approach is to use a uniqueness database file (UDF), a companion to an answer file that allows you to customize an answer file without creating the whole thing from scratch for each set of installation options. Fundamentally used to supply a new computer name to an installation script, a UDF is actually quite a bit more flexible than that. You can use a UDF to edit the values for any keys applied during the graphical portion of Setup. When you create an installation script with a UDF, you'll create a companion BAT file with the same prefix as the answer file and UDF; to initiate the installation, just run the BAT file.

If a key appears in both the answer file and the UDF, or it appears in one but not the other, which value controls? It depends. If a key has a value in the answer file but doesn't appear in the UDF, then the value in the answer file is used. If a key has a value in both the UDF and the answer file, then Setup uses the value in the UDF. However, if a key has a value in the answer file, and the key appears but has no value in the UDF, then Setup uses the *default value for the key*; the answer file does *not* take precedence even though it has a value for that key and the UDF does not. The practical implications of UDFs are this: you can create a standard "server" answer file and use it for installing all your servers, but use UDFs to selectively enable Terminal Services.

> **NOTE** If a section or key appears in the UDF but not the answer file, Setup creates that section in the answer file. Because the section or key already exists in the UDF, the new value in the answer file will not affect that installation. In other words, this scenario won't change the way your scripts work.

The main difference between UDFs and answer files is that the former also have an additional section: [UniqueIDs]. This section indicates the parts of the answer file that you'll be replacing. Each unique section of the installation will be identified by the Unique ID assigned to it at the beginning of the UDF. Initially, a UDF will look something like this:

```
;SetupMgrTag
[UniqueIds]
    TermServ1=UserData
    TermServ2=UserData
    TermServ3=UserData
    TermServ4=UserData

[TermServ1:UserData]
    ComputerName=TermServ1

[TermServ2:UserData]
    ComputerName=TermServ2

[TermServ3:UserData]
    ComputerName=TermServ3

[TermServ4:UserData]
    ComputerName=TermServ4
```

However, you can edit it to add any settings that apply during the graphical portion of Setup. You can even edit the UDF to change the computer names. The title you assign to the individual UDF areas does not need to be the computer name for the server being installed. Therefore, you could create a UDF called "DOSApps" to identify it as a terminal server used for DOS application, apply any settings that applied especially to DOS applications in a multiuser environment, and just edit the computer name each time you ran the "DOSApps" BAT file initiating that script's answer file and UDF.

UDFs have their limitations. They work only for the graphical portion of Setup. You can't use them, say, to customize installation scripts for hardware that doesn't all use the same manufacturer's mass storage driver or keyboard driver. (If the drivers are already on the Win2K CD, then you don't have to worry about this.) You can use only one UDF per installation; there's no way to layer multiple customizations in UDFs to create the ultra-customized installation—if you want that much flexibility in an unattended installation, then use Remote Installation Services. However, UDFs can help you save a lot of time creating situation-specific answer files.

Running a Scripted Installation

The simplest way to run a scripted installation is from the network. Connect to the shared directory that you set up when running Setup Manager. From there, run the BAT file associated with the installation script, supplying the name of the UDF you want to use as an argument. (If you're using UDFs, you can't just click on the BAT file in Explorer, because you'll need to tell the BAT file which UDF to read.) To run the `Server` set of installation instructions from a floppy to install the computer named TERMSERV1, you'd type `server.bat unattend termserv1` from Run or from the command line. If you edited the answer file or UDF to include the Product ID, the installation will begin without further ado. Once you initiate the BAT file, Setup will stop only if you left crucial information out of the installation script or mistyped the product ID.

Unattended installations have one *major* flaw, though: starting them. If you don't mind running the installation from the CD, it's not so bad, but you will install two-year-old drivers, no service packs, and every extra file you want to use must fit on a 1.44MB floppy disk. Running the installation from the network is easier and lets you update the installation files, but you've got to *get* to the network first. If you're reinstalling a computer from one that already has a network-ready OS on it, then this is easy. Install Windows 2000 Server onto a fresh computer, though, and you have to create a bootable floppy, complete with network drivers. Because finding DOS network drivers and creating customized boot floppies is a pain, let's look at an unattended installation option that allows us to skip both: Remote Installation Services.

Remote Installation Services

Remote Installation Services (RIS) is the über-scripted installation, allowing you to store unattended installation files onto a central server to be downloaded to client machines. It's more than that, though. Remember that answer files support only one UDF at a time. RIS allows you a degree of flexibility not possible with answer files. Using RIS, you can do any of the following:

- Create a menu—complete with useful names and detailed explanations—of installations to perform.
- Write a simplified UI to allow the person initiating Setup to define a few settings for the Setup routine, but before the installation starts so that they don't have to either wait for Setup to prompt them for the settings it lacks, or make Setup wait for them.
- Install an operating system over the network—even to a computer with no current operating system, and without having to create a customized boot floppy.

Creating and setting up a RIS installation for a terminal server is a bit more involved than creating and setting up a scripted installation. At its simplest, to make a scripted installation work, you need an installation CD, a cheat sheet to tell you which settings control which parts of the OS installation, and a copy of Notepad. The very basic RIS-based installation requires a DHCP server, a DNS server, a Windows 2000 domain controller, and a RIS server with at least two NTFS-formatted drives in it. (The good news is that the same server can meet all of those requirements.) You can't run RIS off the Setup CD. What you *can* do, however, is create an enormously flexible environment for deploying terminal servers with a variety of configurations with minimal interaction on your part and almost foolproof. (There is no such thing as a completely foolproof system because fools keep getting more ingenious, but this isn't a bad start.)

At its simplest, the process of installing a terminal server using RIS looks like this:

1. On a PXE computer, the client computer displays a `BootP` message indicating that it's requesting an IP address from the DHCP server. On a computer using the generic boot floppy, the computer displays its MAC address.

2. When the client gets an IP address, the word "DHCP" appears on the screen, indicating that the client has an IP address and is waiting to hear from the RIS server.

3. The client PC displays TFTP, indicating that it's connected to the RIS server, and prompts you to click F12. Do this *quickly*, or RIS will decide that you aren't sufficiently eager to perform a remote installation—you really have to *want* this—and will make you reboot the machine to start over.

4. At this point, you should see the beginning screen of the Client Installation Wizard. Now comes the part you do see.

5. Log on with the account name and password of someone with permission to add computers to the domain, and click Enter as prompted.

6. Pick an image to install from the ones in the list.

7. Review the settings that RIS presents to you.

8. If the installation will wipe the hard drive, you'll be warned of this; press Enter to continue.

9. Press Enter to start the installation, and go to lunch. When you come back, the installation should be complete.

That's the basic outline of how the installation works from the perspective of the person initiating it, but of course getting the RIS server to that point (who put up the list of available images? Oh, that's right—you did!) requires some work ahead of time. In this section, I'll talk about the tweaking you can do behind the scenes to make the RIS server present an image for installing a terminal server, or even allowing you to pick and choose settings to apply to the image. That said, RIS is a really big subject; Therefore, I'm going to explain here only the parts that apply directly to using RIS to set up terminal servers. In addition to what you read here, you'll also need to do the following:

- Create a RIS boot floppy to let any servers that don't have PXE ROMs boot from the network and connect to the RIS server.
- Edit the permissions on the shared RIS folders to allow people to see only the image that they are allowed to install.
- Prestage computer accounts so that the person doing the installing doesn't have to have the authority to create user accounts in the domain.

Prep Work: Making Server Files Work with RIS

RIS is really designed for pushing out workstations, not servers. Strictly speaking, it doesn't work for installing server operating systems at all. Left alone, it won't accept server installation files and you can't copy a server with the RIS tools and publish that copy using the service. There is no way to make the image-copying tool work on a server (or if there is, I haven't found it), but you can trick the RIS server into accepting server files for its automatic installations. The only catch is that Microsoft does not officially support this hack.

Part of setting up RIS involves creating a default image from an \i386 directory, and we'll need to trick the service into accepting server files anyway. Therefore, let's save a little time and get the server files ready *now* so that our default image can use the server files needed to back a terminal server installation. First, get the Windows 2000 Server or Advanced Server installation CD and copy the \i386 directory to the RIS server's hard disk. The location doesn't matter, so long as you can get to the files, but label them in such a way that you can easily distinguish them from the Windows 2000 Pro files if you'll also be using the RIS server to install workstations. I call my destination directory something inspired like "Server." I recommend that you slipstream SP2 and any necessary post-SP2 hotfixes into the copied directory as we discussed earlier in this chapter.

Next comes the clever bit. A text file called `txtsetup.sif` is in the \i386 folder containing the server installation files.. Open this file, and look for the line `ProductType = 1`. Edit it to read `ProductType = 0`. Save your changes and exit Notepad. The RIS server will now see the directory as the Windows 2000 Pro files, not Server files, and it will allow you to add them to the RIS server.

> **NOTE** The fact that you're editing `txtsetup.sif` is one reason you can't just use the RIS server's \i386 directory. A Windows 2000 server with this setting would be confused.

Don't do anything else with the copied installation files at this point—it's time to set up RIS.

Setting Up RIS

I don't want to get into a prolonged description of how to use RIS here, so let's concentrate on how to set up and use the service for installing terminal servers. Start by installing the DHCP service on the RIS server and authorize the server for dispensing IP addresses. To do this, open Administrative Tools ➤ DHCP and right-click the server in question, and then pick "Authorize" from the context menu. Next, install RIS on the server, using the Windows Setup portion of Add/Remove Programs, and reboot when prompted to do so.

> **NOTE** If the RIS server backing the installations is a valid DHCP server, it's authorized as a RIS server.

The third step—configuring the RIS server—is a bit more involved. When you restart the server, you'll see the Configure Your Server dialog box prompting you to finish setting up the service. Click the link, or run RISETUP from Start ➤ Run to configure the service. During this short wizard, you'll go through the following steps:

1. Provide a location for the published installation images (that is, the \i386 files backed by an installation script which we'll fine-tune in a moment). These images cannot be on the C: drive; the default location of `D:\RemoteInstall` will probably be fine.
2. Tell RIS that you don't want to start supporting client requests just yet.
3. Set up the default image, using the Windows 2000 Server \i386 files you doctored earlier. Provide a name for the folder in which the image will be stored.
4. Type a name for the default image, for example, **Windows 2000 Server with SP2**.

When you've done all this, you'll have a chance to review your choices. Click Finish to let Windows 2000 set up the service. This takes a few minutes to complete, but you don't need to reboot when it's over.

Creating a Terminal Server Installation

The first part of creating a terminal server installation will look very much like editing a standard unattended installation script. When you set up that default image on the RIS server, you created a folder at \RemoteInstall\Setup\English\Images*foldername*\i386\Templates. In this \Templates folder is a file called `RISTNDRD.SIF`, which looks something like this:

```
[data]
floppyless = "1"
msdosinitiated = "1"
```

```
OriSrc = "\\%SERVERNAME%\RemInst\%INSTALLPATH%\%MACHINETYPE%"
OriTyp = "4"
LocalSourceOnCD = 1

[SetupData]
OsLoadOptions = "/noguiboot /fastdetect"
SetupSourceDevice =
"\Device\LanmanRedirector\%SERVERNAME%\RemInst\%INSTALLPATH%"

[Unattended]
OemPreinstall = no
NoWaitAfterTextMode = 0
FileSystem = LeaveAlone
ExtendOEMPartition = 0
ConfirmHardware = no
NtUpgrade = no
Win31Upgrade = no
TargetPath = \WINNT
OverwriteOemFilesOnUpgrade = no
OemSkipEula = yes
InstallFilesPath =
"\\%SERVERNAME%\RemInst\%INSTALLPATH%\%MACHINETYPE%"

[UserData]
FullName = "%USERFIRSTNAME% %USERLASTNAME%"
OrgName = "%ORGNAME%"
ComputerName = %MACHINENAME%

[GuiUnattended]
OemSkipWelcome = 1
OemSkipRegional = 1
TimeZone = %TIMEZONE%
```

```
AdminPassword = "*"

[LicenseFilePrintData]
AutoMode = PerSeat

[Display]
ConfigureAtLogon = 0
BitsPerPel = 8
XResolution = 640
YResolution = 480
VRefresh = 60
AutoConfirm = 1

[Networking]
ProcessPageSections=Yes

[Identification]
JoinDomain = %MACHINEDOMAIN%
CreateComputerAccountInDomain = No
DoOldStyleDomainJoin = Yes

[NetProtocols]
MS_TCPIP=params.MS_TCPIP

[params.MS_TCPIP]
; transport: TC (TCP/IP Protocol)
InfID=MS_TCPIP
DHCP=Yes

[NetClients]
MS_MSClient=params.MS_MSClient
```

```
[params.MS_MSClient]
InfID=MS_MSClient

[NetServices]
MS_Server=params.MS_Server

[params.MS_Server]
; service: SRV (Server)
InfID=MS_Server
BroadcastsToLanman2Clients = No

[ServicesSection]

[RemoteInstall]
Repartition = Yes
UseWholeDisk = Yes

[OSChooser]
Description ="Windows 2000 Pro with SP2"
Help ="Has SP2 slipstreamed into installation files"
LaunchFile = "%INSTALLPATH%\%MACHINETYPE%\templates\startrom.com"
ImageType =Flat
Version="5.0"
```

Look at this file carefully, and you'll see the key to RIS's flexibility when it comes to setting up servers of any stripe. Many of its keys have variables (e.g., %ServerName%), not fixed values, for their values. These variables come from the answers you supply when prompted by RIS.

The menus you see when you initiate a remote installation session are generated by an HTML-like set of formatting tags, saved as a file with an .osc extension that looks like this:

```
<OSCML>
<TITLE> Client Installation Wizard
Logon</TITLE>
```

```
<FOOTER>  [ENTER] continue    [ESC] clear    [F1] help    [F3] 
restart computer</FOOTER>
<META KEY=F3 ACTION="REBOOT">
<META KEY=F1 HREF="LOGINHLP">
<META KEY=ESC HREF="LOGIN">
<META ACTION="LOGIN">
<BODY left=5 right=75>
<BR>
<BR>
Type a valid user name, password, and domain name. You may use the
Internet-style logon format (for example: Username@Company.com).
<BR>
<BR>
<BR>
<FORM ACTION="CHOICE">
  User name: <INPUT NAME="USERNAME" MAXLENGTH=255>
   Password: <INPUT NAME="*PASSWORD" TYPE=PASSWORD
MAXLENGTH=20><BR>
Domain name: <INPUT NAME="USERDOMAIN" MAXLENGTH=255>
</FORM>
<BR>
<BR>
<BR>
Press the TAB key to move between the User name, Password, and Domain
name fields.
</BODY>
</OSCML>
```

You have quite a bit of flexibility when it comes to editing these OSC files, so long as you begin and end with the <OSCML> tag. OSC files support two classes of tags: formatting and action. Formatting tags control what the document looks like (whether the text is in boldface, flashing, or what have you) and how it's arranged on the screen. Action tags control what the document *does*, accept user input, open another OSC file, or whatever. For our purposes, the action tags are much more important; see Table 4.2 to see them.

Table 4.2 Action Tags Supported by OSC Files

Tag	Function	Example
<FORM>	Creates a form in which you can store INPUT tags.	<FORM> ComputerName: <INPUT NAME="MACHINENAME" SIZE=14 MAXLENGTH=14> </FORM>
<INPUT>	Prompts the user for input and stores it in a variable for later use in the SIF file used for the installation. This tag works with the FORM markup tag, which must enclose the INPUT statements. INPUT supports several parameters: NAME names the variable in which the user input will be stored (required). TYPE indicates whether the user input is text (the default), which can be displayed on the screen), or a password, which makes the user input appear as asterisks (optional). VALUE assigns a preset value to the INPUT box (optional). SIZE delimits the size of the INPUT box in characters (optional). MAXLENGTH specifies the maximum length of the user input in characters (optional).	Games ON or OFF?: <INPUT NAME="GAMES" SIZE=3 MAXLENGTH=3>
<META ACTION = "client-side action">	Takes the action named in the "client-side action" variable.	<META ACTION="LOGIN">
<META KEY= F1 | F3 | ENTER | ESC HREF="screen name">	Opens the OSC file named in the "screen name" variable. You need only the prefix—RIS will automatically append the OSC extension to the filename. Only the F1, F3, ENTER, and ESC keys are supported.	<META KEY= F1 "HELP">

Table 4.2 Action Tags Supported by OSC Files *(continued)*

Tag	Function	Example
`<META SERVER ACTION = "server-side action">`	Takes the action named on the "server-side action" on the server (the action must be in quotation marks). RIS currently supports the following server-side actions: ENUM enumerates the SIF file found in X:\RemoteInstall\Setup\%Language%\"directory"\<some dir name>\%Machinetype%\templates*.SIF and stores the result in the Options variable. WARNING warns the user that the installation will blow away all existing partitions on the client machine. DNRESET resubmits your security credentials as though you'd just logged on. FILTER *name* filters the images you're allowed to see based on the credentials presented to the named page (such as CHOICE). CHECKGUID checks the GUID the client machine is submitting to make sure that it is not already assigned to an Active Directory client.	`<META SERVER ACTION="FILTER CHOICE">`
`<OPTION>`	Shows options in a list from which the user can select one. Supports these parameters: VALUE shows the value of a particular option. TIP shows the help text describing that option.	`<OPTION VALUE="OSAUTO" TIP="This is a tip.">`

Table 4.2 Action Tags Supported by OSC Files *(continued)*

Tag	Function	Example

`<SELECT>`	Creates a list of options from which a user can choose one. If the list contains only one option, the OSChooser selects it automatically and moves on.
	SIZE determines the visible size of the option list (the default is 1, so be sure to edit this to create a list of options).
	VALUE is the name of the option.
	TIP is a description of the chosen option.
		`<SELECT SIZE = 5>`
		`<OPTION VALUE="OSAUTO"`
		`TIP="This is a tip.">`
		`</SELECT>`

Customizing Menus to Make Terminal Services Optional

As you saw earlier, the SIF files that are the unattended installation scripts used with RIS installations use variables to pull information from the Setup screens and insert it into the installation scripts. That is, if you want to name servers during installation, you can request the computer name with an `INPUT` tag and assign that value to the variable `%MACHINENAME%`. If the SIF file makes the computer's name equal to `%MACHINENAME%`, then whatever name the person performing the RIS installation typed will be the one referenced in the installation script. In other words, you can use variables to provide a *very* streamlined set of user prompts, while using default or predefined settings for every other setting.

RIS supports the set of standard variables listed in Table 4.3.

Table 4.3 Standard Variables Supported by RIS

Variable	Meaning
`BOOTFILE`	Sent when a tool is about to be started.
`GUID`	Sent by OSChooser to indicate the GUID address of the client.
`INSTALLPATH`	This is the TFTP relative path to the installation image (for example, Setup\English\Images\win2000.pro).

Table 4.3 Standard Variables Supported by RIS *(continued)*

Variable	Meaning
LANGUAGE	This is the only OSC variable that can be set prior to logon. It indicates the language in which the user wants to view the screens. All OSC screens as well as any ENUM functions the server performs are pulled from that language. The default value of this variable matches the default language of the server. Refer to the Multilng.osc file located in the RemoteInstall\Oschooser directory for an example of how to make the server multilingual.
MAC	Sent by OSChooser to indicate the media access control (MAC) address of the client.
MACHINEDOMAIN	The domain that the new client attempts to join during GUI-mode Setup. This might not correspond to the MACHINEOU variable's domain.
MACHINENAME	Indicates to the server the name of the new machine.
MACHINEOU	Indicates to the server the organizational unit in which the new machine account should be generated.
MACHINETYPE	Sent by OSChooser to indicate the type of hardware on which OSChooser is running. (e.g., INTEL = "i386")
NETBIOSNAME	The NetBIOS name of the new computer (generated using the DnsHostnameToComputerName() call).
OPTIONS	This variable is filled with the results of an ENUM action by the server. It contains OSCML and should be placed between a <SELECT> tag and a </SELECT> tag. See the Tools.osc file located in the RemoteInstall\OSChooser\%Language% directory as an example.
SERVERDOMAIN	Set to the domain name of the server to which OSChooser is connected.
SERVERNAME	Set to the name of the server to which OSChooser is connected.

Table 4.3 Standard Variables Supported by RIS *(continued)*

Variable	Meaning
SIFFILE	Local to the server path of the SIF that the user selected to install the OS. It is similar to the following example: X:\RemoteInstall\Setup\English\Images\win2000.pro\i386\Templates\Ristndrd.sif
SUBERROR	The server sets this internally for any errors it encounters. You can add this variable to an error message screen to diagnose internal failures inside the server.
TIMEZONE	Set by the server to the server's current time zone setting. This setting is helpful if you are replicating images to remote servers in different time zones.
USERNAME, *PASSWORD, USERDOMAIN	OSChooser looks for this value to process the logon request. It is sent to the server after a successful logon. "*PASSWORD" is a short-lived variable that is overwritten as soon as possible on the server and is not accessible to OSC files or SIF files.

This is a lot of options, but you're not limited to these variables. You can create your own and reference them in the SIF file. By exploiting the tags and variables available and editing the accompanying installation scripts a bit, you can do quite a lot to make the RIS installation environment yours. Read on to find out how to edit the default files to make them display a Setup screen you would normally never see and how to create variables for enabling and disabling pieces of an installation script.

> **TIP** When you add new images, RIS will ask if you want to use the old chooser files, replace them with new ones, or save the old ones as backups. If you edit the chooser files, be sure to use the old chooser files or you'll replace all your edits.

A menu called CHOICE.OSC menu theoretically allows you to choose a computer's name before letting Setup rip. This menu is an awfully good template for other customization, but it's got one catch: you never see it because of two commands it contains:

```
<META SERVER ACTION="DNRESET">
<META SERVER ACTION="FILTER CHOICE">
```

Remove those lines from D:\Remote Install\OSChooser\English\CHOICE.OSC (a CHOICE .OSC is in each image folder, but the one to edit is the main one) and the Choice screen will become part of the RIS setup. *Now,* you'll see the Choice screen and with it get access to the Custom Setup option formatted with the CUSTOM.OSC file shown here:

```
<OSCML>
<META KEY=F1 HREF="CUSTHELP">
<META KEY=F3 ACTION="REBOOT">
<META KEY=ESC HREF="CHOICE">
<TITLE>  Client Installation Wizard
Custom Setup</TITLE>
<FOOTER>  [ENTER] continue     [ESC] go back     [F1] help     [F3] restart computer</FOOTER>
<BODY left=5 right=75>
<BR>
<BR>
Type a unique computer name and specify a location within the
directory service in which to create the computer account.
<BR>
<BR>
<FORM ACTION="OSCUST">
Computer name: <INPUT NAME="MACHINENAME" SIZE=63 MAXLENGTH=63><BR>
Directory service path: <INPUT NAME="MACHINEOU" MAXLENGTH=512><BR>
</FORM>
<BR>
<BOLD>Examples:</BOLD><BR>
<PRE>
Computer name:             MyComputer01
Directory service path:    mydomain.com/computers
</PRE>
<BR>
If you leave these fields blank, the default settings selected by the
network administrator will be applied.</BODY>
</OSCML>
```

From this screen, you can choose the machine name and the directory service object to which you want to assign the new account for this computer, rather than having to rely on RIS's machine-naming conventions. As you can see, the name you supply will be assigned to the %MACHINENAME% variable and the directory service path to the %MACHINEOU% variable. The same feature will work for *any* value in a SIF installation file. Because SIF files are very similar to answer files, and answer files have a [Components] section where you can turn on and off selected components, what we'll be doing here is probably pretty clear. We'll add those sections, declare variables for the settings we want to control from the UI, and poof! We'll have a SIF file that could work for both an application server or a regular server, depending on which values you choose. Doing so means that you have to support (and store) fewer images on the RIS server.

For this example, I'm letting the installer choose whether to install games and whether to install Terminal Services in Application Server mode. Rather than creating an entirely new page, I'll just tag along on one of the default ones, with my additions in boldface. I'm editing CUSTOM.OSC here; recall that I had to tweak CHOICE.OSC to make this page available. I could have added the same information—including a prompt for the username—to the main image chooser or created an entirely new page.

```
<OSCML>
<META KEY=F1 HREF="CUSTHELP">
<META KEY=F3 ACTION="REBOOT">
<META KEY=ESC HREF="CHOICE">
<TITLE>  Client Installation Wizard
Custom Setup</TITLE>
<FOOTER>  [ENTER] continue      [ESC] go back      [F1] help      [F3] restart computer</FOOTER>
<BODY left=5 right=75>
<BR>
<BR>
Type a unique computer name and specify a location within the
directory service in which to create the computer account. If you
want to enable or disable components, respond to those boxes.
<BR>
<BR>
<FORM ACTION="OSCUST">
Computer name: <INPUT NAME="MACHINENAME" SIZE=63 MAXLENGTH=63><BR>
Directory service path: <INPUT NAME="MACHINEOU" MAXLENGTH=512><BR>
```

Do you want games turned on or off? <INPUT NAME = "GAMES" SIZE=3 MAXLENGTH=3>

Do you want to turn Terminal Services on or off? <INPUT NAME = "TERMINAL"SIZE=3

If you enabled Terminal Services, type '0' to install Remote Administration or '1' to install Application Server mode <INPUT NAME = "APPSERV" SIZE=1

MAXLENGTH=3>

</FORM>

<BOLD>Examples:</BOLD>

<PRE>

Computer name: MyComputer01

Directory service path: mydomain.com/computers

</PRE>

If you leave these fields blank, the default settings selected by the network administrator will be applied. **Make sure that the directory service path exists—RIS cannot create a new OU during installation.**</BODY>

</OSCML>

> **TIP** To double-check your work without having to start RIS, you can open OSC files in Explorer. They won't look exactly the same as they will during the installation, but you'll be able to tell if the formatting is more or less correct.

That's half the battle. Now I have to edit the SIF file associated with this image to make it accept those variables. So I go to the template folder associated with this image, open `ristndrd.sif`, and make my changes so that it looks like the one shown here (the changes appear in boldface; I'm going to go ahead and make a few other tweaks at the same time):

```
[data]
floppyless = "1"
msdosinitiated = "1"
OriSrc = "\\%SERVERNAME%\RemInst\%INSTALLPATH%\%MACHINETYPE%"
```

```
OriTyp = "4"
LocalSourceOnCD = 1


[SetupData]
OsLoadOptions = "/noguiboot /fastdetect"
SetupSourceDevice =
"\Device\LanmanRedirector\%SERVERNAME%\RemInst\%INSTALLPATH%"


[Unattended]
OemPreinstall = no
NoWaitAfterTextMode = 0
FileSystem = LeaveAlone
ExtendOEMPartition = 0
ConfirmHardware = no
NtUpgrade = no
Win31Upgrade = no
TargetPath = \WINNT
OverwriteOemFilesOnUpgrade = no
OemSkipEula = yes
InstallFilesPath =
"\\%SERVERNAME%\RemInst\%INSTALLPATH%\%MACHINETYPE%"


[UserData]
ProductID = XXXXX-XXXXX-XXXXX-XXXXX-XXXXX
FullName = "%USERFIRSTNAME% %USERLASTNAME%"
OrgName = "%ORGNAME%"
ComputerName = %MACHINENAME%


[GuiUnattended]
OemSkipWelcome = 1
OemSkipRegional = 1
TimeZone = %TIMEZONE%
```

```
AdminPassword = "*"

[LicenseFilePrintData]
AutoMode = PerSeat

[Display]
ConfigureAtLogon = 0
BitsPerPel = 8
XResolution = 1024
YResolution = 768
VRefresh = 75
AutoConfirm = 1

[Networking]
ProcessPageSections=Yes

[Identification]
JoinDomain = %MACHINEDOMAIN%
DomainAdmin=ChristaA
DomainAdminPassword = "*"

[Components]
TSEnable = %TERMINAL%
Solitaire = %GAMES%
Minesweeper = %GAMES%
Freecell = %GAMES%
Pinball = %GAMES%

[NetProtocols]
MS_TCPIP=params.MS_TCPIP
```

```
[params.MS_TCPIP]
; transport: TC (TCP/IP Protocol)
InfID=MS_TCPIP
DHCP=Yes

[NetClients]
MS_MSClient=params.MS_MSClient

[params.MS_MSClient]
InfID=MS_MSClient

[NetServices]
MS_Server=params.MS_Server

[params.MS_Server]
; service: SRV (Server)
InfID=MS_Server
BroadcastsToLanman2Clients = No

[TerminalServices]
ApplicationServer=%APPSERV%

[RemoteInstall]
Repartition = No
UseWholeDisk = No

[OSChooser]
Description ="Windows 2000 Advanced Server"
Help ="Advanced Server with SP2 slipstreamed in"
LaunchFile = "%INSTALLPATH%\%MACHINETYPE%\templates\startrom.com"
ImageType =Flat
Version="5.0"
```

That's it. By editing the OSC and SIF files to use the variables you concocted, you've created an image that allows you to specify the installation of Terminal Services and the mode to install it in, as well as allowing you to turn games on or off wholesale. This method will work for any setting in the SIF file.

Installing MetaFrame XP

If you're using MetaFrame XP, then you'll need to install Terminal Services in Application Server mode and set up a Terminal Services Licensing server… but you *also* need to get MetaFrame installed. I'll cover that here, and also show you how to script that installation so you can be Scripting Whiz and take longer lunches than anyone else.

> **TIP** If you're installing MetaFrame onto a Windows terminal server that's currently in use, kick everyone off and prevent any new connections. (If you're not sure how to do this, check out Chapter 6.)

Several CDs are in the MetaFrame XP package. The one you want is labeled "MetaFrame XP." If you're installing onto a new server, you'll be completing the following steps:

- Agreeing to the EULA
- Setting up or connecting to the data store in the server farm
- Configuring network protocol and shadowing options
- Selecting drive letter mappings

During Setup, you'll also have the option of enabling NFuse support, installing the licenses and product codes you'll need to make the servers accept connections, and updating the ICA client database to make it ready to update older ICA clients (discussed in Chapter 5, "Preparing Client Connections").

Let's look at each of these steps in more detail.

Setting Up The Data Store

If you're performing a new installation of MetaFrame XP, you'll need to set up the data store. (Although the wizard makes it sound as though the data store setup procedure is something that happens all at once, you're really just beginning the process of configuring the farm and zone information that we talked about in Chapters 2 and 3). In the next screen of the Setup Wizard, you'll need to indicate whether you're joining an existing farm or creating a new farm. Choose carefully; to change farms after setup, you'll need to use the chfarm utility on the server. Changing *zones* is no big deal—we'll discuss that in Chapter 6.

The process from here depends on whether you're using the built-in data store or setting up a third-party database, and whether you're creating a new farm or connecting to an existing one. Let's look at how installation works if you're using the default data store.

Creating a New Farm

If you create a new server farm, then you'll need to create a new data store to produce it. Decide whether you want to use a local Access database for the data store or connect to a SQL Server or Oracle-based data store on a separate server. Next, pick a zone name. The default name is based on the subnet ID of the MetaFrame server (meaning that, by default, all MetaFrame servers on the same subnet are in the same zone). You can choose a new zone name by clearing the check box and typing a new name. All servers in the same zone have the same data collector, which means that, if you stick with the defaults, all servers on the same subnet have the same data collector. If this is okay, you can stick with the defaults.

> **TIP** If you're creating a server for cloning and all the servers will be on the same subnet, use the default zone name. However, if you're installing servers from multiple subnets into the same zone, do *not* use the default zone name. The subnet ID determines the automatically created zone name, so if you use the default, then servers on different subnets will be in different zones.

To finish setting up the data store, supply the name of the new farm. Farm names can contain up to 32 characters, including spaces. When you click Next, Setup will warn you that you'll need to use one of MetaFrame's utilities to change farms. Once you tell Setup that you're sure, then Setup will chug away, setting up the data store with the new farm name. This process will take a few minutes. From this point, Setup will be the same whether you're creating or joining a farm.

Joining an Existing Farm

If you're joining an existing farm, you'll need to indicate whether you want direct access to a third-party database or indirect access to an existing data store through another server. In this example, we'll connect to a data store set up on an existing server. Whichever option you choose, Setup will next prompt you to pick a zone name as described in the previous section.

To connect to an existing data store through another server, you'll need to be prepared with some information. First, you'll (obviously) need the name of the server to which you are connecting. Second, you'll need to connect to the port on the server the IMA service is using—2512, unless you edit it. Third, since you'll be prompted to log onto the server farm for management purposes, you'll need the name and password of a valid MetaFrame management account. Just having an Administrator account won't do it—you need an account explicitly permitted to open the Citrix Management Console.

> **TIP** Although Setup will populate the logon screen for the server farm with some information, don't accept it blindly. Setup assumes that the account name used to install MetaFrame XP has authority to manage the server farm, and so populates the user account name section with the name of the person currently logged on. You may not want the person installing MetaFrame XP to be a Citrix Administrator.

When you've successfully created a connection to the intermediate server, the Setup Wizard will show you the server name and port number and ask if you're sure that this setup is what you want. Once you click Next, you won't be able to back up and will have to use MetaFrame command-line tools to change the server's farm membership. Click Next, and Setup will chug away for a few moments, setting up the connection to the data store.

Setting up Network Connections and Shadowing

At this point, you've finished setting up the data store. You can now proceed to the next step: setting up the network.

First, choose the network protocols for which you want to install ICA support (TCP/IP, IPX, SPX, or NetBIOS). You can only install support for protocols that you previously enabled from the Control Panel. However, if you haven't previously installed a protocol that you'd like to use with ICA, you don't have to stop in the middle of Setup and install it; you can add support for other network protocols later so long as you have at least one network protocol installed before installing MetaFrame XP. When you're done, click Next. If you've previously used the Phone and Modem Options applet in the Control Panel to set up Telephony API (TAPI) settings, then MetaFrame Setup will detect them. Otherwise, if you click the Add Modems button in the Setup Wizard, the Phone and Modem Options applet will automatically start, prompting you for the area code and other telephony settings. This setting is optional. If you don't plan to use modems to connect to the MetaFrame server farm, just click through this screen.

The next step, configuring shadowing, is a bit more involved. You can limit ICA session shadowing for this server or disable it altogether. (In case it's not obvious, these restrictions apply only to ICA session shadowing, not to RDP session shadowing.) The way in which any limits you set apply may not be clear. At this point, the shadowing settings you use here apply to *everyone* managing MetaFrame servers. Just to confuse things, however, any restriction you set here apply to this server, not to the entire farm (unless you're building a farm of cloned servers based on this one, of course). In other words, it's possible to set up shadowing with one set of restrictions on one server and with a different set of restrictions on another server. This is not a good idea. Different shadowing permissions will lead to great confusion as you try to shadow user sessions. For the sake of your sanity, apply the same shadowing restrictions to all the servers in the same farm.

> **WARNING** Unlike other Setup options, the shadowing settings you apply now cannot be made more permissive post-Setup. If you disable or limit session shadowing now, you'll need to reinstall MetaFrame to change those settings. Because you can configure shadowing after installing, I'd go ahead and enable shadowing without any caveats now and then tweak after installation.

I think you can grasp the concept of *disabling* shadowing pretty easily, but the options for *restricting* shadowing may be a bit confusing. To those used to Microsoft Terminal Services terminology, it may sound counterintuitive to say, "Okay, you can shadow, but you can't use remote control" because Microsoft's RDP shadowing tools (from the GUI, anyway) are called "remote control." (The command-line shadowing tool in Terminal Services is called "shadow," just to confuse things.) To MetaFrame, however, remote control is only one aspect of shadowing. If you disable remote control while enabling shadowing, anyone shadowing a user session can only watch what the user is doing, rather than taking over the session. If you're trying to curb those controlling tendencies, you can prohibit anyone from taking control of user sessions, but doing so will limit your teaching and Help Desk abilities. There's always some point at which it's easier to stop telling the person what to do and just do it yourself.

Checking the second option means that you can no longer take over—or view —users' sessions without their permission. For Help Desk or training purposes, this option is fine—in my user moments, I'd like to know who's peering over my shoulder and when. The only time that it might not be fine is if you've got someone using the MetaFrame server when they're not supposed to be and you'd like to see what they're doing before you kick them off. The logging option is a security feature that's new to MetaFrame XP. Shadow logging records shadowing attempts, successes, and failures into the Application Log of the Windows 2000 Event Viewer.

I wouldn't disable shadowing except for situations that call for demonstrating ultra-tight security, showing that it is not possible for a second party to view activity in a user session. The only people allowed to shadow user sessions at this point are those with the ability to manage the MetaFrame server farm, so we're talking about people who are trusted. Disabling shadowing means disabling a valuable teaching and Help Desk tool. If you're concerned about security, you can require that the user be notified. In that case, the person whose session is being shadowed can minimize or close any sensitive files before the shadower views his or her desktop. You could also disable remote control so that the user completely controls what happens in his or her session. Choose your options, and click Next to continue.

Configuring Drive Letter Mappings

Because a MetaFrame server already has a C: drive, a client-side C: drive mapped to a terminal session (as is possible with ICA) will need a new name. Therefore, your next task is to configure client drive mappings. MetaFrame XP reassigns the names of drives that conflict with drives on the MetaFrame server, starting from the end of the alphabet and working backward. Although the whole point of reassigning client drive letters in terminal sessions is to avoid conflicts with server drive letters, you can also edit the server drive letter mappings in the next screen of the Setup Wizard. Server drive reassignment is probably not a terrific idea. If you change the server-side mappings, those mappings will persist even if you uninstall MetaFrame. Additionally, changing server drive letters could cause some applications problems if those applications depend on being installed to a particular drive letter. Location-dependent applications cause enough problems in server-based computing, so I hate to create more.

If you're remapping server drives on servers in a farm, Citrix recommends that you clone the servers to make sure that all the drive letter mappings match on all the servers supporting those applications. If you don't, you could break the applications, because they could be using one set of drive letters on one server and another elsewhere. Do *not* remap server drive letters if you're upgrading a MetaFrame 1.8 server whose server drive letters were remapped, as doing so can destroy the installation and make its applications unusable.

Configuring Web Services

Win32 ICA clients get to use a native Program Neighborhood housing all their application and Desktop links. Other ICA clients will need NFuse, MetaFrame's web-based Program Neighborhood. Installing NFuse is a two-step process. To use NFuse, you'll need to install the Citrix XML Service. Generally speaking, you should be fine if you stick with the default HTTP port of 80. If you use another port, you'll need to reconfigure both NFuse and the ICA clients to connect to a port other than 80—so only edit this setting if an application other than IIS is using port 80 and won't share.

After enabling the Citrix XML Service, click Next to indicate whether you want to install support for NFuse. If you choose to install NFuse (installed by default), you'll also have the option of changing the default web page to the NFuse one—which will make sense if you'd like people to run their applications from that page. Either way, make your choice and click Next.

At this point, you're done with the main part of Setup. The next screen will warn you that when you click Next, Setup will begin copying files, and that you cannot reverse the process after doing so. Click Next or cancel out of the operation. Installing the files on the MetaFrame server will take a few minutes.

Final Touches: ICA Files and Licensing

While Setup is copying files to the MetaFrame server's hard disk, it will prompt you to begin the ICA Client Distribution Wizard. This step is an optional part of the base installation—you can initiate it post-Setup—so I'll discuss it later in this chapter. If you click Cancel to halt the wizard, Setup will continue copying files to the server hard disk.

Next, Setup will prompt you for the license serial number. The license serial number can be either a product license number (a license to run a particular version of MetaFrame XP on a server), a connection license (a license for ICA client connections to MetaFrame servers), or both. If you're installing from the CD-ROM pack, the license serial number is the 25-digit code preceded with "Server." To add more than one license serial number during Setup, click the Add button. If you have more than one version of MetaFrame XP in the farm, make sure you supply the license number for the correct version, as the license numbers are product-specific. Adding the license serial number is an optional step; you can add more licenses from the Citrix Management Console.

The final step in Setup is to add the product code. Again, this step is optional. If you added a license serial number, then Setup will suggest a product code for you. Otherwise, you can skip this step (and add the product code later from the Citrix Management Console) or copy the code from the CD-ROM jacket—it's the number enclosed in a rectangular box and labeled "Product Code." (Yes, it would have been simpler had the license serial number been labeled as such, but you can't have everything.)

Now, you're done with the base installation. The server will reboot. When it starts again, MetaFrame XP will be installed on your computer. If you installed the licenses and provided a product code, the computer will be ready to receive connections (although you'll still need to activate them before they expire in 30 days).

Applying Updates to MetaFrame XP

Feature Releases add some additional features to MetaFrame XP and update NFuse if it's installed. Let's take a look at how to install them, using FR1 as an example. When the CD-ROM begins, you'll see a splash screen offering several options: Service Pack 1, Feature Release 1, an updated Citrix Management Console, a web-based Citrix Management Console, and new Network Management components. You can either install the whole thing by installing Feature Release 1, or pick and choose components. Installing FR2 is a nearly identical process, except that you'll need to download Version 2.0 of the Windows Installer from the Microsoft website before you install the feature release.

The first stage of installing FR1 is accepting the licensing agreement. This agreement is the same agreement used for MetaFrame XP's installation. Click I Agree and move on. Next, the first page of the wizard will warn you that you're about to install FR1 and that any active connections will be reset (that is *reset*, not disconnected). If people are already using the MetaFrame server, kick them off the server. Again, this procedure is in Chapter 6.

The next stage of the wizard tells you to click Next to continue or click Cancel to stop. Click Next, and Setup will start copying files to the hard disk and updating MetaFrame and the Citrix Management Console. When Setup finishes, it will prompt you to update the ICA client files, which gives me a good excuse to walk through that process.

Rolling Out the ICA Client

The idea of running the ICA Client Distribution Wizard is to ensure that the ICA client files on the server are the most recent available. When computers running older versions of the client connect to the server, they can be prompted to get the new client files. When you start the wizard, either during installation or from the Citrix Management Console, you'll see the familiar "Congratulations, you've started a wizard and this is what is does" screen before the wizard moves on. I have the ICA Client CD-ROM that comes with FR1, so I'll use it.

When Setup finds the CD-ROM I put in the drive, the wizard will display the available clients and ask how you want older clients to be updated. By default, all clients are selected. You'll definitely want to let people download the most up-to-date clients from the MetaFrame server. The pass-through client is for giving people who don't use the Win32 ICA client access to Program Neighborhood (because, in its non-web form, it's available only to Win32 clients). Copying ICA clients to the web server means that people can get the clients directly from the server, if they're using NFuse to connect to their applications. In other words, if you're not using NFuse and you are supporting only Win32 clients, you only need the client images, the updated client database, and the documentation.

When you've picked the components you want to install and clicked Next, Setup will prompt you with the possible platforms that you can support. Every OS has subclasses. For example, Windows contains both Win32 and Win16 clients. You really don't need all these clients unless you're truly supporting all those OSes. Disk space is cheap, but make your life a little simpler and install only the OS support that you need. Incidentally, there's a Customize object near the bottom of the visible list for creating your own ICA clients. For the average person, this feature option is overkill.

The next stage of the wizard asks you to make a similar choice, except that this time you're updating the ICA client database. Pick from Windows, DOS, Windows CE, UNIX, and Macintosh. When you click Next, Setup will start copying the updated ICA files from the CD-ROM or network share to the local MetaFrame server's ICA client files and database of updates.

Unattended Installations

We just went through an exhaustive look at how to install MetaFrame XP. This thorough approach is a good idea so that you know what your options are.

> **NOTE** Really, do this by hand at least once. If you don't know how to install something manually, automating the process is very difficult because you can't envision what you're doing.

When it comes to unattended installations of MetaFrame, you have two options. You can prepare a script to install MetaFrame, just as you prepared a script to install Windows 2000 earlier, or you can install a MetaFrame member server and then clone that server.

Citrix recommends that no more than 10 servers be simultaneously installed into the same farm because the servers must write to the data store during installation. The more servers installed at once, the more likely it is that two servers will attempt to write to the same area of the data store at the same time, causing a deadlock (a server timeout while waiting to write to the data store). If this happens, it's not a fatal error, because the IMA service will retry the write after waiting a moment. It will slow things down, though. There's also the matter of picking a data collector for that data store. When you're automating the installation of servers into a new zone in a farm, install one server first. Then, from the Citrix Management Console, set that server to Most Preferred. That way, new servers joining the zone will not compete with each other to become the zone's data collector. You don't need to do this if your farm has only one zone, because the first server to join the first zone in a farm is automatically the Most Preferred. However, if you want a specific server to be the data collector (say, the one you juiced up with some more memory), you should fix the election by hand instead of trusting to luck.

Scripting MetaFrame Installations

Installation scripts for MetaFrame XP follow a format similar to those in answer files or the SIF files used with RIS. Citrix makes life easier by providing a sample copy of an installation script called unattend.txt on the MetaFrame XP CD-ROM. First, I'll explain what you need to do to make a scripted installation work, then I'll walk you through a sample script so you can see how to edit the one provided for yourself.

Prep Work   If you'll be setting up a server with direct access to a SQL Server or an Oracle-based data store, use the ODBC Data Source Administrator in Administrative Tools to set up an MF20.DSN file for connecting to the database server. Alternatively, just create one such file in Notepad, using the following format and saving it with the appropriate name. The words in italics should be replaced with the values that apply to your farm.

```
[ODBC]
DRIVER=SQL
ServerUID=SQL_USERNAME
DATABASE=NAME_OF_DATABASE
```

```
WSID=NAME_OF_MF_SERVER
APP=Citrix IMA
SERVER=NAME_OF_SQL_SERVER
```

This file identifies the database driver to use to communicate with the SQL Server database, provides a valid username for the database, identifies the database to connect to, identifies the local server doing the connecting, and identifies the name of the server on which the database is stored.

Next, copy the contents of the MetaFrame XP installation CD-ROM to a server (not a MetaFrame server, but one prepared to field installation requests and use network bandwidth to copy files). Share the folder containing the installation files with the network. Two setup files are on the CD-ROM: one for installing MetaFrame XP on a WTSE terminal server and one for installing MetaFrame XP on a Windows 2000K terminal server. Setup for Windows 2000 is in w2k\mf—just share that folder, and you'll make setups easier. Edit the contents of unattend.txt (the answer file), and place it in a network share.

To start the installation, connect to the appropriate network share and run **setup /u:unattend.txt**. So long as you completely filled out the script, the installation should proceed without any help from you. (If you don't fill in a required value for which there's no default, Setup will stop and wait for you to supply it.) However, the script as it stands is not ready for a completely unattended installation. In the interests of not having Setup wait for you to supply information you could have scripted, let's take a look at the script format.

Dissecting the MetaFrame Installation Script   If you installed Windows 2000 with an unattended installation, the MetaFrame setup file will look familiar. Sections in the script are identified by text in brackets; the data supplied to Setup is arranged in a key=value format. Comments (explanatory text not processed by Setup but there only as reference for the user) are preceded by an asterisk (*) or a semicolon (;).

The first section in the script is the license agreement. Left alone, it looks like this:

```
[MetaFrame License Agreement]
    AcceptLicense=No
```

You must change the value of this key to Yes to accept the license agreement and continue with Setup. Any other value will cause Setup to prompt you for agreement.

In the next section, as in the manual installation, you'll set up the data store, which I've shown here with the default values.

```
[Data Store Configuration]
    CreateFarm=Yes
```

```
DirectConnect=No
ZoneName=
```

What you say here depends on whether you're setting up a new farm or attaching to an existing one, and whether this server will have a direct or indirect connection to the data store. As it stands now, this script will install a new farm and use the default zone name. Table 4.4 explains which values you should supply based on what you want to do. Only provide a value for the ZoneName key if you don't want to use the default zone name based on the server's subnet; as it is, Setup will assume that you want to use the default.

Table 4.4 Options for Setting Up the Data Store

If You Want to...	CreateFarm	DirectConnect	Additional Sections Required
Create a farm using an Access database.	Yes	No	[Farm Settings]
Create a farm using an Oracle or SQL Server database to back the data store.	Yes	Yes	[Direct Connect Settings] [Farm Settings]
Join a farm using an Oracle or SQL Server database to back the data store and using direct connection.	No	Yes	[Direct Connect Settings]
Join a farm using an Access database.	No	No	[Indirect Connect Settings]
Join a farm using an Oracle or SQL Server database to back the data store and using indirect connection.	No	No	[Indirect Connect Settings]

You'll only need to work with the Direct Connect Settings Section (next) for servers with a direct connection to the data store. Otherwise, Setup will ignore the values in this section:

```
[Direct Connect Settings]
DSNFilePath=
```

```
    UserName=
    Password=
```

The `DSNFilePath` key is the path where you stored the DSN file when setting it up (by default, \Program Files\Common Files\ODBC\Data Sources). The `UserName` key needs either the database logon ID or, if you're using Windows NT authentication, the logon ID in the form *domainname\username*. The password is self-explanatory; the only thing you really need to keep in mind is that it's not encrypted or displayed in "asterisk mode"—this file is stored in plaintext. (A friend of mine jokingly suggests using a password of ten asterisks for answer files of any kind, the idea being that people will *think* it's encrypted.)

If you're using the Indirect Connect Settings options, fill out the next section. If the values in the `[Data Store Configuration]` section don't apply to indirect connections, Setup will ignore the values in this section:

```
[Indirect Connect Settings]
    IndirectServerName=
    IndirectServerPort=2512
    UserName=
    Password=
```

If you read the walkthrough of a manual installation, you can probably figure this section out. The key `IndirectServerName` refers to the name of the server that has the direct connection to the data store. The `IndirectServerPort` is the default port value; only edit this value if you edited the direct-connection server's Registry to point to a new port, as explained earlier. The username and password asked for here are the username and password of someone permitted to manage the server farm. As we've discussed to death in the past, just being a member of the Administrators group does not permit this level of access—you need someone authorized to manage the server farm. You must include the user account's domain in the value of UserName, like this: *domainname\username*.

The Farm Settings section applies only if you're creating a new Access-based server farm using the settings in Table 4.4. Otherwise, Setup will ignore it.

```
[Farm Settings]
    FarmName=Farm
    InteroperabilityMode=No
    FarmAdministratorUsername=Administrator
    FarmAdministratorDomain=
```

This section gives the farm a name, tells MetaFrame whether the farm will need to cooperate with MetaFrame 1.8 server farms, and supplies the name and domain of a person authorized to manage the farm. You can add more accounts to the list of managers later. Notice that, if you keep the default settings, the default farm manager may not be the same user as the person logged on to perform the installation. Also, because this person is authenticated in the domain, you don't need to provide a password in the script for them.

Moving right along, the next step is to set up ICA for use with network protocols. Supply values of Yes or No to the keys (already provided in the template script). If a protocol is not already installed on the MetaFrame server, then setting up ICA to work with the protocol won't work; you'll need to use the Citrix Management Console to add this support after adding the protocol. You must enable ICA support for at least one network protocol.

```
[ICA Network Protocols]
    TCP=Yes
    IPX=Yes
    SPX=No
    NETBIOS=Yes
```

The unattended installation script skips right over TAPI configuration with ICA and goes right on to shadowing. I described the meanings of these settings while walking through the manual installation. The main point here is that, if you set the value of `AllowShadowing` to No, then (of course) Setup will ignore the other keys. Again, being too loose is better than being too tight during Setup, because you can tighten shadowing post-Setup but you cannot loosen restrictions on it. If you do restrict shadowing, be consistent in the farm so that you don't run into strange shadowing problems caused by unevenly applied restrictions.

```
[Shadowing Restrictions]
    AllowShadowing=Yes
    ProhibitRemoteControl=No
    ProhibitNotificationOff=No
    ProhibitLoggingOff=No
```

Next, it's time for drive reassignment settings. MetaFrame automatically reassigns client mapped drives (so that they don't conflict with the drive letters for server drives), so the settings here apply to server drive remappings. The value of `NewDriveLetter` is only used if the value of `ReassignDriveLetters` is Yes and represents the beginning drive letter for server drive letter remapping (with subsequent remappings being N, O, P, and so on).

```
[Drive Reassignment]
```

ReassignDriveLetters=No

NewDriveLetter=M

The next section allows you to specify how you want to add the Citrix XML Service to MetaFrame XP (required for using NFuse). As we discussed earlier, you can share the default port (80) with IIS. Changing this port will require you to tweak all the ICA clients that will use NFuse and the MetaFrame servers supplying applications to NFuse. Therefore, the best practice is to leave this setting alone unless you are sure that the port can't be 80.

[Citrix XML Service]

ExtendIIS=No

DedicatedPortNumber=80

Setup only refers to the value of `DedicatedPortNumber` if the value of `ExtendIIS` is No. If you have IIS 4 or later installed (if you set up Windows 2000K with the default settings and you have IIS 4 or later installed, you do), then Setup will read the NFuse section to see whether it should install NFuse. If the value of `SetDefaultPage` is Yes, then Setup will make `servername/citrix/metaframe/index.htm` the default home page. You can't change the default home page from the script.

[NFuse]

InstallNFuse=Yes

SetDefaultPage=Yes

The section for updating the ICA clients lets you set up a typical installation of ICA clients and populate the Client Update Database.

[Update ICA Clients]

UpdateClients=No

ClientPath=

If you walked through the manual installation, you know we're almost done. Next, you can (this is optional) provide license serial numbers, the 25-digit codes on the inside of the CD-ROM flap. Just as you can use the Add button to install multiple license packs for the server farm during manual installation, you can supply as many license codes as you need here, using the following format:

[License Serial Numbers]

XXXXX-XXXXX-XXXXX-XXXXX-XXXXX=

YYYYY-YYYYY-YYYYY-YYYYY-YYYYY=

If you choose to supply the license numbers, Setup can figure out the product code for you, just as it does during manual installation. The server will need a product code before it can start accepting connections, so save yourself some time and include it here.

```
[MetaFrame Product Code]
    ProductCode=
```

Finally, you can specify whether to have Setup automatically reboot the server when it's done (which it will need to do in order to get the IMA service running) or wait. By default, Setup will reboot; change the value to No if you have other things to do to the server before rebooting it.

```
[Options]
    RebootOnFinish=Yes
```

The final option applies only if you're upgrading a previous version of MetaFrame to MetaFrame XP. If you stick with the default value of Yes, Setup will check for installed applications and try to migrate them. Otherwise, you'll need to publish applications from the Citrix Management Console.

```
[Upgrade Settings]
    MigrateApplications=Yes
```

Put all these pieces together in the same order, save the file as **unattend.txt**, and you've got a MetaFrame unattended installation script.

Scripting FR1 Installation If you're applying FR1 separately to a MetaFrame XP installation, you can script its installation, too. The file follows the same format as the larger MetaFrame XP setup script, and you can initiate it in the same way (barring the difference in the answer file name, of course). What we have here is simple. You need to agree to the license agreement in order to install FR1. You can optionally update the ICA clients. (If you do, you'll need to provide the path to the updated ICA client files. I recommend that you copy them to the installation network share so that you don't need to keep running around with the CD-ROM.) You also need to specify whether you want Setup to reboot the server when it's done or wait for you to reboot manually.

```
[License Agreement]
    Accept=No
[Client CD]
    UpdateClients=No
    ClientCDPath=
[Reboot]
    RebootAutomatically=Yes
```

Preparing a MetaFrame Server for Cloning

Another way to create MetaFrame servers without sitting through the Installation Wizard (or sitting through the Windows 2000K Setup Wizard, for that matter) is to clone the computer with a disk-imaging tool such as Symantec's Norton Ghost or PowerQuest's Disk Image. You can't just clone a MetaFrame server blindly, however. In addition to the preparation you'd normally do to make a Windows 2000 server ready for cloning, you have some MetaFrame-specific settings to adjust as well.

First, choose your server carefully. The server you clone must be in a zone with the default IMA zone name (so that the name can be generated based on the subnet on which the server's located) and must not be the first server in a farm using the Access-based data store, because cloning this server will also clone the data store. We haven't yet discussed SSL certificates, but don't image a server that has an SSL certificate installed, because this certificate is unique to the computer hardware. (If you have not explicitly installed one, you don't need to worry about this.) In addition, you should not clone a server with remapped server drives.

If you're cloning a server using Access to back its data store, follow these steps:

1. Delete `wfcname.ini` in the root directory of the system drive. This file identifies the server by name, so you don't want this information as part of the cloning process.
2. Stop the IMA Service, and set it to start manually.
3. Delete the following values from the Windows Registry:

    HKLM\Software\Citrix\IMA\Runtime\HostId

    HKLM \ Software \Citrix\IMA\Runtime\ImaPort

    HKLM \ Software \Citrix\IMA\Runtime\MasterRanking

    HKLM \ Software \Citrix\IMA\Runtime\PSRequired

    HKLM \ Software \Citrix\IMA\Runtime\RassPort

    HKEY_LOCAL_MACHINE\ Software\Citrix\IMA\Runtime\ZoneName

4. When you've completed the cloning steps for Windows 2000 (including running SyspPrep to make the server generate a new SID, server name, and Administrator password), image the server using the cloning software, and then install the image on additional servers.
5. Change the Independent Management Architecture service to start automatically.

To configure MetaFrame XP on a newly imaged server, follow these steps:

1. Add the Registry key HKLM \Software\Citrix\IMA\ServerHost, and set the value to the name of the server.
2. Edit the `wfcname.ini` file on the root of the drive on which you installed MetaFrame XP, and replace the name with the name of the machine.

3. Set the Independent Management Architecture service to start automatically.
4. Reboot the machine, and use the `qfarm` utility to make sure that the server joined the farm as expected.

Cloning a server using a SQL Server or Oracle-based data store is much the same as cloning one using the Access data store, but there are a couple of differences. First, when using a SQL Server or Oracle-based data store, you *can* clone the first server in the farm, because the data store won't be on this server. Second, you'll need to edit the `mf20.dsn` file found in \ProgramFiles\Citrix\Independent Management Architecture, just as you did in preparation for automating the installation of a MetaFrame server. To clone this computer, we'll need to delete the line beginning `WSID=`, so that the clones of this server aren't misidentified.

If the servers in your farm use a mixture of direct and indirect access to reach the SQL Server or Oracle database, be sure to clone the correct type. Access to the data store will be included in the cloning.

Upgrading to MetaFrame XP

So far, I've assumed that you're performing a fresh installation. If you've been using MetaFrame for a while, however, you're not going to want to start from scratch, you're going to want to use the settings from your existing servers as much as possible. Upgrading is complicated by differences between the way that servers using previous versions of MetaFrame and MetaFrame XP servers communicate. As we've discussed at length in previous chapters, not only does MetaFrame XP introduce a new organizational model, it introduces a new communications protocol to make the model work. In other words, assuming that you don't want to take every single MetaFrame server offline all at once and upgrade them all at once, keeping the server farm usable while migrating to MetaFrame XP presents a problem—the two versions of software do not have the same native language.

One way to do this would be to have, for a time, two completely separate server farms, one running MetaFrame 1.8 and one running MetaFrame XP. Doing so would allow you to avoid any migration issues with applications on servers migrated from MetaFrame 1.8 to MetaFrame XP, and would keep traffic at the levels you'd expect with MetaFrame 1.8 and MetaFrame XP server farms. The disadvantages are pretty obvious, however. Any load balancing you're using will be crippled because of the smaller number of servers in each farm. You'll need to make sure that people connect to the proper farm to get to their applications, and you'll have to manage the two farms separately. Having two server farms would probably be your best bet only if you were supporting a MetaFrame environment that extended over multiple physical sites. If bandwidth between sites is already strained, it's better to have temporarily separated server farms than to double up on communication traffic sent between servers—which, as you'll see, your other options will do.

> **TIP** If you must maintain two farms, NFuse will let you provide a single UI for access to the published applications in those farms.

Now, if you're upgrading from MetaFrame 1 or WinFrame, parallel server farms are your only option. If you're migrating to MetaFrame XP from MetaFrame 1.8, however, you can run the MetaFrame XP server farm in Mixed mode while upgrading. Mixed mode makes MetaFrame XP servers bilingual. The MetaFrame XP servers use IMA to talk to other MetaFrame XP servers, and they use UDP to talk to MetaFrame 1.8 servers. Therefore, at a cost of increased network traffic (because all broadcasts sent from MetaFrame XP servers will use both protocols), MetaFrame 1.8 and MetaFrame XP servers can coexist in the same farm. You can upgrade servers one at a time, running them all in Mixed mode, until the last server has been upgraded and you're ready to switch to Native mode, MetaFrame XP's normal operation mode. Table 4.5 contrasts the two modes in more detail.

Table 4.5 Contrasting Native Mode and Mixed Mode

Native Mode	Mixed Mode
The Program Neighborhood and ICA Browser services are disabled on all farm servers by default.	The Program Neighborhood and ICA Browser services are enabled on all farm servers by default. MetaFrame XP servers will always win the ICA Browser elections.
MetaFrame XP servers do not share Program Neighborhood or ICA Browser information with MetaFrame 1.8 servers.	MetaFrame XP servers send Program Neighborhood information to MetaFrame 1.8 servers that have the same farm name and are on the same subnet.
MetaFrame XP servers do not send Program Neighborhood information to every other server in the farm, just to the data collector. MetaFrame XP servers do not share dynamic information through the ICA Browser service. Instead, the IMA service notifies the data collectors of dynamic changes.	In order to share Program Neighborhood data, every server running the Program Neighborhood service maintains a connection with every other server with the same farm name. MetaFrame XP servers with the same farm name as MetaFrame 1.8 servers appear to ICA Clients as the same application set.

Table 4.5 Contrasting Native Mode and Mixed Mode *(continued)*

Native Mode	Mixed Mode
Servers communicate through the IMA service, not UDP, and cannot "hear" UDP broadcasts.	MetaFrame XP servers answer ICA Client UDP broadcasts and generate IMA traffic.
MetaFrame XP connection licenses are not pooled with MetaFrame 1.8 servers.	MetaFrame XP servers and MetaFrame 1.8 servers on the same subnet can pool licenses.
Published applications are not load balanced across both MetaFrame XP and MetaFrame 1.8 servers.	Published applications in the same application set can be load balanced across MetaFrame XP and MetaFrame 1.8 servers that share the same farm name. That said, MetaFrame XP has load-balancing rules that MetaFrame 1.8 does not. If you've published an application from the Citrix Management Console in MetaFrame XP, you can't publish an application with the same name using the MetaFrame 1.8 Published Application Manager—the application will already exist in the data store.

To migrate MetaFrame 1.8 servers to MetaFrame XP, follow these steps:

1. If you're using Microsoft SQL Server or Oracle for the MetaFrame XP server farm's data store, configure the data store server.

2. Identify the current master ICA browser in the MetaFrame 1.8 server farm. Install MetaFrame XP onto another server, not the master ICA browser. When you get the MetaFrame XP server up and running in Mixed mode, it's going to initiate (and win) an election. However, if you take down the master browser for upgrading, then you'll initiate an election among the remaining MetaFrame 1.8 servers anyway.

   You can use the query server command-line utility to discover the Citrix server acting as the master browser. An "M" next to the network address of a server (as shown in boldface below) indicates that the server is the master browser in the MetaFrame 1.8 server farm. Again, avoid this server when choosing the first one to migrate to MetaFrame XP.

```
Server              Transport  Conns  Free  Total  Network Address
----------          -----      ----------   ----------

TERMSERV*           TCP/IP     0      0     0      10.0.0.7 M
```

3. Install MetaFrame XP after hours, so that the inevitable elections for master browser don't interfere with anyone's work. During the installation, create a new IMA-based server farm with the same name as the MetaFrame 1.8 server farm. When prompted, enter the serial numbers and product code for your migration license. This server will become the new master ICA Browser.

4. Choose to operate the server in Mixed mode, and then complete the installation as described in this chapter. When prompted, choose to migrate applications.

5. Make sure that you can connect to the MetaFrame XP server and check the migration log file (%systemroot%\System32; the name of the file will be displayed during Setup) to confirm that all applications were migrated successfully.

6. Install MetaFrame XP on more MetaFrame 1.8 servers, choosing to join an existing farm.

After all MetaFrame 1.8 servers have been migrated to MetaFrame XP, change the server farm to operate in Native mode by right-clicking the farm node in the Citrix Management Console and choosing Properties from the context menu. Go to the Interoperability tab, and clear the check box under MetaFrame Interoperability. This change stops license sharing with license gateways.

Running a Mixed-Mode Server Farm Running a server farm in Mixed mode isn't just a matter of checking a box on a server. You'll need to do a little finagling to make the servers work together well. Again, running a server farm in Mixed mode is a temporary measure, but "temporary" can last longer than you may have originally planned. If it does, then you'll be glad to have a working server farm.

First, and most obviously, the MetaFrame XP servers must be configured to work in Mixed mode. Otherwise, even if the MetaFrame XP farm has the same name as the MetaFrame 1.8 farm, the two farms will be separate. MetaFrame XP servers running in Native mode don't use the ICA Browser service to communicate, so they can't share information with MetaFrame 1.8 servers. Once the MetaFrame XP servers are running in Mixed mode, they must be in a farm that has the same name as the MetaFrame 1.8 servers.

> **TIP** When MetaFrame XP servers are operating in Mixed mode, use the qserver command from both MetaFrame 1.8 and MetaFrame XP servers to display ICA Browser information.

Second, there's managing. Because the Citrix Management Console is new to MetaFrame XP, you can't manage a Mixed-mode server farm with the CMC. When you installed MetaFrame XP, you may have noticed a new Citrix program group that, in addition to containing a link to the CMC, contained links to other tools that you apparently don't need with MetaFrame XP, such as the Published Application Manager. Generally speaking, you're right—you only need them for managing a Mixed-mode server farm. For the most part, these tools will not work with MetaFrame XP servers. To manage MetaFrame XP servers, or to configure or manage printers in the farm, use the Citrix Management Console.

Speaking of application management, this topic can get a bit complex in a Mixed-mode farm. When the first MetaFrame 1.8 server is migrated to MetaFrame XP in Mixed mode, a "snapshot" of the current MetaFrame 1.8 environment is taken and saved for reference during future migrations into the same MetaFrame XP farm. This snapshot includes published applications. Therefore, you have to be careful about how you add and modify applications to a Mixed-mode server farm. If you plan to load balance the same published application across MetaFrame XP servers and MetaFrame 1.8 servers, you must publish the application first on the MetaFrame 1.8 servers, and then add the application (with the same published name) to the MetaFrame XP servers using the Citrix Management Console. If you add the applications first with the Citrix Management Console, they'll already exist in the data store and you won't be able to add them with the Published Application Manager. If you modify published applications with the version of Published Application Manager installed with MetaFrame XP, you can't modify those same applications with the Published Application Manager installed on MetaFrame 1.8 servers. Citrix doesn't recommend that you modify applications in the farm if you're planning on upgrading the servers, because the applications might not upgrade properly if they've been modified. Finally, published applications on migrated servers will still appear within the PAM until removed manually.

The bottom line is this: Don't plan on running a Mixed-mode farm for very long. Running a farm in Mixed mode is a migration measure only, not the way to run a production environment. Using Mixed mode complicates management and increases network traffic. Frankly, if you're planning to run MetaFrame XP in Mixed mode forever, you might as well stick with MetaFrame 1.8 and save yourself some money and work.

Summary

In this chapter, you've learned how to install Terminal Services in just about every imaginable way, ranging from installations on servers that are already set up to installing the service during an automated installation. For those using MetaFrame XP, we also discussed how to install that software. Now that the server side is taken care of, Chapter 5 will concentrate on configuring the clients.

5

Preparing Client Connections

Chapter 4, "Rolling Out Terminal Services," discussed the process of setting up the server, but that still leaves us without any connection to the terminal server. In this chapter, I'll talk about the many ways you can get RDP and ICA to the client computer.

Creating Client Connections

We discussed the feature differences between the Remote Desktop Protocol (RDP) and the Independent Computing Architecture (ICA) display protocols in Chapter 1. The procedure for installing the RDP or ICA protocol on a client computer varies slightly depending on whether you're talking about PC clients, handheld PCs, or Windows-based terminals. Because the connection settings are so similar for the RDP and ICA clients, I'll mix up the discussion here a bit. If you're not using one or the other, just skip ahead.

> **TIP** Set up RDP and ICA support not just on clients, but also on terminal servers. You can't remotely control user sessions from the console, but only from within another session. If you're working on the console, you can shadow a session only by starting a terminal server session—even if it's one on the same terminal server whose console you're logged into.

I've explained how to install both current versions of the RDP client, but there are so many versions of ICA that I simply don't have room to walk you through the installation and configuration of them all. Therefore, I've chosen the Win32 clients for examples.

Setting Up PC Support

To connect a PC-based client to Terminal Services, you must run a short installation program on the PC to install client support for the display protocol—RDP or ICA. This process is quite simple and (wonder of wonders in the Windows world) does not require that you reboot the computer afterward to use the client. The only catch is that you have to *get* those installation files to the client.

How you go about this depends on the operating system your clients are using and how many clients you have to install the display protocol client on (and, by extension, the effort that you're willing to put into creating a deployment plan). You can install the client either manually or automatically. If you don't mind filling out Setup by hand, and want to save yourself the time required to set up an automated installation, you can run the installation using Setup disks that you make with a tool on the terminal server or (better yet) by sharing the same installation files from the network and running Setup from there. To automate the installation, you must do a little prep work first, creating a batch file, setting up an IIS server to issue RDP ActiveX controls, or creating Group Policy Objects (GPOs) to send automatic installer packages to client computers or to specific users. This is more work for you, but less work on the client side. I'll look at both approaches here.

> **NOTE** Incidentally, everything I'm saying here applies to installing or updating the *client* display protocol software, not the server. Early in 2002, there were rumors that Microsoft might issue an update to Windows 2000 Terminal Services to give it the same capabilities as Terminal Services with .NET Server. When I asked Microsoft about it, they told me point blank that there were no plans to issue such a patch. It's not really surprising, because there is no update for WTS to make it RDP5-compatible, either. A patch to update the terminal service on previous generations of servers to the latest capabilities wouldn't make sense from Microsoft's perspective, because such a patch would remove one incentive to upgrade. Sorry.

Manual Installation

When you're first starting out, or if you only have to install display protocol clients on a few computers, you'll probably install the RDP or ICA clients manually.

Making Setup Files Accessible to Client Computers When you're manually installing client-side support for a display protocol, the first step is getting the setup files onto the client computer. The easiest way to distribute a terminal server client is via network share. Installing clients this way requires only that you create a network share to the installation files. The client OS doesn't have to be anything in particular (as is required with Group Policy Objects—GPOs work only with Windows 2000 and Windows XP clients, and Windows XP clients come with an RDP client installed). Nor do you need to perform any extra setup, as you will if you want to deploy the RDP client through Internet Explorer. And setting up via the network is certainly a lot easier than making floppy disks! You can even create a batch file to automatically install the files from the network without requiring any user interaction, perhaps as a RunOnce option while installing the terminal server itself, as described in Chapter 4.

To make the RDP or ICA client files accessible to client computers, follow these steps:

1. From the terminal server, share the folder *%systemroot%*\system32\clients\tsclient\net. There are two folders within the Net folder: Win16 (for Windows for Workgroups clients) and Win32 (for *x*86-based Windows 9*x*, ME, and NT operating system clients). Once you've installed MetaFrame on a terminal server, the ICA files are located in almost exactly the same place as the RDP client files: \system32\clients\ica.

> **TIP** To avoid providing access to a subfolder of \system32, copy the \net or \ica folder to another location on the server—perhaps the data drive instead of the system drive—and share the files from there. Also, share only the installation files you need. If you're only supporting Win32 clients for ICA or RDP, then share only those directories.

   If you're having your users install their own client files, it's important to make sure they install the right files for their operating system. To avoid user misunderstandings about which installation files to use, you could share each client installation set individually. If you *really* want to eliminate the possibility that someone will install the wrong files, put people in groups according to the operating system of the computer they use, then set user- or group-specific permissions on the shares so that only those who need access to each client type have access.

2. From each client computer, locate and connect to the share, drilling down to the Disk 1 folder within the appropriate directory. You'll run Setup.exe (for either ICA or RDP) from there.

If you simply can't get a client computer connected to a terminal server with the installation files—and, if you can't, it's hard to see why you're installing a network-dependent display protocol in the first place—then you'll need to create Setup floppies. Both Windows Terminal Services and MetaFrame XP have tools that you can use to create Setup disks for client PCs. To make RDP installation disks, run the Terminal Services Client Creator located in the Administrative Tools program group on a terminal server with the client support files installed. You'll see a dialog box such as the one shown in Figure 5.1.

Figure 5.1 Creating RDP client Setup floppies for a Win32 client

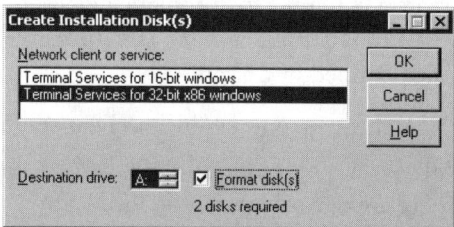

Notice that each client type requires a different number of disks: the Win16 client requires four, and the Win32 client requires two. Notice also that only Intel clients are supported for Win2K Terminal Services, even though NT4 could, technically, run on other operating systems. The client creator tool doesn't format the disks by default, but I choose to format mine on general principles (after making sure that nothing important is on the disks, of course). I'm unlikely to remember that anything else important is on a disk labeled "RDP Client for Windows NT (Intel)."

NOTE You can't fit the entire client on a single disk. Because you can't create a disk to any location other than a floppy drive, creating a Setup CD isn't an option with this tool.

MetaFrame XP has a very similar tool, called the ICA Client Creator. It works almost identically to the Windows 2000 tool, except that you have more choices (because you have more ICA clients than RDP clients) and both Win16 and Win32 clients require three disks, instead of four and two, respectively. The ICA Client Creator shown in Figure 5.2 is accessible either from the MetaFrame XP toolbar or from Program Files ➢ Citrix ➢ MetaFrame XP. To create the floppies, just choose the appropriate client type, check the box to format the disks, click OK, and follow the instructions.

Figure 5.2 ICA Client

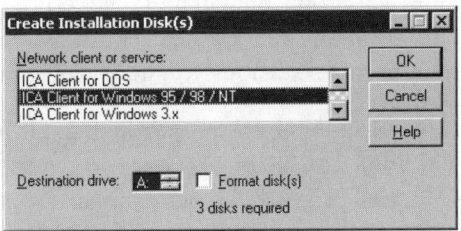

Manually Installing RDP Once you've created the network share or have gotten the floppy disks, installing the Windows 2000 RDP client is a matter of running Setup. Supply your name and the name of your company, agree to the EULA requirements, and choose a destination directory for the files if you don't like the default location of a new folder in the Program Files directory. Start the copying process, and that's the end of it. A few seconds later, you'll see a message box stating that the client was successfully installed. Click OK, and you're ready to use the client—no reboot is required. Win32 computers will keep the client in the Terminal Services Client program group on the client.

The previous process will install the RDP client that comes with Windows 2000, but a newer client is available for all Win32 operating systems and preinstalled on Windows XP. (This client is not available for Windows for Workgroups.) When used with a Windows 2000 application server, the newer client won't have all the bells and whistles possible with the latest version of RDP's server component, but the new client has a nice UI, it feels a little faster than previous versions of RDP, and having it already distributed will make it easier if/when you get around to installing .NET Server—your clients will already have the updated RDP client. Download msrdpcli.exe, currently available from http://www.microsoft.com/windowsxp/pro/downloads/rdclientdl.asp, and run the executable to install Remote Desktop. Any previously installed RDP clients will disappear, so you'll either need to back up and reapply any saved client configuration settings or restore them for use with the Remote Desktop.

> **TIP** Reboot the Windows 2000 terminal server after upgrading any clients to Remote Desktop. I've seen some strange errors—mostly cookies that no longer worked—after installing Remote Desktop, but they went away after a reboot.

Installing Remote Desktop is pretty much identical to installing previous versions of the client. Agree to the terms of the EULA, enter your name and company if Setup does not populate these fields for you, indicate whether you want the Remote Desktop available to anyone who uses the computer or just you, and click Install to let the Setup Wizard copy the files. The Remote Desktop icon will be added to Programs/Accessories/Communications. Again, you don't need to reboot the client to use Remote Desktop, but if you encounter Odd Things in terminal sessions you may want to reboot the terminal server.

Manually Installing ICA   Installing ICA support by hand is much like installing RDP, with one exception. When you run SETUP.EXE, once you click Next to leave the Welcome screen, most of the installation process will look familiar to anyone who's installed a program lately. You'll need to agree to the terms of the EULA and opt to install fresh or (if the client is already installed) upgrade the existing client or install a second copy of the present one. If you're installing fresh, choose a location for the files—the default is c:\program files\citrix\ica client—and a program folder for the ICA client to go into. So far, the process is pretty much like installing RDP.

However, an extra feature of the ICA client requires an additional query in Setup. The ICA client can optionally use the name and password of the currently logged-in user to authenticate access to the MetaFrame server (see Figure 5.3). The default is to not support pass-through authentication, because it is less secure. However, enabling this authentication-passing will make using applications published from a MetaFrame server more seamless than they would be otherwise, since the people using them won't have to log in twice to use them. That said, if you don't want to allow *all* ICA connections to use pass-through authentication, you can enable it for individual connections. I'll explain how to do that shortly.

Figure 5.3   Pass-through authentication reduces the number of logons required to use published applications.

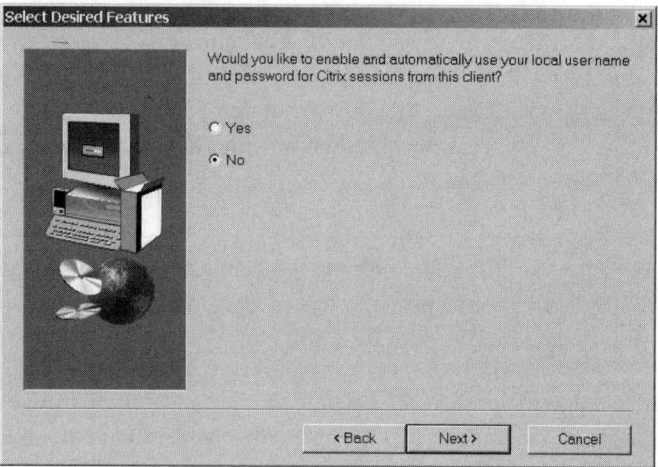

When you make your choice and click Next, ICA Setup will start copying files to your hard disk. When it's done, the ICA client will be installed on your computer—no reboot required.

If you're using FR2 and the version of NFuse Classic that comes with it (1.7), then you've got another option for supporting Win32 clients: the Program Neighborhood Agent. Unlike other versions of the Program Neighborhood that open windows on the client computer, the Program Neighborhood Agent can give users access to remote applications, desktops, and content from icons on their local Desktop, in the System Tray, or from the Start menu, all through a MetaFrame server with NFuse 1.7 installed. The ICA client is mostly invisible to the user apart from an icon in the System Tray. But the really interesting part about the Program Neighborhood Agent is that it's largely controlled from a file located on the MetaFrame server it's configured to point to. In other words, instead of configuring it on the client, you configure it on the NFuse server in a file called config.xml, located in \Inetpub\wwwroot\Citrix\PNagent. Being able to centrally configure clients—and to centrally prevent users from reconfiguring their agents if you need to—can save a lot of time.

Installing the Program Neighborhood Agent is largely painless. The installation files are on the Components CD that comes with FR2; drill down to Icaweb\language\ica32 or Icainst\language\ica32\pnagent—same files. Run ica32a.msi or ica32a.exe. Agree to the license agreement, choose an installation location (Program Files\Citrix\PNAgent, if you stick with the defaults). The only entry really likely to cause confusion is the entry for the server address, which is the name of the NFuse 1.7 server the client should be connecting to. Since the agent supports both secured and non-secured Web access, supply the name of the server as either http://servername or https://servername (the second is secured communication; the first isn't) and click Next. Unless you're connecting to a server named PNAgent, you will need to edit this value.

> **NOTE** The agent will accept just a plain server name (e.g. "TERMSERV") so long as that server exists on the network, but will convert that entry to http://termserv—that is, it won't be set up to use secure communications.

After pointing the client to the proper server, it's all downhill from there. Setup will create a new program folder for the client (called Citrix Program Neighborhood Agent if you stick with the defaults), ask for a unique name for your computer—prompting you with your computer's name—and ask if you'd like to use pass-through authentication so that the agent will use the name and password you used to log on to log onto the NFuse server. (If you want to have the option, enable single-sign on now. Otherwise, you won't be able to use it unless you reinstall the agent.) Click Next, and that's it. Setup will start copying files. When you reboot—Setup will prompt you to do so—the agent will be installed and will appear as an icon in the System Tray.

Deploying the Client Automatically

That's how you install RDP or ICA support manually, but let's face it: the easiest way to install a display protocol is to automate the process. You can do this with just Win2K in any of a few ways: use the TSAC to distribute client connection files through web pages, distribute the Terminal Services client files using Group Policy (this requires using Active Directory and clients that can connect to Active Directory), or run a simple logon script that you can use whether or not you've set up group policies. If you're using ICA, you can deploy the client with a web-based installation, or get an MSI file from the Download section of the Citrix Web site and deploy that file with GPOs. You can also, of course, install RDP or ICA support while automatically deploying clients.

> **WARNING** As I've mentioned before and will no doubt mention again, access to a Windows 2000 application server is licensed on a per-seat basis, regardless of whether you're using ICA or RDP to connect to the terminal server. Although SP3 for Windows 2000 prevents a server from issuing TSCALs to a computer before the person initiating the session has successfully logged on, a person authorized to use the terminal server and automatically installing display protocols can really suck down TSCALs onto machines that shouldn't have them. If the people in your organization may use more than one computer and you don't have enough licenses for all those computers, you'll need to control the automatic distribution of display protocols to go only to computers, not users.

Installing Clients via Browser Both RDP and ICA support installation from a browser, although only ICA has an option to let you install the full-fledged client from a web browser—this install from RDP will install only the version that only works within IE.

> **NOTE** The Terminal Services Advanced Client (TSAC), the ActiveX version of RDP, works only with Win32 operating systems running 32-bit IE.

To install RDP, you'll need to download the file labeled "Web Package" that's currently available from http://www.microsoft.com/windows2000/downloads/recommended/TSAC/default.asp. (If they've rearranged the site, then look for "TSAC" and "download" and you should be able to find the right page.) Put this on a server running IIS 4 or later, as discussed in Chapter 4. For clients to connect to a terminal server from Internet Explorer, they need to navigate to the location where the page including the connection ActiveX control is located, even if it's just like this: *servername**sharename**tspage.htm*. Say, for example, that you're just using the `Default.HTM` page that comes with TSAC, and this page is located on gammawin2K in the shared tsweb folder—the UNC would look like this: `\\gammawin2K\tsweb\Default.HTM`. When someone connects to this page, they'll see a screen prompting them to supply the name of the server they want to connect to and the resolution. There's also a slot to provide security credentials: username and logon domain. When you click the Connect button, if the TSAC ActiveX control isn't already installed on your computer, you'll see a dialog box asking if you want to install and run the Terminal Services ActiveX Control. Click OK to install it. You should see the usual domain logon screen prompting you for your name and password.

Installing ICA with a web browser is similar. Although there is a web-based Program Neighborhood for MetaFrame users called NFuse, you don't have to use NFuse to install the ICA client via browser; you could just use Web-based installation to make it easy to install ICA support on a client. Unlike the TSAC, you can use this method to install either the web-only version of ICA or the full version used to connect to MetaFrame servers outside a browser. Install support for web-based installation on the server as described in Chapter 4, and then somewhere on a page that ICA users will see, publish a link to the `setup.htm` web page shown in Figure 5.4.

Figure 5.4 Web UI for installing ICA support

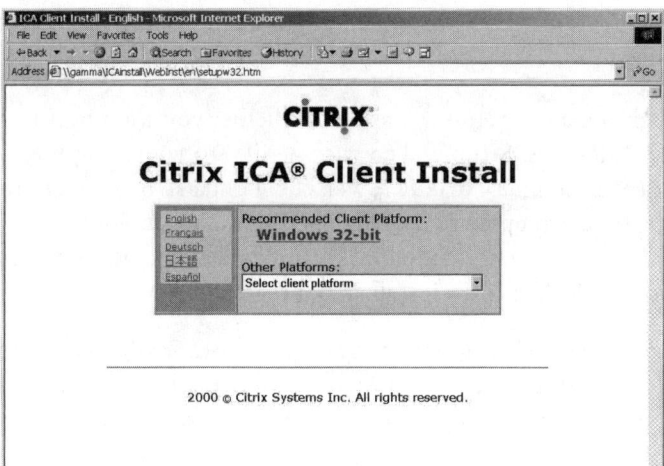

In this case, Setup is recommending that you install the Win32 ICA client (the boldface link) because this Web page is displaying on a client running Windows 2000 Professional.

NOTE As it stands, this page will install only the English-language version of ICA. Clicking the other language links gives you a page explaining that other language support is not available—that is, I assume that that's what the Japanese says. To install support for French, German, Spanish, or Japanese, copy the appropriate folder (e.g., the Spanish folder is \es) from the ICA Web folder, or follow the link from http:/www.citrix.com\download to copy the files from the Citrix website.

Assuming that you follow this suggestion (other platforms are visible in the Other Platforms drop-down menu) and click the link. You'll next see a screen giving you the option of installing either the full ICA client (ica32.exe), which you'll need to use Program Neighborhood and direct server connections, or just the web client (ica32t.exe), which is smaller but useful only for those who will be initiating applications exclusively from the browser. Click the button for the appropriate client. If you're running Netscape, you'll need to download the executable and run it manually; if you're running IE, you can run the executable or download it for running offline.

TIP If users should definitely download only one particular client, consider editing setup.htm to display only the button for downloading the client you want them to use.

Whichever link you click, Setup will ask you whether you want to trust content from Citrix. When you click Yes, Setup will copy some files to your computer and then tell you that it's about to install the Citrix ICA web client and ask if you want to continue? Click Yes. You'll next be prompted to agree to the EULA. When you do so, Setup will copy some files in the background without asking any more questions and install the ICA client. That's it—the ICA client is installed and ready to go.

Using Group Policies If you have a lot of Windows 2000 Professional clients to get a display protocol to but don't want to use the web interface to RDP, you can use Windows 2000 Group Policy Objects (GPOs) to automatically install the RDP and ICA clients.

Microsoft Installer (.msi) files can automatically install applications with a preset group of settings. If you're using Active Directory, you can use GPOs to automatically deploy the MSI files to computers (my preference, because of the Terminal Service's per-seat licensing) or to users. To make this work, you'll need to create an organizational unit (OU) for all the computers allowed to access the terminal server or MetaFrame server, then apply this GPO to that OU and refresh the domain policy. You can download an MSI file from the same place you got the TSAC file: http://www.microsoft.com/windows2000/downloads/recommended/TSAC/default.asp–just select MSI Package from the drop-down list on the right side of the page and follow the instructions. MSI packages for some ICA clients are available from the Citrix download section, currently at http://www.citrix.com/download/bin/download.asp.

When a member of the OU you assign the MSI file to next connects to the network, the client will automatically install onto the computer.

Using the Command Prompt If you're only distributing the client to a few people, aren't using Windows 2000 Professional clients, and/or don't have Active Directory set up, you can just create an unattended installation for the display protocol. RDP has its own command-line tools for enabling this, or you can use the msiexec command to silently install MSI files for the RDP or ICA clients, so long as the Windows Installer service is installed on that computer. It's installed by default on Windows 2000 and later computers, and you can download it for free from the Microsoft Web site.

To install RDP from the command prompt, make sure you're in the path for the right version of the Setup files on the terminal server and type **setup /q1** to install the RDP client. This method ensures that when the installation is done, the user has to click OK on the Installation Was Completed Successfully box. To install without any user interaction, go to the command prompt and type **setup /qt**. (I suppose that this means that you're installing RDP "on the QT." I crack myself up sometimes.)

So, for example, you could create a short script to automate this process:

```
net use j: \\sandworm\net /persistent:no
j:\win32
setup /qt
c:
net use j: /delete
```

In this example, sandworm is the terminal server where the client installation files are located, and \net is the share name for *%systemroot%*\system32\clients\tsclient\ net.

As you can see, this script connects you to the share, changes to the Win32 directory in that share (because \NET contains files for both Win16 and Win32 clients; obviously, to install the Win16 version you'd change to the Win16 directory), runs a silent unattended install, changes back to a local drive, and then disconnects from the remote drive. Put this script in the [RunOnce] section of an unattended installation of a computer connected to the network, and you've got yourself an installed RDP client, without having to set up Active Directory *or* configure group policies.

To uninstall the RDP client from the command line, type **setup /u /qnt**.

`msiexec /i` works to install both the ICA and RDP clients for which you have MSI files. The syntax looks like this:

```
msiexec /I <MSI_Package> /qn+ [Key=Value]
```

This example will install the MSI package located at the name and path within the triangular brackets, showing only a dialog box at the end of the installation. (To install without displaying the ending dialog box, replace the qn+ with a q or qn.) The keys and values that replace [Key=Value] depend on what you're trying to do and the package you're installing. If you're installing the Program Neighborhood Agent, for example, you'll have the option of these keys:.

- INSTALLDIR=<Installation_Path>, where <Installation_Path> is the path to the directory where the ICA Client software is installed. By default, the client will install into Program Files\Citrix\PNAgent.
- PROGRAM_FOLDER_NAME=<Start Menu Program Folder Name>, where <Start Menu Program Folder Name> is the name of the Programs folder on the Start menu containing the shortcut to the Program Neighborhood Agent software. The default value is Citrix Program Neighborhood Agent.
- CLIENT_UPGRADE={Yes | No}. The default value is Yes.
- INSTALLDIR=<Installation_Path>, where <Installation_Path> is the path to the directory where the ICA Client software is installed. The Program Neighborhood Agent software is installed in the directory Program Files\Citrix\PNAgent by default.
- SERVER_LOCATION=<NFuse Classic_server_URL>. The default value is PNAgent. Enter the URL of the NFuse Classic server hosting the Config.xml file in the format http://<servername> or https://<servername>.

NOTE The Program Neighborhood Agent appends to the server URL the default path and filename of the agent's configuration file (config.xml) on the NFuse Classic server. If you move the configuration file, you must enter the new path in the SERVER_LOCATION key.

- ENABLE_SSON={Yes | No}. The default value is No. If you enable the SSON (Single-Sign-On—it's the property enabling pass-through authentication) property, set ALLOW_REBOOT to No to avoid rebooting the client system.
- ALLOW_REBOOT={Yes | No}. The default value is Yes.
- DEFAULT_NDSCONTEXT=<Context1 [,–]>. Include this parameter if you want to set a default context for NDS. If you are including more than one context, place the entire value in quotation marks, and separate the contexts by a comma.

Creating, Deleting, and Modifying RDP Connections

Now that the client is installed, you're ready to connect to the terminal server. Let's take a look at how to do this from a PC or NTE-based Windows terminal. (Because Windows terminals running NTE are running a stripped-down version of NT, they use the same versions of RDP that work with any other Win32 operating system.)

Connections with the RDP5 Client If you're using the RDP5 client that comes with Windows 2000, then the simplest way to connect to a terminal server is to run the Terminal Services Client found in the Terminal Services Client program group. When you do, you'll see a dialog box like the one in Figure 5.5, showing all available terminal servers on the network.

Figure 5.5 Use the Terminal Services Client to connect to a terminal server using default settings.

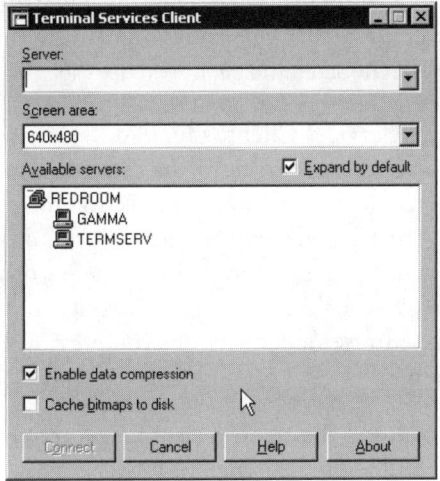

To connect to a server, select its icon in the list. I find that the RDP5 client isn't always great about finding servers across domains, even trusted domains. If the server you want isn't listed, try typing its name or IP address in the Server box at the top of the dialog box. You'll also need to choose a resolution for the terminal window. For first-timers, this setting could be confusing. A lower resolution doesn't give you a lower-resolution full-screen client session; it gives you a smaller window. For example, if your client computer's local resolution is 1024×768 and you choose a terminal server session resolution of 800×600, the session window will be smaller than your Desktop. However, it will have the same resolution as the local Desktop, instead of looking as it would if you changed your display settings to make the display 800×600. You can't choose a terminal session resolution greater than the one you're using locally.

> **NOTE** If you choose a resolution identical to the one you're using locally, you won't be able to see the entire screen at once unless you press Ctrl+Alt+Break to run the session in Full Screen mode. Run it in a window and you'll spend a lot of time scrolling up and down looking for icons and menu bars. Which option you choose depends on whether it's more important to your user base to be able to quickly switch between locally installed applications and a terminal session or to be able to see the entire Desktop without scrolling.

Once you click the Connect button, the client should find the selected terminal server and display the usual domain logon screen in the session window. Type your name and password, and pick a domain or server to log onto, and you're in.

> **TIP** If the client gets an error message saying that the terminal server is busy and try again later, check the client TCP/IP settings and make sure that it has a valid IP address and subnet. If it doesn't, the client will get the "too busy" message.

Easy... but the Terminal Services Client is limited. It only connects you to a complete Desktop rather than to a single application, you can't save settings to use at a later time, and you can't save user credentials with the connection to skip the logon step. To set up client custom settings, skip the Terminal Services Client and choose the Client Connection Manager from the same program group. From there, you can create new connections with personalized settings, save those connection settings for future reference or to use on another computer, edit settings for connections you previously connected, and delete session settings if you no longer want to use them.

Creating a New Connection To create a customized connection, choose New Connection from the File menu and complete the following steps:

1. Choose a name for the new connection and a server to which to connect, as in Figure 5.6. If your network includes a WINS or DNS server, you can use the name of the server. If not, then supply the terminal server's IP address. If you don't know which terminal servers are available, click the Browse button to display a list of available terminal servers in the domain. Again, the RDP5 client doesn't always browse across domains successfully, but I've found that typing in the name of the terminal server I want to connect to works so long as it's in a trusted domain. Click Next.

Figure 5.6 Naming a terminal connection

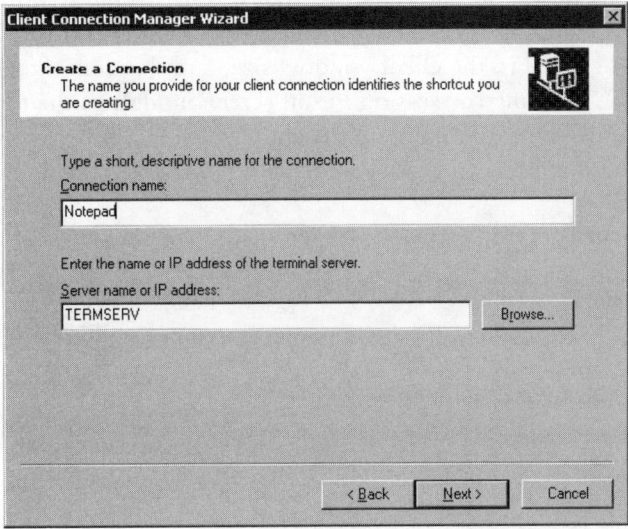

2. If you want to automatically log onto the server when starting the connection, check the box and fill in the appropriate account name, password, and domain or workgroup. As you can see in Figure 5.7, the password is displayed in asterisks. Sadly, there's no setting here to tell RDP to use the credentials of the currently logged-on user, as is possible with ICA. Click Next.

Figure 5.7 Supplying a name and password for the connection

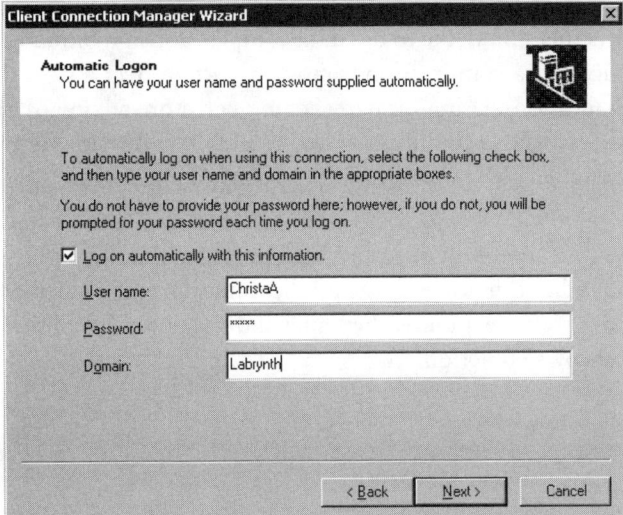

3. Choose the session display settings, including the session display resolution and whether the session should run in a window or take up the entire screen. Some settings in Figure 5.8 are grayed out because you can only choose a session resolution less than or equal to the client window size, and this computer's display is set to 1024×768. Running the session in full-screen mode sets the terminal session to automatically start up taking up the entire screen, hiding the local Desktop, but you can always press Ctrl+Alt+Break to run the session in a window.

Figure 5.8 Choosing a display resolution for a terminal session

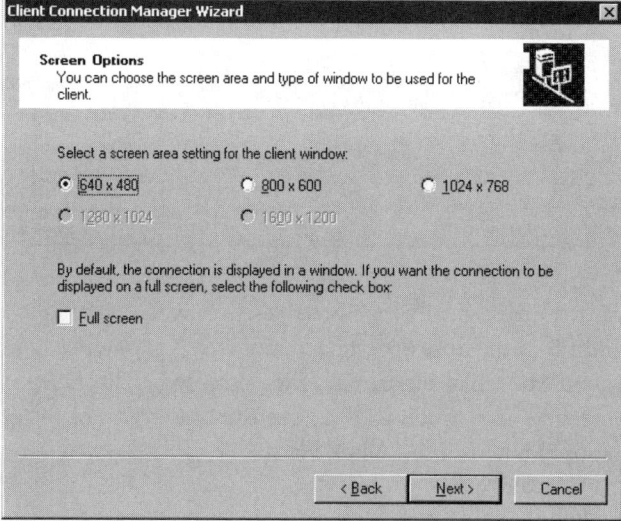

4. Indicate whether you'd like to use data compression and bitmap caching to improve performance. Data compression is most important over a slow network (such as a dial-up connection). Using bitmap caching will store a copy of bitmapped images locally, so that RDP will only have to update them if there are changes.

5. Specify whether you want the session to display an application or the entire Desktop. If you choose the Desktop, you'll be able to run any application accessible to your user account. Running a single application means that only that application will be displayed, and that if you exit the application, the session will end. As you can see in Figure 5.9, you must know the name and path of the application to connect to—there's no Browse function.

Figure 5.9 Selecting an application to display

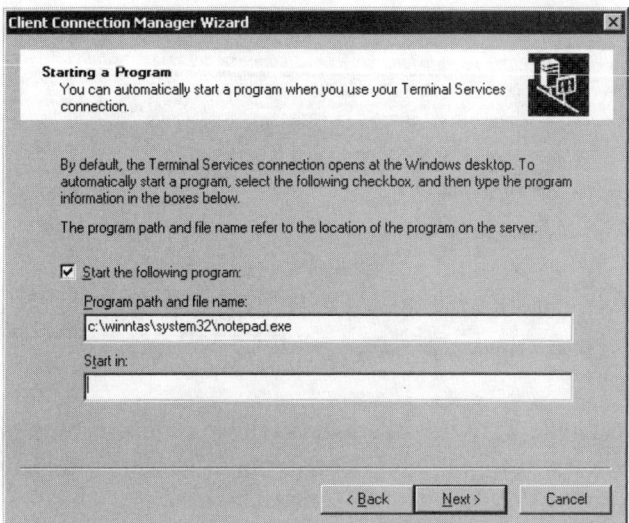

NOTE Although it might seem logical to name the application location by its Unicode name, this isn't how it works. Instead, because you're connecting to the application locally, not via the network, you must enter the path as it appears from the terminal server's perspective (for example, `C:\winntas\system32\notepad.exe`).

6. Specify how the session will be displayed. You can add the connection to the Terminal Services Client program group (or to another program group that you specify if, for example, you'd like users to be unaware that they're running the application from the terminal server) so that you can use it without running the Client Connection Manager. To improve the illusion that applications running in a terminal session are running locally, you can edit the connection's icon as I've done in Figure 5.10 to use the one for the application that the session will open.

TIP Icons have an `.ico` extension, so you can find them with the Win32 Search utility accessible from the Start menu. Alternatively, just browse to the application's location and select the executable.

Figure 5.10 Assigning a new icon to a published application

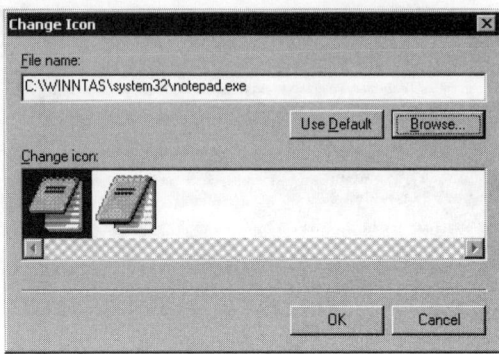

When you've entered all this information, you'll see a Finish screen. When you click Finish, the connection will appear in the Connection Manager as in Figure 5.11. The client connection settings will be ready to use immediately.

Figure 5.11 Client Connection Manager with a new custom RDP connection to run Notepad

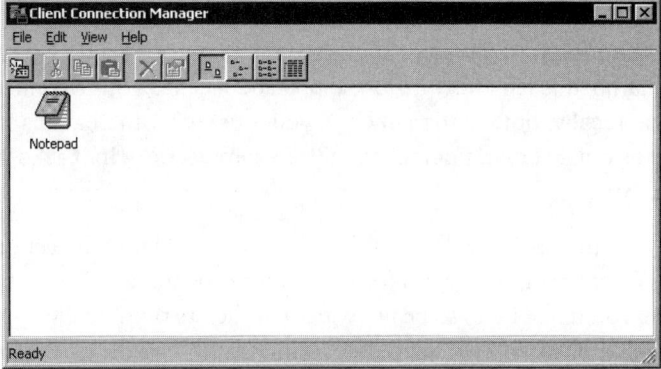

TIP So that user's don't have to look in the Connection Manager to find their applications, drag the terminal connection's icon to the Desktop or to the Start menu. Also, if you right-click on a connection's icon, you'll see an option to copy the connection to the local Desktop.

You can make as many connection settings as you need to different terminal servers or different applications or at different resolutions. Just keep in mind that each separate session running on the terminal server, whether it's an application or a full Desktop, uses resources on the terminal server and gets a timeslice of the CPU cycles. Multiple connections to the same server do not pool server resources.

Reusing Connections on Other Computers You can also transfer connection settings to another client computer without typing them in again. First, save the connection to a file. Highlight it in the Client Connection Manager, and choose Export from the File menu. Choose a name for the file, and click Save. If password information was part of the connection settings, you'll be asked whether you want to save the password along with the rest of the configuration information for that connection. If you do, then click Yes—just don't forget that doing so means that anyone logging on to the terminal server with that connection will use the identity of the person for whom you originally created the connection. The exported connection will be saved with a .cns extension and will be quite small—around a kilobyte.

> **NOTE** Sadly, RDP5 connections export with a .cns extension, and the new Remote Desktop connection saves and imports files with an .rdp extension. Each client version can only open its particular saved file type; even changing the saved connection's extension doesn't do the trick. Therefore, when upgrading to Remote Desktop you can't save all your connection information in the Connection Manager and import it to the Remote Desktop tool.

To use that connection on another computer, open the Client Connection Manager at the client computer that you want to have access to the terminal server. Choose Import from the File menu, browse to the location of the saved connection, and select it. Annoyingly, any special icons that you assigned to the connection will *not* be saved—it'll revert to the normal connection icon, but you can tweak the icons by hand from the connection's Properties screen.

Coincidentally, that leads us to the next topic.

Editing and Deleting Connection Information Not all session settings are engraved in stone after you've created the connection. In fact, as you can see in the case of imported CNS files with non-default icons that mysteriously revert to the default icon when imported, they may not even be set in wet concrete. Even after you set up a connection, you can easily tweak it, which means that you can create a template connection and copy it as the basis of slightly different connections. To edit a connection, right-click on it in the Client Connection Manager and Properties from the context menu (see Figures 5.12-5.14).

194 Chapter 5 Preparing Client Connections

Figure 5.12 The General tab is for editing the name of the server, its description, and any automatic logon information.

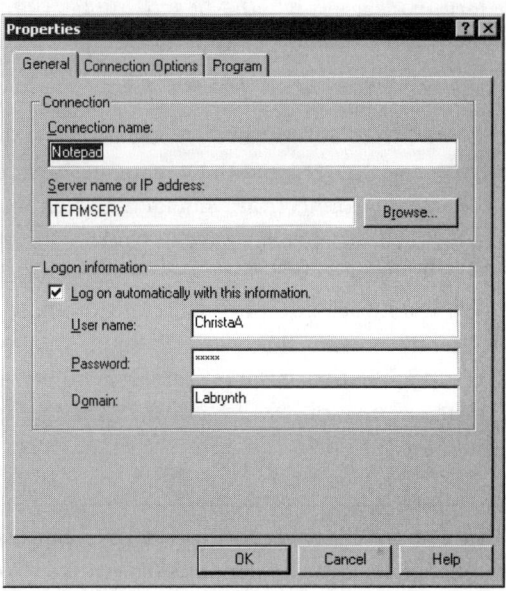

Figure 5.13 The Connection Options tab covers session display settings, including the size of the window and the speed of the connection between server and client.

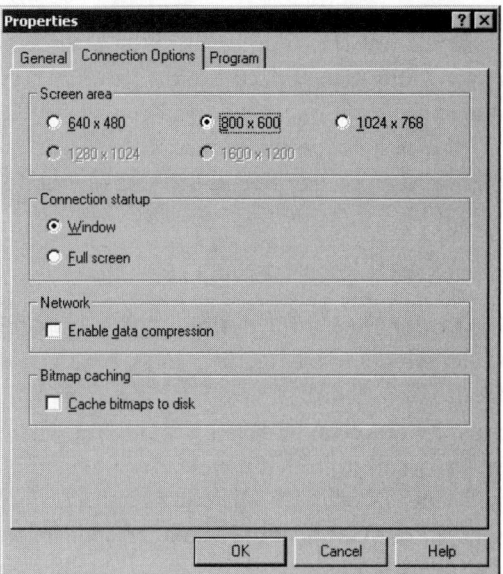

Figure 5.14 In the Program tab, choose a new application to run in the terminal server session, or change the icon or program group associated with the session settings.

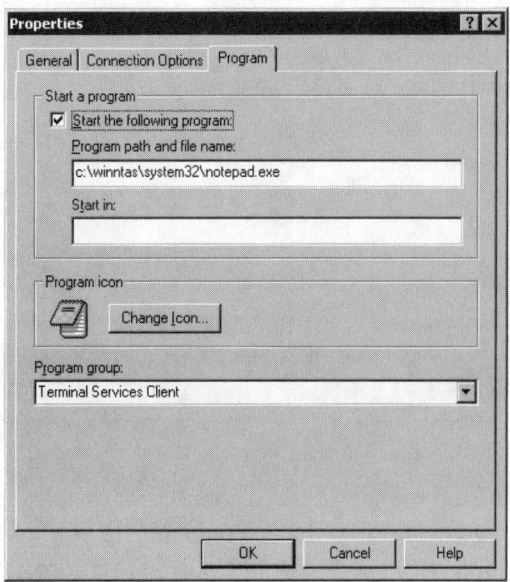

Finally, to delete a session from the Connection Manager, just highlight it and press the Delete key.

Connections with the Remote Desktop If you install the Remote Desktop RDP client, the setup and adjustment procedures will look a little different from those in the RDP5 client, partially because of the change in UI and partially because of the new options. (Sadly, however, these new options will not actually *do* anything unless you're using the Remote Desktop to connect to a Windows XP or .NET Server RDP connection.)

To use the Remote Desktop client, open it (its default location is Programs ≻ Accessories ≻ Communications ≻ Remote Desktop Connection, but I like to move it to the Start menu or Desktop to make it a bit more accessible). When you first run the tool, no servers will be selected, but you can either type a server's name or browse for them by clicking the down-arrow button in the Computer box and choosing Browse for More… to open the dialog box shown in Figure 5.15.

Figure 5.15 Browsing for terminal servers from the Remote Desktop

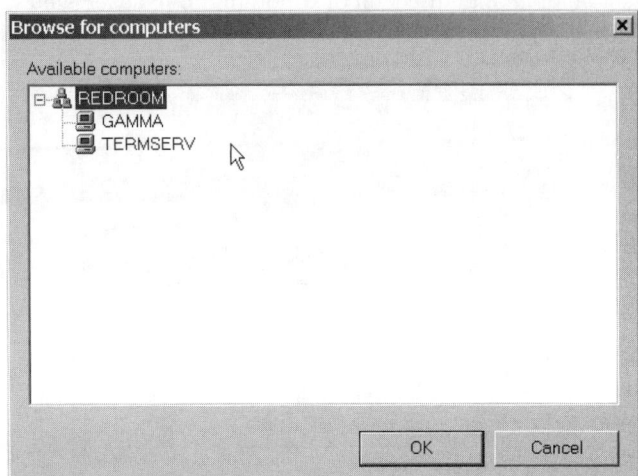

When you've found the terminal server to connect to, double-click on it or click OK to return to the main logon window, which should now have a server selected, as shown in Figure 5.16. To connect to this server with the default settings, just click the Connect button. This will connect you to the selected terminal server and prompt you to log on. When you have successfully logged on, by default the session will run in full-screen mode with a window-sizing bar at the top so that you can easily minimize or resize the window to show the local Desktop.

Figure 5.16 To use the selected terminal server with the default settings, click the Connect button.

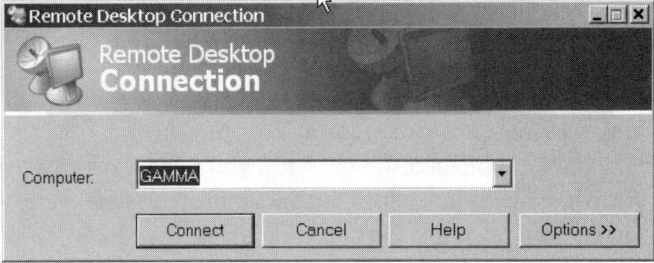

Notice that I didn't touch the Options button in Figure 5.16. If you're using the default settings, you'll never *need* to touch it—think of the Terminal Services Client tool for RDP5 that we discussed a little earlier. However, as with the TSC, using the default settings doesn't allow you a whole lot of flexibility. Let's take a look at what those settings involve.

When you first click the Options button, you'll see the General tab, shown in Figure 5.17. From here, you can choose user credentials to log on with, save or open shared connection settings, and pick another server to log into, if you like. The only part that might cause confusion (and with reason—it doesn't make a whole lot of sense) is the box prompting you for your user password. Even if you supply this information, you'll still be prompted for your password when you connect to the terminal server.

Recall that we saved RDP5 connections on other computers to reuse them on other computers. You can do the same thing from the General tab of the Remote Desktop—when you click the Save As button, you'll be prompted to save the connection information in My Documents. To use a saved RDP connection file, click the Open button, browse for it, and open the file. Sadly, the formats for Remote Desktop and the RDP4 Connection Manager are incompatible, so you can't create settings in one tool and use them in another.

Figure 5.17 Use the General tab to supply user credentials and save connection settings to a file.

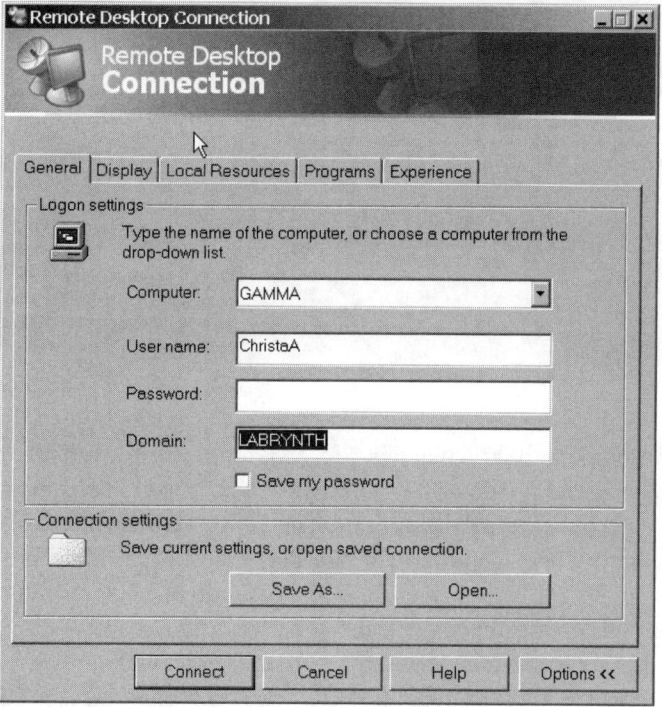

The Display tab controls all session settings relating to display. The default settings shown in Figure 5.18 may not apply to the terminal session you create. For example, when connecting to a Windows 2000 application server, 24-bit color will not work, but full-screen mode will. The connection bar at the top of the terminal session window is useful for full-screen sessions, as it offers an easy way to minimize the session and reach the local Desktop. As with RDP5, the resolution for the setting will depend on the local client settings—the settings for Remote Desktop size apply only to the window's size.

Figure 5.18 The Remote Desktop display settings are intended to mimic a user's local Desktop.

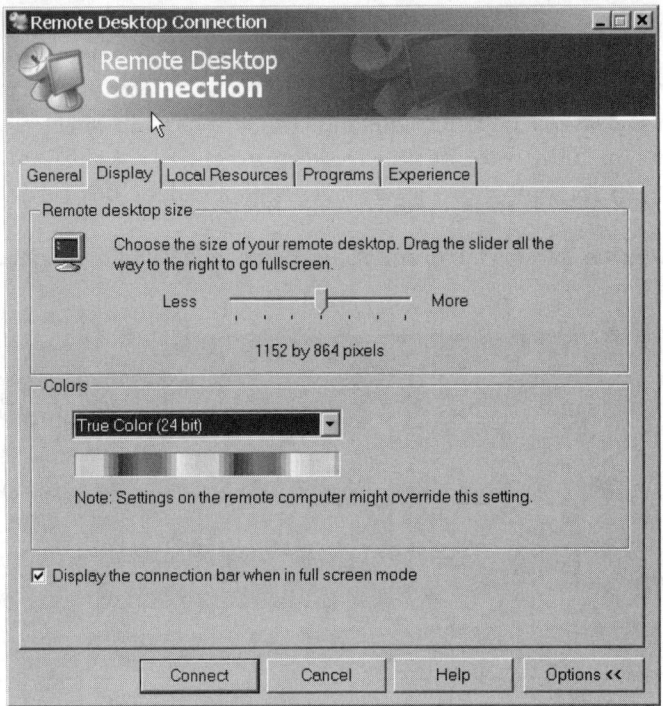

The Local Resources tab shown in Figure 5.19 is a little more in-depth, but (again) unless you're connecting to a Windows XP Desktop or .NET Server application server, you don't need to worry about most of the options. The Sound settings at the top offer you three options—Bring to This Computer, Do Not Play, and Leave at Remote Computer—but these settings don't apply to sessions hosted by Windows 2000 terminal servers. The key combinations settings do apply all the time or always to the local session. The settings also specify whether standard Windows key combinations should apply to the remote session only in full-screen mode. The default option of full-screen mode is probably the one that people will find easiest to use because it will send the keystrokes to whichever view of the Desktop is most prominent. Finally, the Local Devices settings may or may not apply.

Printer mappings (enabled by default) will work with Windows 2000 terminal sessions, as will serial mappings, but local drive mappings are only available with the newest version of the RDP server component, on Windows XP and .NET Server only.

> **TIP** When creating a connection to work over a limited-bandwidth network, seriously consider disabling printer mapping unless you're using some form of print job compression tool. Print jobs take up a lot of bandwidth and, because they use RDP channels, will impede the performance of the terminal session while crawling from the terminal server to the client.

Figure 5.19 Not all Local Resources settings will be available to sessions hosted by a Windows 2000 terminal server.

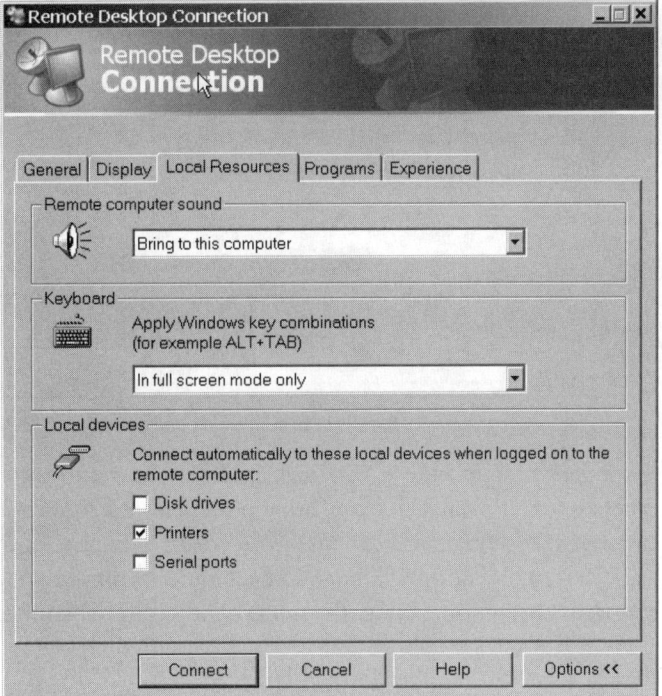

The Programs tab displayed in Figure 5.20 is pretty self-explanatory if you've used Terminal Services before. If you choose a program to run here, that program will be the only one available—if the user closes it, they'll end their session. The starting folder settings supply a working directory for the program that you can use if you don't want to use the default (often My Documents), but this setting is optional.

Figure 5.20 Choose a single program for terminal sessions.

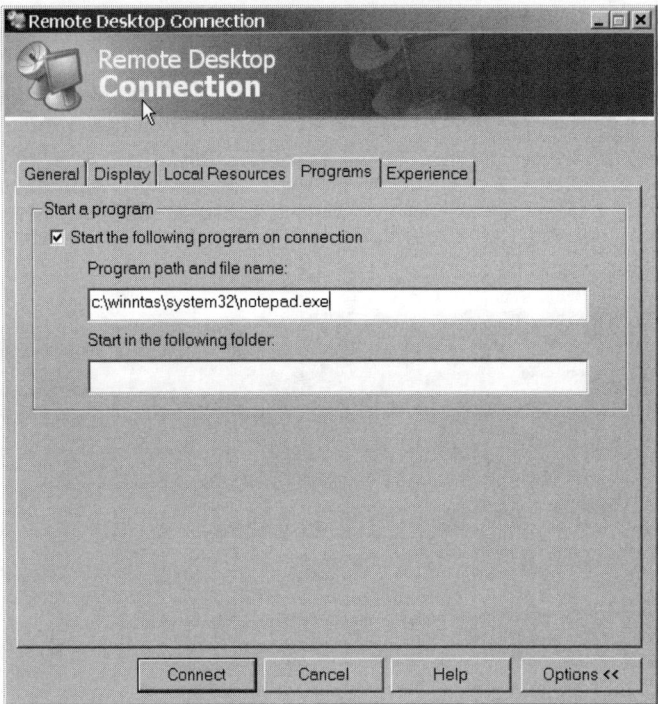

Finally, the Experience tab in Figure 5.21 determines some features to enable based on Microsoft's guesses about what will work best on the selected connection speeds, shown in the drop-down list. Although you can manually check or uncheck boxes to enable and disable features, Remote Desktop will have some default settings for each network speed offered. The more features you enable, the more bandwidth the connection will require.

Client Catch-22s By and large, using a connection to the terminal server is largely idiot-proof once you've got everything set up. However, your users should be aware of a few things before they use one of their terminal server connections. Some apply to all PC users (but not to Windows terminals), and one applies only to Win16 clients.

Figure 5.21 Enable or disable session features depending on the network speed the connection will be using.

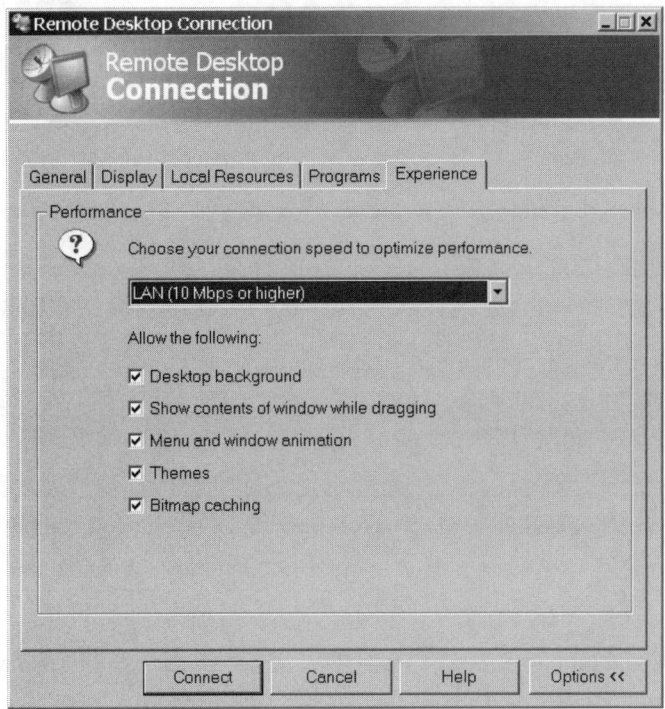

Normal Keyboard Shortcuts Don't Work with RDP5 Sessions You're accustomed to using keyboard shortcuts to navigate between applications on your Desktop, and you can see how to enable Desktop shortcuts for use with Remote Desktop. You may wonder how to make the shortcuts work in your terminal server session running on your PC and using the RDP5 display protocol. The simple answer is that you can't—those shortcuts are picked up by the local buffer for use on the local console. Instead, you'll need to substitute keyboard shortcuts as shown in Table 5.1.

Table 5.1 Keyboard Shortcuts in Terminal Services Client Sessions

Function	Locally Used Combination	Session-Specific Combination
Brings up application selector and moves selection to the right	Alt+Tab	Alt+PgUp

Table 5.1 Keyboard Shortcuts in Terminal Services Client Sessions *(continued)*

Function	Locally Used Combination	Session-Specific Combination
Brings up application selector and moves selection to the left	Alt+Shift+Tab	Alt+PgDn
Swaps between running applications	Alt+Esc	Alt+Insert
Opens the Start menu	Ctrl+Esc	Alt+Home
Right-clicks the active application's icon button in the upper left of the application window	Alt+spacebar	Alt+Del
Brings up the Windows NT Security window	Ctrl+Alt+Del	Ctrl+Alt+End

The Copy, Cut, and Paste commands will work as usual in both local and remote sessions. The commands will apply to whichever session is in the foreground. If you copy in one session and then move the other session to the foreground to paste, the text will be pasted in the second session.

You Must Log Off to End a Session Just closing the terminal server window doesn't terminate the session; it disconnects it so it's in a sort of trance state on the server, maintaining the user's session until the user decides to come back to it. If you want to *terminate* a session, then log out as you would if logging out of the domain.

> **WARNING** Be sure to train users to terminate sessions correctly, not just disconnect them. Every user connected to the terminal server has their own HKEY_CURRENT_USER section in the server's Registry, left open until the session is terminated. If you're having trouble with painful, swollen Registries, then disconnected-and-never-terminated sessions could be a factor. You can configure Windows 2000 Terminal Services to automatically terminate disconnected sessions after a predetermined period of inactivity.

Problems with Password-Protected Screensavers Frankly, you shouldn't be using screensavers with terminal sessions anyway, because generating the output takes a toll on the processor for no good reason. But if you do, and if a user minimizes the session, they'll get a blank screen in the session window when they try to log back on to the password-protected screensaver. Nothing can be done about this; the user will need to terminate the session and then restart it. All in all, it's just one more reason not to use screensavers with terminal sessions. If a user needs to secure a session without terminating it, tell them to disconnect. They'll need to log on again to reconnect to the session.

Connecting with the Win16 Client Windows for Workgroups clients must save their domain password in their password list when logging on (a check box in the logon screen allows them to do this). Otherwise, they'll get an unhelpful error message: "Error code: 0x906 SL_ERR_SECCTXTINITFAILED (0x906) SL: InitSecurityContext call failed." All this means is that the domain controller can't find the password. This does not apply if your network is organized as a workgroup, only if it's using domain security.

Troubleshooting Connection Problems When you set up a connection properly, it should work—but *should* is a nice word that doesn't always apply to reality. Table 5.2 lists some error messages that users might encounter when trying to access a terminal server.

Table 5.2 Connection Error Messages

Error Message	Probable Meaning
The local policy of this system does not allow you to log on interactively.	The user attempting to log on does not have the Log On Locally permission available under `Security Settings\Local Policies\User Rights Assignment\Log On Locally`. Modify the appropriate GPO to grant the user or group this permission. Remember, using a terminal server counts as logging onto the console, so if you disabled local logons then people can't use the terminal server.
You do not have access to this session.	The user attempting to log on does not have sufficient permissions on the RDP-TCP connection. Modify the RDP-TCP permissions by using Terminal Services Configuration to grant the user or group the logon permission.

Table 5.2 Connection Error Messages *(continued)*

Error Message	Probable Meaning
Your interactive logon privilege has been disabled. Please contact your system administrator.	The user attempting to log on does not have the Allow Logon to Terminal Server check box selected on the Terminal Services Profile tab of their account. Use Active Directory Users and Computers to modify this setting.
The terminal server has exceeded the maximum number of allowed connections. The system cannot log you on (1B8E). Please try again or consult your system administrator.	The user is attempting to log on to a terminal server in Remote Administration mode, but the server has reached its connection limit. Terminal servers in Remote Administration mode allow a maximum of two concurrent sessions, active or disconnected.
Terminal server sessions disabled. Remote logons are currently disabled.	The user is attempting to log on to a terminal server where an administrator has disabled additional logons by issuing the CHANGE LOGON /DISABLE command. To enable logon, run CHANGE LOGON /ENABLE.
Because of a network error, the session will be disconnected. Please try to reconnect.	The user is attempting to log on to a terminal server where an administrator has specified a maximum connection limit, and the limit has been reached. To change this value, open the Terminal Services Configuration MMC snap-in, click Connections, double-click a connection (i.e., RDP-TCP), then select the Network Adapter tab. At the bottom of this tab are two options, Unlimited connections and Maximum connections.

Table 5.2 Connection Error Messages *(continued)*

Error Message	Probable Meaning
The client could not connect to the terminal server. The server may be too busy. Please try connecting later.	The user is attempting to log on to a terminal server where an administrator has disabled one or more connections. To check this, open the Terminal Services Configuration MMC snap-in, click Connections, right-click a connection (i.e., RDP-TCP—and select All Tasks). If Enable Connection is an option, the connection is currently disabled. There will also be a red *X* over the icon for the specified connection when disabled. This is also known as the World's Most Unhelpful Error Message because it will appear for any number of problems that don't have anything to do with the server being busy. For example, if your client can't find the subnet where your terminal server is, you'll see this error message.
ICA clients unexpectedly disconnect.	This is a MetaFrame problem, not an RDP one, but because both Microsoft and Citrix have addressed it, it's worth including. Install SP2 for Windows 2000 Server, and get the hotfix from Citrix.

Connecting with the ICA Client

Because you now have a way to get ICA clients to everyone and can update those clients as needed, you're ready to create connections to MetaFrame servers. We'll start with connecting to a server's entire desktop. From there, we'll move to connecting to individually published applications. (No, you haven't published any applications yet. We'll get to that in Chapter 7, "Installing and Tuning Applications on an Application Server.")

No matter which client operating system you're running—DOS, Linux, Win32, Macintosh, or any other ICA-supporting operating system—you'll need to provide some basic information to create a direct connection to a MetaFrame server. I'll use a Windows 2000 Professional client to illustrate the connection process. The specifics of the process of gathering connection-specific information may differ with the operating system. However, the basic routine remains the same: to create a client connection, you need to tell ICA which server to connect to, what you want the session to look like, and (optionally) who you are. The basic routine is summarized as follows:

1. Open the Citrix Program Neighborhood, located by default in Programs ➤ Citrix ICA Client. The first time you open it after installing, you may see a dialog box prompting you to pick the default application set. If we had already published applications, then we would need to worry about this, but for right now, we're just connecting to a MetaFrame server's desktop. If you see this dialog box, just click Cancel.

2. Once in the Program Neighborhood, you'll see two icons: "Find New Application Set" and "Custom ICA Connections." We don't *have* a published application set yet, so we'll set up a custom ICA connection. When you click on that icon, the dialog box will display an icon labeled "Add ICA Connection." Click on that to begin the Connection Wizard.

3. Most of this process is similar to the wizard you used to create an RDP5 terminal connection. First, as shown in Figure 5.22, you'll pick a connection type—LAN, WAN, dial-up networking, or ICA dial-in. Choose dial-up networking if you're connecting to the MetaFrame server through PPP or RAS; choose ICA dial-in if you configured a modem to work with a MetaFrame server and accept incoming calls.

Figure 5.22 Choosing a network type for an ICA session

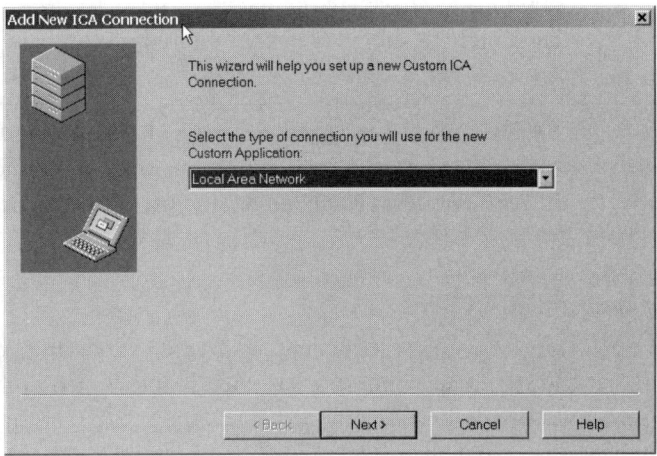

> **NOTE** Knowledge Base article Q303432 describes a problem where direct dial-in connections may hang while trying to connect, and provides a link the post-SP2 hotfix for this problem. If you're using dial-up connections with MetaFrame, make sure you download this fix.

4. Next, you'll name the connection, choose the network protocol you'll use to connect to the server, and name the server to which you want to connect. When you choose to connect to a server, you should see the names of all available MetaFrame servers when you click the drop-down arrow. (If you choose a server from the list, that server's name is the default name of the connection. See Figure 5.23.)

Figure 5.23 Available servers will appear in the browse list.

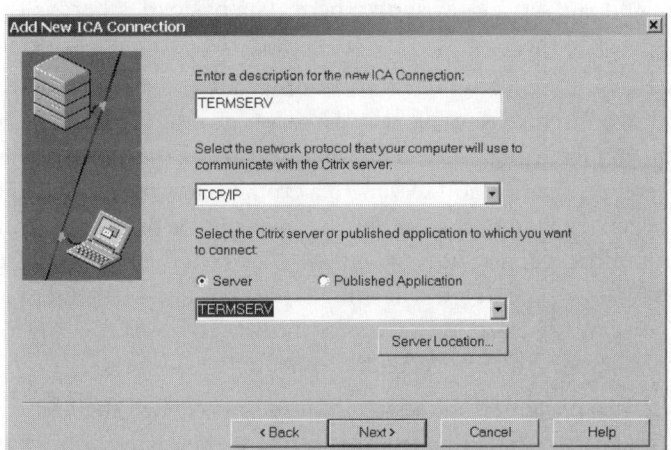

About the only part of the section of the wizard that might throw you is the Server Location button, which opens a dialog box allowing you to configure server groups. You'd use server groups to cut down on network traffic. If you stick with the default settings, then with every protocol except TCP/IP+HTTP, the ICA client finds servers by broadcasting on the network. (The sidebar "Using Server Groups to Reduce Network Traffic" explains how server groups work.) To do so, click the Server Location button to open the dialog box shown in Figure 5.24.

Figure 5.24 You can configure server location to minimize network broadcasts.

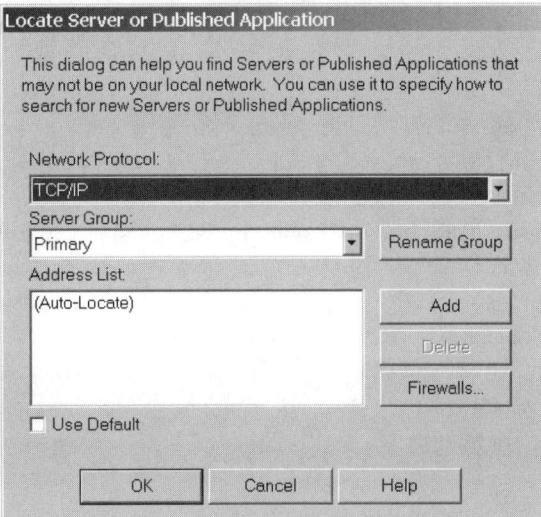

Normally, the Use Default check box in this dialog box is checked; uncheck it so that you can edit the settings as shown here. The basic idea here is to send ICA client requests *only* to the servers in the list, not to the entire network.

First, we've got the Network Protocol drop-down list; if you're using TCP/IP, you can stick with that setting. Next is the server group. Click the down arrow for this box, and you'll see that you can organize servers on the network into up to three separate server groups. To add servers to a group, select the group from the drop-down list and click the Add button to type a server's name or IP address in the Add Server Location Address dialog box. When you click OK, the Address List text box will no longer say (Auto-Locate); it will contain the IP address or server name that you supplied. You can add up to five servers to the list. To revert to using auto-location, just use the Delete key to remove all entries from the Address list.

Once you've configured the server locations and exited the Locate Server or Published Application dialog box, pick a server from the drop-down list in the wizard screen shown in Figure 5.23 and click Next.

Using Server Groups to Reduce Network Traffic

When you're setting up ICA connections to applications or desktops, the ICA client has to find a MetaFrame server to support that application. When using the TCP/IP, IPX/SPX, and NetBIOS protocols, the client locates servers by issuing broadcasts to the local network. The first MetaFrame server that responds (allowing for load balancing and the presence of any individual applications the ICA client is attempting to connect to) then accepts the connection.

This method of discovery works fine, and is the only method that *can* work using the default settings—if you uncritically click Next throughout the wizard, you can set up a working ICA connection. But if a lot of ICA clients attempt to connect to MetaFrame servers, then all these auto-location broadcasts necessarily take up a lot of bandwidth. Even load balancing doesn't help, because the load-balancing manager evaluates server load after getting the ICA client requests. You can reduce network traffic by disabling Auto-Locate and instead giving ICA clients a suggested list of servers. The ICA client will still send requests to all the listed servers, but only *those* servers will hear the request—not the entire network. For connecting to a MetaFrame server desktop, as we're doing here, the server listed will be the one to which you connect. For running published applications, the server the ICA client connects to will find the data collector, which will then discover from which MetaFrame server the ICA client should run the connection.

Using Server Groups to Reduce Network Traffic *(continued)*

The way the ICA client uses server groups depends on whether it's using an application set. You can organize servers into three groups (Primary, Backup 1, and Backup 2) of up to five servers each. When an ICA client using any network protocol other than TCP/IP+HTTP tries to connect to a MetaFrame server, it first sends one packet requesting the zone data collector (native mode) or ICA master browser (compatibility mode) to each MetaFrame server in the Primary group. If one answers, then great—it's made the connection. If no servers answer after three tries, then it sends packets to the servers in Backup 1 three times, and then Backup 2 once before giving up.

Which servers go in which group depends on what you're trying to do. In smaller networks with less competition for bandwidth, you can point the ICA clients to a single zone data collectors (native mode) or ICA master browser (compatibility mode) and then let the data collector sort out which server should accept the connection. For busier networks that spread over a wider area, give the ICA clients an option of more than one data collector (if there is more than one in the farm) and also some backup servers to accept the connection if the data collectors are busy. Either way, if ICA clients are spread out over multiple locations, then make sure that the servers in the Primary and Backup 1 groups are at the same location as the ICA client computer. You can include servers from another location in Backup 2 if letting the ICA client establish a connection is your top priority. As you can see, you could also use the server groups as a form of static load balancing, by spreading out the servers in a farm among different server groups and prioritizing those servers differently for different saved client connections.

Note that that's the way server groups are treated for all LAN protocols *other* than TCP/IP+HTTP. TCP/IP+HTTP uses server groups differently, treating them as a single-entry list rather than three separate groups. When an ICA client attempts to find a MetaFrame server via TCP/IP+HTTP, it works down the list of MetaFrame servers one by one until it can establish a connection, beginning with the first server it finds in the Primary group and ending with the last server in the Backup 2 group. (TCP/IP+HTTP cannot use Auto-Locate at all.) Therefore, when using this protocol, put the servers most likely to respond at the top of the list and avoid listing too many servers—the ICA client won't complain that it can't find a MetaFrame server until it has tried *all* of them. (This can be a time-consuming process if you listed 15 servers.) Also, make sure that all the servers in the list are in the same farm.

5. In the next screen, you'll set the encryption level for the connection. If you stick with the default settings visible in Figure 5.25, you'll use Basic encryption, which does not protect the data stream. Uncheck the box to change the settings. The 128-bit setting (Login Only) protects the initial logon, but it does not encrypt any data transfer after that. Other than that, the higher the level of encryption, the more secure the connection, but the slower it will be. The Citrix server must be configured to allow the selected encryption level or greater as the settings you pick for the client connection.

Figure 5.25 Setting the client encryption level

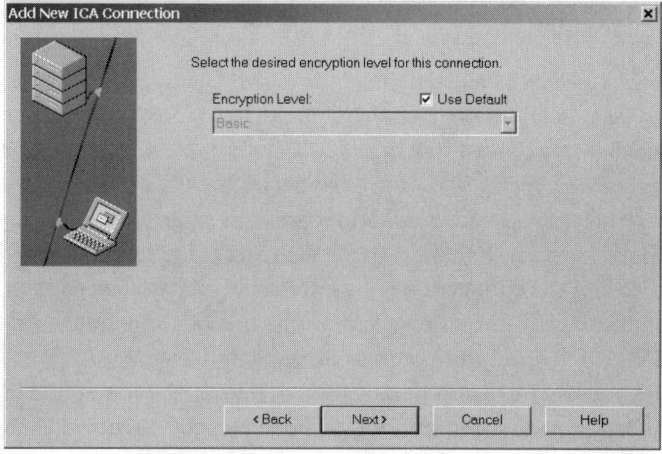

NOTE FR1 for MetaFrame XP supports RC5 (40-bit) encryption. If you use the 40-bit encryption supported with FR1, you cannot use automatic logon to the MetaFrame server.

6. Next (unless you chose 40-bit encryption), the wizard will prompt you for your logon credentials as in Figure 5.26 and, if you set up the ICA client with this option, a box to check to use the local logon information. Logging on explicitly is more secure and makes it easier to copy ICA connection configuration from one computer to another, but if you're more concerned with ease of use than security, pass-through authorization is a good idea. This option is disabled here because, when I installed ICA, I set it up to not use pass-through authentication. To have the option of pass-through encryption, I'd need to have enabled it when installing the ICA client.

Figure 5.26 Providing logon data (or at least pass-through authentication) makes ICA sessions easier to use.

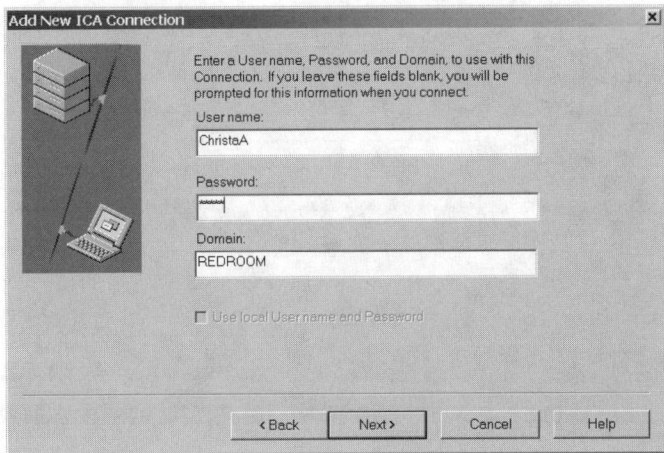

7. The wizard will next prompt you for the size of window and color depth you want to use. As you can see in Figure 5.27, by default the ICA client connection window will be 75 percent of the screen size and use a True Color display. To change either of these settings, uncheck the Use Default box and select your options from the list. You cannot configure a custom ICA connection to use Seamless Windows, just with published applications or desktops, described in Chapter 7. However, you *can't* use a video mode the MetaFrame server won't support. If you set up a connection to run in full-screen mode but the server can't support the resolution the client's using, when you connect you'll see an error message telling you that the requested video mode was not available and telling you what video mode the session is using instead. For example, on one client that supports 1400×1050, the ICA session displayed at 1212×863.

8. Next, if you want the server to display only a single application (and then close the ICA connection if the user closes that application), provide a path here. You'll need to know the exact path information, formatted with absolute paths as in Figure 5.28. As with connecting to a single application for an RDP connection, you can't browse for the app because you're not connected to the MetaFrame server. That Browse button only works if the application is located in a folder that's shared with the network.

That's it. (Finally.) Now, review your choices if need be, then click Finish to complete the process and add an icon for this connection to the Citrix program group or Program Neighborhood. To start that connection, you'll just double-click on it and log on as prompted if you didn't include name and password settings in the ICA connection setup.

Figure 5.27 Choosing a window size and resolution for an ICA session

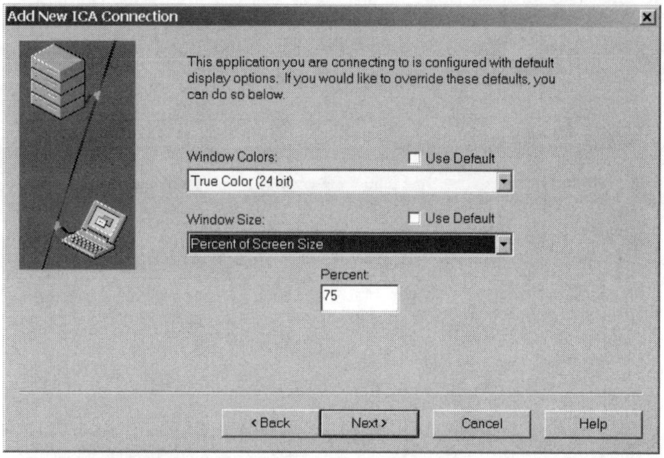

Figure 5.28 You can opt to run a single application instead of a desktop.

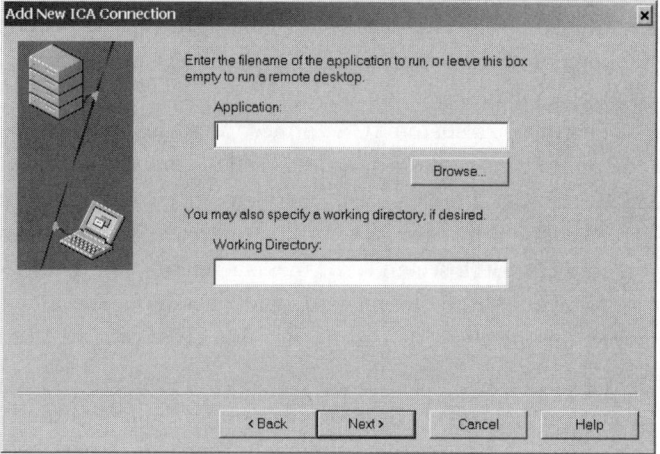

Setting Up and Creating Connections on a Windows Terminal

Setting up a Windows terminal for the first time is pretty simple. It's largely a matter of plugging everything in (power supply, monitor, network connection, mouse, and keyboard) and supplying the information the terminal needs to interact with the terminal server. For this example, I'll set up a Windows CE–based Windows terminal on a LAN. Although some Windows have more options from others (for example, NCD thin clients have an extra Management tab and Wyse clients have some additional security options that other terminals don't have), the basic setup information required is pretty much the same on all CE-based Windows terminals.

> **NOTE** Setting up Linux-based Windows terminals gets a bit more complicated. Sadly, there is no standardized way of doing this, so you'll need to peruse your Linux terminal's documentation for instructions. You'll be providing much the same information to the Linux-based terminal that you're providing to the Windows-based terminal, but the *way* that you'll present the data depends on the terminal's Linux distribution. I've seen four different models for setting up Linux-based Windows terminals—three GUIs and one command-line—and none of them were organized like the CE-based terminal settings.

Tuning Terminal Settings

When you first get a Windows terminal fresh from the manufacturer, it's unlikely to have all the settings enabled that you'll want to use. Some terminals, such as NCD's, will walk you through a short wizard to help you configure DHCP settings, display resolution and refresh rate, and network speed, and help you set up an initial connection. Other terminals will come preconfigured, even including a default RDP and ICA setting that you'll need to tweak to connect to *your* terminal servers. To edit a terminal's general settings, turn the terminal on, wait for its Connection Manager to appear, and then press F2 to open the Terminal Properties dialog box, a series of tabs. Again, the tabs you see depend on the model of terminal you're using, but the basic tabs described in Table 5.3 are standard on all CE-based Windows terminals.

Table 5.3 Location of Standard Windows Terminal Configuration Settings

Setting	Properties Tab
Return to factory default settings	General
Keyboard language, character repeat, mouse properties	Input
General device version and RAM information	General
Desktop display and screen saver settings	Display
DHCP settings, network speed	Network

Table 5.3 Location of Standard Windows Terminal Configuration Settings *(continued)*

Setting	Properties Tab
Terminal name (for management purposes)	Network
Printer installation	Printers
Touch screen settings (if any)	Input
Security settings	Security or Administration (depends on the terminal)
Inventory information for software and hardware	Inventory or SysInfo (depends on the terminal)

Some of these settings may be on different tabs than the ones I've listed here, if they're not controlled by Microsoft's rules for how CE-based Windows terminals must be organized. Some terminals will have settings that others will not—a terminal that does not support touch screen input will not have any touch screen settings. However, most standard settings are on the same tabs on the CE-based Windows terminals from three different manufacturers that I've been using lately.

Creating New RDP Connections

Some Windows terminals come with default connections that you can tweak, but others require that you create all connections yourself. To create a new connection, follow these steps:

1. Choose a name for the new connection and the name of the terminal server to which you're connecting. If you're using a dial-up connection instead of a LAN, be sure to check the Low-Speed Connection box so that RDP will compress the data. Bitmap caching is not an option, because terminals don't have hard disks.

2. To configure the terminal for automatic logon to the terminal server session, fill in the name, password, and domain of the person using the terminal. If you leave this section blank, you'll have to explicitly log on each time you connect to the terminal server. For tighter security, leave it blank; if it doesn't matter whether someone can log on to the terminal server, you can set it up for automatic logon.

3. Choose whether you want the terminal server session to display a Desktop or run a single application. Once again, there's no browse function, so you need to know the name and path (from the server's perspective) of any application you choose. If you don't provide the correct path information, the connection will fail.

At this point, the connection is set up and you're ready to go. The Connection Manager displays a list of the available connections. To use one, select it and click the Connect button. You'll see the usual blue logon screen (assuming you didn't set up the connection for an automatic logon). Type your name and password, and you're in.

Creating a New ICA Connection

Creating an ICA connection is almost identical to creating an RDP connection, allowing for the differences in the two protocols. From the Configure tab of the terminal's main screen, click the Add button, and choose Citrix ICA Connection from the drop-down list. Choose a connection type (Network or Dial-Up are the options), and the terminal will send out an ICA broadcast looking for MetaFrame servers. Assuming that you have the right DHCP settings and subnet mask, the terminal will respond with a list of available servers (if you click Citrix Server) or available published applications (if you click Published Application).

> **TIP** The ICA client for CE supports server grouping, therefore, if you'd like to minimize ICA broadcasts on the network, you can use the same grouping technique that we discussed earlier for the Win32 ICA client.

When you pick a server to connect to and click Next, you'll be prompted for a name for the connection. Supply it and click Next to (optionally) provide path information, if you want the session to display only a single application, not an entire desktop. (Of course, another, simpler, option would be to connect to a published application.) Next, supply logon credentials if you'd like to automate the connection, as well as the color depth for the session.

> **NOTE** The CE-compatible ICA clients on the terminals I have come with a maximum color depth of 256 colors, not the 64-bit color possible with the Win32 ICA client.

Finally, choose whether you'd like to use compression and whether or not you'd like to enable sound, and finally end by setting up any required use of SOCKs or network address translation to deal with a firewall. When you're done, click Finish. The new connection will appear on the Connections and Configure tabs with its display protocol displayed; to use it, turn to Connections and double-click.

Setting Up a Handheld PC

The Pocket PC 2002 comes with an RDP client pre-installed, but to use a handheld PC (H/PC) to connect to a terminal server, you must first install the RDP client on the H/PC and then create a session on the client. To get the client, go to the Microsoft website and navigate to the Downloads section of the WinCE section. You'll have to go through some screens where you agree that you understand that having the RDP client installed does not imply that you're licensed to access a terminal server. (There's also a link to a place where you can buy more licenses if needed.) Download the 1MB-client setup program (hpcrdp.exe) to the Desktop partner of the H/PC.

> **NOTE** As of this writing, the Windows CE RDP client is located at www.microsoft.com/mobile/downloads/ts.asp, but it may have moved by the time you read this. It's also on your Win2K Server CD in the \valueadd\msft\mgmt\mstsc_hpc directory.

To install the RDP client on the H/PC, follow these steps.

1. Turn on the H/PC, and connect it to the Desktop partner. Make sure that they're connected.
2. Run hpcrdp.exe to start the Installation Wizard.
3. Click Yes to agree to the EULA.
4. Choose an installation folder for the client on the Desktop partner. The default location is a subfolder of the Windows CE Services folder, which you'll have installed in the course of partnering the desktop machine and the H/PC.
5. The installation program will start copying the files to the H/PC. This may take a few minutes if you're using the sync cable instead of a network connection—a sync cable is a serial connection.
6. Once the files have been copied, click Finish on the Desktop side to end the Setup program.

To set up a connection, go to the H/PC and look in Start/Programs/Terminal Server Client. There are two options here: the Client Connection Wizard and the Terminal Server Client.

To use the default connection settings, click the Terminal Server Client and type the name or IP address of the terminal server to which you want to connect. Click the Connect button, and the client will search for that terminal server. You'll need to log on as if you were logging onto the server or domain.

For a little more control over the connection settings, run the Client Connection Wizard. You don't have as many options as you do when running the similar wizard for the PC client, but you can specify a connection name, provide your username and password for automatic logon, and choose whether to run an application or display the entire Desktop. Click the Finish button, and the wizard will put a shortcut to that connection on your H/PC's Desktop.

Updating Client Display Protocols

We've discussed how to install RDP and ICA once on a PC or handheld PC. The clients come preinstalled on Windows terminals. But from time to time, Microsoft and Citrix come out with new versions of their display protocols that have new capabilities the older clients don't have. Do you really have to go through the whole process again to get the new versions of the display protocols on the client computers? Are you stuck with the versions of the display protocols on the Windows terminals you have?

The answers, respectively, are "Maybe" and "No." When it comes to updating PCs, upgrading ICA clients is definitely easier. MetaFrame XP maintains an ICA Client database that you can update. When a client computer connects to the application server with ICA, the version of the ICA client is compared with that in the database. If the database version is more recent, then (depending on how you've configured it) it can either ignore the discrepancy, ask the user if they'd like to install the newer version of ICA, or just go ahead and install without asking. Windows Terminal Services does not have a similar feature for RDP. If you have a newer version of RDP available, you'll need to install it either by hand or automatically, using one of the techniques we've already discussed.

One of the reasons to get Windows terminals is to exit the upgrade rat race, so you'll be glad to know that you can update the display protocols on the terminals, using management software designed to work with the terminals. *How* you'll do this depends on the management software you're using. However, the basic idea will be downloading the new client from Microsoft or Citrix, or getting it from the terminals' manufacturer, packaging it up, and then distributing the package to the terminals for automatic installation. Just make sure that you thoroughly test any new clients before you disseminate them, to avoid any problems with buggy early versions. (Come to think of it, that caveat applies to *any* display protocol, regardless of the hardware platform on which it's running.)

Editing Server-Side Session Settings

Everything's ready to go on the client side, but you may still have some work to do to get the server side configured. The following are optional—but useful—settings that allow you to define how long a session may last, determine whether someone can take remote control of a user's terminal session, define how the display protocol is configured, and input client path and profile information. The location of these settings depends on whether you're editing RDP settings or ICA. If the former, then the settings are part of user account properties. If the latter, then you'll need to use some Citrix tools available when you install MetaFrame XP.

Configuring RDP Settings

You can configure RDP settings on both a per-user and per-protocol basis. Here's how.

Account-Level Settings

Individual RDP settings are in different places if you've set up the member accounts on the terminal server itself (as a member server) or are editing the main user database on a Win2K domain controller. If the former, the settings will be in the Local Users and Groups section of the Computer Management tool in the Administrative Tools folder. If the latter, the settings will be in the Active Directory Users and Computers tool in the Administrative Tools folder. In this example, I'll use the Active Directory Users and Groups tool. The settings for user accounts in the Local Users and Groups option are the same as the ones in the user accounts stored in the Active Directory, the only difference being that the Active Directory account properties have tabs related to user contact information.

> **NOTE** If you're using NT4 domain controllers to store user accounts, then you'll need to copy the usrmgr tool from the Windows 2000 installation CD and copy it to the domain controller to make the Terminal Services-specific settings available.

Open the Users folder, find the user you want, right-click it, and choose the Properties item. This properties page controls all user settings, so I'll concentrate on the settings that apply to Terminal Services.

> **NOTE** Unfortunately, in Windows 2000, you have to configure all user settings—for Terminal Services and in general—individually, rather than configuring settings for groups or organizational units. (Terminal Services Configuration allows you to edit all settings and override the user-specific settings, but you can't apply protocol-wide settings with any discretion.) This is not the way that you'd apply settings in a perfect world, but that's the way it is. This is fixed in .NET Server, allowing you to use group policies to apply these user settings to organizational units.

Remote Control The ability to take remote control of a user's session comes in handy when troubleshooting time comes. With remote control, you don't need to blindly talk someone through a series of commands ("OK, find the Programs folder. Got it? Now look for the icon that says 'Microsoft Word.' ") You can take over the session, manipulating it from your session while also displaying it for the user. The person whose session you're controlling will be able to see exactly how the task is completed, and it will be done for them.

The settings for the kind of remote control that you can take are defined on the Remote Control tab of each user's properties pages, shown in Figure 5.29.

Figure 5.29 Setting remote control options for taking over user sessions

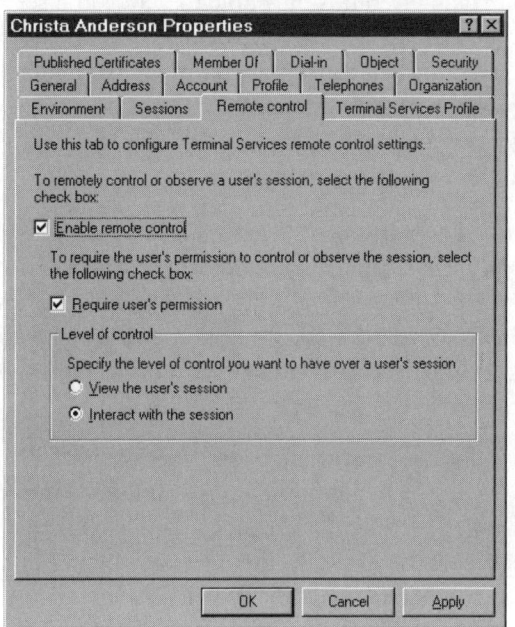

First, you must specify whether remote control is even permitted for the session (by default, you can take control of any session, no matter what rights the owner of the session has). Specify also whether the user whose session is being shadowed must permit the action before the remote control can begin. If you choose this option, the person who originated the session will see a message box telling them that such and such person of such and such domain is attempting to control their session, offering the chance to accept or refuse the control.

> **NOTE** If a user refuses the remote control connection, you can't control or view the session even from an account with Administrator privileges.

The final option on this tab determines what kind of control you can have over this user's session. For troubleshooting purposes, you'll find it most useful to be able to interact with the session, so you can actually show the user how to do something (or just do it for them). Choosing this option means that both the original user and the person with remote control over the session can send mouse clicks and keystrokes to the terminal server for interpretation. Graphical output is displayed on both the original session and the remote control view of the session.

If you choose the option to view the user's session, the person remotely controlling the session isn't really controlling it, but is only able to watch and see what the original user is doing. The person who set up remote control can't use the mouse or keyboard with the remotely controlled session. This could potentially be a troubleshooting tool if you're trying to find out exactly what someone's doing wrong and help them correct it, while making sure that you can't interfere. Most often, however, I find the option to take control of the session more useful than the ability to watch.

Session Time-Outs The status of a client session isn't a binary proposition. Rather than On/Off, the state of a client session may be active, disconnected, or reset. An *active* session is what it sounds like: a session that's actively in use. In a *disconnected* session, the client has shut off the client interface to the session, but the session—and all its applications—is still running on the server. When a client *resets* a session with the Logoff command, the session ends and all applications in the session are shut down.

Although the distinction may not sound significant at first, it's important. When clients disconnect from their sessions, all their data is still loaded into memory and their applications are running, exactly as they left them. This means that a client can disconnect while going to lunch and, therefore, secure the session without having to start over. The only catch to a disconnected session is that it still uses up processor cycles and some memory because the session thread still gets its crack at the processor and because all the user data is still active. However, as the data stops being accessed, Win2K will swap it out to the paging file on the hard disk and replace it in physical memory with more recent data. When the client reconnects to the session and tries to use the data, the data will be paged back in. The still-running client session won't impact available network bandwidth much because the terminal server will detect that the session is idle and stop sending video updates to the client machine.

If a user attempts to reconnect to the terminal server with more than one disconnected session running, a dialog box will display the disconnected sessions, their resolution, and the length of time that they've been disconnected. The user can then pick the session to reconnect. If the user doesn't pick a session in a minute or so, the highlighted session will be reestablished. The other session will remain on the terminal server, still in its inactive state.

Win2K gives you the option of controlling how long a session may stay active, how long it may stay disconnected without being terminated, how long active but idle sessions may stay active before they're disconnected, and even whether a particular user may connect to the server at all. These settings are controlled from the Sessions tab, as shown in Figure 5.30.

Figure 5.30 Configuring session connection settings

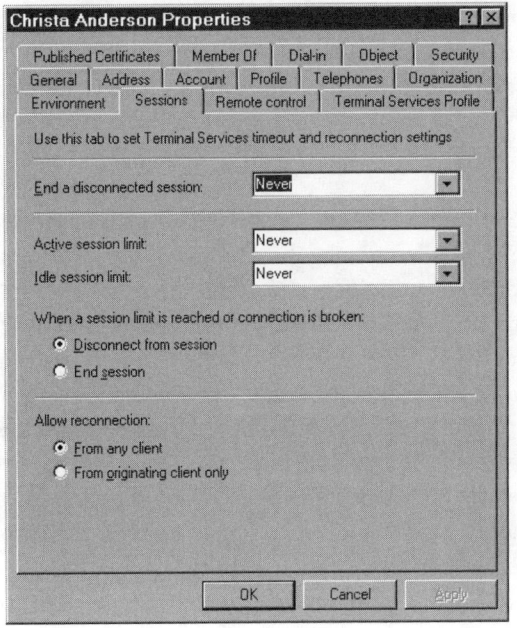

You can control how long the setting may remain active before being disconnected or terminated. If you want to prevent people from forgetting to log out from their terminal session at the end of the day or at lunch, use this setting.

As I already discussed, a disconnected session still uses up some application server resources—in the page file if nowhere else. This is by design, so that users can reconnect to a session and have all their applications and data still loaded. However, if a session is permanently abandoned, there's no point in leaving it up. Choose a time-out period that reflects the amount of time you're willing to give a user to get back and use their connection before their applications are all closed.

You can determine also how long a session can be idle before being disconnected or terminated. This isn't quite the same setting as the first one, which limits connection time whether or not the session is still getting input. Rather, this setting limits the amount of time that a session can be idle before being shut down. This setting is a little more useful in most cases, given that the session must be unused for a certain period before it is shut down.

The default for all three settings is Never, meaning there's no restriction on how long a session may be running, disconnected, or idle. The maximum time-out period is two days.

> **TIP** If you want to gather some statistics about how long people are staying logged on or how long disconnected sessions are remaining idle on the server, you can get this information from the Terminal Services Manager. System Monitor can tell you how many active or inactive sessions are currently running on a given terminal server.

The settings on the bottom of the tab determine how disconnected and reestablished connections should be handled. You may have noticed that two of the time-out options gave you the choice of disconnecting or terminating the session at the end of the time-out session, but no option for specifying which it should be—disconnection or resetting the connection. The answer depends on whether you pick Disconnect (the default) or End (which resets the connection) for broken or timed-out connections. The other option controls how users may reconnect to disconnected sessions. By default, they can reconnect to their client session from any client machine, but you can specify that users may only reestablish the connection from the same machine from which they started. If this option is selected and they try to reconnect from a different client machine, they'll start a new session and their current session will still be running on the terminal server. If a user has more than one disconnected session running on the same terminal server, they'll have a choice of which session they want to use when they reconnect. The session(s) not chosen will continue to run on the terminal server.

Setting Client Path Information   Win2K spreads per-user files all over the place. Unless you specify otherwise, user home directories are in subfolders of the terminal server's Profiles folder and are identified by username. Their temporary directories are subfolders of the terminal server's temporary directory and identified by session ID. To keep all per-user information in a single place, you may want to specify a new home directory. This will give you a fighting chance of applying per-user system quotas and keeping all files in one place for easier recovery—not to mention keeping the home directories off the terminal server, which could ultimately take up a lot of room.

Roaming profiles are stored on a profile server instead of a local machine, so the user can log on with the same settings wherever she connects to the network. The other option is locally stored profiles, stored on the computer where they're displayed. When a profile is applied, it makes per-user changes (applying only to that user) to the Registry of the computer the person is logged onto. So far, this is the same as NT profiles have been for years.

With Terminal Services, the profiles still work more or less the same way. They may still be stored either locally or on a profile server—but in this case *locally* means on the terminal server. As you probably know, you must use a profile with Win2K—if you don't specify one, you'll get the Default User profile.

You have a couple of options when it comes to profiles and Terminal Services. If you only provide a path for the user profile, then that path applies to both "normal" user settings and settings for terminal sessions that the user starts up. Filling in only the information the Profile tab in a user's profile will have this effect—the person will have the same profile path and home directory for terminal sessions as they do normally.

Making the same profile do double duty may sound like a good plan, but in most cases it's not. What works well when logging on from a Win2K Pro computer may not work well when logging onto a terminal session. For one example, the screensaver you might use without a second thought on Win2K Pro is a resource-draining vanity in a terminal session. For another, the colors that look great in a 16-million color environment look odd when the maximum color depth is 256 colors. Both color scheme and preferred screensaver are part of the profile. For another, using the same profile for both ordinary sessions and terminal sessions leaves you exposed to lost profile changes. Consider how profiles work. When you open a profile and make changes to it, those changes are stored locally and aren't written back to the profile server until you log out. So what happens if you have two copies open, make a change in one and then log out, then make a change in the other copy and then log out? Right—you lose all the changes made to the first one because the copy you saved last to the profile server overwrote the copy you saved first. This can happen any time you open a profile more than once—it's not just a problem with Terminal Services—but you're not likely to log on two or more times when you're logging on to the domain from a fat client. Log on to both the fat client (since you needed to log on to the domain to get to a computer from which you could run the terminal session) and to the terminal server, and you immediately have two copies open. For these reasons, it's probably best to use different profiles for terminal sessions and fat client sessions.

How about roaming profiles for terminal sessions, if those profiles are different from the ordinary user profiles? This may still not be a good idea because of the possibility that you'll have multiple copies of your profile open at once. Particularly, if your terminal session is set up to only serve applications and you use more than one application, you're likely to open multiple copies of your profile at the same time.

So does this mean that local profiles are the way to go? Nope—not if you have many users to support and those users won't always log on to the same server. When you use local profiles, they're stored on the terminal server. If you have 60 users, each with his or her own profile, and you can't predict which of four servers those 60 users will connect to, you've got to store those 60 profiles on each server. That's a lot of room to munch up on the terminal server's system drive. It can also lead to inconsistency in the user environment if a user changes his profile on one server and not on another. If you're using load balancing of any kind, it's especially important that you don't keep user profiles locally because doing so would mean that people would never know which profile they'd get.

For this reason, the best plan might be to use mandatory profiles, which are just ordinary profiles with a .man extension. Users can edit mandatory profiles to the degree their system policies allow them to, but those changes won't be saved to the server. This may limit the user experience, perhaps; however, if you use mandatory profiles with terminal sessions, you avoid the problems of lost profile edits from multiple copies of the profile being opened. To specify a profile location, set the path location for the Terminal Services profile from each user's properties pages, as shown in Figure 5.31.

Figure 5.31 Specify the path to the user profile and home directory in the Terminal Services Profile tab.

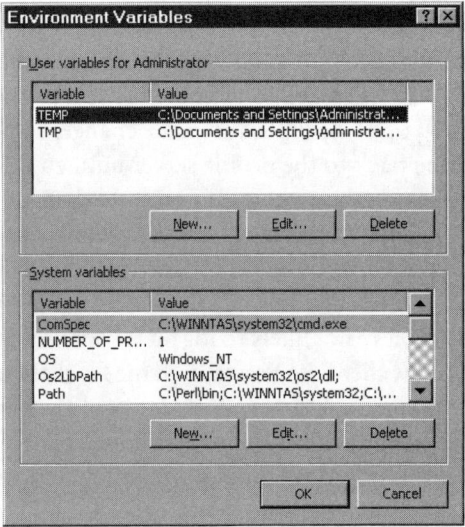

The Allow Logon to Terminal Server check box controls whether the person is permitted to log on to the terminal server at all. By default, anyone with an account on the domain or server may do so.

Command-Line Updates to Profile Information

To change or set user profile information for one user account is no big deal: Open Active Directory Users and Computers, open the user account's Properties sheet, turn to the Terminal Services Profile tab, and make the change. Multiply this procedure by 50, 500, or 5,000 users, however, and it gets more difficult. ADSI doesn't expose the Terminal Services profile path for user accounts, so you can't use VBScript to programmatically change user account profile information. However, all is not lost. You can make these edits with the `tsprof` command-line tool.

Command-Line Updates to Profile Information *(continued)*

Tsprof supports three actions: You can update account profile information, you can copy it to another user account, or you can query a user account to make sure your changes took or see what the current profile settings are. The basic syntax for these commands looks like this:

```
TSPROF /UPDATE [/DOMAIN:domainname|/LOCAL] /PROFILE:<path> username

TSPROF /COPY    [/DOMAIN:domainname|/LOCAL] [/PROFILE:<path>] sourceuser destinationuser

TSPROF /Q       [/DOMAIN:domainname|/LOCAL] username
```

Make sure you don't include extra spaces in the command, or you could accidentally query the domain name as though it were a username.

For example, say that my Terminal Services users don't have session-explicit user accounts; they're using the same accounts they typically use to log on to the domain. The profile settings that work well for a full-color session on a single-user computer might not translate well to a terminal session, so I want to edit that account information to C:\profiles. I can do so from the command line, like this:

```
tsprof /update /domain:redroom /profile:c:\profiles\profile.man christa
```

In this example, the user account is in the REDROOM domain, the profile path is C:\profiles, and the user account I'm editing is named Christa. This command will spit back the following information:

```
Terminal Services Profile Path for redroom\christa is { c:\profiles\profile.man }
```

If the curly brackets don't contain any information, I haven't set a Terminal Services profile for that user account. The /update argument doesn't tell you what the profile path information was *before* you changed it, so if you want to ensure that it needs to be updated, query the account. To perform the query, use the /q argument, like this:

```
tsprof /q /domain:labrynth christa
```

If you used `tsprof` with TSE, notice that the command now is /q, not /query. The command changed in Windows 2000.

> **Command-Line Updates to Profile Information** *(continued)*
>
> Finally, you can copy profile-path information from one account to another. The /copy command works similar to /update, except you must provide the source and destination account names, in this case, Christa and Vera, respectively:
>
>   Tsprof /copy /domain:redroom christa vera
>
> The system will now copy Christa's profile account information to Vera's user account; if I query Vera's account, the profile information will be there.

Be careful when you use these tools. Tsprof can't tell whether a profile path is valid any more than the graphical user account management tools can; tsprof will enter whatever information you give it. If the account name is invalid, tsprof will generate an error when it attempts to update the information:

    Failed setting User Configuration, Error = 1332 (0x534)

However, it won't show any problems when you perform a query.

Defining the Session Environment   The Environment tab in the properties pages (see Figure 5.32) sets the Terminal Services environment for the user, replacing any related settings (such as an application to run at logon) that might already appear in a user's client logon settings. If you want to automatically run an application at logon, type its path in the Program File Name box (sadly, there's no browse function). The working directory goes in the Start In box. Notice that supplying the name of an application does not limit the terminal server session to only running that application and then ending when the application is terminated. All this does is run the application when the session starts—the main Desktop still remains available. If you want to provide a terminal session running only a single application, and then closing when that application closes, you'll need to set that up when configuring the client connections, as described earlier in this chapter.

The settings in the Client Devices section at the bottom of this tab don't all apply to Win2K clients. The first one, Connect Client Drives at Logon, applies only to sessions where remapping client drives for use in terminal server sessions is enabled—meaning that it *doesn't* apply to RDP5 sessions. The printing options, however, do apply to RDP5 clients. Checking Connect Client Printers at Logon specifies that any printers mapped from the terminal server session should be reconnected. Default to Main Client Printer specifies that the client should use its own default printer, not the one defined for the terminal server.

Figure 5.32 You can choose to map all or no client-side devices to terminal sessions.

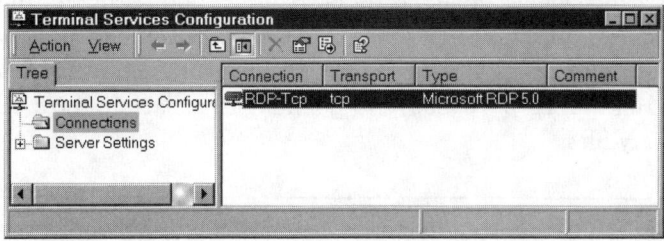

Setting the Location of Temporary Directories Rather than using the default location for user temporary files, you can specify a new one in the user's home directory. Unlike the other settings we've discussed, this one is not set from the user properties pages. Instead, you'll use the `flattemp` command and edit user system settings.

First, log on as the user for whom you're making the change and open the System applet in the Control Panel. Turn to the Advanced tab, and click the Environment Variables button to open the dialog box shown in Figure 5.33.

Figure 5.33 Editing the location of temporary files

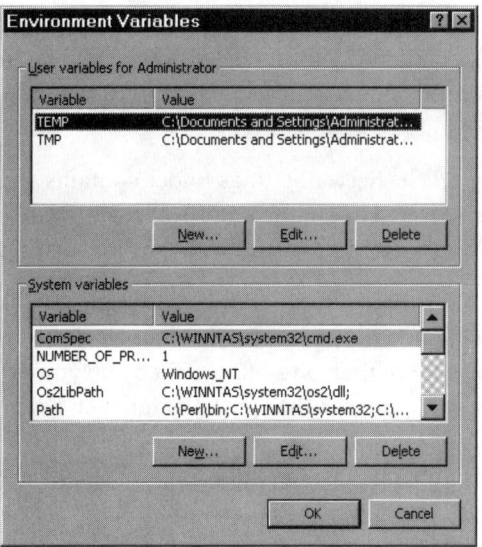

TIP Rather than logging on as the person whose environment you're editing, you can remotely control a terminal server session that that person is running. This allows you to edit their settings as though you were that person.

Double-click the values of TEMP and TMP, and type the new location in the dialog box that appears. When you've done this for every user, you're ready for the next step. From the command line, run `flattemp /enable`. This will tell Win2K to point all users either to a single temporary directory or to one specified for them in the System applet. To reverse this, run `flattemp /disable` to point all users back to the default location for their temporary files.

> **WARNING** If user home directories are located on a network share instead of on the terminal server, you'll be vulnerable to application errors if an application attempts to write to the temporary directory when there's a network error. This won't hurt the disk volume, but the application will respond as it would if the disk had died, and you may lose data. You can avoid this problem by keeping terminal server home directories on the terminal server, but you'll end up with a lot of data clogging up the server. Sadly, you can't use Offline Files with a terminal session. As you no doubt have noticed if your office keeps a community laptop for people to take on the road, Offline Files is a machine-specific setting.

Configuring RDP for All Connections

You can configure general settings for all Terminal Services connections from the Terminal Services Configuration tool in the Administrative Tools folder. If you're running Terminal Services alone, you'll have only the RDP connection in this folder; if you have other multiuser Windows components added (like MetaFrame's ICA protocol, or direct video streaming), they'll be in the folder as well.

What can you do here? The Server Settings folder contains settings that apply to all connections made to the server. The Connections folder shows all installed display protocols (if you're running Win2K only, then RDP will be the only object in this folder).

> **NOTE** Win2K supports only one RDP connection per network adapter. If your terminal server has more than one NIC installed and you're using RDP with both of them, you can configure the RDP protocol for each adapter separately.

The Server Settings Folder The Server Settings folder (see Figure 5.34) contains options that control the creation and deletion of per-session temporary files and the types of access permitted to the terminal server. The options here are identical whether the server is set up to be an ordinary server with remote administration capabilities or an application server.

Figure 5.34 The Server Settings folder for a terminal server in Application Server mode

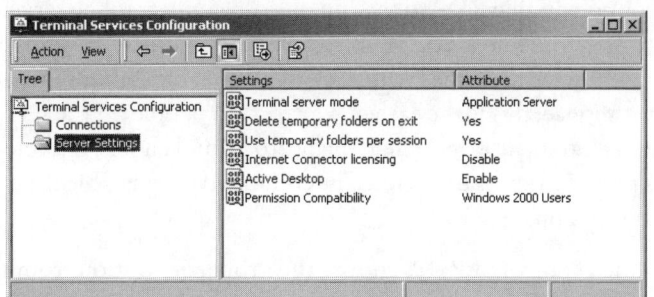

As discussed in Chapter 4, the terminal server mode indicates what kind of access is permitted to the terminal server. The server may be set up as an application server or as an ordinary server that can be remotely administered. Application servers permit as many users as you have licenses for to run terminal sessions on the server. Remote Administration mode is for administrative work only. (Well, mostly. It's also a more-or-less free way of giving two people access to a test server, if you're interested in development work and don't mind them having Administrator-level access to the server.)

Deleting the temporary folders on exit means that when a user logs out of a terminal server session, the temporary folder they used—and all the TMP files in it—is deleted. This setting, set to Yes by default, keeps the terminal server from getting cluttered with TMP files, and it ensures that those files are only deleted when they're no longer needed. Using temporary folders per session means that a separate TMP folder will be created for each session started, with those new folders (identified by Session ID) being placed by default in subfolders to the main Win2K Temporary Files directory.

The Internet Connector licensing option affects *all* terminal server sessions, not just those that come through the Internet, so only enable this option for terminal servers accepting only Internet connections. Frankly, the useful application I've seen for this license type is for ISVs offering their software via the Web for people to sample on an anonymous basis. Even application service providers (ASPs) have a different licensing scheme.

The second-to-last option lets you turn off Active Desktop on the terminal server sessions. Unless you really need it for some reason, I'd turn it off and save the resources. Finally, you can choose the type of permissions you want to apply to this terminal server: TSE 4 file access is compatible with all applications (but may leave some system folders vulnerable to changes from user applications) or Win2K file access that may not work with all applications (because it denies permissions to some system folders) but does not allow users—or applications—to tamper with those files.

The Connections Folder Use the Connections folder to configure protocol-wide settings. First, you can disable RDP so that no one can connect to the server—something you might want to do if you know you're going to be taking the server down for maintenance and don't want to have to bother with kicking people off. Because you can't turn off the terminal server service, this is the easiest way to keep people off the server while still keeping it running. To do so, just right-click the protocol and choose Disable Connection from the All Tasks part of the pop-up menu. The command to re-enable the connection is in the same All Tasks section.

For more detailed control of RDP, choose the Properties option from the pop-up menu. Most settings in the RDP-T dialog box work the same way as their counterparts in the per-user connection settings, which normally take precedence. For a more uniform set of protocol configurations, you may edit the settings here and check the boxes that tell the protocol properties not to inherit their settings according to the user. The two settings that aren't configurable on a per-user basis control security are found on the General and Permissions tabs.

The General tab shown in Figure 5.35 controls the degree of encryption used with RDP.

Figure 5.35 Configuring RDP access security

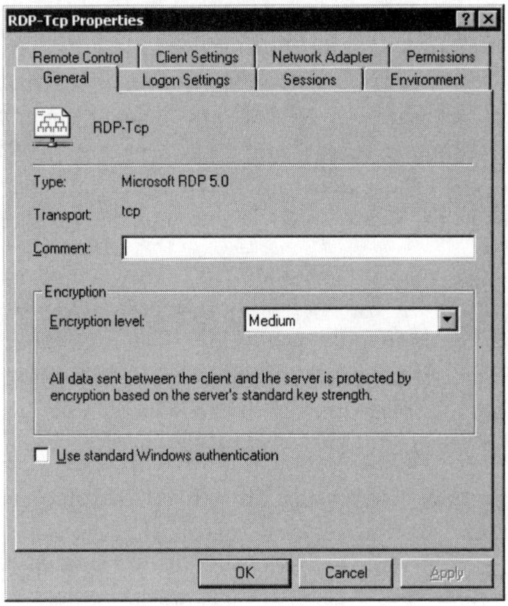

By default, the protocol is set for Medium encryption, meaning that all communications between client and server are encrypted with the standard 40-bit algorithm (56-bit if the client is running Win2K Professional). Low encryption only protects communications from the client to the server—not the other way around. High encryption protects communications in both directions with 128-bit encryption. The level of encryption depends on the server—the RDP client will negotiate the security level that the server's using.

> **TIP** The greater the level of encryption, the worse the session performance will be, due to the encryption/decryption overhead at both ends of the connection. Only use Medium or High encryption over slow networks if you're concerned about the signal being intercepted.

You don't need to worry about the Use Standard Windows Authentication check box unless you've installed a third-party authentication package on the server. In that case, checking this box tells Win2K to use its native authentication scheme to validate terminal session user logons, rather than using the third-party package. If you have a third-party Gina.dll file installed, however, you'll want to be sure you've applied SP2 to the Windows 2000 terminal server; otherwise the server will use the third-party authentication package for console logons regardless of your settings.

Those familiar with the NT/Win2K argot will remember that you secure a Win2K network by defining user rights for what people can *do* on the network and setting permissions for the resources that people can *use*. Terminal Services security is controlled with permissions, on a per-group or per-user basis.

Editing ICA Settings

Once the ICA client is installed, it will work, but there is some server and client-side tuning that you might want to do.

Client-Side ICA Settings

On the client side, there's not a lot to be done. If you go into the Program Neighborhood and choose Tools ➢ ICA Settings, you'll open a tabbed dialog box like the one in Figure 5.36.

You won't need to edit most of the settings here. The Bitmap Cache tab controls the size and location of the bitmap cache—a small area on the client computer's hard disk where the ICA client stores frequently used bitmaps so that it doesn't have to keep downloading them from the MetaFrame server. The Hotkeys tab sets the hotkeys used to control menu selections from within the MetaFrame session. Event Logging controls the way that connections and errors are logged to a client-side file, stored by default in C:\Documents and Settings\%UserName%\Application Data\ICAClient\wfcwin32.log.

Figure 5.36 Some ICA settings are adjustable on a per-client basis.

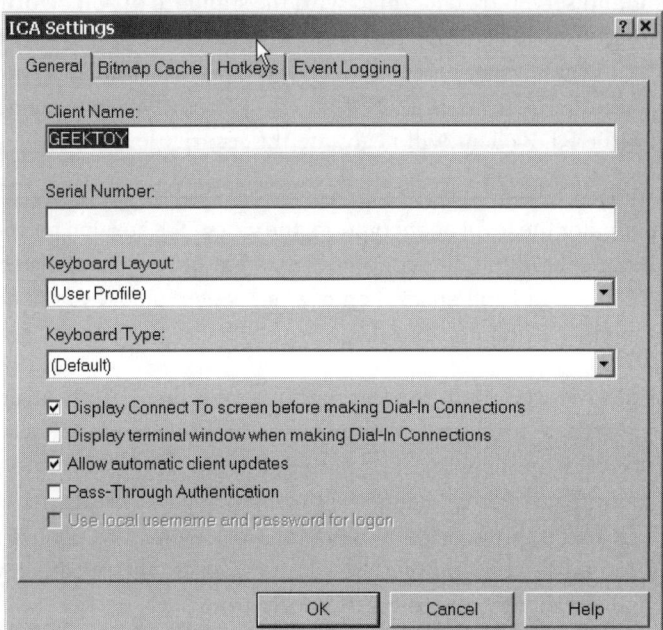

If you spend much time on the client-side ICA settings at all, you'll probably spend it on the General tab, where you can edit some of the settings you applied while installing the ICA client and add a few more. For example, the Windows 2000 user account Properties sheet displays an option wherein users may only reconnect disconnected sessions from the same computer from which the session was originally started. You can set this option from the Sessions tab of a user's account properties or on a global basis for the ICA protocol as a whole from Terminal Services Configuration. However, this setting will only have an effect if a client serial number is entered on the General tab. Similarly, you can change the settings on this tab to permit pass-through authentication for single sign-on, even if you didn't enable it when you originally set up ICA.

The Program Neighborhood Agent requires even less configuring because most of the configuration information is on the server. If you right-click on the agent's icon in the System Tray, you'll see a Properties entry in the context menu. Open it, and you'll see a three-tabbed sheet: Server, Application Display, and ICA Options.

> **TIP** You can edit the server-side configuration settings to disable some or all of these tabs, or to add the (normally disabled) Application Refresh tab.

From the Server tab, you can view the server location that the agent is pointing to, or click the Browse button to enter a new server. (An NFuse server can be backed by more than one MetaFrame server, so using the agent does not disable load balancing.) This tab also has the password settings for the agent: Prompt user, which provides a normal log-in screen; Pass-through authentication, which uses the login credentials that the user already provided to log onto the domain; Smart-card logon, which prompts the user to swipe a card; and Smart-card pass-through authentication, which uses smart-card credentials. Even if you enabled single sign on when installing the agent, the default is Prompt user.

> **NOTE** As the administrator, you can edit the server-side configuration settings to enable a fifth option: Anonymous logon. This option is disabled by default.

The Application Display tab controls the placement of icons linking the user to published content and applications: on the Start menu (or in a Programs folder off the Start button), in a desktop folder which you can name, and/or in the System Tray. Personally, I prefer putting the icons in folders on the Start menu so that applications are both easy to get to when you've got other applications open and don't clutter the System Tray, but you do have other options. By default, application icons appear in both the system tray and the Start menu.

Finally, the ICA Options tab contains settings for the size of the user window, the color depth, and the audio quality. All these settings are normally configured on the server, but you can override those settings here.

Server-Side ICA Settings

You can do a lot more ICA tuning from the server side. First, when publishing applications (as we'll discuss in Chapter 7), you can affect the way those applications are presented and encrypted. Second, using the Windows 2000 Terminal Services Administration tools, MetaFrame ICA graphical configuration tools, and some command-line utilities, you can direct the way that ICA sessions should present data and make client-side devices available. Table 5.4 shows which settings are available where.

Table 5.4 Terminal Setting Availability

Setting	Global Location	Per-User Location	Default Setting
Client Drive and Printer Mapping	Client Settings tab of ICA Properties (Terminal Services Configuration) and ICA Settings	Environment	Enabled

Table 5.4 Terminal Setting Availability *(continued)*

Setting	Global Location	Per-User Location	Default Setting
Client Disconnection and Reconnection Settings	Session tab of ICA Properties (Terminal Services Configuration)	Environment	Disconnect broken sessions rather than resetting them
Port Mapping	Client Settings tab of ICA Properties (Terminal Services Configuration)	None	Enabled
Clipboard Mapping	Client Settings tab of ICA Properties (Terminal Services Configuration)	None	Enabled
Idle Session Limits	Session tab of ICA Properties (Terminal Services Configuration)	Sessions	Never end idle sessions
Terminal Services Profile and Home Directory	N/None	Terminal Services Profile	None
Default to Main Client Printer	Environment tab of ICA Properties (Terminal Services Configuration)	Environment (User)	Enabled
Startup Program	Environment tab of ICA Properties (Terminal Services Configuration)	Environment (User)	None
Encryption Level	General tab of ICA Properties (Terminal Services Configuration)	ICA client settings	Basic

Table 5.4 Terminal Setting Availability *(continued)*

Setting	Global Location	Per-User Location	Default Setting
User Logon Settings	Logon tab of ICA Properties (Terminal Services Configuration)	In ICA client connection setup	No account information provided

Unless you explicitly choose to override them, client-specific settings control all options that exist on both a client and ICA-wide level.

In addition to the graphical tools used for tuning the ICA client, there are also a couple of command-line tools. One, change client, will display or edit the ICA client device and port mappings for terminal sessions. The other, icaport, changes the port to which ICA clients will connect. Anyone with administrative rights to the MetaFrame server (not the CMC, but the server) can run change client, but only Citrix Administrators can run icaport.

> **WARNING** If you change the ICA port on a MetaFrame server, you'll need to change the default port on all ICA clients that will connect to that server. Also, if you change the ICA port, you'll need to restart the server to establish the change.

If you're using FR2's NFuse 1.7. and Program Neighborhood Agent, you'll do server-side configuration with both the standard tools and by editing an XML file called config.xml, located in \Inetpub\wwwroot\Citrix\PNagent. When you first open this file, you may be intimidated by the mass of brackets. However, set Notepad to a large font so you don't go blind (I must be getting old) and look at the individual pieces, and you'll see that it's organized fairly logically.

> **WARNING** When you install NFuse 1.7, the installation will create two copies of this file: one in the normal location and a backup in \Program Files\Citrix\NFuse\BackedUpBy17. If you edit the file once in a way that works and later need to edit it again, *always* back up first. You're editing a text file, so it's easy to screw up, and there's no easy way to reverse changes once you've saved the file.

All the settings within config.xml are displayed as tags that look like HTML tags, except that instead of describing formatting settings (e.g. <title></title>) they describe configuration settings described in the schema associated with the XML document. The tagged configuration settings are nested; for example, the <ServerSettings> tag is subordinate to the

`<UserInterface>` tag. The tags can contain only a single value or many values—it depends on the setting controlled by the tag. The form of the value also varies with the type of data needed to control a particular setting. For example, whether the Server tab appears on the client is a true/false setting, like this: `<ServerSettings>true</ServerSettings>`. Including an 800x600 display window in the client's list of session displays is controlled with width and height tags containing numeric values, like this: `<Height>600</Height>`. And listing logon methods requires a string value like this one: `<LogonMethod>smartcard_sson</LogonMethod>`.

You may not actually need to edit these settings much if you plan a sort of laissez-faire attitude toward client configuration of the agent. Contrary to some of the Win32 ICA Client documentation, the use of smart cards is already enabled in config.xml (it's controlled with the `<LogonMethod>smartcard_prompt</LogonMethod>` and `<LogonMethod>smartcard_sson</LogonMethod>` tags within `<Logon>`. And clients already have an extended list of session window settings that they can choose from. However, as you've seen users normally have a fair amount of discretion in picking an NFuse server to connect to for their applications, and in configuring client environment settings. If you'd prefer to give end-users less control (or no control) over these settings, then you'll want to edit config.xml to hide those tabs in the Properties sheet for the agent installed on their computer, or to make some of those settings mandated from the central server.

> **NOTE** If you change settings that affect the agent properties, those changes will not take effect until the client restarts. Either have people reboot their computers after a change (simple, but time-consuming), or have them right-click on the agent's icon in the System Tray, choose Exit from the context menu, and then restart the agent from the Program Neighborhood agent off the Start menu.

To hide tabs entirely, go to the `<UserSettings>` tab in config.xml. You'll see a list of three settings: `<ServerSettings>true</ServerSettings>`, controlling the appearance of the Server tab, `<FolderDisplaySettings>true</FolderDisplaySettings>` controlling the appearance of the Application Display tab, and `<RefreshSettings>false</RefreshSettings>`, controlling the appearance of an Application Refresh tab that you *haven't* already seen, because it's hidden by default. (You don't need to display this tab unless you want clients to be able to adjust the refresh rate from the normal every six hours and/or at user logon.) To show an entire tab, make the value of the tag `true`, as in the first two examples here. To hide it, make its value `false`.

Controlling individual settings on a tab is a bit more involved. Most of the XML elements controlling user-customizable options contain two attributes: `modifiable` and `forcedefault`. The values assigned to these two attributes determine if and how users can set preferences for the associated option, but do it in slightly different ways. The modifiable attribute determines whether the option it's associated with is enabled or disabled. To enable an option, set the modifiable attribute's value to "true."

> **NOTE** Notice that you need quotation marks in the values of the modifiable and forcedefault attributes (e.g., "true") although you do *not* need them to hide tabs.

The value of the modifiable attribute determines whether the associated option is enabled or disabled. Set the value of the `modifiable` attribute to "true" (include the quotation marks) to enable the associated option. Set the value of the modifiable attribute to "false" (include the quotation marks) to disable the associated option, or "true" to enable it. The `forcedefault` attribute controls whether the user-defined settings are saved to be reapplied each time the agent starts, or whether the settings on the server replace user-defined settings. For example, the following values allow users to configure whether the agent's icon appears in the System Tray and does not reapply a server-default setting each time the agent starts.

```
<SystemTrayMenuDisplay>
    <Enabled modifiable="true" forcedefault="false">true</Enabled>
</SystemTrayMenuDisplay>
```

Summary

This chapter has examined the process of getting ICA and RDP configured on the client and server. I've discussed the various deployment methods at your disposal and noted when each is appropriate, showed you how to create connections on PCs, Windows terminals, and handheld PCs, and explained the session settings available on the client and server. Because you should now be able to connect to the terminal server, Chapter 6, "Managing Terminal Sessions," will discuss server-side management, using the graphical and command line tools at your disposal.

6

Managing Terminal Sessions

At this point, you have a working terminal server, whether it's using MetaFrame or just Windows 2000 Terminal Services. It's all ready to install applications and let people go to work. But before you do that, you should know how to manage the servers available to you and any user sessions on those servers. That's what we'll talk about in this chapter, and we'll include the tools that come with Windows 2000 and those available only with MetaFrame XP. The only catch to these tools is that they'll work only on the application servers—you can't remotely manage servers from a workstation.

You can take either—or both—of two approaches to server management. Windows 2000 and MetaFrame XP both come with graphical and command-line tools you can use to extract information about and control the application server environment. I'll be discussing those approaches in this chapter.

> **NOTE** With MetaFrame XP and .NET Server, you have a third option: you can script some server administration. Administrative scripting is a big topic and one that requires at least some background in a supported scripting language, so I've included an appendix of the scripting interfaces currently available that apply to MetaFrame and .NET Server Terminal Services scripting and points you to more information about VBScript.

Using Standard Management Tools

First, we'll tackle the standard tools. Both Windows 2000 and MetaFrame XP come with one main tool that you'll use to do most session administration, and a couple of other ones you'll use for supplementary work.

Permitting People to Manage Servers

First, though, you need to be able to manage the servers. If you're using the Remote Desktop Protocol (RDP) for terminal sessions, this isn't an issue. Windows 2000 assumes that anyone allowed to access the Administrative Tools section of a Windows 2000 server is permitted to manage application servers. That's not a bad assumption, but MetaFrame works under different rules—at least in part because the Citrix management tool isn't necessarily installed on a MetaFrame server, or even on a server. If the management tool for the servers supporting dozens or hundreds of people can be installed on a workstation, you'd better require a separate explicit logon to use that tool.

To add user accounts to the list of Citrix administrators, log onto the Citrix Management Console with the existing valid account, and then go to the Citrix Administrators section. When you select the icon, the list of user accounts allowed to manage the server farm will appear in the right-hand pane. To add a new account, right-click on the Citrix Administrators icon and choose Add Citrix Administrator from the context menu. You'll open a dialog box like the one in Figure 6.1.

Figure 6.1 You can add new Citrix Administrators by username or group.

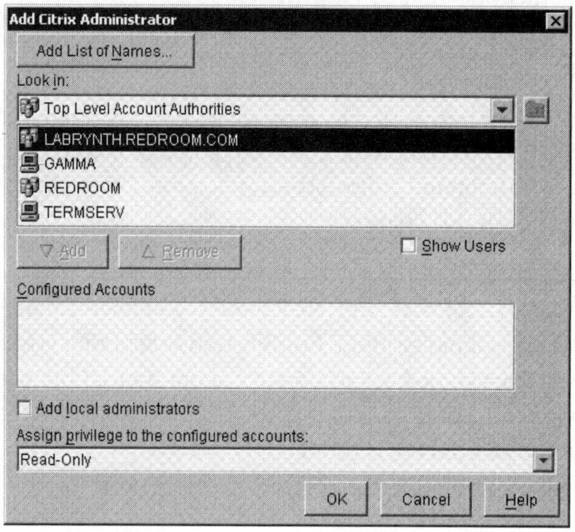

As you can see, you've got several options for how you can add new administrators. The most exact way is to choose the security authority you want to use from the drop-down Look In list. Whichever authority you choose—domain or server—you'll see a list of user and group accounts for that authority that you can add to the list of trusted accounts. If you've installed FR1 or later for MetaFrame XP, any NDS authorities will also be listed. The Show Users check box works as it does in Windows 2000 dialog boxes of the same kind. If you leave it unchecked, you'll see only group accounts. If you check it, you'll enumerate all user accounts within those groups so that you can pick and choose.

You can also categorically add all local administrators for each MetaFrame server to the list of people allowed to manage the server farm. Checking the Add Local Administrators box does not allow local administrators for a workstation to log on if you've installed the Citrix Management Console on a workstation.

Finally, if you've installed FR1, you'll see the Add List of Names button at the top of the dialog box. This option is most useful if you know specifically which user accounts you want to add and don't want the trouble of browsing through more than one account authority. A Check Names button in the Add List Of Names dialog box (see Figure 6.2) allows you to verify that the accounts exist before you officially add them to the list of Citrix administrators. If you've misspelled an account name, or haven't formatted it properly (all account names must take the *servername\username* format for NT4 domains, or the *username@servername.com* format for Windows 2000 domains), then you'll see an error message when you check the names.

Figure 6.2 Check names before adding them to the list of Citrix administrators.

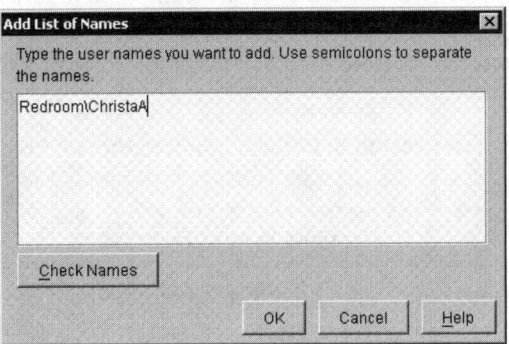

As you can see at the bottom of the screen, adding someone to the list of administrators doesn't mean that you have to give them full control over the farm. If you choose Read-Write permissions for the configured accounts, they have full control over the server farm. Read-Only permission allows them only to view current settings without editing any of them. Those with Read-Only views can't even *see* the editing options—for example, the menu option for adding new published applications won't exist. If you need to change a user's or group's permission level after adding them to the list of Citrix Administrators, right-click their icon in the Citrix Management Console. Choose Properties to open a dialog box where you can choose the appropriate permission level from a drop-down list.

If you've got FR2 for MetaFrame XP installed, rather than choosing between Read/Write or Read Only access for Citrix Administrators, you can choose the components that new administrators have access to. (The first Citrix Administrator you created while installing MetaFrame will always have full access to everything.) The process for creating new Citrix Administrator accounts is a little more elaborate than it is for previous versions of MetaFrame XP. While you start out the same (choosing Add Citrix Administrator and having a list of available account authorities to choose from) the path changes from that point.

When you choose the Next button after having chosen individual or group accounts to configure as Citrix Administrators, you'll next see a list of all the possible tasks that can be performed from the Citrix Management Console and three options of providing access to them: View Only (the former Read Only), Full Administration (the former Read/Write), and Custom. Full Administration gives people full access to all parts of the Citrix Management Console; View Only lets them see settings but not edit them, and with Custom you can pick the settings for the user or group accounts you're configuring. You can see the settings and the various sub-options in Table 6.1.

NOTE The settings you apply during this wizard will apply to every user or group account you selected in the first screen. To apply settings differently to different accounts, you'll need to either walk through the wizard separately for each group or edit the account settings for a group or user account after you've completed the wizard.

Table 6.1 Tasks you can assign to Citrix Administrators on FR2 MetaFrame XP server farms

Task	Options Within Task	View Only Setting
Citrix Administrators	Log on to Citrix Management Console; View Citrix Administrators	Log on to Citrix Management Console; View Citrix Administrators
Farm Management	View Farm Management; Edit Zone Settings; Edit Interoperability Settings; Edit All Other Farm Settings	View Farm Management

Table 6.1 Tasks you can assign to Citrix Administrators on FR2 MetaFrame XP server farms *(continued)*

Task	Options Within Task	View Only Setting
Installation Manager (XPe only)	View Installation Manager; Edit Installation Manager	View Installation Manager
Licenses	View License Information; Assign Licenses; Edit Licenses and Product Code	View License Information
Load Manager (XPa and XPe only)	View Load Evaluators; Assign Load Evaluators; Edit Load Evaluators	View Load Evaluators
Printers	View Printers and Printer Drivers; Replicate Printer Drivers; Edit Printers; Edit All Other Printer Settings; Edit Printer Drivers	View Printers and Printer Drivers
Published Applications	View Published Applications and Content; Publish Applications and Edit Properties	View Published Applications and Content
Resource Management (XPe only)	View Resource Management Configuration; Configure Resource Management	View Resource Management Configuration
Servers	View Server Information; Server Folder Management; Remove Server; Edit SNMP Settings; Edit Other Server Settings	View Server Information
Sessions	View Session Management; Reset Sessions; Send Messages; Log Off Users; Disconnect Users; Connect Sessions.	View Session Management
User Policies	View User Policies; Edit User Policies	View User Policies

These aren't system policies like the ones you can configure with the Windows 2000 Group Policy Editor, but application-level policies applying only to the Citrix Management Console. That is, if a task done through the Citrix Management Console can be done through the Windows 2000 Terminal Services Management or Terminal Services Configuration tool, then even if the task is blocked to a Citrix Administrator that person will still be able to perform the task.

> **WARNING** Do not remove the right to log onto the Citrix Management Console unless you've created some other way for that group of Citrix Administrators to get to the tools they need. The set of command line tools isn't complete. If you prevent an administrator from logging onto the Citrix Management Console, when they try they'll see an error message telling them that they failed, but not why.

From the same screen where you can choose tasks to assign to new Citrix Administrator accounts, you can also choose to disable administrator accounts if you need to keep that group of people off the Citrix Management Console for a while.

You can get to all the FR2-specific settings from the Citrix Management Console. To enable a disabled account, right-click on the group name in the Citrix Administrators section of the Citrix Management Console and choose Enable Account. You can also disable accounts by right-clicking on them and choosing the appropriate option from the context menu. To edit the tasks assigned to a user or group account, choose Properties from the context menu for that account to open the same dialog box you edited to assign tasks in the first place.

Now that everyone who needs the ability to manage servers has it, let's move on.

Gathering User and Process Information

We had to install FreeCell onto the application servers, since the person signing the checks wanted it there, but people are only supposed to play during lunch. Today, however, someone is playing FreeCell from the application servers during work hours. I feel it in my bones.

To find the culprit, I'll need to know who's using the application servers and what processes are running in their sessions. I can gather this information from either the graphical tools or from the command line. As you'll see, although the tools available depend on the software you have installed, the information available does not. So long as the information you're looking for is not specific to one display protocol, you can get information for RDP or ICA sessions from the tools I'll mention here.

Using Graphical Tools

If I'm using Windows 2000 Terminal Services in isolation, I'll use the Terminal Services Manager to find a particular process. All the trusted domains are visible in the left-hand pane of the tool; since I don't know which servers people are logging onto, I'll start from there. When I've selected a domain (I do need to know which domain I'm starting from—Windows 2000 doesn't list process or session information across domains), three tabs will become visible in the right-hand pane: one listing users currently logged onto the terminal server, one showing the current active and disconnected sessions, and one showing the processes currently running on the terminal server. Because I'm interested in finding out whether or not someone is running a particular process and who it is, I'll flip to the Processes tab shown in Figure 6.3. From here, I can see a complete list of all processes running in the domain, the server they're running on, the session they're in, and the name of the user who owns that session. This screen will also show the process ID (PID), which will come in handy when it comes time to terminate processes. By clicking the column header for any column, I can sort the items in alphabetical/numerical order, making it easier to find the information I'm seeking.

Figure 6.3 Viewing processes running on a terminal server

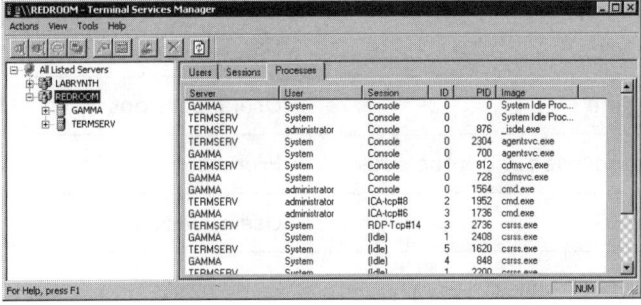

If you found the server running the FreeCell process, you're home free. As you can see here, all the processes running on that server are listed according to who's running them, the Session ID of the process in which they're running, and the Process ID. As you'll see, this information can be useful if you need to shut down a specific instance of a process.

Because my focus here is on finding a particular process, I'm most interested in the Processes tab, but the other two tabs are also useful for some purposes. If I want to find out who is using what application servers in the domain, I can select the Users tab. It will show me the servers in the domain, the usernames of the people logged onto them (showing more than once if a person had more than one active session), the session status and ID, any idle time, and the time and date someone logged on. The Sessions tab's information is similar (if more detailed) to that of the Users tab, but its focus is different. In addition to finding out which sessions are running on which servers, you can use this tab to find out which client computers are connecting to which terminal servers. Table 6.2 shows you the information available on a per-domain and per-server basis, and the tab on which it's located.

Table 6.2 Finding Domain or Server Information in the Terminal Services Manager

Data Type	Tab
Client computer name	Sessions
Image names for processes	Processes
Process IDs	Processes
Protocol used for each session	Sessions
Session idle time	Users
Session IDs associated with processes	Processes
Session status	Users, Sessions
User logon time	Users, Sessions
Username associated with processes	Processes
User session IDs	Users, Sessions

Everything you need to find out—which user and which PID is associated with which session, and how busy that session is—is here.

Even though the Terminal Server Manager comes with Windows 2000 Terminal Services and isn't MetaFrame-specific, it's actually the better tool for finding processes across multiple servers, even for MetaFrame servers. Given the farm organizational structure, you'd expect that finding process information from the Citrix Management Console across multiple servers would be simple, but this isn't the case. To find a process from the Citrix Management Console, you must first find out which server the FreeCell enthusiast might be using and then look for the server there. In a small server farm, that's not a real problem, but if we're talking about hunting down one process over fifty servers that's quite a bit of work.

To find out who's playing FreeCell from the Citrix Management Console, you'll need to select each server in turn from the Servers icon and turn to the Processes tab in Figure 6.4. You'll see a list of all the processes running on the selected server and the name of the person running each process. Again, you can sort the information in any column by clicking on the column header.

Figure 6.4 You'll need to look for processes on individual MetaFrame servers.

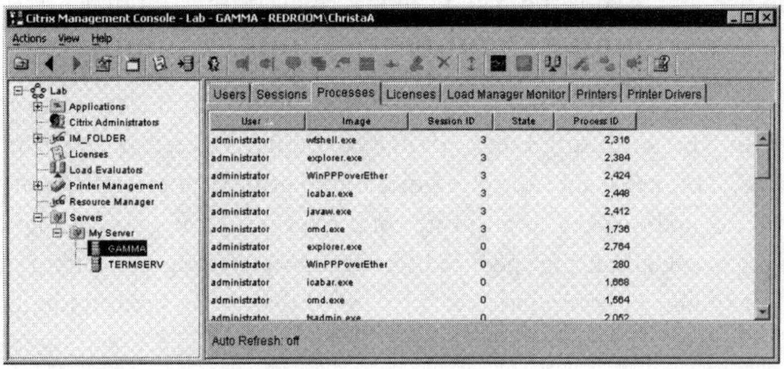

Command-Line Tools

Farm-wide process information for MetaFrame servers *is* available from the command line. If you type **query farm /process**, you'll get a complete list of all processes running in the farm (arranged by Process ID for each server, so you may need to do a bit of skimming to find the process you're looking for) and the server each process is running on. Once you know the server on which a process is running, it's much easier to get more details—like who's running it and what its process ID is. A small snippet of the output from query farm /process could look like this:

```
  2504  notepad.exe                              GAMMA
  2896  tsadmin.exe                              GAMMA
  2324  query.exe                                GAMMA
   860  qfarm.exe                                GAMMA
     0                                           TERMSERV
     8  System                                   TERMSERV
   312  smss.exe                                 TERMSERV
   340  csrss.exe                                TERMSERV
```

So, if you're using MetaFrame XP, you can track down processes running across multiple servers. Sadly, the Windows 2000 Terminal Server command-line tools do not have any way of helping you do this.

Once you know where a process is running, you can get more detailed information using the Windows 2000 Terminal Services tools. If you run **query process** (a Windows 2000 tool, even though it starts with the query prefix) without arguments, you'll create a list of all the processes currently running on the currently selected server. (To view the processes running on another application server in the domain, type **query process /server:servername**, where *servername* is the name of the server you want to query.) The output will tell you the user account running the process, the session ID in which the process is running, the name of the session, the process ID, and the name of the image supporting the process.

The information you get from **query process** is awfully broad, so let's refine it a little. We want to find out who's running FreeCell on a particular server, so we'll type **query process freecell.exe**. You must include the .exe extension. If you don't, **query process** will complain that no such process is running on the server. Doing so will net us a list of all the people running FreeCell on the specified server (again, you can specify a different server by including the */server:servername* switch) and show us the session identifier and number, as well as the Process ID for each instance, like this:

USERNAME	SESSIONNAME	ID	PID	IMAGE
administrator	console	0	1268	freecell.exe
administrator		3	2356	freecell.exe
scott		4	2504	freecell.exe

To find out what processes a particular person was running, I'd substitute the name of the person I was investigating—say, Scott, since I'm not going to quarrel with the system administrator's need to run FreeCell—to find out what else they were doing while playing games. You can also list processes associated with a particular session name or Session ID, but for most purposes I find it easier to reference user account names. Querying by session will only help you if you care what processes are running within a given session, as opposed to what processes are running on a particular application server.

Sending Messages

Once you've got your list of people running FreeCell, you can let them know that they're caught. From both the GUI and the command line, you can send messages to a single person or multiple people—even across domains.

Using Graphical Tools

Both Terminal Services Manager and the Citrix Management Console come with a messaging component. From the left pane of the Terminal Services Manager tool, select the terminal server or domain that the people you want to message are logged onto. In the right, select the people to whom you want to send a massage (Ctrl+click to select multiple usernames). From the Actions menu, or the context menu that appears when you right-click the selected usernames, choose Send Message to open the dialog box shown in Figure 6.5. Type your message, and click OK. The message will instantly pop up on the screen of everyone you included on the recipient list.

Figure 6.5 Sending a message to users from the Windows 2000 Terminal Services Manager

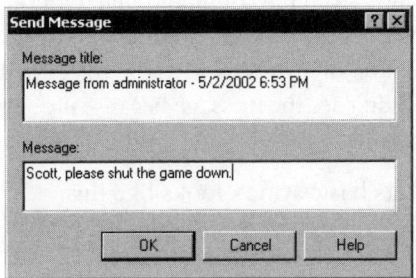

The procedure for messaging doesn't change a whole lot for Citrix Management Console users. Go to the Users tab for the server or server group, as shown in Figure 6.5, right-click the name of the person you want to message, and choose Send Message from the context menu to open the box in Figure 6.6. Edit the title information if you like and type a message. When you click OK, that message will go to every session associated with that username. So if Scott's running more than one session on servers in the selected group, he'll get nagged in each one.

Figure 6.6 The message-sending tool in the Citrix Management Console is almost identical to the one in Windows 2000.

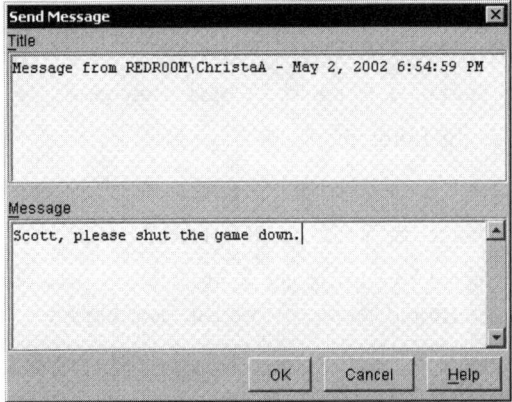

> **TIP** To send the same message to more than one person, just Ctrl+click to select all the names, and then right-click and choose Send Message, as you did in the previous example.

Command-Line Options

You can also send messages from the command line with the Windows 2000 `msg` utility. This works much like `msg` did in single-user Windows, with one exception: messages sent to a username will be sent to all instances of that name, not just one. Scott is not going to be able to claim that he didn't see the message because it popped up in a session other than the one he was looking at.

`msg` has lots of options. Its basic syntax looks like this:

    msg {identifier}[/SERVER:servername] [/TIME:sec] [/v] [/w] [message]

The *identifier* can be a username, Session ID, session name, or a filename containing an ASCII list of all users to whom the message should go. The /TIME parameter doesn't delay the message; rather, it's a time-out period that cooperates with the /w switch that makes the command wait for a user response before giving control of the command prompt back to the message's sender.

> **NOTE** Like the other command-line utilities, `msg` runs on the server that you're connected to unless you specify otherwise.

To send a message to a single user, run `msg` using the user's name as an argument, like this:

    msg Scott Scott, please close FreeCell. You're wasting processor time.

If you want some kind of record that Scott saw the message—or at least clicked OK—use the /v (for "verbose") switch as follows:

    msg Scott /v Scott, I mean it. Close the game.

You'll see output like the following:

    Sending message to session RDP-Tcp#1, display time 60
    Timeout on message to session RDP-Tcp#1 before user response

Let's apply a little external pressure to get Scott back to work. To send a message to everyone logged onto that terminal server, use an asterisk, like so:

    msg * Hey, everyone—Scott's got enough free time to play FreeCell.
    Anyone got anything for him to do?

Alternatively, send a message to a preset group by typing all recipient names into a Notepad file and saving it, and then referencing the file (in this case, called "users") like this:

```
msg @users Hey, everyone—Scott has enough free time to play FreeCell.
Anyone got anything for him to do?
```

The only catch to sending messages to multiple users is that if you add the /w option, msg works sequentially. That is, it will send the message to the first person in the list (going in order of Session ID) and wait for either a response or a time-out before sending the message to the second person in the list.

Terminating Applications

Scott and the other FreeCell players aren't paying attention to your pleas. Time to get tough and terminate the application. Every instance of FreeCell that you close will exit immediately, with no warning to the user. Were FreeCell capable of saving games, they wouldn't get a chance to save, either.

> **NOTE** Before I get into this, let me distinguish again between "terminating" and "resetting." Both options close applications with no warning, but single processes are "terminated" and entire sessions are "reset."

Using Graphical Tools

To kill a single application from Terminal Services Manager, select the server or domain in the left pane and turn to the Processes tab in the right. All running processes will appear here, identified by the name of the server they're running on, who's got them open, the PIDs of the processes, and other relevant information. As elsewhere, you can Ctrl+click to select multiple processes. When you've selected every process to be terminated, right-click and choose End Process from the context menu (it's the only option). The selected applications will close instantly.

To kill a single application from the Citrix Management Console, go back to the Processes tab. Find the process you want to terminate—sort instances by user to make sure that you've got the right one!—and then right-click and choose Terminate. The CMC will ask if you're sure that you want to terminate the selected process. Assuming that you are sure, click OK. The process will disappear from the user's session, ending the session if you terminated a published application or just ending a single process if you terminated an application running from a desktop.

Using the Command Line

You can also terminate applications from the command line. Just be careful. This procedure is open to error, and you will make people unhappy if you accidentally close the wrong process and lose all their data.

The command to kill terminal server applications is `tskill`, related to the `kill` command that appeared for the first time in NT 3.5's Resource Kit and which stops an application by terminating its process with extreme prejudice. Like the Terminate menu command, `tskill` will stop an application as soon as the tool is executed, with no time allowed for saving data or other tasks. It's very intrusive, so you should use it only when there's simply no other way of getting an application to stop.

The syntax of `tskill` is as follows:

```
tskill processid | processname [/SERVER:servername] [/ID:sessionid |
/a] [/v]
```

Notice that you can reference a process either by its name or its process ID. The former is easier and necessary if you're using the /a switch to close all instances of an application on the terminal server. The latter is necessary if you're only trying to close specific instances of the application, perhaps leaving untouched the instance of TSQUAKE that your boss has open.

So, to kill all instances of TSQUAKE running on the currently selected server, you type:

tskill tsquake /a

To kill only selected instances, get the PID by running query process or query user and plug it in, like this:

tskill 1875

Sadly, you can't list several PIDs at once to kill, so if you need to pick and choose processes without killing all instances, you'll need to terminate instances of a process one at a time.

> **TIP** Although you need to supply the executable extension with query process, the command won't work if you supply the extension with tskill. So, use **query process tsquake.exe**, but use **tskill tsquake**.

Taking Control of User Sessions

Sometimes, the best plan isn't to just shut down applications from the terminal server. Instead, you can take control of a user session and see what they're doing (as opposed to listing processes, which just tells you what processes are active in the context of a given session). This can be especially helpful for troubleshooting purposes, such as if Scott says he didn't mean to run FreeCell but couldn't figure out how to shut it down once he had it running. (Okay, I'm reaching here, but work with me on this.) Taking remote control of the session gives you the same degree of control that you'd have if logged on as that user.

Using Graphical Tools

You can remotely control a user's session in one of two ways: from the Terminal Services Manager or from the command line.

> **TIP** You can only take remote control of a terminal server session from another terminal server session using the same display protocol, not from the console and not from a session using ICA when the session you want to shadow is using RDP (or vice versa). The remote control option in the Terminal Services Manager and the shadow command-line utility won't work from the console. The session must be running at the same resolution as the session you're trying to control; you can't shadow a 1024×768 session from one running at 800×600.

To shadow an RDP session, start another session, logging on with an account with Administrator privileges. From within that session, start the Terminal Services Manager. Select a terminal server in the left pane and switch to the Users tab so that user sessions are showing. Find the session you want to shadow, and choose Remote Control from the Actions menu. A dialog box like the one shown in Figure 6.7 will prompt you for the hotkey combination you want to use to end remote control of your own session (so you can get back to the original session).

Figure 6.7 Choose a hotkey combination to toggle back to your original RDP session.

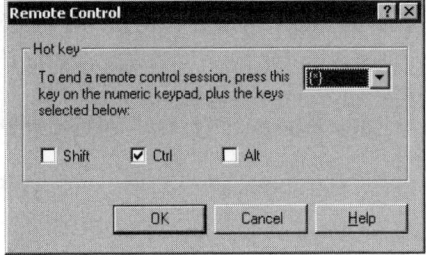

If the user session is configured to require user permission for control, a dialog box will appear on the screen, letting the user know that someone has requested permission to control their session. If they permit the control, you're in charge of their session without further ado. If they don't permit the control, you'll see an error message telling you that you couldn't get permission to control the session.

So far as MetaFrame shadowing goes, I've found the Citrix Management Console to be a better shadowing tool than the command line. To shadow a session from the Citrix Management Console, go to the Users tab for a server or server group, right-click the name of the person you want to shadow, and choose Shadow from the context menu to open the dialog box in Figure 6.8. When you've done so, click OK to begin shadowing.

> **NOTE** You can only shadow from an ICA session, but you can initiate the shadow from the CMC. You'll just be prompted to start an ICA session before the shadow becomes available. With FR2, you may be better off starting the ICA session ahead of time—I'm finding that the Citrix Management Console complains that you can't initiate shadowing from the Citrix Management Console when I try.

Figure 6.8 ICA shadowing will use a hotkey independent of RDP shadowing.

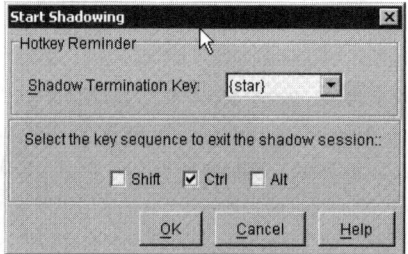

If the person has to grant you permission to shadow their session, you'll see an hourglass for a few seconds until they accept the shadow. Once they see the message telling them of the shadowing request and click OK to accept it, you'll see their desktop exactly as they do. Both of you will also see a dialog box in the session, making it easy for the person being shadowed to tell that they *are* being shadowed. This button also makes it easy to stop shadowing, since you don't need to use the hotkey to leave the shadowed session.

What if they don't accept the shadow or don't see your request within a minute or two? If they *don't* accept it, you'll see error code 7044—the request to shadow was denied. I've also seen an error code 2 telling me that the resource was unavailable.

The Citrix Management Console isn't the only interface for shadowing ICA sessions—MetaFrame XP actually comes with another option I like better—the Shadowing tool that's in the ICA toolbar and in the Citrix program group. (Why do I like it better? It's not a Java application, for one thing, and it stays neatly out of the way at the top of the screen until you need it for another.) When you open the Shadow Toolbar, you'll be prompted for your password to be used for accessing other user sessions. After logging on, you'll see a thin taskbar along the top of your screen with a Shadow button on it. Click the button, and you'll open the dialog box in Figure 6.9.

Figure 6.9 The Shadow Session tool allows you to sort by server, application, or username when you're trying to find the session to shadow.

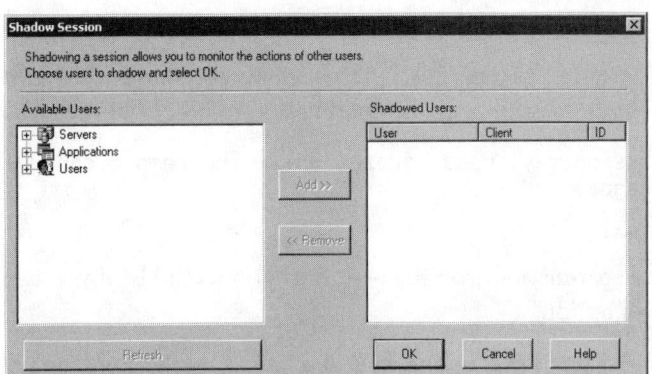

This dialog box makes it a lot easier to find the session you want to shadow. If the person whose session you need to shadow is running a published application, you can search for that application in the appropriate folder, and then choose their session (identified by username and the client computer they're using) from the list. If they've created a custom connection to a MetaFrame server, you can look up that server and find their connection. If the user isn't running a published application and doesn't know which server they're connected to, you can still find them—the Users section of the Shadow Session tool will list all current user connections in the farm.

Once you've found a session in the left-hand pane, click the Add button to move it to the right, where it will display the username, client machine, and Session ID. Click OK, and you'll be connected to the selected session. From here, everything works as it does when you're shadowing from the Citrix Management Console.

Using Command-Line Tools

Both Windows 2000 and MetaFrame XP have their own shadowing tools; Windows 2000's is called **shadow**, and MetaFrame's is called **cshadow**. The **shadow** syntax is as follows:

    shadow {sessionname | sessionid} [/SERVER:servername] [/v]

To use it, start an RDP session with administrative privileges. Open the command prompt and run **query user** *username* or **query session** *username* to find the session ID or session name of the user whose session you want to shadow. You can't shadow from the command line based on *username* (because a user might have more than one session open), so you'll need the session identifiers even if you know the account name of the person whose session you're shadowing.

If you're shadowing a session on the same terminal server that you're logged on to, the command syntax for shadowing session ID 1 looks like this:

```
shadow 1
```

If that session requires user permission to be remotely controlled, you'll see the following message while your session waits for permission to take over the remote one:

```
Your session may appear frozen while the remote control approval is
being negotiated.

Please wait...
```

Once you have permission, you're in—just as you would be if you were using the GUI remote control option.

The only tricky part to shadowing RDP sessions from the command prompt is that you should do it at least once from the GUI before trying the command-line utility so that you can find your way back. The `shadow` and `cshadow` commands do not prompt you for a hotkey combination to end remote control and return to your session. They will use the one defined for the GUI, so if you know what that hotkey combination is, you can use it. Just make sure you know how to return to your own session from the remote control. (For ICA sessions, this caveat doesn't apply—ICA shadowed sessions have a Stop Shadowing button.)

Tuning Shadowing Permissions

I've mentioned user permissions that permit shadowing, prohibit shadowing, or restrict it, but I haven't discussed *how* to edit or view these permissions. The answer depends on the display protocol you're using for terminal sessions. RDP and ICA shadowing permissions are configured differently.

To configure shadowing settings for RDP sessions, open the Terminal Services Configuration tool in Administrative Tools. Right-click the RDP protocol visible from the Connections folder, and open the Properties sheet. From the Remote Control tab in Figure 6.10, you can disable shadowing altogether, disable the need for users to explicitly agree to the shadowing, permit shadowers only to view events in a user's session, choose not to interact with them, or leave the shadow settings at the defaults visible here.

If you want to configure the shadowing settings for all RDP sessions, be sure to choose the Use Remote Control With the Following Settings option. If you stick with the defaults, then all remote control settings are inherited from the per-user settings configured from the Remote Control tab on each user account's Properties sheet. You can't apply remote control settings to groups or organizational units, just to individual accounts. Therefore, for terminal servers with more than a few users, it is much simpler to configure RDP settings and override individual account settings.

Figure 6.10 Set protocol-wide remote control settings from Terminal Services Configuration.

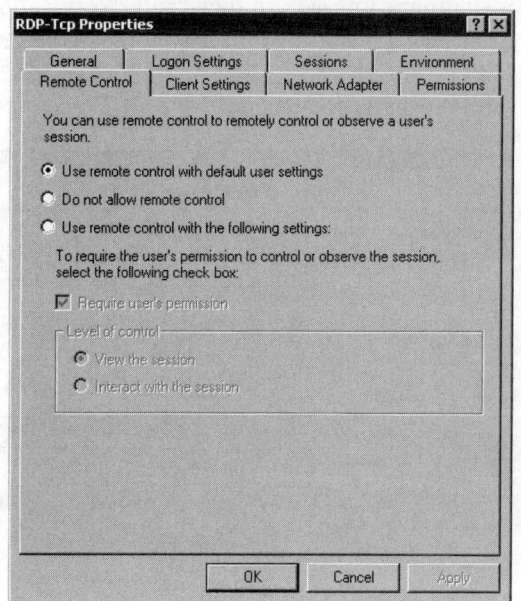

When you were installing MetaFrame XP, you had the chance to configure shadowing settings then, but you can also do it post-Setup. If you're already using Terminal Services Configuration, just configure the shadowing settings from the Remote Control tab as you just saw for RDP. Shadowing settings are also available from the Citrix Connection Configuration tool in the Citrix program group. Select the display protocol you want to configure (bearing in mind that there will be more than one instance of ICA if you enabled support for multiple network protocols when installing MetaFrame), and choose Edit from its context menu to open the Edit Connection dialog box. Click the Advanced button, and you'll open the Advanced Connection Settings dialog box in Figure 6.11.

This is a pretty busy dialog box; the settings you're looking for are in a drop-down list at the very bottom. Uncheck the Inherit User Config box next to the Shadowing drop-down list, and you'll see these settings:

- Is disabled
- Is enabled; input OFF notify ON
- Is enabled; input OFF notify OFF
- Is enabled; input ON notify OFF
- Is enabled: input ON notify ON

Basically, input ON or OFF indicates whether the person doing the shadowing can interact with the session—if input is turned off, they can't. Notification refers to whether the person who's being shadowed is notified of the shadowing before it happens.

Figure 6.11 The Advanced Connection settings tune all ICA connection information.

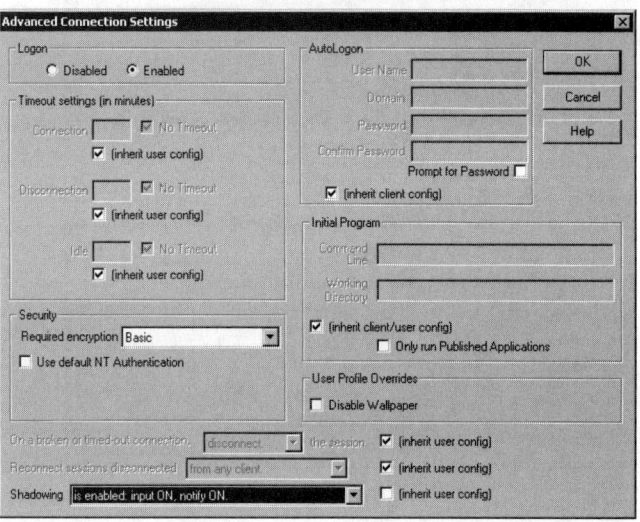

If you have FR2 installed, you can configure shadowing settings for groups of user or group accounts by using MetaFrame User Policies. You'll need to create a policy, configure it, and then assign that policy to the user or group accounts to which you want it to apply.

For example, to configure shadowing settings for a subset of all users in the farm, right-click on the Policies section in the Citrix Management Console and choose Create Policy from the context menu. When prompted, choose a name for the policy such as "Shadowing" and click OK. The new policy will now be in the Policies section, but it won't be configured. Right-click on it and choose Properties from the context menu to open its Properties sheet, and choose Configure User Shadowing, located in the Shadowing folder in the list on the left-hand side of the screen. You'll see three choices on the right: Rule Not Configured, Rule Disabled, and Rule Enabled. Click Rule Enabled, and you'll activate the shadowing options in the lower right of the screen. When you've configured them, click OK to return to the Citrix Management Console. To assign the configured policy to user or group accounts, right-click on its entry in the Policies section and choose Assign Users from the context menu. From the familiar dialog box showing the available account authorities, choose the user or group accounts to which you want the policy to apply. The shadowing settings you set here will apply to those accounts.

> **NOTE** Enabled or Disabled settings override settings applied elsewhere. Not Configured settings are overridden by external settings.

Ending—or Preventing—User Sessions

That's it—Scott's kicked off the server until he can learn to use it correctly.

If you want to stop an entire terminal session, not just a single process within it, you can either disconnect or reset the connection. Disconnecting, you recall, cuts the user off from the session and closes the session window on the client computer (although there's normally nothing to keep a user from reconnecting), but it leaves all applications running and data in memory. When the user reconnects to a session they were disconnected from, then they're right back where they left off. A reset connection, in contrast, closes all of the applications the person had open. Disconnected sessions still use some system resources, albeit not much because their data will eventually be paged to disk and they won't have new user input to process. Reset sessions use no resources—they don't exist.

Using Graphical Tools

To disconnect or reset a session from the Terminal Services Manager tool, select it in the left pane and choose Reset or Disconnect from the Action menu. You'll see a dialog box warning you that the session will be disconnected or reset. Click OK, and the selected session or sessions will be ended.

To reset or disconnect a session from the Citrix Management Console, find the session on the Users tab for a particular published application or a server or server group, then right-click and choose Disconnect or Reset from the context menu. A dialog box will ask if you're sure. If you indicate that you are, the session will reset or disconnect immediately.

Want to kick everyone off the server? As I explained in Chapter 2, "Core Parts of Windows Terminal Services," both Windows 2000 and MetaFrame XP maintain "listener" sessions that listen for incoming session requests so that user sessions can be created more quickly. When a user connects to a listener session, Windows 2000 or MetaFrame XP creates another listener session for that display protocol so that there are always two available. You can see all listener sessions from Terminal Services Manager.

If you reset a listener session, you will reset *all* sessions associated with that display protocol. It's very abrupt—the people you reset will have no chance to save their data—but it's one way to quickly and easily end all current connections without having to go through session by session. Just make sure that you pick the right server before resetting a listener session, or you'll have a lot of people after your head. Sadly, you can't use the same technique to just disconnect everybody—this only works for resetting all sessions.

Using Command-Line Tools

You can also end user sessions from the command line with the Windows 2000 `tsdiscon` and `reset session` commands. The syntax for `tsdiscon` is as follows:

```
tsdiscon [sessionid | sessionname] [/SERVER:servername] [/v]
```

Once again, you can choose to identify sessions to close by session name or Session ID. To find out both, run `query session` to get output like the following:

```
SESSIONNAME USERNAME ID STATE TYPE DEVICE
console 0 Conn wdcon
ica-tcp 65536 Listen wdica
ChristaA 2 Disc wdica
 >ica-tcp#3 Administrator 3 Active wdica
4 Idle
5 Idle
rdp-tcp 65538 Listen rdpwd
```

Notice that I can see both ICA and RDP sessions in this list. Find the session name or ID you want, and plug it into the `tsdiscon` command like this: **tsdiscon 2**. Once you've pressed the Enter key, the user of the selected session sees a message telling them that the remote server has ended the connection (the exact wording depends on the client type and version they're using) and is given a Close button to click.

> **TIP** I find it easiest to reference Session IDs. You always have to use a number—you can't choose to disconnect a session attached to a particular username—so you might as well choose the shortest identifier possible.

The syntax for resetting a session is similar to that used for disconnecting it:

```
reset session {sessionname | sessionid} [/SERVER:servername] [/v]
```

Once again, the user will see a dialog box telling them that the terminal server ended the connection and prompting them to close.

What if you'd like to keep people off the terminal server altogether, perhaps while you're installing new applications on it? If no one's yet connected, you can disable the RDP protocol from the Terminal Services Configuration tool located in the Administrative Tools program group without any harm. Open the tool so that it looks like the window in Figure 6.12, and right-click the RDP protocol. From the pop-up menu that appears, choose All Tasks/ Disable Connection. Disabling the ICA protocol works the same way; you can perform either task either from here or from Citrix Connection Manager.

Figure 6.12 Disabling the RDP protocol

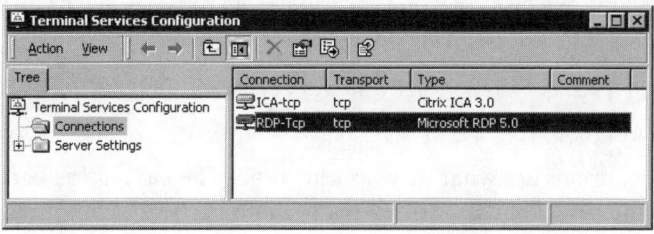

> **WARNING** If you disable the connection from the Terminal Services Configuration tool, you'll reset any existing sessions. This works just like resetting a listening session.

To disable the protocol for new sessions without disturbing the ones already in place, you'll need to use the change logon command-line utility. This tool isn't disabling RDP; it's merely disabling logons, so no current sessions will be affected. Its syntax is as follows:

```
change logon {/QUERY | /ENABLE | /DISABLE}
    /QUERY      Query current terminal session login mode.
    /ENABLE     Enable user login from terminal sessions.
    /DISABLE    Disable user login from terminal sessions.
```

Typing **change logon /disable** prevents any further connections from being made until you re-enable logons. Anyone who tries to connect will see an error message telling them that remote logons are currently disabled. Disabling RDP does not, obviously, affect the console session as it's not dependent on RDP. As I mentioned earlier, you'll need to disable logons if you want to keep people off the terminal server, as the service itself does not shut off.

Shutting Down the Server

If you've reset all connections in preparation for shutting down the server, you can do that either from the GUI or from the command line. From the GUI, just click the Start button as though you were going to log off, and choose Shut Down or Restart (you shouldn't have these options unless you're a server administrator). That works from either the console or a remote session, although (obviously) the remote session won't last very long after you do this.

Shutting down sessions with the `tsshutdn` command-line tool gives you a little more control over the shutdown process than is possible from the GUI, since you can delay the time for shutting down the server. The `tsshutdn` syntax is as follows:

```
tsshutdn [wait_time] [/SERVER:servername] [/REBOOT] [/POWERDOWN]
➥[/DELAY:logoffdelay] [/v]
```

Most of these options are what they appear to be. The `wait_time` variable specifies the amount of time (in seconds) until all sessions on the server are disconnected, with a default of 60. `Servername` specifies a server if you don't want to shut down the one you're currently logged on to. `/REBOOT` reboots the server, and `/POWERDOWN` shuts it down if the server has Advanced Power Management drivers (if not, the server shuts down all server processes and displays the Click to Restart message). `/Delay` specifies the time to wait after all sessions are terminated before the server should start shutting down/rebooting.

So, for example, you could combine `tsshutdn` and `msg` to tell everyone that the server's going to be rebooted in five minutes. First, send the following message:

```
Msg * The server will go down in 5 minutes for maintenance. Please
save your work and log out.
```

Second, run the `tshutdn` command with the following parameters, which will terminate all user sessions in 5 minutes and then delay 30 seconds before shutting down the server.

```
tshutdn 300 /powerdown /delay:30
```

Controlling User Connections

If you're using Windows 2000 Terminal Services, you cannot limit the number of connections that clients make to the application server. Opening multiple sessions can lead to profile confusion, overusing application or ICA connection licenses, and even overusing the more-or-less permanently assigned TSCALs (if a user is connecting from more than one computer). Not good. The only way to avoid this problem is through user education and perhaps the threat of flogging. .NET Server includes a machine policy you can apply to application servers that permits users to have only a single connection to an application server.

MetaFrame XP administrators can control the number of sessions or application instances that people run... *if* they've installed FR1 or later on the farm servers. Anyone trying to run applications or sessions outside their limit will see a chiding message telling them that they're not allowed to do so.

To limit the number of concurrent sessions that a person can run, right-click the farm's icon in the Citrix Management Console and choose Properties from the context menu. On the MetaFrame Settings tab shown in Figure 6.13, check the box in the Connection Limits section (again, this section and the NDS ones will be present only if you've installed FR1 or later) and then choose a session limit. Although Citrix Administrators can normally disregard these limits, you can check the box here to make them play by the same rules as everyone else.

Figure 6.13 Enabling session limits for all farm servers

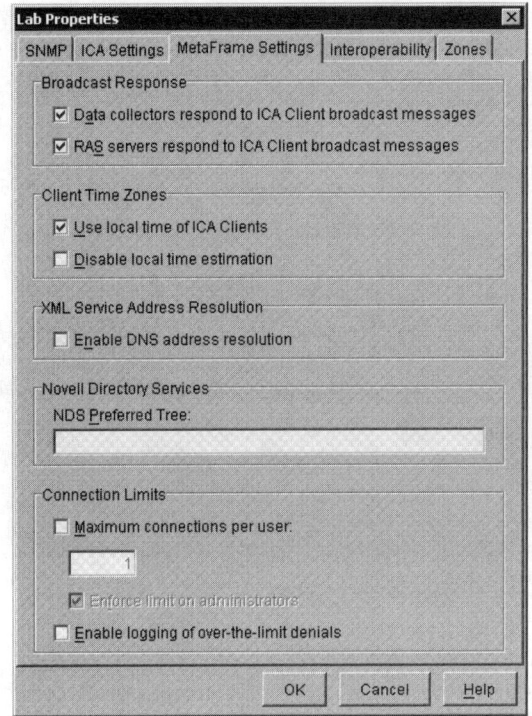

Connection control doesn't apply to seamless windows, because all sessions running in seamless windows use the same core environment (thereby saving system resources). Therefore, simple connection control won't help you here. To limit the number of instances of a published application that people can run, go to the Application icon in the Citrix Management Console, right-click on an application you want to limit access to, and from the Properties sheet, go to the Application Limits tab visible in Figure 6.14.

From here, just pick the maximum number of instances of an application that you want people using the farm to be able to run. For example, if you have 10 licenses for WordCrusher, you can set the limit to 10 connections for the entire farm and not worry about ever exceeding your licenses. To keep one person from using up those 10 licenses, check the box to keep individuals from running more than one copy of an application.

> **NOTE** You can also configure application connection limits while publishing an application. I'll explain how to do that in Chapter 7, "Installing and Tuning Applications on an Application Server."

Figure 6.14 Configuring published application limits

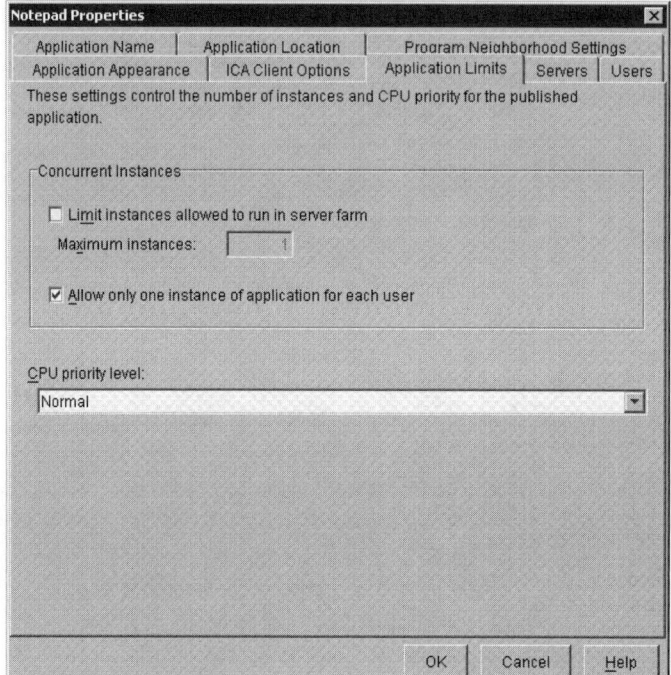

If you enable connection limits, you can also log attempts to exceed those limits to the System log in the Windows 2000 Event Viewer.

Through the use of policies, those with FR2 installed on their MetaFrame XP servers can edit these session limitations on a per-group basis. As described earlier in "Tuning Shadowing Permissions," create a new user policy. When editing its properties, look in the Resource Limits folder to find the Limit Concurrent Logon Sessions Policy. Enable this policy and set a logon limit, and the user and group accounts for which you set this policy will have those logon limits.

Summary

In this chapter, I've walked you through the management tools in Windows 2000 Terminal Services and MetaFrame XP that you'll be using for session management. In the next chapter, we'll talk about configuring applications to run within those sessions.

Installing and Tuning Applications on an Application Server

At this point, you have a working application server, but no one can use it for anything other than running Notepad—and perhaps playing Solitaire, if you're feeling indulgent. In this chapter, we'll talk about building the application part of the application server. By the end of this chapter, you should understand how applications share settings on an application server, and you should be able to choose applications for a multiuser environment. We will also discuss publishing desktops and individual applications, and automating application installations to terminal servers.

How Applications Work in a Shared Environment

We talked about how Windows 2000 allocates processor cycles and memory to individual sessions in an earlier chapter. As you can probably guess, shared resources affect how applications run, but using them also means that shared applications are installed a little differently than applications for use by one person at a time. Using them also means your choice of applications may be more limited than if you were running the applications on a single-user computer.

Choosing Applications

Not all applications work equally well on an application server. An application suitable for a shared environment fits the following profile:

- Undemanding of processor cycles and memory
- Modular in video output for better caching
- Identifies users by username, not computer name
- Stores global data in global locations, not local ones
- Can run more than one instance on the same computer

As you'll see, any of these factors can be a problem for Win32 applications, but some are more likely to be an issue for applications designed for older operating systems where a shared environment or remote display wasn't an option. If an application doesn't perform well in some of these categories, you may be able to fix it. I'll explain how a little later in this chapter. Ideally, this is what you should be looking for in new applications or what you should be designing into homegrown applications that you'd like to install on an application server.

Resource Efficiency

The reasons for this one are probably obvious. Although each session maintains its own memory space and the sessions cooperate to allocate processor time as equitably as possible, the less competition for memory and processor time, the better. You can avoid some crowding by installing a lot of memory and fast processors, but you know how it is—there is no such thing as too many resources. Ever.

Incidentally, the way that Windows 2000 is designed means that application servers are much more likely to be memory-bound than processor-bound. Part of the reason has to do with system architecture. Processor cycles are effectively unlimited, even though the return you get for a faster processor gets smaller the faster the processor you're talking about is—that is, the jump from 33MHz processors to 66MHz processors made more of a difference than going from 700MHz to 1GHz. Memory space, however, is *not* unlimited. Windows 2000 and other 32-bit operating systems can address only 4GB of memory. When 64-bit Windows becomes available, memory will gain some breathing room—and make application servers more likely to be processor-bound.

The other reason that application servers are more likely to be memory-bound is the way that applications themselves work. Most applications normally only use up a lot of processor time when they're performing calculations—working a spreadsheet, perhaps, or rendering a CAD design—but they're *always* using memory. If I'm running PowerPoint in the background, it's not using processor cycles, but it's still using memory to maintain the application and store any files that I have open. If I ignore the application for a long time, the memory manager may page that application's data out to the paging file on the hard disk because there doesn't seem to be any immediate call for it, but the paging file uses part of the 4GB of available memory addresses. People who've been using PCs are used to being able to run a lot of applications simultaneously, and they aren't likely to change that in their terminal sessions without duly applied thwacking—er, user training.

> **WARNING** Watch for application memory leaks. The effect of memory leaks in an application server is exponentially increased because multiple instances of the application—all leaking—may be running.

The operating system that an application is designed for matters, too. All else being equal, Win16 and DOS applications will use more resources than Win32 applications. The reason for this has to do with how Win2K runs Win32 and Win16 applications. As a Win32 operating system, Windows 2000 can't run Win16 applications on its own. Instead, it creates a Virtual DOS Machine (VDM) with a process called NTVDM.EXE, and it runs the Win16 application within the context of that VDM. Whereas Win32 applications running normally on Win2K can share files and structures among themselves, so long as they're not changing those files or structures, applications running within VDMs can't "see" each other to share files, because their processes are spawned by the main VDM process. The practical upshot of this, combined with the fact that translating 16-bit calls to the operating system into 32-bit calls takes some overhead, means that Win16 applications perform less well in this environment than Win32 applications. They'll work—a good thing because you may not have a choice about running them if that's what you're using—but they'll use more memory than equivalent Win32 apps.

> **NOTE** As pointed out in an earlier chapter, all things usually *aren't* equal. DOS and Win16 applications were designed for computers with a tiny fraction of the memory installed in today's computers, so they're much more parsimonious about their demands than modern applications are. This isn't a recommendation to use 16-bit applications over 32-bit applications (even if doing so is an option for you), just an observation about relative memory usage.

In addition to running within VDMs and thereby using more memory proportionate to their needs than Win32 applications, DOS applications present another kind of problem. Because they were written for a single-user, single-tasking environment in a relatively slow computer, some DOS applications constantly poll the keyboard buffer, looking for input that's meant for them. This means such an application in the foreground, even when not doing anything, can use an astounding amount of processor time. This is acceptable in a single-user environment, but it won't work when that processor time has to be shared with dozens of people.

Video Output Tuned for Remote Updates

When you're running an application from the console, graphical output for that application can go straight from the graphical device interface (GDI) component of the operating system to the video driver responsible for getting it onscreen. Applications running from within sessions can't do that. If the session is RDP-based, the GDI commands travel from application server to client via an RDP channel, to be processed on the client. ICA-based sessions work more like "screen-scraping," taking an image of the screen and then sending updates to the client computer as required. (This difference is why ICA is more client-OS agnostic than RDP is—native RDP depends on the client OS knowing how to process GDI commands.) Both display protocols have the option of caching bitmaps to speed up screen updates. Either way, though, the bitmaps or the GDI commands have to get to the client computer for processing, and a network connection is slower than the video connections internal to a computer. The fewer updates that need to go through that connection, the better. Applications that require a lot of visual updates—the System Monitor is one readily available example—may look jerky when running from a terminal session.

Again, DOS applications—or any application that runs in DOS mode, such as some games—have additional graphical issues. DOS applications with a graphical UI don't use Windows graphics rendering instructions, but bitmaps. Bitmaps take much longer to download to the client than GDI rendering instructions, so session responsiveness will suffer. I've found bitmap-displaying applications to be jerky at best in a terminal server environment and more often completely unusable, particularly on slower connections. Another problem with DOS applications in a multiuser environment is that you can't run them in full-screen mode. Because full-screen mode requires loading a different font set from the Windows set used for DOS applications running in a window (and thereby increasing memory overhead), Microsoft decided not to permit this.

Per-User Information Storage

If many people are running the same application on the same computer, you don't want them to share their personal settings. Sharing per-user settings could become a security issue. In addition, if Jane has set up her application settings the way she wants them, you want those application settings stored for her—not in a location where Joe can overwrite them when he's using the application installed on the same application server.

Identification of Users, Not Computers

Finally, applications that work best on an application server identify their users by their logon names or other per-user identifier, not by the IP address or computer name of the application server on which they're running. The reasons for this are probably apparent: every instance of an application running on an application server is associated with the same computer name and IP address, but each instance has a unique username.

Supports Multiple Instances

Some applications are designed to detect previously loaded copies of themselves and will refuse to run more than one. Obviously, this is a deal-breaker on an application server.

How Application Installation Works

Even if an application doesn't need any massaging to make it work well when shared among multiple people, you can't usually install it in the same way you would if you were installing it for a single person's use. The reason why has to do with the way the Windows 2000 Registry works. As you probably know, the Registry has several parts: HKEY_LOCAL_MACHINE (HKLM), HKEY_CURRENT_USER (HKCU), HKEY_USERS (HU), HKEY_CLASSES_ROOT (HCR), and HKEY_CURRENT_CONFIG (HCC). The two that matter to us now are HKLM, which contains the settings that apply to the entire computer, and HKCU, which applies to the person who's currently logged onto the computer. If more than one person is logged on at a time, then the Registry may contain multiple HKCU sections (each visible only to its session), but it will always maintain only a single HKLM section. HKCU settings include profile information.

The problem with installing applications on an application server is that we want *some* settings to apply to everybody using the same computer, but we also want some to apply to individuals. For example, everyone connecting to the same application server needs to know where the files supporting the installed applications are located—that's good per-machine information. Similarly, the location of a shared database is good per-machine information—if you made that information per-user, then everyone would have their own copy of the database and they couldn't share information. But the people using the applications on that server may have different per-user settings—for example, whether or not they want to use grammar checking in Word or where they're storing their spreadsheet files. *That* information should not be shared, both because you don't want people overwriting each other's settings and because you don't want everyone to know how many Star Wars pages Joe User has bookmarked from Internet Explorer.

The question, therefore, is how to install applications to make some settings machine-wide (HKLM) and some settings user-specific (HKCU). The way that Windows 2000 accomplishes this is to support a special installation routine for multiuser servers.

An application server has two operating modes: Execute and Install. As you can probably guess, Execute mode is for running applications, and Install mode is for installing applications to be available to multiple users. The mechanics of installing an application depend on which mode you're in when running the application's Setup program. If you install an application while in Execute mode, it installs and edits the Registry as it would if you installed it for use on a single-user computer. That's not the clever bit. The clever bit comes when you put a session into *Install* mode.

> **NOTE** The entire application server doesn't go into Install or Execute mode, individual sessions do.

When a session is in Install mode, all Registry entries created or edited within the session are shadowed under HKLM\Software\Microsoft\Windows NT\CurrentVersion\Terminal Server\Install. Any edits that an application makes to HKCU or HKLM are copied to HKLM\Software\ Microsoft\Windows NT\CurrentVersion\Terminal Server\Install\Machine. You don't need to know all this to install applications. What you *do* need to know is that when the session is in Execute mode, if an application attempts to read an HKCU Registry entry that doesn't exist, Terminal Services will look in HKLM\Software\Microsoft\ Windows NT\CurrentVersion\Terminal Server\Install for the missing key. If the key is there, Terminal Services will copy it and its subkeys to the appropriate location under HKCU, and copy any INI files or user-specific DLLs to the user's home directory. For users without home directories, the files go to a personal folder within c:\documents and settings*username* (where *username* is their logon name) on the application server to which they're connected. In short, Windows 2000 makes the basic settings for each application machine-specific. It then copies these base settings into the user Registry entries so that the user can customize the application. Notice that this doesn't mean the application keeps returning to its pristine state every time the user runs it—the keys are copied from their Install mode location to their user location only if the keys don't already exist under HKCU.

> **NOTE** Unfortunately, there's no way to spoof a user's identity to install an application for an individual while logged on with another account (if you logged on as Administrator and wanted to install an application for a particular user, for example). Nor can you specify a subset of users who should have access to a particular application, if you're using only Windows 2000 (those using MetaFrame on their application servers can restrict access to published applications). If you only want some people to use an application stored on a terminal server and you're using only Windows 2000, the easiest way to manage that is to limit the people allowed to use that server.

So how do you put the server into Install mode? If you're installing from an executable called SETUP.EXE, it's easy. If you attempt to run Setup without using Add/Remove Programs, the installation will fail and Win2K will nag you to run the Add/Remove Programs applet to put Win2K into Install mode (and provide a link to help you do so). When you use Add/Remove Programs, the session goes into Install mode automatically. Returning to Execute mode is also automated. When the application's Setup program finishes running, you'll go back to the wizard, which will prompt you to click the Next button. Finally, you'll see a dire-looking dialog box (see Figure 7.1) telling you to click the Finish button or the Cancel button when the installation process is complete, and warning you in capital letters not to do so *until* the installation is complete. Clicking Finish or Cancel returns the session to Execute mode.

Figure 7.1 Don't click the Finish button until the application is completely installed, or the settings won't all be copied.

Windows 2000 isn't smart enough to recognize an installation routine, just smart enough to tell when someone tries to start a program called SETUP.EXE. If the installation routine you're using doesn't use this executable name, you'll need to put the session into Install mode manually. (You'll also need to do this if you want to tune the application in ways that you can't do during base Setup. You can put a session into Install mode with the change user command-line utility, which has three options:

- /execute, the default, in which applications install in single-user mode
- /install, used to put the session into Install mode so that applications will be available to all users
- /query, which reports the mode that the session is in, like this:

    Application EXECUTE mode is enabled.

So, before running a setup program not called SETUP.EXE, open a command prompt and type **change user /install**. This will cause Windows 2000 to shadow new Registry entries as I described earlier, so that they'll be copied to each user's personal Registry settings as the user runs the application for the first time. Just bear in mind that *any* changes you make to an application while your session is in Install mode will be copied to the shadowing location and will, therefore, apply to all users using the application for the first time.

Installing Multiuser-Enabled Applications

As Terminal Services becomes more widespread, more applications will probably come with multiuser installation packages. Microsoft Office 2000 is one that presently does. If you try to run the normal installation program on a terminal server, you'll see a nag screen telling you that you can't do that and prompting you to use the installation files provided with the Office 2000 Resource Kit. You'll need to follow these steps:

1. First, get the terminal server transform file, TermSrvr.mst, and place it in an accessible location for the installation. You can obtain the transform file from the \ORK\PFiles\ORKTools\Toolbox\Tools\TermSrvr folder of the Office 2000 Resource Kit CD, or in \Program Files\ORKtools\Toolbox\Terminal Server Tools if you installed the Resource Kit.

2. Install Office Disc 1 on the Terminal Server computer.

3. In the Control Panel, double-click Add/Remove Programs, click Add New Programs, and then click CD or Floppy. Click Next, click Browse, and then move to the root folder of the installation CD and select Setup.exe. Click Open to add Setup.exe to the Run Installation Program box.

4. Don't run it yet. On the command line, append the following command after Setup.exe, separated by a space: **TRANSFORMS=*path*\TermSrvr.mst**, where *path* is the location where you copied TermSrvr.mst.

5. From here, all goes as expected. In successive windows of the Installation Wizard, provide your customer information and accept the EULA, and then choose Install Now. When you see a message telling you that the installation completed successfully, click OK, click Next, and then click Finish.

Tuning Installed Applications

Once applications are installed, you may have to mess around with them a bit to make them work properly—use the right path information, do not use animations that create unnecessary graphical changes, and the like. You can do this by directly editing application settings from a session in Install mode, running application compatibility scripts, or editing the Registry directly.

Why Do We Need to Tune Applications?

Considering that we don't need to tune applications for single-user installations, and that Windows 2000 has this elaborate mechanism for copying Registry keys and DLLs to the places where they need to be, it may frustrate you that you can't just install those applications and leave it at that. Unfortunately, while some applications will work without trouble—particularly newer ones developed by people who knew that their code might run on an application server—some will not. These older applications may have problems with putting information in the wrong place in the Registry (again, putting per-user settings in per-machine locations), using paths that are specific to a particular computer, not a user, and, due to the way that Windows 2000 creates and names objects created from within terminal sessions, being unable to communicate with services to run.

Misplaced Registry Entries

You may encounter a couple of different Registry problems: installations that apply only to the person who ran them, applications that don't create their user-specific entries until actually run, and applications that want to store all settings in a machine-wide space.

User-Specific Installations An application that installs itself only for the current user is a problem, because its settings will apply only to the person installing it. This situation is handled with Install mode, as described earlier. The only things you need to watch out for are installation programs not called SETUP.EXE, since they won't trigger Windows 2000 to remind you to use Add/Remove Programs to install the application and, therefore, automatically put the application server into Install mode. In that case, you'll need to remember yourself and run change user to install the application properly, and then restore the session to Execution mode when it's done.

Applications that Don't Customize until Run Once If an application doesn't create its per-user entries until the first time it's run, those per-user entries won't be copied to the shadow key in HKLM unless the computer happens to be in Install mode at the time. (You can tell that this is happening if you installed the application with specific settings and you discover that it's reverted to the defaults for all the people who use it.) If this is the case, you'll need to run the application once after installing it—but first run change user /install to put the session into Install mode. Again, restore the session to Execute mode when you're finished.

Machine-Specific Settings If an application puts per-user data in HKLM, then all users will share that information. As you've seen, sometimes this is desirable, and sometimes it isn't. If an application *does* include this information and it's not shadowed properly, there may be nothing much you can do about it. You can fix options like path information with an application compatibility script; however, if color (for example) is determined on a per-machine basis, you may not be able to create per-user color settings. That will be a limitation of the application on a shared server, and (for some settings) that could mean that the application works best when installed locally, not on an application server.

File-Specific Problems

Path and file problems are usually in older applications. You may find that users can't find an application, or that they don't have permission to access a file required to run an application. Specifically, you may find the following problems.

Common Paths Some shared path information is helpful. If you'd like to be sure that everyone is using the same version of a word processing or slide show template, then pointing everyone to the same template location is easiest. (You might want to make templates read-only, but sharing a Templates folder does simplify document sharing and avoids funky formatting issues that can arise from mismatched templates.) The same goes for executable files—the whole point of installing applications on a shared server is to make updates apply to everyone connecting to the server, so it's only sensible to have them share those files. However, if an application uses the same pathname for files containing user-specific *configuration* data (e.g., an INI file), then people may be able to overwrite each other's settings. Not good.

Fixing this can be more difficult than it may seem at first. To resolve problems of common path and filenames, first you must notice that there *is* a problem, since this is the kind of thing that can pop up after people have been using an application for weeks without incident. One day, everything's fine, and the next day everybody's application settings have gone haywire. (This gets even more exciting if no one admits to having changed anything.) Once you've noticed that there is a problem, you'll have to find out which files are being edited. Finally, you'll have to figure out what to change the path to so as to make the configuration files user-specific.

I can't tell you a lot about finding out whether or not there is a problem, other than suggesting that you keep your eyes and ears open for complaints from people whose settings have changed unexpectedly. Tracking down changed files is a bit more concrete. To do that, you can turn on folder and file auditing for the location of the problem child's configuration files. Go to the folder for that application and open its Properties sheet, turning to the Security tab. From there, click the Advanced button, turn to the Auditing tab, and click the Advanced button to show the settings visible in Figure 7.2.

Monitor the successes for the Everyone group creating or writing to files. Such events will show up in the Security Log portion of the Event Viewer.

Figure 7.2 Turning on file auditing for a folder

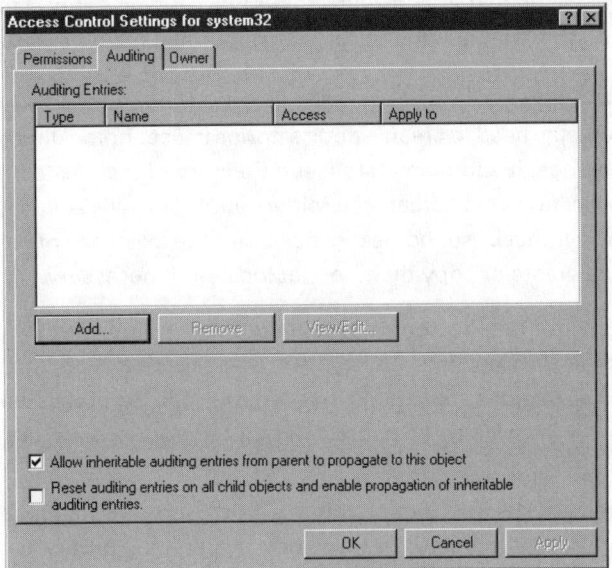

> **NOTE** To audit file access, you'll need to enable security logging for the domain or local server. You'll also need to use NTFS, because it is the only Windows 2000 file system that supports file auditing.

When you've found the files being edited for that program, you'll need to find out how the application is pointing to those files. If you're lucky, the information will be accessible from somewhere in the GUI itself (for example, the Options menu setting in the Tools menu in Word where all path information is stored). If it is accessible, you can change the path information there. If the application UI doesn't expose configuration path information, you can check the Software tree of HKLM and HKCU for that application's entry, and then look for the path to the configuration files there. Even if there isn't any path information there, you may be able to add it—check with the application's developer if you can.

Whether you can change it from the application UI or you need to edit the Registry by hand, path information stored in HKCU doesn't present any problems. Just go into Install mode and change it so that the settings are shadowed to HKLM and will be automatically copied to HKCU for each user when they next start the application. Changing path information stored in HKLM is a little more complicated, because it applies to everyone using the application server. In that case, you'll probably need to map a driver letter to user home directories when people connect to the terminal server. You can do this with a logon script that runs when the user starts their session.

> **NOTE** You may need to create subdirectories in user home directories for some program settings, if you pointed to a subdirectory of the user's home directory and the application won't create the folders automatically. Again, you can create a script that will check user home directories for the existence of particular folders and files and create or copy them to that location if necessary.

This applies not only to configuration data, but to user files as well. If applications are accessing the same temporary directories, users can potentially overwrite each other's data. Again, applications that can't use the normal temporary directory and create their own need to be redirected to a temporary directory in the user's home directory.

Application Works for Administrators, Not Users If an application works when you log on as an administrator, but not when you log on as a user, it could be doing so for a couple of reasons.

One reason might be the way the application is written. If it's automatically remapping the system root directory to a location in user home directories—but not doing this for administrators, who have access to the system root—the application won't work if the files aren't present in the expected location. You can take a couple of tacks to fix this. If the file access is read-only, you can turn off automatic remapping by editing the Registry. If people need write access to the files, you'll need to copy them to the expected location in a user's home directory.

Another possible explanation is that the users don't have the kind of access to the system root they need, and therefore the applications, which run in the user security context, don't either. This is most likely to be a problem with older applications; newer ones don't write to the system root directory. You can confirm that this is the problem by auditing the system root directory for failed file writes. In this case, you can change the security settings for Terminal Services from Terminal Services Configuration. Alternatively, try remapping the configuration files to the user home directories as described earlier. If the applications really are writing to the files stored in the system root, one user's writes could affect everybody using the application.

Applications Only Run from the Console

What if an application will run from the console, but it refuses to run from within a terminal session? In that case, the problem may have to do with how Windows 2000 deals with objects created within terminal sessions. As we discussed in Chapter 2, "Core

Parts of Windows Terminal Services," Windows 2000 has to identify objects created within a terminal session for that session, so that it can tell which particular instance of that object—there may be several, all using the same name—it's dealing with. It does this by appending the Session ID to each object that it creates from within a session. Objects identified by the session in which they were created are *user global objects*. Console objects, on the other hand, don't have a Session ID and, therefore, have just their own names—they're *system global objects*.

Most of the time, this is as it should be—by renaming session-specific objects, Windows 2000 keeps its Object Manager from being confused as to which objects belong to which session. However, some kinds of applications—generally, those running as services—want to deal with system global objects only. Therefore, these applications won't run from a terminal session, even when you're logged on as an administrator. The terminal session object doesn't have the right name.

To run such applications from a terminal session, you'll need to register the DLL or EXE for the application as system global so that Windows 2000's Object Manager doesn't rename it according to its session. Windows 2000 has a command-line utility called `register` that you can use to register a program as system global. Once you've registered an image file as system global, every object created in the context of that image's process will be system global. (If you do this to a process that should be user global, then you can use the same `register` command to make the image user global.)

So that's a look at what can go wrong with applications running on an application server. How do we *fix* these problems?

Editing Application Settings Manually

The simplest way to tune applications, of course, is to just run them and configure them the way you want the application to appear to everyone else. This takes longer than running a script, but it does mean that you don't have to *write* the script in the first place.

Terminal servers are designed to squeeze every last bit of juice out of system resources so that nothing is wasted. Therefore, they're often stressed—they're *supposed* to be stressed. Given that, don't waste processor cycles on producing effects that don't necessarily add any real content to the end product, and don't waste network bandwidth on sending those useless effects to the client. In Microsoft Office, for example, turn off sparkle text and the Office Assistant. In other applications, look for pretty effects that don't do anything constructive and see whether you can disable them.

Many applications have settings for file locations—places to save files to, places to open files from, template locations, and so forth. However, those locations will often be different for different users. To make sure that file locations for each user are correct, enter a drive letter—and then map that drive letter to different locations for each user. For example, the Save As location for all Word users could be the H: drive, but H: would direct each user to their private home directory *mapped* to the H: drive.

Application Compatibility Scripts

Given that just about all of the applications the terminal server users will be running were originally designed for a single-user environment, many applications require a little manipulation to get them optimized for a multiuser system. Windows 2000 Server includes application compatibility scripts for some commonly used applications. (Well, they used to be commonly used, when Windows 2000 came out in February 2000. By now, they're getting a bit dated.) These scripts tweak application settings for known problems with the applications themselves. You can find the scripts for the applications in Table 7.1 in %systemroot%\Application Compatibility Scripts\Install.

Table 7.1 Compatibility Scripts Included with Win2K

Application	Script
Corel Office 7	Coffice7.cmd
Corel Office 8	Not supported
Eudora Pro 4	Eudora4.cmd
Lotus Notes 4.*x*	Lnote4u.cmd
Lotus Smart Suite 9	Ssuite9.cmd
Lotus Smart Suite 97	Ssuite97.cmd
Microsoft Access 2	Office43.cmd
Microsoft Access 7	Office95.cmd
Microsoft Access 97	Office97.cmd
Microsoft Excel 5.0z	Office43.cmd
Microsoft Excel 7	Office95.cmd
Microsoft Excel 97	Office97.cmd
Microsoft Excel 97 (stand-alone installation)	Msexcl97.cmd

Table 7.1 Compatibility Scripts Included with Win2K *(continued)*

Application	Script
Microsoft Exchange 5 and higher	`Winmsg.cmd`
Microsoft ODBC	`ODBC.cmd`
Microsoft Office 4.3	`Office43.cmd`
Microsoft Office 95	`Office95.cmd`
Microsoft Office 97	`Office97.cmd`
Microsoft Office 2000	Requires Transform file
Microsoft Outlook 97	`Outlk98.cmd`
Microsoft Outlook 98	`Outlk98.cmd`
Microsoft Outlook Express	`Outlk98.cmd`
Microsoft PowerPoint 4	`Office43.cmd`
Microsoft PowerPoint 7	`Office95.cmd`
Microsoft PowerPoint 97	`Office97.cmd`
Microsoft Project 95	`Msproj95.cmd`
Microsoft Project 98	`Msproj98.cmd`
Microsoft Schedule+ 7	`Office95.cmd`
Microsoft SNA Client 4	`Sna40cli.cmd`
Microsoft SNA Server 3	`Mssna30.cmd`
Microsoft SNA Server 4	`Sna40srv.cmd`
Microsoft Visual Studio 6	`MSVS6.cmd`
Microsoft Word 6	`Office43.cmd`
Microsoft Word 7	`Office95.cmd`

Table 7.1 Compatibility Scripts Included with Win2K *(continued)*

Application	Script
Microsoft Word 97	Office97.cmd
Microsoft Word 97 (stand-alone installation)	Msword97.cmd
Netscape Communicator 4.0*x*	Netcom40.cmd
Netscape Communicator 4.5*x*	Netcom40.cmd
Netscape Communicator 4.6*x*	Netcom40.cmd
Netscape Navigator 3.*x*	Netnav30.cmd
Peachtree Complete Accounting 6	PchTree6.cmd
PowerBuilder 6	PwrBldr6.cmd
Visio 5	Visio5.cmd

These scripts are designed to customize the application's setup to be appropriate for terminal server users, first setting up the command environment, then making sure that the session is in Install mode, checking the Registry for evidence of the application to be configured, and finally editing the Registry as needed. The contents of the scripts vary based on the application. Generally speaking, they do things such as turn off processor-intensive features (for example, the FindFast utility that comes with Microsoft Office), add multi-user support to the application, and set user-specific application directories for applications that may be set up for machine-wide directories.

Using Application Compatibility Scripts

Using application compatibility scripts is a bit more complex than just running a CMD file. You may have noticed that, whenever you log onto a terminal session, a small command-line window at the bottom left of the screen does something quickly and then exits. It is running usrlogon.cmd. Now, usrlogon.cmd doesn't necessarily do much on its own. What it *can* do, however, is call on other command files to do things. *Which* command files it calls on depends on what application compatibility scripts you've already run.

To use the scripts, just run them right after you install the application they customize, while the session is still in Install mode and before anyone has a chance to use the application themselves. If you've run any application compatibility script that depends on the existence of a mapped root drive, you created a file called rootdrv2.cmd and opened it with Notepad when you ran it. `Rootdrv2.cmd` prompts you for the drive letter you want application compatibility scripts to use for their root drive information. Type a letter—no spaces, pleases—and save the file as prompted. Doing so will create a Registry entry HKLM\Software\Microsoft\Windows NT\CurrentVersion\Terminal Server\RootDrive with a value of whatever letter you supplied—say W. Now, any application compatibility script that needs root drive information can call on that drive letter. The information will be available to all sessions because the root drive key is in HKLM.

> **WARNING** Do *not* use the same drive letter for application compatibility scripts that you used for user home directories. If you do, you'll overwrite that mapping and screw up your home directories for terminal sessions. The drive letter you supply now should not be used for anything else on the application server.

In addition to creating `rootdrv2.cmd`, running an application compatibility script that requires root drive information also creates a new CMD file called `usrlogn2.cmd`, which calls on scripts that require root drive mapping. Any time you run these scripts, they're added to `usrlogon2.cmd` if they're not already there.

When you run an application compatibility script that doesn't require drive mapping information, it creates (and adds itself to) `usrlogn1.cmd`, so that when this command file runs it launches that application compatibility script.

When you log onto a terminal session, the following takes place:

1. The `usrlogon.cmd` script runs and checks to see if `usrlogn1.cmd` exists. If it does, then `usrlogn1.cmd` runs, launching the application compatibility scripts it references.
2. When `usrlogon1.cmd` has run (or if it didn't exist), `usrlogon.cmd` calls `rootdrive.cmd` to see if there's a root drive mapping. If there isn't, `userlogon.cmd` ends and your session starts. If there is, `rootdrive.cmd` calls `rootdrv2.cmd`, which sets the drive letter and returns control to `rootdrive.cmd`. `Rootdrive.cmd` then removes any mappings to that drive letter, substitutes root drive for home drive and home path information, and checks for the existence of `usrlogn2.cmd`.
3. If `usrlogn2.cmd` exists, then it runs, launching all the application compatibility scripts it's set up to call.
4. When `userlogn.cmd` finishes, the session begins, with the environment set up for that user.

Editing or Creating Scripts

Microsoft came up with its scripts in time for Windows 2000's release in early 2000. What do you do for the many applications that have been released since then and for which Microsoft has not developed a script, or for applications that aren't on that list? What if *they* need tweaking?

The answer's probably obvious: you roll up your sleeves and start writing your own scripts. Luckily, the mechanics of writing the application compatibility scripts aren't terribly difficult—the harder part is identifying the problem in the first place so you can script a solution. Getting into this seriously requires some knowledge of batch file language, but here are some basics to help you get started.

Built-In Script Support First of all, you don't have to hand-write everything. The mkdir and copy commands work fine in scripts, but you can also call on the pre-made scripts for doing this called, respectively, tsmkudir.cmd and tsmkufil.cmd. You can call on these scripted commands from within *your* scripts with the Call command, like these commands to create application-specific directories in the user's home directory (mapped to the root drive letter). What you're doing here is calling on an external script and supplying the path as an argument.

```
call TsMkUDir "%RootDrive%\Office97"
call TsMkUDir "%RootDrive%\Office97\Templates"
call TsMkUDir "%RootDrive%\%MY_DOCUMENTS%"
call TsMkUDir "%RootDrive%\Office97\XLStart"
```

In addition to these simple commands, Windows 2000 Terminal Services includes some Resource Kit utilities in the Application Compatibility Scripts folder that you can use: ACREGL, ACSR and ACINIUPD.

ACREGL looks up a key and string value in the Registry (optionally stripping it to a particular bit, if you don't want the whole thing). Then it sets this value to a variable and stores this information in a user-defined file. For example, this command:

```
ACREGL OfficeNfo.Cmd INSTLOC
"HKLM\Software\Microsoft\Office\9.0\Common\InstallRoot" "" ""
```

creates a file called Officenfo.cmd that contains the statement:

```
SET INSTLOC=C:\Program Files\Microsoft Office\Office
```

Not so exciting on its own, but you can use the Call command to retrieve this information when you need it for scripts.

ACSR performs simple text replacement, reading from an input file and writing the changed text to an output file. For example, #ROOTDRIVE# in a script doesn't mean anything; but if you use ACSR to replace it, you can change the string to the actual value of the variable. It's similar to ACREGL in that you can use it to populate variables with meaningful values, but different in that it allows you to include a placeholder variable in scripts. As with ACREGL, you can then call on this new output file from a script.

ACINIUPD is useful when you need to edit INI files. You're probably familiar with the basic structure of an INI file, where you've got a lot of key=value statements that tune the user environment. Using ACINIUPD, you can change either the key or the value if necessary. For example, the following (wrapped to fit on the page) updates the value of the USER-DOT-PATH key in the Microsoft Word section of WinWord6.ini:

```
Aciniupd /e "Winword6.ini" "Microsoft Word" USER-DOT-PATH
"%RootDrive%\OFFICE43\WINWORD"
```

Changing the Flow of Information   You can make a script check for the existence of a file or directory before you copy it as well, by employing the If Exist and If Not Exist statements. You'll use these statements to determine whether an application is installed (important before running an application compatibility script) and whether certain directories already exist at the suggested location. For example, the following (wrapped to fit on the page) tells the script to check for the existence of a particular template in the user's profile directory and, if it's not there, copy it from the All Users profile directory to the named location without prompting:

```
If Not Exist "%UserProfile%\%TEMPLATES%\WINWORD8.DOC" copy
"%ALLUSERSPROFILE%\%TEMPLATES%\WINWORD8.DOC"
"%UserProfile%\%Templates%\" /Y
```

If you're doing conditional actions, you'll probably want the script to react differently depending on what the conditions are. To that end, you can include Goto statements pointing to user-defined sections of the script. For example, Goto End sends the script right to the line beginning :End, ignoring any other commands in between the Goto statement and that line.

> **WARNING**   Inspect any script before running it, even if it's one of the scripts that come with Windows 2000. The path information for the script may not be correct if you installed the application in question in a location other than the one the script expects. You may want to echo off the script's output so that it runs without showing what it's doing.

Registry Settings for Application Tuning

Of course, if an application doesn't have a setting in its interface, you can't use Install mode to tune that setting. However, all is not necessarily lost. You can edit some application settings directly within the Registry, in HKLM\Software\Microsoft\Windows NT \CurrentVersion\Terminal Server\Compatibility\Applications. (The obligatory warning follows.)

> **WARNING** Be careful when you're editing the Registry. Neither REGEDIT nor REGEDT32 has an Undo feature, and neither will tell you if you edit a value to a meaningless entry. Back up the Registry before you edit it, and remember that a mistyped entry in the wrong place can wipe out needed information or render Win2K unbootable.

More specifically, keep the following in mind:

- When editing value data, notice whether the values are shown in hex, decimal, or binary. When you're editing string values, you can choose to display them in any of those formats. Just be sure that you're entering the data in the chosen format. The numeral 15 decimal is F hex, but 15 hex is 21 decimal. You can guess how mixing up hex and decimal could get very ugly very quickly.

- If you're replacing a key (and, if you try out these hacks, you will be), be sure that the key that's selected is the one you want to replace. Restoring a key deletes all the present information in the key and replaces it with what's in the restored key. For example, say that you want to replace the contents of the MSOFFICE key that's a subkey of Applications. If you have Applications selected when you restore the saved REG file, you will wipe out every subkey of Applications and replace it with the information that should have gone into MSOFFICE.

- Never run a REG file unless you know exactly what it contains and what it will do. Executing a REG file imports the contents of that file into the Registry—permanently. There is no Undo feature. You *can* undo an MSI file by removing it from the computer with Add/Remove Programs, which is one reason why I earlier suggested that you package Registry edits as MSI files instead of REG files.

Now that you're thoroughly intimidated, read on to see how to make your applications play well with others and call you by your name.

Sample Registry Values

To make applications work the way you want them to, you may have to edit Registry values associated with those applications. Sadly, the values aren't always something easy to remember, like, "Make this application use system global objects." More often, they're hexadecimal values that, to Windows 2000, mean "Make this application use system global objects." There is a reason for this other than a desire on the part of the Microsoft developers to complicate your life. The part of application settings you'll directly edit from the Registry most often is a key called Flags, and Flags can contain more than one setting at a time. To make it do so, you'll add the values of the Registry edits together and enter the result as the value for Flags. For example, a 32-bit Windows application has a

Flags value of 8 hex, and the value that tells Windows 2000 to make the application reference usernames instead of computer names is 10 hex. A value of 18 hex, therefore, tells Windows 2000 that a particular application is a Win32 application that should reference usernames, not computer names. (You have to tell Windows 2000 that the application is a 32-bit version to make sure it knows which version of that application to edit, in case there's more than one application using the same image name.)

These values are set under HKLM\SOFTWARE \Microsoft\Windows NT\CurrentVersion\ Terminal Server\Compatibility\Applications*appname*, where *appname* is the name of the application's executable file. For example, if the executable filename for an application is WINWORD.EXE, the key will be WINWORD. Table 7.2 contains some values of Flags; in the next sections I'll explain more about how and when to apply these values.

Table 7.2 Some Values for Flags

Flag meaning	Value
DOS application	0x00000001
Win16 application	0x00000004
Win32 application	0x00000008
Win16 or Win32 application	0x0000000c
Return username instead of computername	0x00000010
Disable Registry mapping for this application	0x00000100
Instruct application to create System Global Objects	0x00000200
Return systemroot, not user's WINDOWS directory	0x00000400
Limit the reported physical memory (GlobalMemoryStatus) for applications that can't use more than 32MB	0x00000800
Don't put app to sleep on unsuccessful keyboard polling (WIN16 only)	0x20000000

Bad! Bad Application! Go to Sleep! Reducing Demands of Windows Applications

Even if you turn off processor-hogging effects, some applications are just more cycle-hungry than others. In a terminal server environment, this is a Bad Thing. Not only do processor-sucking applications themselves underperform in a multiuser environment because they're contending with other applications, they hurt other applications' performance by denying them cycles. You can edit the Registry to make Windows 2000 keep a closer eye on Windows application management, denying processor cycles to applications that use too many, known internally as Bad Applications. Doing so will give more cycles to the other applications that the processor-sucker was starving, but it will also make the errant application less responsive itself.

To make the edit, open REGEDT32 and turn to HKLM\Software\Microsoft\Windows NT\CurrentVersion\Terminal Server\Compatibility\Applications. As you can see in Figure 7.3, within the Applications key, you'll see a long list of keys for installed applications.

Figure 7.3 The contents of the Applications subkey

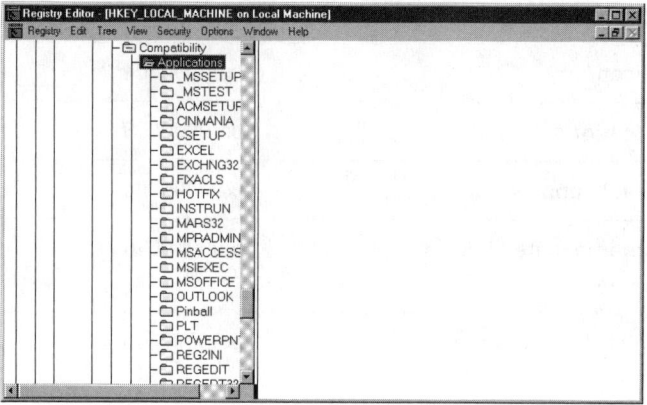

> **NOTE** Use REGEDT32, not REGEDIT, for this process. You'll need tools found only in REGEDIT32.

First, check to see whether the application you want to configure is already listed; if it is, then a key with the name of the application will be present. If the key exists, open it. If the key doesn't exist, or doesn't include the values you need to edit, then you'll need to get the values elsewhere. Find the SETUP key, designed for Win32 applications.

> **NOTE** SETUP1 is almost identical to SETUP. The only difference is in its Flags value, which is set for both Win16 and Win32 applications.

Open SETUP and look at the values within it, which are described in Table 7.3.

Table 7.3 Bad Application Registry Values

Value Name	Description	Default Value
FirstCountMsgQPeeksSleepBadApp	Number of times that the application will query the message queue before Win2K decides the application is a Bad Application. The lower this value, the sooner Win2K will decide that the application is bad, and the more quickly the other two values will apply.	0xf (15 decimal)
MsgQBadAppSleepTimeInMillisec	The number of milliseconds that a suspended application will be denied CPU cycles. The higher this value is, the longer the application will sleep.	0
NthCountMsgQPeeksSleepBadApp	The number of times that a Bad Application can query the message queue before Win2K will put it to sleep again. The lower this number, the more often the misbehaving application will go to sleep.	0x5 (5 decimal)
Flags	Describes the type of application to which these settings apply. Your options are 0x4 for Win16 applications, 0x8 for Win32 applications, or 0xc for both types.	0x8 (Win32 only)

288   Chapter 7   Installing and Tuning Applications on an Application Server

Assuming you're starting from scratch, you're going to save the SETUP key, import the key to a new (or existing) key for the application, and then edit these settings:

1. First, highlight SETUP, choose Save Key from the Registry menu, and as shown in Figure 7.4, and save the key to the default directory with some name and a `.reg` extension.

Figure 7.4   Saving a Registry key

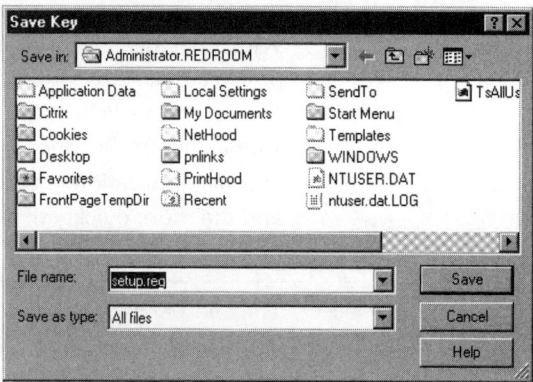

2. Now, highlight the Applications key and choose Add Key from the Edit menu. In the dialog box shown in Figure 7.5, name the new key the filename of the application you're configuring, minus the extension—for example, wordstar.exe's key would be named wordstar. Leave the Class field blank, and click OK. The new key will appear below Applications.

Figure 7.5   Creating a new application key

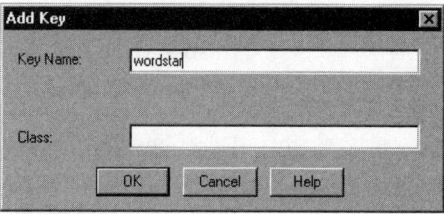

3. Now, with your new key highlighted, pick Restore from the Registry menu and choose the REG file you created earlier. The Registry Editor will warn you that you're about to replace the contents of the selected key with the contents of the file you're importing. Once you're sure you're replacing the right key, click Yes.

4. Finally, double-click value data entries to make your edits in the dialog box shown in Figure 7.6, bearing in mind what those edits will do. Make sure you've set the flags properly according to whether the application you're editing is a 16-bit or 32-bit application, and don't forget to notice whether you're making changes in hex or decimal (or binary, if you're a true glutton for punishment).

Figure 7.6 Edit string values to set the Bad Application parameters you want.

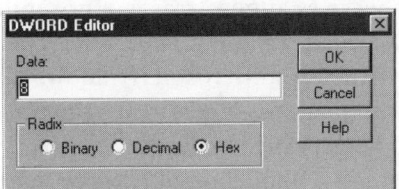

The settings will take effect when you next open the application. Because you edited a key in HKLM, the changes will apply to all instances of the application running on this terminal server.

TAMEing DOS Applications

Windows NT, Terminal Server Edition (TSE), includes a utility called DOSKBD that modifies a program's keyboard polling to improve system performance when you run DOS-based programs. Essentially, DOSKBD puts a program to sleep when it polls the keyboard buffer too often and negatively affects server performance. Win2K doesn't include a copy of DOSKBD, and the TSE version doesn't work with Win2K Server Terminal Services.

A while ago, I was told that the Win2K Resource Kit would eventually include a Win2K-compatible version of DOSKBD, but it doesn't now. Until and unless it does, according to Microsoft, people who need to use DOSKBD can't upgrade to Win2K Terminal Services—they're stuck with TSE. (And this means that new users of Terminal Services are out of luck, as Microsoft stopped making TSE in August 2000, and the only copies for sale are those made before that time.) However, there's another option. Go to http://www.mindspring.com/~dgthomas/tame.htm and check out Tame, a tool for tuning DOS applications in a Win2K environment. Until the resource kit utility is ready—and at this point I would not hold my breath—that's the advice you'll get from Microsoft Support if you ask about tuning DOS applications. According to the Microsoft Terminal Services team, .NET Server will not include a version of DOSKBD either.

Making Applications Reference Usernames Instead of Computer Names

Windows Terminal Server, and terminal sessions running on early betas of Win2K Server, had a little problem when it came to running WinChat, the graphical chat application that comes with Windows. Because WinChat referenced computers, not users, you couldn't use it from a terminal server session to talk to someone running another terminal session. If you tried to connect to someone, you'd see a list of computers from which to choose.

The intrepid Terminal Services administrator is not foiled by such petty machinations, however. You can make an application reference usernames instead of computer names. In HKLM\Software\Microsoft\Windows NT\CurrentVersion\Terminal Server\Compatibility\Applications, where you just edited the Bad Application settings, there's a value for Flags, which in the previous section was *8* or *c*, signifying that the settings applied to either a Win32 application or to both Win16 and Win32 applications. Make it **18** (8 for being a Win32 application and 10 for referencing usernames instead of computer names), and the application will accept usernames as input. You won't change the application UI—that would have been handy, but no dice—but if you plug a username into the browse function, it will find that user and place the call.

> **NOTE** You're probably thinking that I'm going to tell you that Microsoft fixed this problem in Win2K. In a way, you would be correct. You will no longer have problems running WinChat in a terminal server session and only being able to reference computers. This is because Microsoft has evidently decided there was no point in having a messaging application that "didn't work" from terminal server sessions available to those sessions.

At this point, you should be able to make applications run on an application server, whether that server is running only Windows 2000 Server or also MetaFrame XP. However, MetaFrame XP has some additional application-presenting features not found in Windows 2000 alone, so let's take a look at how to configure those before we get around to configuring RDP or ICA client connections.

Publishing Applications with MetaFrame XP

When you present applications from a Windows 2000 application server with no helper software, people get two kinds of views of applications on that server: an entire Desktop, from which they can launch applications, or single connections to applications installed on a particular application server. Either one of those options is possible with MetaFrame, but MetaFrame has another option as well: published applications.

The ability to publish applications is really useful for a server-based computing environment, especially one where people may be using a mix of locally installed applications and ones made available from an application server.

First, they present well. Published applications using Seamless Windows fit nicely into a Win32 Desktop alongside locally running applications, maximizing to the same size as the local applications. Providing published applications keeps people from having to navigate two Desktops. Published applications make a dynamically updated menu of all the applications available to a person, based on their user or group membership. Single-application connections, on the other hand, are not dynamic and are entirely user-driven—you have to create such connections by hand. If you install a new application on an application server, users won't know about it until they connect to a full Desktop or you create a connection for them—and the reverse is true if you uninstall an application. With published applications, users always have a complete and updated list of the applications they're allowed to run.

Published applications are also good from the server's perspective. Using Seamless Windows to present applications means that all the applications are actually running from the same session (if they're running from the same application server, anyway), so that they can use the same Windows environment and, therefore, save memory. In contrast, if you set up an RDP connection to single applications, the application displays in a terminal window and each application connection needs its own Windows environment. In other words, single-application connections use more memory than accessing the same applications from a Desktop. And, since published applications can be backed by any MetaFrame server in the server farm, you can potentially use load balancing to make the connection always to the server best equipped to handle it when the user launches it.

> **NOTE** The shared Windows environment used by published applications applies only to applications using Seamless Windows. Applications published in regular session windows from a MetaFrame server all need their own environment and will use as much memory as RDP connections to single applications.

Publishing Applications to Program Neighborhood

MetaFrame XP can publish applications, entire desktops (you'd do this to make the desktop window fit into the user's local desktop), or, with FR1 or later installed, publish content to be viewed on the user's computer using locally installed applications. Most often, you'll publish individual applications, and the process for publishing desktops and content is similar, so let's start with that. To publish a new application, go to the Applications folder in the Citrix Management Console. No applications are published by default, so right-click the Applications folder, and choose Publish Application from the menu to begin the Application Publishing Wizard. Follow these steps:

1. First, you'll need to provide a name and description for the published application, as in Figure 7.7. The name will identify the application in the Program Neighborhood; the optional description will appear in the bottom of the Program Neighborhood when the published application's icon is selected.

2. Next, you'll need to specify what you're publishing (application, desktop, or, with FR1 installed, content) and provide a command-line path for the published application. Because you're working from the console, you can browse for the correct path using the button visible in Figure 7.8, rather than having to know the path as you do when configuring the ICA Client. Because the Citrix Management Console connects to all servers in the farm—not just the one you're running the console from—when browsing, you'll need to select a server to browse on, and then dig until you get to the right path. (Obviously, if you'll be publishing an application from more than one server in the farm, either the application path must be the same on all servers or you'll need to edit individual server configurations later in the wizard—I'll point out where to do so.) The publishing server will not be identified in the command-line information. When you've filled in the information, click Next.

Figure 7.7 Choose a name and description for the published application.

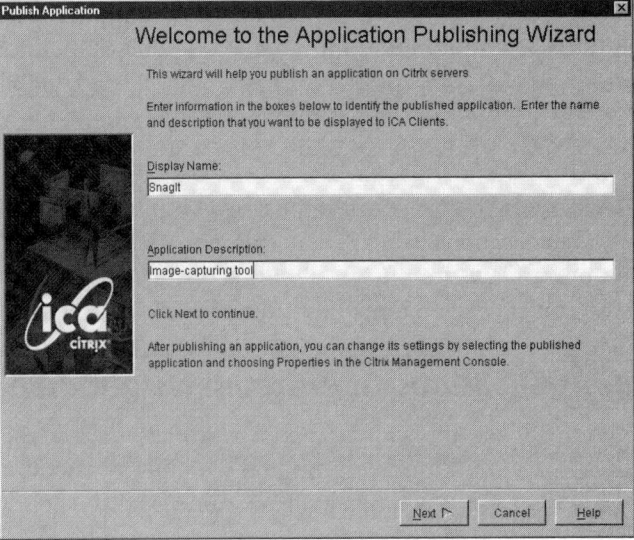

Figure 7.8 Provide command-line information for the published application.

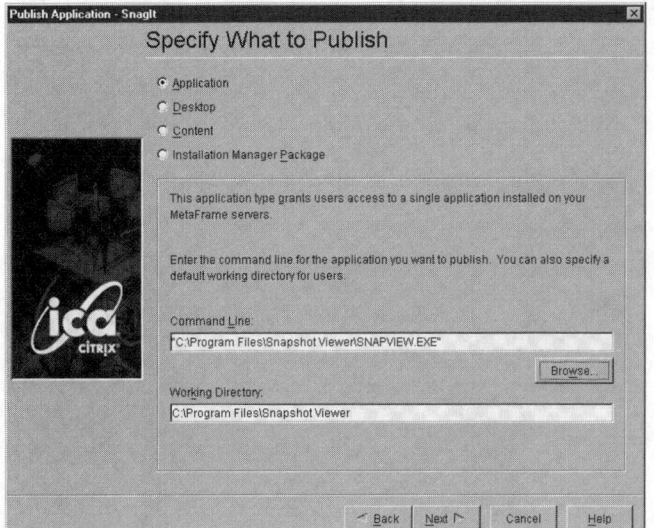

TIP You can configure a client computer to associate a published application with a local file extension. If you're going to do so, append the command line with a %* token at the end to let the published application accept application parameters from the client. In this example, the command-line information would look like this: `c:\winntas\system32\"notepad.exe %*"`.

3. In the next screen, you'll configure the Program Neighborhood settings for the published application, assuming that at least some of the people using this application will use Program Neighborhood to connect to the application. Most of the settings here (see Figure 7.9) are self-explanatory. Ordinarily, published applications will appear in the folder for the client's server farm in the Program Neighborhood. If you want them in a new or different folder, provide the new location in this window. If you want to put a link to the application on client Start menus, in the Programs folder, or even on the desktop, select the appropriate check box. Finally, although the icon normally associated with the application should be selected, you can change it in this window and browse for a new one. When you're done, click Next.

NOTE If you put published applications on user desktops or in the Start menu, you'll minimize the differences between using local applications and published applications.

Figure 7.9 Edit settings to control how the application is presented to users of the Program Neighborhood.

4. The next group of settings controls the way that the published application appears on the client's desktop. From here, you can edit the window size (from 640×480 to Full Screen) and the color depth. MetaFrame has offered True Color support since FR1 for MetaFrame 1.8, but for slower connections, consider reducing the color depth. The more colors you're using, the more bits have to pass over the wire every time there's a screen update.

If a client can support a greater screen resolution than the server can, Full Screen settings will drop to a level the server can support. The client will know if this happens; the ICA session will display a message to this effect.

> **TIP** For task-based workers who will use only a single application, consider running the application in full-screen mode and disabling the window bar. Doing so will make it effectively impossible for people to lose their application window.

5. When you click Next, you'll have a chance to set the minimum ICA connection settings for the published application. Those with FR1 will have an additional option—enabling SSL support if the client wants to use it. The settings you apply here don't override the ICA Client settings; they just establish a minimum. If you check the box to disable audio, and a client connects with audio enabled, the client setting will take precedence.

6. Only those servers with FR1 installed will next see the page of the wizard in Figure 7.10, but this feature is important enough that it's worth looking at even if you haven't yet installed the feature release. FR1 introduced the ability to control application impact on the server farm not just with the application-specific load balancing tools available to anyone using MetaFrame XP, but by limiting the number of *instances* of an application per user and/or per farm. Limiting the total number of instances makes it easier to keep within application licensing limits; limiting the per-user instances to one prevents people from losing their applications and starting numerous instances of the same application.

   You can also edit application processor priority levels to give them more or less access to processor cycles, but in general, I'd leave that setting alone. In fact, that's worth a warning.

   WARNING Do not edit the processor priority settings unless you are *very* sure of what you are doing. Applications normally run in the Normal range of processor priority. Set an application's priority too low, and it will run at a snail's pace. Offhand, the only time I would reduce an application's processor priority would be if people planned to start a calculation, disconnect, drive to another location, and reconnect to keep working—reducing the application's priority might permit the calculations to finish without impacting the other people using the MetaFrame server. (However, at that point, you'd want to jack the processor priority back up.) Set an application's priority too high, and you will not only interfere with other applications running on the same MetaFrame server, you can impact the way the OS operates. It's a neat feature, but one best avoided unless you have very specific and well-thought-out reasons for using it.

7. At this point, you're ready to choose servers to publish the application from. When you click Next, you'll see a screen like the one in Figure 7.11.

   This screen is a bit more complicated than some of the others. To add servers to the list of configured servers, click the appropriate button. The Filter Servers By button lets you control which servers appear. Normally, every server in the farm will appear regardless of whether it's capable of running the published application, but you can edit the filters to display only servers running Installation Management (that is, only MetaFrame XPe servers) or only those running a specific OS—at this point, either WTS or Win2K.

   The Edit Configuration button in Figure 7.11 is grayed because I haven't yet selected any servers. When I've done so, clicking this button will let me edit the application command line and working directory, using the dialog box in Figure 7.12. This way, even if an application isn't installed in the same place on all servers in the farm, you can still use those servers to back a published application.

Figure 7.10 Servers with FR1 installed can control application impact on the server farm.

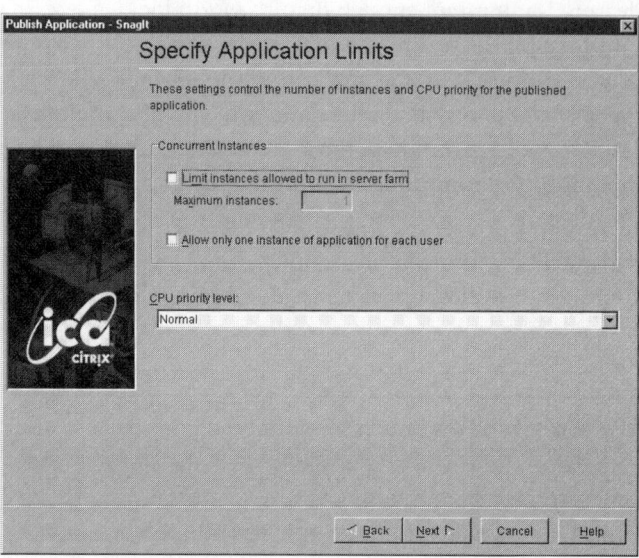

Figure 7.11 Choosing servers from which to publish the application

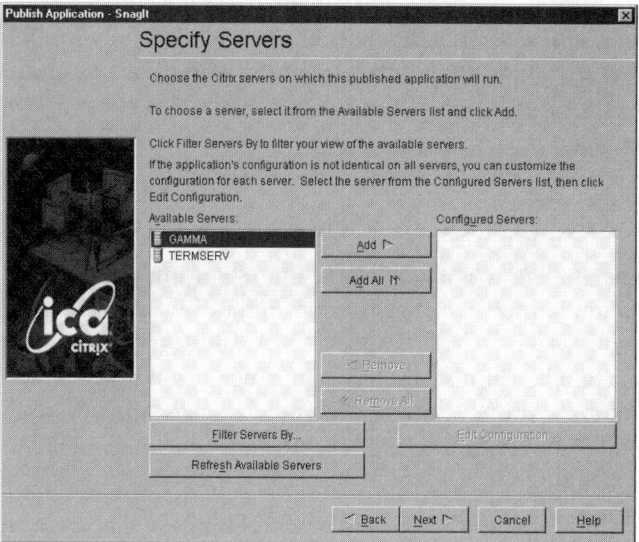

Figure 7.12 If the published application is not installed in the same place on all MetaFrame servers in the farm, edit the path information.

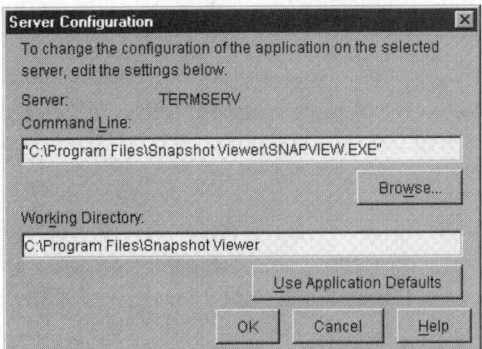

8. Finally, you get to determine who gets access to the published application (see Figure 7.13). Most of what's here should be pretty familiar to anyone who's worked with Windows 2000: Look in the drop-down list for the domains you want to add support for, clicking the groups or individuals who should be permitted access.

Figure 7.13 End the wizard by choosing the users and groups able to access the application.

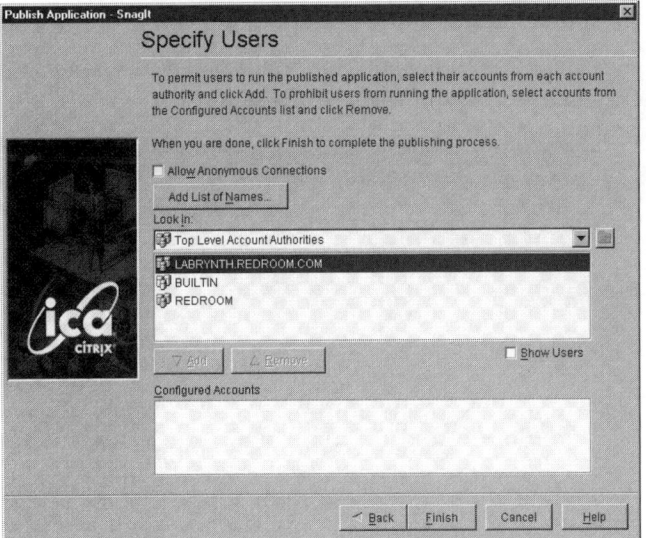

Some of the features shown in this page of the wizard are only available to those with FR1 installed. For example, NDS support is only available with the feature release—those using MetaFrame XP unenhanced will see only NT/Win2K domains in the drop-down list. FR1 users will also have more options when it comes to allowing anonymous connections; users have to authenticate to the server, but they don't need a domain account and password. Normally, when you choose to allow anonymous connections to an application, you can't *also* permit access via named accounts. Those with FR1 installed will see the Add List of Names button in Figure 7.13.

When you click this button, you'll have the chance to add domain accounts using the *name@domainname.com* or *domainname\username* format. Separate all added names with semicolons, as I've done in Figure 7.14, and be sure to click Check Names to make sure that you've entered the names in the right format and the account names you've selected actually exist. If everything's okay, you'll see a message telling you that the account names have been validated. If the Publish Application Wizard cannot validate some or all the account names, you'll see an error message indicating the problem (wrong format or an account name that does not exist). When you click OK, the names will appear in the Configured Accounts list.

NOTE Generally speaking, a MetaFrame server will not be a domain controller. However, if the server is a domain controller, you can't enable anonymous accounts on it.

Figure 7.14 Those using FR1 or later can select named accounts to access anonymous-access published applications.

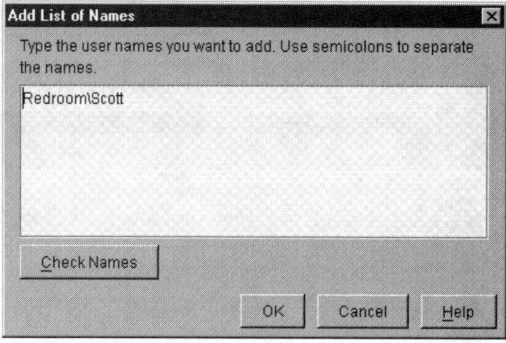

Those with FR2 installed will see an additional screen in the wizard at this point: one to choose file type associations for the published application. (These associations are used for client to server content redirection.) Choose the file extensions with which you want to associate the published application.

> **WARNING** Redirecting content associates the published application with the ICA Client—with the Program Neighborhood Agent, if you installed it on the client. If the application server is not available when the client starts a linked application, the application may not open unless the user employs Open With and chooses a functioning local application.

When you click Finish, the wizard will close and the application—complete with the icon and name you assigned it—will appear subordinate to the Applications section of the Citrix Management Console. Users who are using the Program Neighborhood and refresh their connection to the server farm (and have permission to use the application) will see the published application's icon and can double-click the icon to log on and use the application.

If you need to edit any of the settings of a published application, right-click its icon in the Citrix Management Console and choose Properties from the context menu. You'll see a tabbed properties sheet containing all the settings you established when you originally set up the application, organized by subject.

Publishing Desktops

You can publish access to an entire desktop just as you can publish access to a single application. (If you do so, you'll need to be very careful about securing the MetaFrame server.) The process is very similar to publishing an application, so I won't walk you through the whole procedure again, just the following core steps:

1. Name the desktop, and give it a description.
2. Specify that you want to publish a desktop.
3. Choose the Program Neighborhood, Application Appearance, ICA Client, Application Limits (if you have FR1 installed), servers, permitted users for the published desktop, and click Finish.

Publishing Content

If you have FR1 or later for MetaFrame XP installed, you can publish content—not just applications, but actual files or links to websites—for people to connect to via the Program Neighborhood. Publishing content is not spectacularly different from ordinary network access, though. You can publish content stored on any network file, FTP, or web server, not just MetaFrame servers. The users accessing the content will use their locally installed applications (and computer resources) to view it, and must have permission to access the files on the server.

The main advantage of publishing content instead of permitting network access to a file is that it makes it easier to give people file access over slow connections. When people connect to published content, the file is not downloaded to their computer, just displayed there, so those using slow connections to view files on the network (perhaps by connecting to the office while on the road) won't have to wait for a huge file to make it to their computer. However, it appears that you could accomplish exactly the same thing by publishing access to an application without requiring people to have the application loaded locally—publishing access to content just makes it easier to find specific files.

Load Balancing Application Servers

If you've got more than one application server, you'd like to distribute the load among those servers so that no single server is getting hammered while another one is going idle. One way to make this happen is to assign people to servers, so that Joe always logs onto Server A and Susan always logs onto Server B. So long as Joe and his compatriots stress a server about as much as Susan and her compatriots—and the servers are more or less identical when it comes to memory and processing power—this approach works. But it's limited and a lot of work, because you have to figure out who should be using which servers and make changes if the server loads change. This approach doesn't make it easy to add new application servers, because a new server means redistributing your user load. In short, if you're not managing a small static farm with a homogenous user base, you can think about how to apply MetaFrame XP's load-management capabilities, available in MetaFrame XPa and XPe.

MetaFrame XP's load management is different from the load balancing tools available with MetaFrame 1.8. First, the new GUI is an improvement; those hard-to-manipulate slider bars that controlled the loads are gone; they have been replaced with numbers that you input. Second, the new load management has more options—called *rules*—for creating load balancing *evaluators*, or combinations of rules. A rule is a small module of executable code that queries specific conditions and performance metrics (often usage) for servers or published applications. The expanded rule set gives you a lot more load-management flexibility than MetaFrame could offer previously.

How Load Manager Determines Where to Start an ICA Session

The load manager is the part of MetaFrame XP that handles load balancing. When you're load balancing server connections to entire desktops or published applications, the load manager must attach new ICA sessions to the server that's currently least stressed according to applied rules. Let's take a look at how this process works.

For most load balancing rules, you can set two thresholds:

- A lower threshold below which the server (or application) appears to the load manager as having no load
- An upper threshold at or above which load manager sees the server as having a full load and no longer manages it using that rule

Not all rules work this way. As you'll see, you can set rules that, for example, define the hours that a server is available, determine the maximum number of simultaneous connections, or limit the IP addresses from which the server will accept connections. However, for most rules this explanation is a pretty good general description.

Let's say that you're trying to connect to a published version of Solitaire so that you can, er, work on your mouse coordination skills. Rather than connecting to a specific server, you initiate a connection to the published application Solitaire using the ICA Client. When you do, the client contacts the server farm you specified to find a server hosting Solitaire. The data store for the farm knows which servers are publishing Solitaire, so the data store will offer those servers for possible connections. If the servers are load managed on a server basis, the load manager for the farm reports the loads as follows:

- A server with a load below the threshold defined in the rule will report itself as having no load and will, therefore, be the more attractive candidate for new connections.
- A server with a load somewhere between its lowest and highest thresholds will report its load as a percentage of a total. The lower the percentage, the better candidate the server is for getting new connections.
- A server with a load at or above its upper threshold (possible if its load evaluator includes rules such as memory usage or processor time) is reported as being at full load and will not accept any more connections. In fact, it won't even be in the load manager's list of available servers.

Once it identifies the server with the lowest load (whether at no load or as a percentage of a full load), the load manager picks one of those servers and returns the address of that server to the ICA Client to begin the connection.

What Happens If Load Management Forbids Access?

Most of the time, you probably won't be able to tell whether a server is unavailable because it has exceeded a load balancing threshold or for some other reason. If someone is unable to connect to a chosen server or application because of the load balancing rules, the user will see two error messages when that user tries to connect.

> **What Happens If Load Management Forbids Access?** *(continued)*
>
> When the person denied access clicks OK, the system will present the error message here.
>
>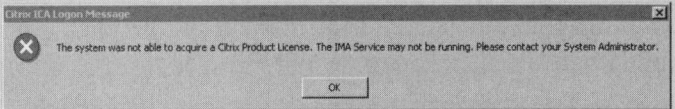
>
> It's obvious that the server isn't working, but it's far from obvious *why*. I'm not sure whether these messages reflect good or bad design. On the one hand, the error messages don't really tell users what the problem is—just that they're not able to get a license. On the other hand, the vagueness of the messages might encourage users to try again a minute later, which, given the minute-by-minute sampling done by the load manager, may be enough to get them a connection. Just make sure that the Help Desk people know which error messages appear when load management keeps people off the server farm, so that they can advise users to wait a minute or two and try again.

Understanding the Built-In Load Balancing Evaluators

MetaFrame XP comes with two built-in load balancing evaluators: Default and Advanced. Let's take a look at these to help you determine whether you need to build your own evaluators and, if so, which rules you should include. To view the rules for any load evaluator, go to the Contents tab of the Load Evaluators section of the Citrix Management Console, right-click the evaluator's icon, and choose Load Evaluator Properties from the context menu.

> **NOTE** You can't edit or delete the built-in load evaluators. If you want a load evaluator similar to one that's built in, you'll need to create a new one.

The Default load evaluator has just one rule: Server User Load. This rule means that ICA Client connections are load balanced according to the number of users on each server, with servers refusing connections when they hit 100. Within that restriction, the servers will accept connections as they would normally—that is, based on which viable server answers the request for connection first.

The Advanced load evaluator is more complex than the default and includes three rules instead of one: CPU Utilization, Memory Usage, and Page Swaps. According to the thresholds set, servers using the advanced load evaluator will report a full load when any of the following are true: the processor is running at 90 percent or more capacity; 90 percent or more of virtual memory (not physical memory) is in use; and the server's memory manager is making 100 or more page swaps per second. The server will appear with *no* load so long as all of the following are true: the processor is running at less than 10 percent capacity; less than 10 percent of virtual memory is in use, and the virtual memory manager is not swapping any data out to the paging file. In other words, it's *very* unlikely that a server using the Advanced load evaluator will ever report no load. The Memory Usage rule alone will take care of that.

> **NOTE** Although the comment for the Advanced load evaluator says that it also uses the Context Switches rule, this rule is in the list of available rules, not the list of rules assigned to the load evaluator.

Applying Load Evaluators

To apply a load evaluator to a server, turn to the Usage Reports tab in the Load Evaluators section, as in Figure 7.15. As you would expect, when load balancing is first installed, the default load evaluator is applied to all servers in the farm.

Figure 7.15 Change the assigned load evaluators from the Usage Reports tab.

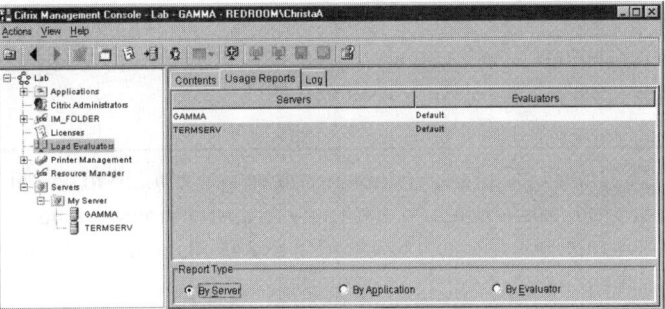

To change the assigned load evaluator for a server, right-click its icon to choose the Load Manage Server option from the context menu (it will be the only option in the context menu) and open the dialog box in Figure 7.16.

To assign a new load evaluator, just select it from the list, and click OK. When you do, you'll return to the Usage Report tab, which will display the new load evaluator. You can't change the load evaluator for all servers in a farm at once; only change one by one. Check this tab to be sure that all load-balanced servers that you want to act as a team are using the same evaluator.

Figure 7.16 Choose the load evaluator you want from the list.

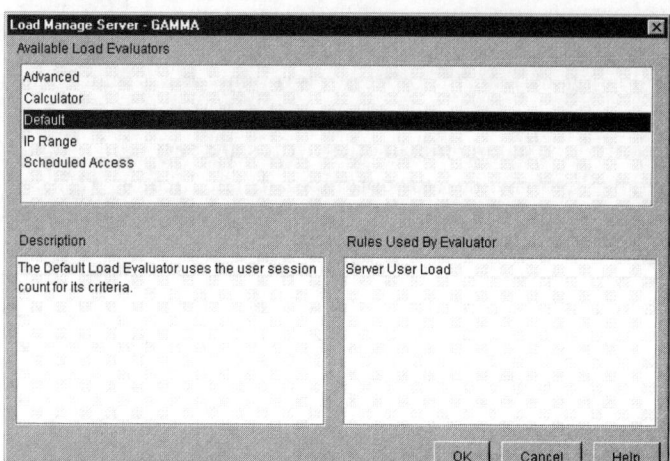

If you're publishing applications from a server, you can apply load evaluators not only at a server level, but also at an application level. To load balance applications, go to the Applications folder in the Citrix Management Console, and right-click the application you want to load balance, choosing Load Manage Application from the context menu. You'll open a dialog box like the one in Figure 7.17, showing the available load evaluators. Choose one, select the servers among which you want to load balance the application (only those servers publishing the application will be listed), and click OK.

> **NOTE** The built-in load evaluators are more appropriate to servers than to applications, but this procedure will apply to custom load evaluators as well. Once you've built them, they'll be listed in the Available Load Evaluators section alongside the others.

Once you've chosen to load manage a published application, it will appear on the Usage Reports tab of the Load Evaluator section of the Citrix Management Console when you click the By Application option at the bottom of the screen. To change the load evaluator for an application, right-click it to open the same dialog box you saw when you initially chose to load manage the application (see Figure 7.15), and pick a new one.

> **TIP** To stop load balancing an application entirely, just make the load evaluator <None>.

Figure 7.17 Load manage published applications from the Applications folder in the Citrix Management Console.

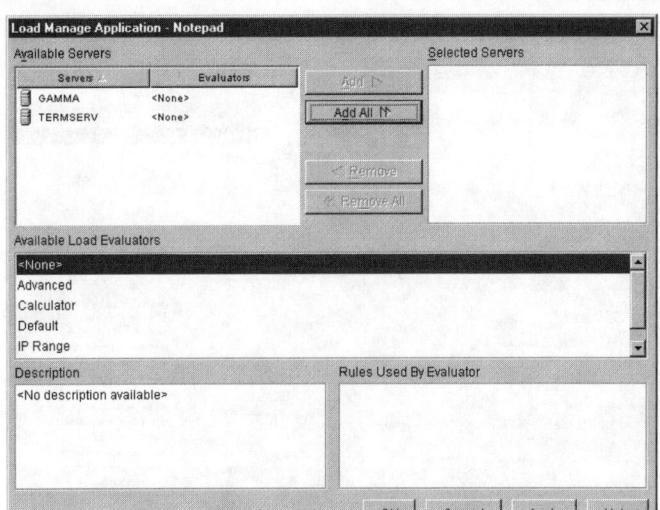

Creating Custom Load Evaluators

You can create your own load evaluators, making them as simple or as complex as you'd like.

Editing Existing Load Evaluators

The simplest way to create a new load evaluator is to copy one that already exists, and then make your changes. For example, what if the default load evaluator works well for you, but you want to reduce the maximum number of connections allowed from 100 to 50? The built-in load evaluators are read-only, so you can't edit either of them. But you *can* copy the default load evaluator, make your changes, and then apply the new load evaluator to your servers. To do so, follow these steps:

1. Turn to the Contents tab of the Load Evaluators section of the Citrix Management Console. Assuming that you haven't yet added any custom load evaluators to the server farm, you should see the two built-in load evaluators: Default and Advanced.

2. Right-click Default, and choose Duplicate Load Evaluator from the pop-up menu. This action will open the screen in Figure 7.18. Click Server User Load in the Assigned Rules box to display the information in the lower half of the screen.

3. Type a name and description for the new load evaluator. The description is optional, but using it is a good idea.

Figure 7.18 To make load evaluators similar to existing ones, just create duplicates and edit them.

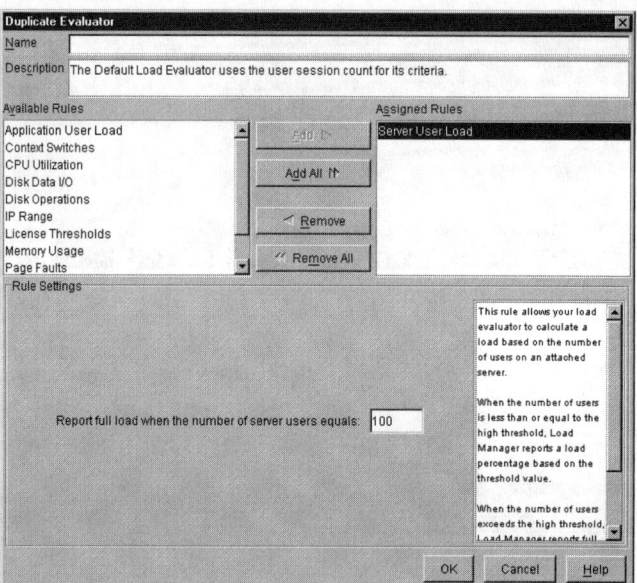

4. When we previously examined this rule, we couldn't edit the numbers in the Report Full Load When box in the lower center of the screen. Because this rule is a duplicate, though, we can. Enter the lower number—in this example, I'll set it to 50—and click OK. The dialog box will close, and your new evaluator will appear on the Contents tab alongside Default and Advanced, and you can now apply it to servers or to published applications.

> **TIP** If, when you click OK, you see an error message chastising you that the highlighted value is incorrect but nothing is highlighted, you probably forgot to name the duplicated load evaluator. Click OK to close the message box, add a name, and click OK again.

That's the easy way to create a new load evaluator. This method will work not only for changing existing rules, but for adding new ones. You can, however, also start from scratch. Doing so is a two-part process. The first (and hardest) part is figuring out which load balancing rules to use. The second, and considerably easier, part is adding those rules to the load evaluator.

Understanding Load Balancing Rules

The basis of all load balancing evaluators are the load balancing rules listed in Table 7.4. Using these rules, you can create evaluators for just about any situation.

Table 7.4 Supported Load Balancing Rules with FR1 or later installed

Counter	Description	More Information
Application User Load	Calculates a load based on the number of users accessing a specific published application on the attached server. Use this load evaluator to restrict the number of instances of a single application running on a MetaFrame server.	Useful for keeping people from overloading a server with many instances of a resource-intensive application. Also useful for licensing because you can restrict access to the number of people for whom you have licenses.
Context Switches	Calculates a load based on the processor context switches. A context switch occurs every time the OS switches from one executing process to another. The valid range for the high and low thresholds is 0 to 2,147,483,647.	A Win2K server normally performs a lot of context switches. Although context switches do cause an infinitesimal delay before the processor starts working on a process's data, they're a normal part of the functioning of a Windows OS. Don't use this rule unless you are familiar with context switches and know what you're doing. If you do use it, apply it to servers, not applications.
CPU Utilization	Calculates a load based on how busy the processor is. The valid range for the high and low thresholds is 0 to 100.	Best for servers, not applications.
Disk Data I/O	Calculates a load based on physical disk I/O throughput (in kilobytes).	Best for servers, not applications.

Table 7.4 Supported Load Balancing Rules with FR1 or later installed *(continued)*

Counter	Description	More Information
Disk Operations	Calculates a load based on the number of physical disk operations per second. This rule is similar to Disk Data I/O, but it counts the number of operations the disk is doing, not how much data it's passing.	Best for servers, not applications.
IP Range	Allows your load evaluator to enable or disable access to a published application based on whether the IP addresses of the ICA Clients are within the specified IP address ranges. If the IP address of the ICA Client is greater than or equal to the specified starting IP Address, and the IP address of the ICA Client is less than or equal to the specified ending IP Address, the client is considered a part of the specified range and the client machine will be permitted or denied access—depending on your approach.	Use this rule to restrict access to the MetaFrame XP servers or applications. You'll generally use this rule in combination with another rule because this rule will not actually load balance connections, just restrict access—it's a security thing. This rule is more useful for granting access than denying it.
License Thresholds	Calculates a load based on the number of assigned or pooled connection licenses used on each server.	These licenses are MetaFrame XP licenses, so this rule is a server rule. You cannot use this rule to manage application access.
Memory Usage	Allows your load evaluator to calculate a load based on memory utilization.	Best for servers, not applications.

Table 7.4 Supported Load Balancing Rules with FR1 or later installed *(continued)*

Counter	Description	More Information
Page Faults	Calculates a load based on the number of page faults each second. Page faults take place when a process tries to read data that has been flushed from memory to the paging file on the hard disk.	Best for servers, not applications.
Page Swaps	Like the Page Faults rule, this rule uses paging actions to determine server load. The difference is that Page Faults counts the number of times each second. This rule allows your load evaluator to calculate a load based on the number of page swaps per second. A page swap occurs every time the OS swaps physical memory to virtual memory on disk.	Best for servers, not applications.
Scheduling	Enables or disables availability of a server or published application during certain days of the week and certain hours of the day. Outside the permitted hours, existing connections are not deleted but new connections aren't allowed.	Use this rule for servers or applications. More of a security option than a performance one.
Server User Load	Calculates a load based on the number of users on an attached server. Basically, it works like the Application User Load rule, except on a server basis.	Best for servers, not applications.

The rules you pick and thresholds you apply depend on where you're most concerned about stress. If you'd like to keep people from running many instances of a resource-intensive application, you'll use the Application User Load rule. To prevent people from getting frustrated by processor-bound or memory-bound servers, you'll use the CPU Usage or Memory Usage rules—always bearing in mind that the one thing more likely to frustrate a potential user more than a slow server is no server connection at all. When designing new load evaluators, think about how you want to load balance and work backward from there.

> **TIP** One way you can tune settings is to use the Windows 2000 System Monitor to get an idea of normal values for your MetaFrame XP servers so that you can more easily set reasonable upper and lower thresholds. I'll talk more about performance monitoring application servers in Chapter 9, "Ongoing Server Management."

Load evaluators suggest load balancing patterns, but real life may change the way that model is applied. Rules with upper and lower thresholds (for example, Memory Usage) will be reported as a percentage of their upper limit. These percentages will change constantly, depending on the state of the server *right then* when a user initiates an ICA connection. If your evaluators contain rules taking into account values that could easily change (for example, processor utilization), a server might accept connections at 8:00 A.M., reject them at 8:02 A.M. because it's over its threshold while people log on, and accept connections again at 8:05 A.M. If a user begins a session on one server and runs an application in Seamless Windows, that user's other Seamless Windows applications will run on that server if at all possible because doing so derives performance benefits. If you apply more than one rule to a server, bear in mind that *all* rules must be below their threshold for a server to register no load, but only *one* rule must be above its threshold to register full load. This is good or bad depending on just how quickly you want your MetaFrame servers to brush aside ICA Client requests with a "Not now, Sonny—I'm busy."

Creating a New Load Evaluator

The mechanics of creating the load evaluator are very simple:

1. Right-click any existing load evaluator or the Load Evaluator icon in the Citrix Management Console, and choose New Load Evaluator from the context menu.
2. Type a name and (optionally) a description for the new load evaluator in the dialog box that appears.
3. From the Available Rules list, choose a rule, and click the Add button to put the rule into the Assigned Rules list.

4. Select the rule in the Assigned Rules list so that you can enter the thresholds for the rule (if applicable) or the range of hours or IP addresses for which the server or application using this load evaluator will be available.

What happens at this point will depend on the kind of rule you're applying. For server-wide rules with upper and lower thresholds, you'll enter the lower threshold (below which the server will report no load) and the upper threshold (at or above which the server will report a full load and be unavailable for new connections). For other types of rules, the options will be different. For example, if you're creating a load evaluator for a server farm that already has some published applications, the screen will look like the one in Figure 7.19 when you choose the Application User Load rule and move it to the Assigned Rules list.

Figure 7.19 After publishing an application, you can set an upper limit of people to use that application.

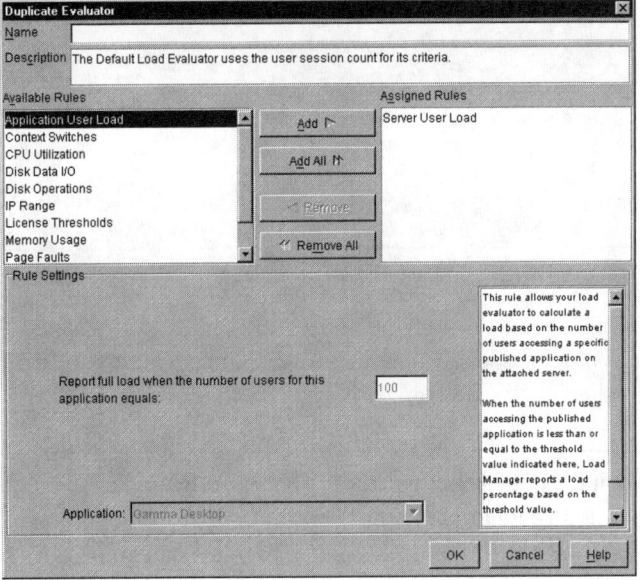

The Application User Load rule works very much like the Server User Load rule in the default load evaluator, defining the maximum number of users running a single application. (And yes, this setting is really for *users*, not connections. A single user can connect many times to the same application without counting more than once, assuming that you do not restrict the number of instances of an application that a single user may run.) A drop-down list at the bottom of the screen shows all published applications. Just pick one—you can't use this evaluator to load manage more than one application—and pick the appropriate maximum number of connections.

If you picked the IP Range rule, when you move the rule to the Assigned Rule list and select it, your screen will look like the one in Figure 7.20.

Figure 7.20 Choose the IP Range rule to specify the machines explicitly forbidden or permitted to access the server or application.

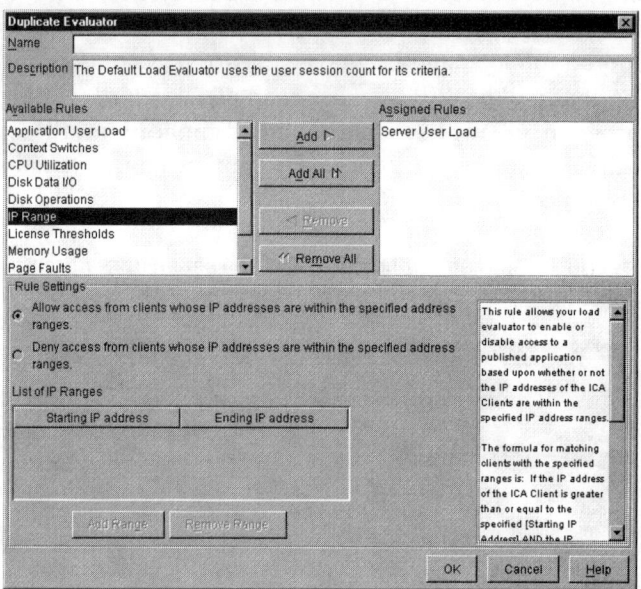

Assigning IP ranges works a bit like specifying a range of available IP addresses on a DHCP server. To do so, decide whether you're going to allow or deny access to the specific range, then click Add Range to open the dialog box in Figure 7.21.

NOTE Generally speaking, *permitting* access only to a specific range of IP addresses will give you much more control than *denying* access—you're telling people what they can do, rather what they can't. You cannot both permit and restrict IP address ranges using the same load evaluator.

Figure 7.21 Set the range of IP addresses to which you're granting or denying access.

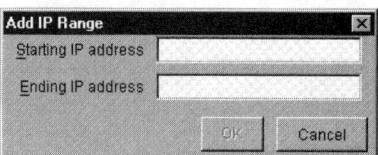

When you click OK, you'll return to the Evaluator Properties dialog box, and the IP address range will appear in the list of IP ranges. If you need to edit a range after adding it, you can do so from the Evaluator Properties dialog box—just select the range to edit. To delete a range, just select it, and click Remove Range. Be very careful when you do so because there's no confirmation dialog box asking if you're sure.

The last rule that works a little differently from the upper and lower thresholds we've already seen is the Scheduling rule. As you can see in Figure 7.22, when you select this rule, you'll open a sort of clock/calendar view of server access.

Figure 7.22 Use the Scheduling rule to restrict access to farm servers by time or date.

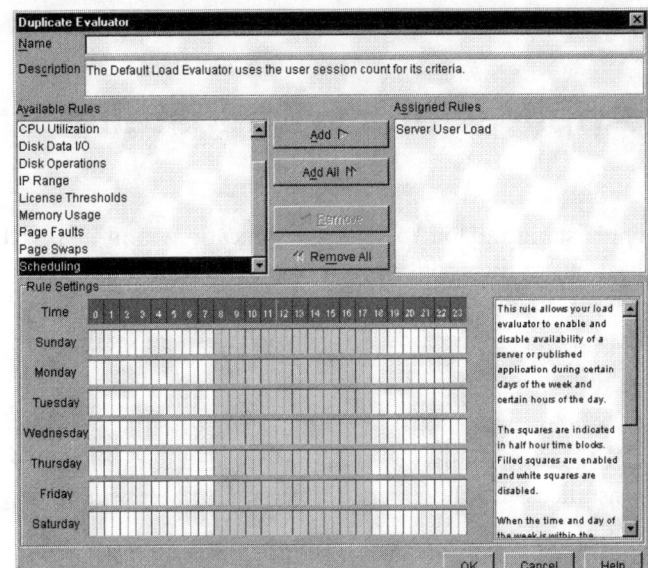

Hours when the servers or applications using this rule are available are displayed in green; hours when servers or applications are unavailable are shown in white. MetaFrame XP's Load Manager begins by assuming that the people in your company work 7 days a week, 8 hours a day (on a 24-hour clock). To add permitted hours, click them until they turn green. To delete them, click them until they turn white.

One way or another, when you've picked the rules you want to apply (no more than one instance of each rule per load evaluator), click OK, and you can now apply the load evaluator to servers or applications.

Renaming and Deleting Load Evaluators

You can rename or delete any load evaluator you create, but the default and advanced load evaluators are there to stay. To rename a load evaluator, right-click it, and choose Load Evaluator Properties from the context menu. When its properties sheet opens, type a new name for the evaluator, and click OK.

To delete a custom load evaluator, right-click it and choose Delete Load Evaluator(s) from the context menu. (You can press Ctrl+click to select more than one load evaluator at a time.) You can also just highlight the load evaluator's name and press the Delete key. Just be sure of what you're doing. There's no Undo button, and the confirmation dialog box asking if you're sure does not identify the load evaluator you're deleting, so it's easy to accidentally delete the wrong load evaluator.

Installing Applications with Installation Manager

All this talk of publishing and load balancing applications is all very well, but how do you *get* those applications to the application servers? You can install all the applications by hand. You can use Windows 2000 Group Policy objects to install applications on application servers based on computer identity. If you're using MetaFrame XPe, you can also use the Installation Manager.

MetaFrame 1.8 administrators will recall the Installation Manager as an add-on, but in MetaFrame XP it's been repackaged to be included with MetaFrame XPe. It's not automatically installed with the enterprise version of MetaFrame XP, but the installation CD is part of the package.

For those who aren't familiar with the concept of Installation Manager, it's an enterprise tool meant for those who have a lot of servers that need applications and hotfixes installed on them. You might not need it yourself. Setting up and maintaining a couple of MetaFrame servers—installing MetaFrame XP, installing and tuning the applications to publish, and applying service packs and hotfixes—is no big deal. Make that couple of MetaFrame servers 20, however, and installing applications and hotfixes on all those servers becomes a larger task. Make those 20 MetaFrame servers 200, and you have a lot of work on your hands.

Installation Manager allows you to streamline the process of deploying applications and hotfixes to MetaFrame servers. After creating packages in MetaFrame's native ADF format or getting MSI files from the manufacturer (or making them yourself with Windows 2000's version of WinInstaller), you can deploy those packages for automatic installation to MetaFrame XP servers with the Installation Manager service installed, managing the whole process from a central console. Using an ADF file, you can perform all of the following tasks from a centralized console:

- Install an application without using the product CD.
- Repair a damaged application.
- Remove or uninstall an application.
- Describe the application and its requirements.
- Tell the Installer service how to access the application files.

In other words, the reason for using Installation Manager is the same reason that you'd use Windows 2000's Remote Installation Services to install servers or Intellimirror to install applications—simplicity. Using Installation Manager or any other automated installation tool requires some up-front time, but when it comes to repetitive tasks that you'll need to perform many times and in exactly the same way, that initial setup time saves steps in the long run.

Using Installation Manager isn't just a matter of installing the service on one MetaFrame server and letting it rip. To use the service, your network will need four types of servers. A file server stores the ADF and MSI packages used to distribute applications and hot-fixes. A server with the CMC installed manages the packages. A packager machine—preferably one not used for anything else, for reasons that I'll explain when we talk about packaging—wraps applications into Windows Installer MSI files or Citrix Installation Manager ADF files. The MetaFrame servers receiving those packaged files for automated installation need the Citrix Installer service on them, and they must all have a network protocol in common. Once you have all that in place, the process of distributing applications with the Installation Manager looks like this:

1. Create installation packages (ADF and/or MSI files) and store them on a file server.
2. From the CMC, a Citrix administrator assigns applications to MetaFrame servers with the Installation Manager service installed.
3. When you initiate the installation, the MetaFrame servers connect to the file server and install the assigned applications.

In other words, to use Installation Manager, you'll need all the following:

- Administrative rights to manage farm servers
- A management console to assign packages to MetaFrame servers
- A packager computer, definitely running Windows 2000 and preferably also running MetaFrame XP, used to create installation packages
- A file server with enough room to store all the packages
- The Installer service installed on every MetaFrame XP server that you want to be able to receive packaged installations

Installing Installation Manager

Installation Manager isn't automatically installed when you install MetaFrame XPe. Get the CD from your MetaFrame XPe package, and put it in the CD-ROM drive of one server in the farm. From the initial window that appears, choose Installation Manager 2.0 Setup. As advised in the next screen, shut other applications down if you haven't already done so and click Next to arrive at the Setup screen in Figure 7.23.

WARNING Only install Installation Manager during off hours. During this process, you'll shut down the IMA Service.

Figure 7.23 Choose components of Installation Manager to install.

Do *not* blindly click through this screen. All the options are selected by default, as shown here, but you don't need all of them and probably don't want them all on the same server. To set up an application publishing manager, install the console plug-in that's highlighted in the figure. To set up a MetaFrame server to receive applications, select the Installer service. To create a packaging server—which should not, under any circumstances, be a working MetaFrame XP or Windows 2000 server even though you should have both Windows 2000 Server and MetaFrame XPe installed on it—choose to install the Citrix Packager. (See the sidebar for more information about the packaging server.) Because we're setting up the application management server and we also want this server to be able to accept automated installation instructions, choose to install the Installer service.

Doing so will install both the service and the plug-in. When you've checked the boxes for those components, click Next. When you click Next, Setup stops the IMA Service for that server and copies the appropriate files. When you click Finish, the service is installed. When you restart the CMC, you'll see a new part of the console: the Citrix Installation Manager. You don't need to reboot.

However, you can't set up applications from the Installation Manager—in fact, right now you can't do much of anything because no applications are available; Installation Manager uses MSI and WFS files (derived from ADF) to remotely install applications. Some applications come with MSI files that you can publish, but not all—so before we try adding packages, let's look at how to create them with the Installation Manager.

> **TIP** Although I've explained here how to use Installation Manager's Citrix Packager to create installation packages, I recommend that you use MSI files so far as possible. They're more flexible—you can use them outside of Installation Manager—and the publication jobs based on MSI packages offer more detail about the process of installation, which can be helpful for troubleshooting installation failures.

To create packages, you'll need a packaging server. To set up the server, put the CD in the drive of a server that has a partition large enough for installing any one of the applications that you'll be packaging. Citrix suggests that the partition be at least 500MB—this shouldn't be a problem, given the size and cheapness of hard disks available today. Again, choose the component you want to install, let Setup copy the relevant files, and click Finish when prompted. You don't need to reboot—the packaging server is now set up and ready to go.

Why Does the Packager Need to Be a Single-Purpose Server?

Although MetaFrame XP's per-connection, no-server-fees licensing model means that you aren't financially penalized for installing MetaFrame XPe on more than one server, having to maintain separate servers does mean that you need to supply additional hardware. Is it *really* necessary to maintain a separate packaging server?

> **Why Does the Packager Need to Be a Single-Purpose Server?** *(continued)*
>
> Unfortunately, it really is. Making the server single-purpose means that it's easier to keep it unsullied. Both packaging applications—Citrix Packager and WinInstall—work more or less the same way. The packaging tool takes a "before" snapshot of the computer you're using to package applications, records the file and Registry changes needed to install a file or hotfix, and then packages those changes by comparing the "before" snapshot with the "after" status of the computer. When you run a package on a target computer, those differences are applied to the computer. Because of the way this process works, the packaging computer must be as similar to the computers that will be using those packages as possible. At the very least, they should not assume the presence of any files, Registry changes, or the like that the target computers may not have. For example, say that a particular application needs MYDLL.DLL to run. If a version of that DLL that is the same age or newer than the one the application requires is already on the packaging server (perhaps because another, already-installed, application uses the same DLL), then the Setup routine for the application won't install MYDLL.DLL because it's already there. Ergo, the packaging application won't record the installation of that DLL. Because that recording does not include the instruction "install MYDLL.DLL," that file won't be installed when the package runs on the target computer—and the application won't run. (For similar reasons, the packaging server should use the same version of the operating system that the target computers will use, complete with all applicable service packs. You want all the DLLs and system files on the packaging server to be the same as the ones on the target computers.) Every time you finish packaging an application, you're going to roll back the changes that the installation made to the packaging server, so that those changes won't impact later packagings.
>
> Keeping the server single-purpose also means that nothing happening in the background will change the packaging server without you knowing it. People using applications in the background on a MetaFrame server could conceivably change the packaging server during the recording period, meaning that those changes will become part of the package. This might not happen, or matter if it did—but this kind of thing could mess up your packaging operations.
>
> The short version of all this is that packaging will be much more predictable if you keep a MetaFrame XP server to do nothing but package applications. You're going to the trouble of using Installation Manager to simplify the process of deploying applications, so you might as well do what you can to make the deployment work the first time.

Packaging Applications and Hotfixes for Installation

Now that we have a packaging server, let's take a look at the tools we've got to use it and see how to use this tool to package applications or patches to the core OS. On the packaging server, go to the Citrix program group and choose Citrix Installation Manager to open the Citrix Packager. Right now, it's not too exciting—you don't have any packages available. To get make it somewhat more exciting, walk through the Project Wizard. Click the Project Wizard button, fourth from the left on the toolbar. You can use this wizard to record three different kinds of installation routines. As you'd expect, Installation Recordings and Unattended Program packages record the process of installing applications or service packs. Packaging Files might be less obvious. You could use the file packaging option to automate the installation of applications that don't have special Setup routines, as is the case with some older applications that just have you copy files to a specified folder. You could also use this option to copy data files such as templates to MetaFrame servers that needed to have local access to those files.

Let's start by creating an ADF file to install Adobe Acrobat Reader, Adobe software's free PDF reader. Make the setup file available to the packaging server and follow the steps in the next section.

> **NOTE** If an application you need to install has an MSI file available, you can just publish that file with Installation Manager. Creating ADF files is mostly necessary when you don't have an MSI file available, or you need to modify the application's Setup routine with installation scripts or adding extra files. You also can't automatically uninstall ADF files; you need MSI uninstallation routines to do that.

Packaging an Installation Recording

In the first stage of the Project Wizard (see Figure 7.24), you'll need to choose the kind of project you want to create. For this instance, we want to package an installation recording, so choose that option and click Next.

Next, you'll need to choose a name and location for the package. In the example in Figure 7.25, I've created a shared folder on a file server to store all the packages. When I named the project Adobe Acrobat, the Project Wizard automatically created a folder with that name for that project.

Next, you'll need to find the path to the application setup files as in Figure 7.26. Don't map a drive letter to this path—use UNC names if you need to get to network-accessible files. For a drive letter to work, that drive letter would have to be mapped on every MetaFrame server you planned to install this application.

Figure 7.24 Choose a type of installation to record.

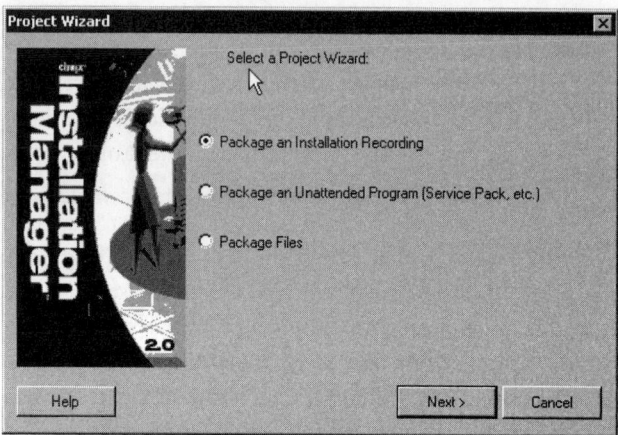

Figure 7.25 Choose a location for the package files.

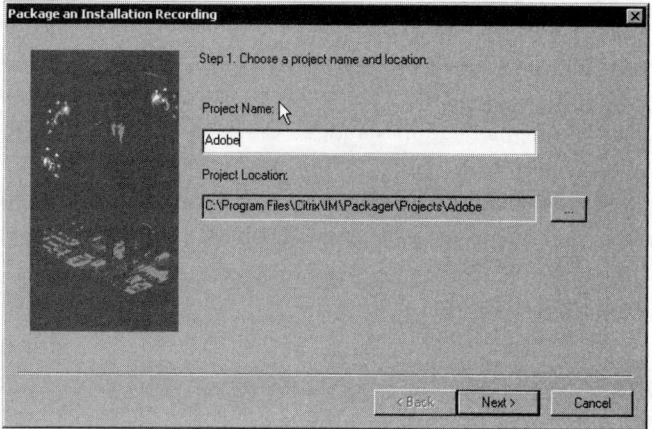

As we discussed earlier in this chapter, some applications need application compatibility scripts to run properly in a multiuser environment. If the application you're packaging is one of them, the next screen of the wizard (see Figure 7.27) is the place where you'll name the script. In this case, we don't need one, but if you do need one, then select the Include Compatibility Script option and click the Find Script button to choose the script from the list in Figure 7.28.

Figure 7.26 Provide the path to the installation files.

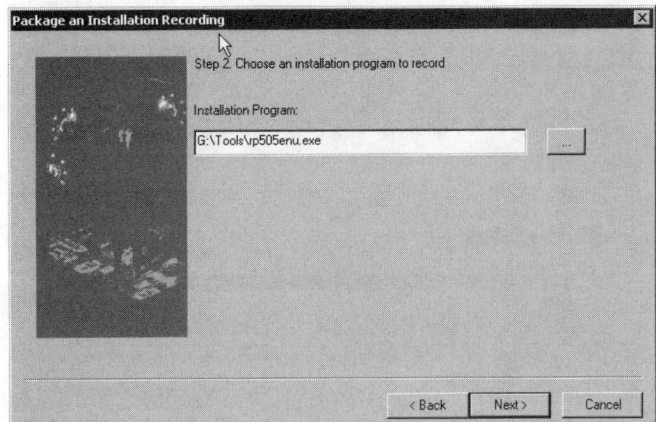

NOTE Note that these are not the application compatibility scripts that come with Windows 2000—they're in the Citrix directory.

Figure 7.27 If an application needs a compatibility script, choose it here.

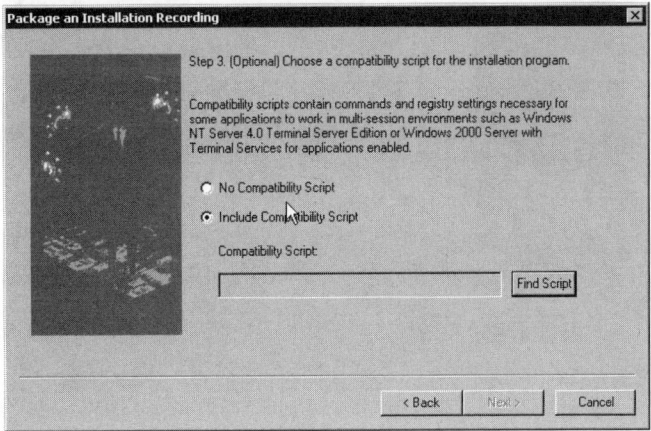

Next, you'll need to choose a location for the real build of the application. As you can see from Figure 7.29, this location is by default the folder that you specified when choosing a location for the package files.

Figure 7.28 Compatibility scripts may come with instructions.

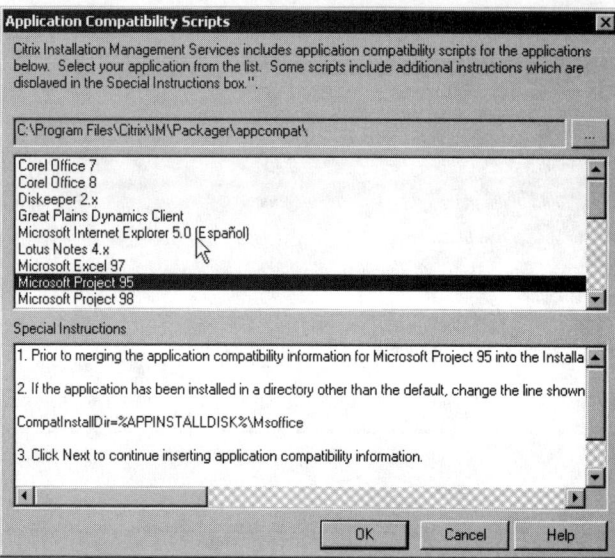

Figure 7.29 Choose a build location for the application.

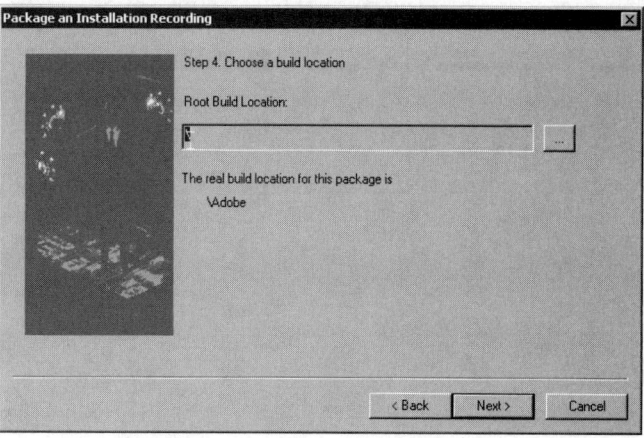

Finally, review the installation packaging settings as in Figure 7.30. When you click the Finish button, you'll see a dialog box asking if you want to save the changes to No Project (named that since we didn't give the project a name before running the Packaging Wizard). The project settings are separate from the package, so choose a location and filename for the project file and click Save. I named the file Adobe 5-5 so I could easily tell which application the project file was meant to install.

Figure 7.30 Review your packaging choices and click Finish to begin packaging.

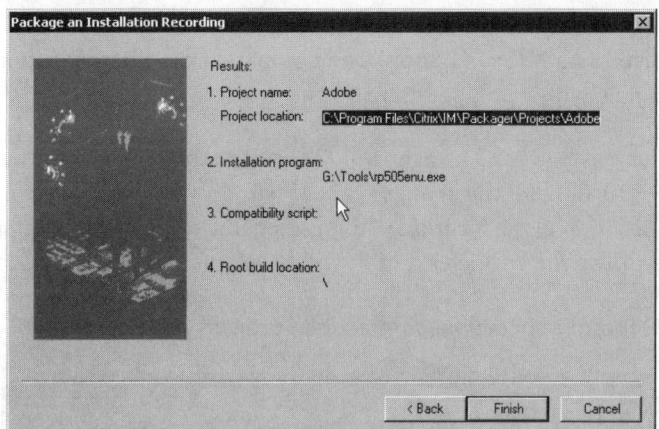

When you save the project file, the recording process will begin, as in Figure 7.31. In this case, Adobe Acrobat Reader Setup shows a dialog box monitoring the process of copying installation files. When it's done, the normal Setup routine that you've probably seen before will begin. Go through the Setup program as you would normally, making sure to choose file locations that will apply to all target servers.

Figure 7.31 You can watch the process of recording changes.

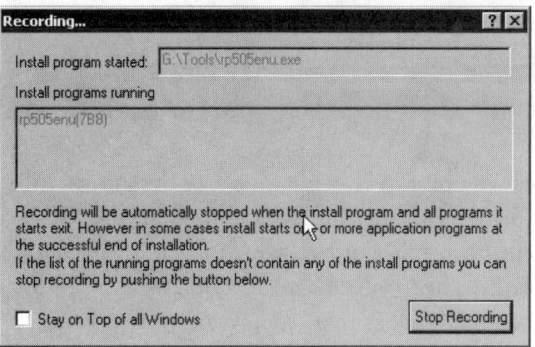

When you've finished running Setup and all the Setup files have exited (you can monitor their progress by looking at the list of Install Programs Running in the Recording dialog box), the button in the same dialog box will change to a Done.

> **WARNING** Setup may finish (from your perspective) before the Recording dialog box displays a "Done" button. Don't stop recording before Citrix Packager thinks it's finished—it will get there.

When you click this button, Packager will analyze the changes that it made and then create the ADF file recording all the changes. There will now be a complete installation of the packaged application in the location you specified, including the project and package files. When you return to the Packager tool, it will have a project loaded, as in Figure 7.32.

Figure 7.32 Packager application with an open project

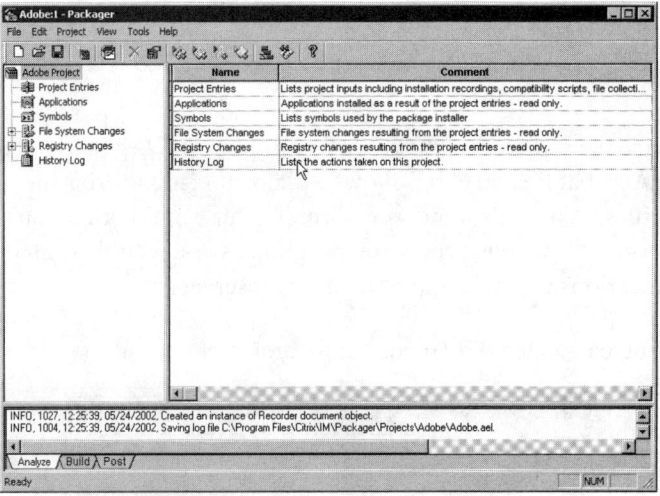

You shouldn't need to look too closely at most of the information here once you've successfully created a project. It's just a record of the changes that the installation made to the packaging server during installation and which will be applied to the target server to which you apply the package. The Project Entries section lists the Setup programs used to create the project—there could be more than one, if you were creating a project that was a complete set of applications for a MetaFrame server. The Applications folder lists the applications installed as a result of applying the package to a server. The Symbols folder contains installation path and manufacturer information. You might need to change the path information here if your application installation demands it.

The File System Changes and Registry Changes folders contain copies of the respective folders or Registry entries that are changed in the process of installing the application.

You could inspect these folders to find out how installing the application changes the computer on which it is installed. Finally, the History Log section walks you through the process of creating the project and associated ADF file, including installation analysis, Registry changes, creation of the ADF file, and any errors that might have taken place while recording the changes.

Packaging a Service Pack or Hotfix

Strictly speaking, the point of this option is not just packaging service packs and hotfixes, but to package *any* unattended file installation. Most of this process is similar to that of recording an application installation, but let's take a look at how this works.

The first couple of the steps will be familiar to you. When prompted, choose the type of project you want to create, then choose a name and location for the files. As with the recorded installation, Packager will plan to create a folder subordinate to the location you specify with the same name that you assigned to the project.

Next, though, you'll do something different. As you can see in Figure 7.33, you'll have the chance to supply any necessary parameters when packaging an unattended installation. In this example, I'm packaging Service Pack 2 to distribute to any MetaFrame member servers that don't already have it, but this tool will work for any unattended program you're using to install applications, including batch files. Make sure that you include any necessary command-line arguments in the appropriate section. Here, I'm telling the Service Pack 2 Update tool to update the /i386 folder on the C: drive.

> **NOTE** Hopefully, by the time you read this you'll have long since installed Service Pack 2 and can instead apply Service Pack 3. Service Pack 2 is important to some functioning of Terminal Services, so you should have it installed already.

Next, you'll need to choose the location from which you want the unattended program to run—that is, whether you want it to run from the network location or whether you want to copy the files to the MetaFrame server and *then* run them. In this case, I'll choose to run Update from a network location, as you can see in Figure 7.34. The installation works fine, and I won't have to worry about copying all the support files to the MetaFrame member servers. Nor will I need to worry that the service pack won't install properly because the files aren't locally available. (The copying process won't copy all the supporting files for the unattended program unless I add them from this dialog box, just the one I specified to run.) To add files or folders to the list of things to copy to the target MetaFrame servers, just click the appropriate button and browse to add them to the list. Notice that I've also got the option of rebooting the server after running the unattended program on the target MetaFrame server.

Figure 7.33 When you're packaging unattended installations, be sure to include any necessary command-line arguments.

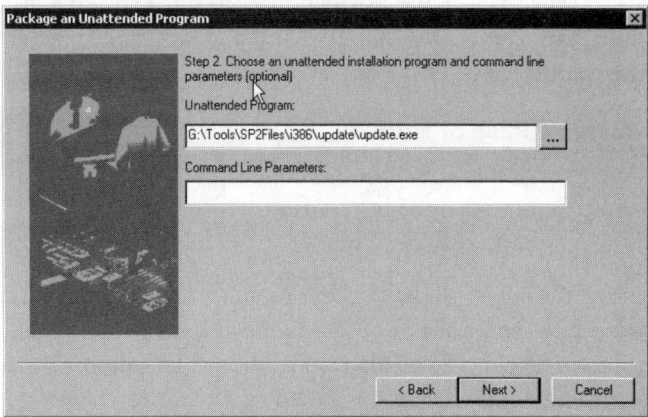

> **TIP** Always experiment with any installation—attended or unattended—that you're packaging so that you know how it will react in a given situation (rebooting versus not rebooting, running from the network versus running locally, that kind of thing).

Figure 7.34 You can run the unattended program across the network or copy it to the target server.

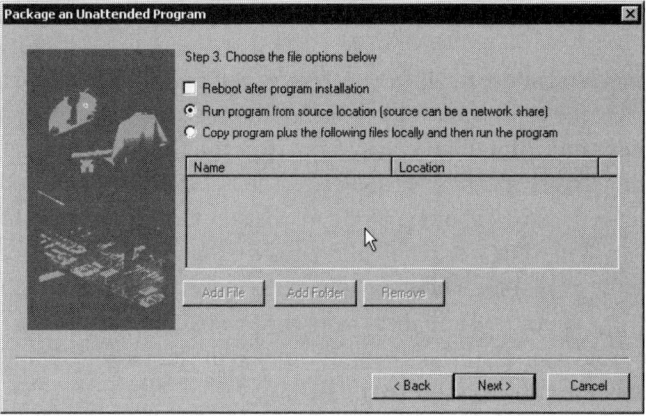

As a final step, you'll choose a build location for the packaged files, just as you did when packaging an application. Double-check your settings, and then click Next to get to the last page of the wizard where you can review all your settings before clicking Finish to begin the packaging. This process is different from packaging an installation, as you won't need to run through the installation here to package the files.

Packaging Files to Copy

Finally, you can package files to copy to MetaFrame servers. Again, you can do this from the Project Wizard as we've already done with the other two. When starting the wizard, choose to copy files. As before, choose a name for the project. Next, add a file collection using the dialog box in Figure 7.35. This dialog box is essentially the same one that you used to add files when packaging an unattended program in the previous section, except that you don't have the option here to reboot the server after applying the package—this is a copy-only tool. As when choosing files to copy with the unattended program packaging, choose carefully when copying a folder. If you add the contents of a folder to the list of files to copy, you'll need to delete each file (Ctrl+click to select more than one file) rather than just choosing the folder name.

NOTE Map the file copy location to a local drive letter, rather than copying from a UNC name.

Figure 7.35 You package single files or entire folders.

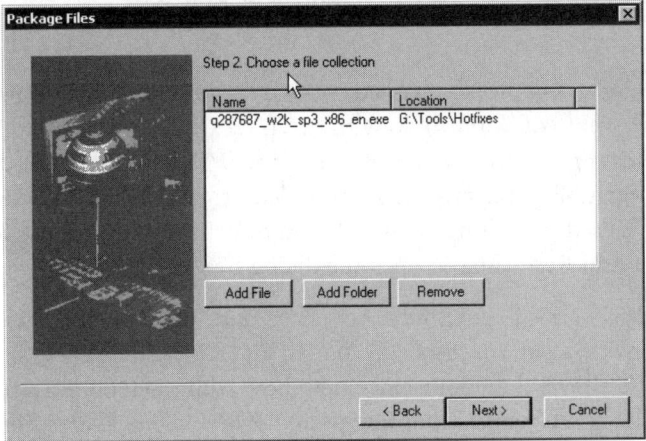

Next, you'll choose the build location as we've done for the other two kinds of packages. Make sure that you're building in the right location, and then in the next screen review the choices before you click Finish to create the package. That's it. The Packager will ask you if you want to save the changes to the packaging file and then package the files and create the directory.

Using Citrix Packager to Build or Edit Project Files

You don't have to use the Project Wizard to build a package. Once you're familiar with the process and know what you're doing, you may find it faster to skip it and build the package manually. You'll also need to use the manual method if you want to edit a project you created with the Project Wizard or add a compatibility script after the project's created. The process of packaging in this way doesn't differ much from using the wizards, so I'll stick with one example: packaging an application—in this example, WinZip.

From the Citrix Packager, choose New from the File menu or click the leftmost icon in the toolbar to begin a new project in the dialog box shown in Figure 7.36.

Figure 7.36 First, give the package a name.

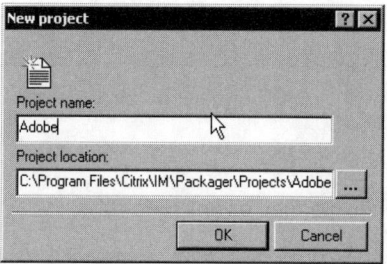

Now you've got a new project that's displayed in Citrix Packager, but you haven't yet told Packager what you want to do with it. To create a new installation package, right-click the Project Entries icon in the left-hand pane. You'll see four options: Add Recording, Add Compatibility Script, Add Unattended Program, and Add Files. (Add Compatibility Script is used for editing an installation recording package, not for creating a new one.) Choose Add Recording to open the dialog box in Figure 7.37.

Unless you expand this box with the Advanced button as I've done here, you'll just have a space to provide a path to the setup routine and a description for the project. Most of the time, that's all you'll need. I've included these additional options so you can see what Packager is doing during the recording period. The Include Events For box lists all the available drives on the packaging computer, but it checks only those that you've given Packager some reason to believe are involved with the packaging process. (In this case, the Windows 2000 installation I'm using is based on drive E: and some files I was using were on drive F:, so it looked at both of those.) Although drives mapped from the network are included in this list, they're not monitored for events unless you explicitly decide to monitor them by checking their box here. The These Types Of Actions box lists the events to monitor. Most of them are pretty self-explanatory, and you won't need to change their settings. File Reads and File Read Attributes record the event when files or their attributes are read during the installation process. File Set Attributes records the event when Setup makes changes to file attributes (e.g., read-only, hidden, system, or archive). Wildcard File Searches records any Find First or Find Next actions that use wildcards (e.g., *). Registry Value Reads records the values read when Setup reads the Registry. You can safely not record these actions—Setup will do them anyway if that's part of the routine. INI file changes and Service changes (such as the addition of a new service or the stopping or pausing of an existing one) are recorded by default, because this kind of information is important to the functioning of Setup. Finally, scrolled down where you can't see it in the figure, is a last option called Consecutive Duplicates. Unselected, as it normally is, Packager will record only the first time an action is taken if it's taken more than once in a row. If you select this option, Packager will record every single time that it records duplicate actions. The final box at the bottom of the dialog box controls the recording of events not related to the Setup routine. When this box is checked, as it is by default, Packager only records processes related to the Setup routine you identify and any other processes that that program spawns. Other changes to INI files or service changes that are not initiated by that Setup routine won't be recorded. This is as it should be—keeping this box checked keeps Packager from recording actions that are not relevant to the installation process. If the server is single-purpose, this shouldn't be too much of a problem. There probably won't be any reason to record changes *not* initiated by the application's Setup routine. Leave this box checked unless you have real reason for doing otherwise.

Figure 7.37 Choose the drives and events that you want Citrix Packager to monitor.

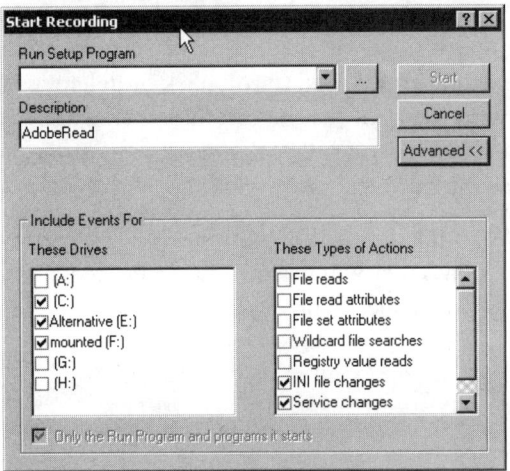

When you click the Start button on this dialog box, the Recording dialog box you saw when packaging an application with the wizard will appear, and the Setup routine will begin. Install the application using the options that you want to use for all instances of that application, and click the Done button when the Packager is finished. When you do so, Packager will analyze the log file it created while you were installing the application. When it's done, press F7 to build the project and create the project directory. The package will appear in Packager as it did after you created it with the Packaging Wizard.

You can also load packages that you previously saved and view or edit them, and then rebuild the package. Choose Open Package from the File menu, and browse to the location where you've been saving the project packages. There will be a folder for each package; the file you need is in the root of its project folder and will have an .aep extension.

Restoring the Packaging Server

Every time you create a project on the packaging server, you're potentially screwing up later projects by editing the Registry and installing files. Therefore, every time you finish creating a package and have saved the project file, you should roll back the changes to the server before creating another project. The process for doing so is pretty simple and will not affect the project you created—it just undoes the changes you made to the packaging server during the installation.

To roll back changes, choose Rollback from the Tools menu to open the dialog box in Figure 7.38. The difference between deleting a session (recording instance) and rolling it back may not be immediately obvious. Generally speaking, you'll want to roll back changes, which undoes the changes made to the packaging server when you recorded the installation. Deleting a session just removes it from the list without removing the changes that installation made to the packaging server. You might delete a session if you don't want to uninstall the files that you applied during an installation but need to roll back a session that is lower on the list. As you can see from the dialog box, if more than one session is listed, you'll need to roll back or delete the sessions in reverse order of the one you created them in. Just be careful—there is no "undo" option for either rollbacks or deletions. Once you roll back a session, it's gone, and once you delete a session, you cannot roll it back.

When you click OK to the dialog box warning you that you can't reverse rollback or delete actions, Citrix Packager will perform the requested action. It takes only a couple of seconds—this is a pretty speedy process.

Figure 7.38 After creating a package, roll back the changes before creating a new one.

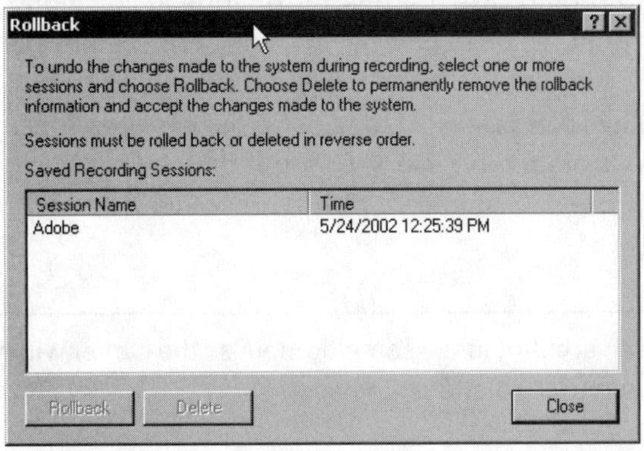

Publishing Packages

Now that we have packages, make sure that they're network-accessible to the MetaFrame server acting as Installation Manager, and we'll get them published. In the Citrix Management Console, go to the Citrix Installation Manager section. You'll see three icons here: Packages, Server Groups, and Summary.

First, we need to configure Installation Manager to deliver packages. It needs an account to connect to the published files, and you have the option of tuning a couple of installation settings. Right-click the Installation Manager icon, and choose Properties from the context menu to open the dialog box in Figure 7.39.

Figure 7.39 Tune the Installation Manager Properties before publishing packages.

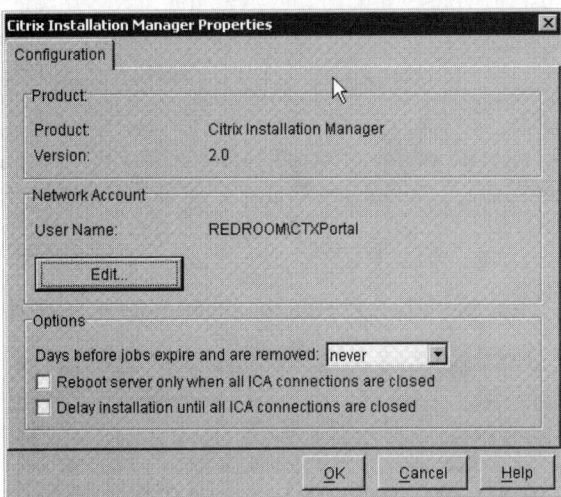

You might have already given Installation Manager an account to use, because when you first start the tool it prompts you for this information. If you didn't provide it, or you need to change the account, you can edit the account settings here. Click the Edit button to open the Network Account dialog box. Choose the domain where the account you want to access the package files is located, and enter the password for that account. You can't add new accounts from the Network Account dialog box, so you'll need to set up the account ahead of time. When you've picked an account, you'll return to the main Properties dialog box.

TIP Choose an account in the same domain as the server with the package files, so you can avoid trust relationship hassles.

The other settings are options. The jobs mentioned here are installation jobs—packages to be deployed. The amount of time you want to keep them around (anywhere from 7 to 90 days, or indefinitely) depends on how long you're willing to wait for a job to get a chance to complete, or how long you'd like to have to view the progress of a past job (success or failure). By default, jobs are never deleted. The other two options have to do with the timing for the job. Normally, a publishing job will begin when it's scheduled to begin, and do what's necessary to finish. If you check the boxes at the bottom of the screen, you can delay the installation until people are through using the server.

To create a package, right-click Packages and choose Add Package from the context menu to open the dialog box. Enter the path to the package files (MSI or WDF) as shown in Figure 7.40, and give the package a name. Make sure you've entered the path to the package files as a UNC name, as I've shown here. Although Installation Manager will accept logical drive letters as paths with some whining, forcing it to do so is not a good idea. Installation Manager just provides a link to files available across the network, and unless you map the same drive letters to the same network share on all managed MetaFrame servers, installations dependent on those mapped drive letters won't work.

TIP Give the package a name that will help you identify its application and version information. All application packages of the same file type (MSI or WDF) look alike.

Figure 7.40 Provide a UNC path to the package files and name the package.

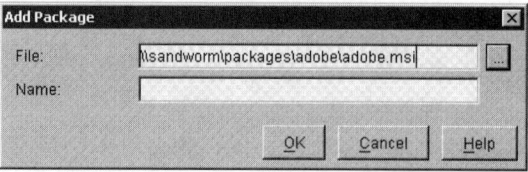

NOTE Installation Manager will sometimes get stubborn and only show computer icons in the Browse dialog box—not folders on shared computers. If it does this to you, you can either close the dialog box and try again (sometimes this works, but not always) or type the UNC path to the shared files in the Add Package dialog box.

The appearance of the packaged applications will depend on the type of package. If you made the package with Citrix Packager, the package's icon will have the envelope icon you can see in Figure 7.41. If the package is an MSI file, it will have the Windows Installer icon you've probably seen before. (I just gave the MSI package a distinctive name to make the point; the package names are what you call them and do not reflect the type of package file.)

Figure 7.41 MSI and Citrix packages have different icons.

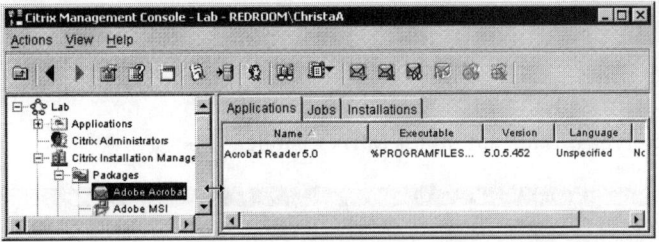

You're not stuck with packages once you add them to the server. To delete a package, just right-click it and choose Remove Package from the context menu.

Creating Server Groups for Application Deployment

You can apply installation packages to individual application servers; however, if you've got enough servers to make using Installation Manager an attractive option, you'll likely find it easier to apply those packages to *groups* of servers. To create a group, right-click the (you guessed it) Server Groups icon in Citrix Installation Manager and choose Create from the context menu to open the dialog box in Figure 7.42.

Give the new group a name, and to move an available server to the new server group, click the Add or Add All buttons. To remove servers in the group, select the server and click the Remove or Remove All button. A server can be in more than one group at the same time—just make sure that you don't accidentally apply conflicting packages to servers with membership in more than one group. All the new groups you create will appear in the Server Groups section, as in Figure 7.43.

Figure 7.42 Creating a new server group

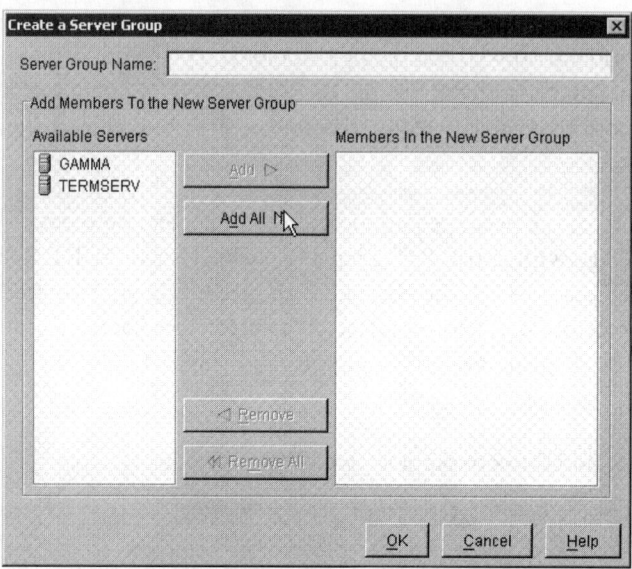

Figure 7.43 Server groups set up for Citrix Installer

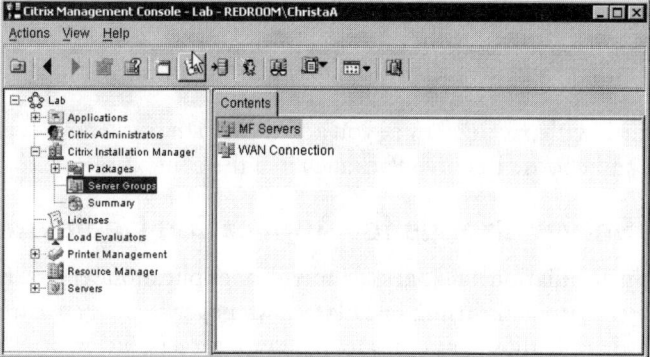

Organizing servers is the easy part. Choosing *how* to organize them is harder. The way that you'll do it, of course, depends on your circumstances. If you are working with MetaFrame servers based on a mixture of Windows 2000 and TSE-based servers, you'd be wise to organize the servers into groups according to their base operating systems, because the packages created for NT and Windows 2000–based computers will be slightly different. You can organize server groups based on user application needs, because not all MetaFrame servers will need a complete set of applications. If one group of servers is located at a remote site in a different time zone, you can group those servers together to make it easy to remember their location, and then schedule the updates accordingly. Because servers can be in more than one group, you've got a lot of flexibility when it comes to organizing.

Incidentally, server group membership matters only until the installation job has been completed. If you add a server to a server group after a job applied to that server group finishes, or remove a server from a server group, the change in membership does not change how the packages were applied. That is, removing a server from a server group after installing a package won't uninstall the package, and adding a server to a server group after installing a package to that group won't install the package. Installations and uninstallations are a one-time deal—every time you want to perform them, you'll need to initiate them explicitly.

Scheduling Installation Jobs

You have packages, and you have server groups. Now you need some deployed packages. To schedule a deployment job, right-click the package's icon and choose Install Package from the context menu to begin the wizard with the opening screen in Figure 7.44.

Figure 7.44 You can install packages to individual servers or server groups.

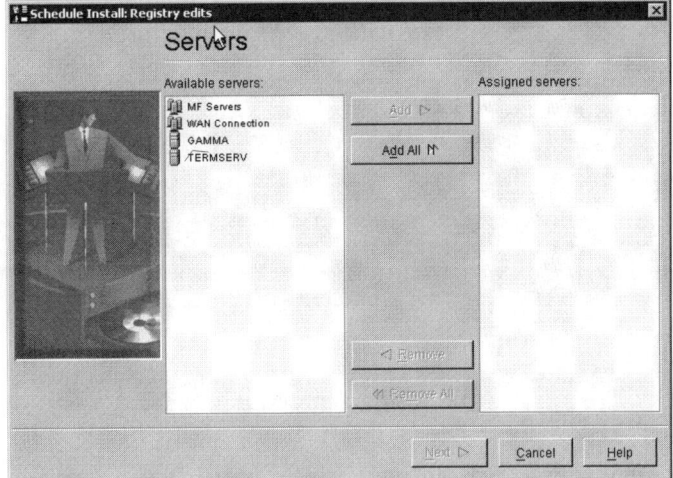

Pick a server or server group to install the package on, then click Next to move to the scheduling screen in Figure 7.45.

Normally, packages will install very shortly after you click the Finish button. You can, of course, change the scheduling. Click the Edit button to open the Schedule Details dialog box in Figure 7.46. Choose Schedule Later and pick a date, hour, and minute for the installation. Click OK when you're done to return to the previous dialog box, and click Finish to end the Scheduling Wizard. When you've done so, you should see a dialog box telling you that the package has been successfully scheduled.

Figure 7.45 Packages normally install immediately.

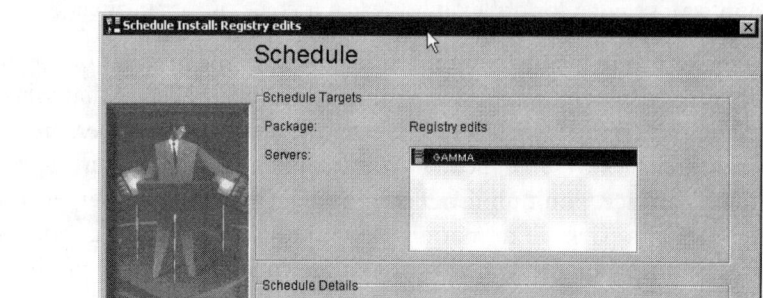

Figure 7.46 Scheduling package installation for non-busy times

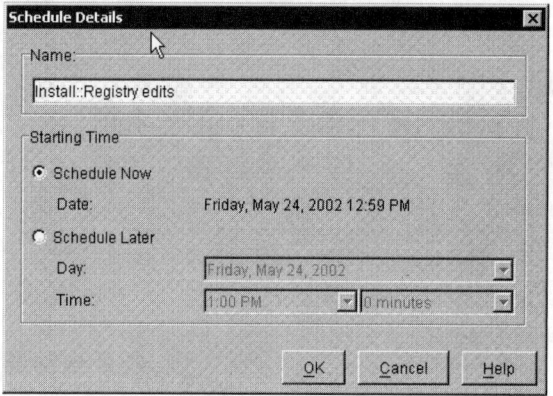

When you're done with the Scheduling Wizard, the job will appear in the Summary section of Installation Manager, on the All Jobs tab. Scheduled jobs and their status will appear here until you delete them or they expire (you had the option of setting expiration dates when you first configured Installation Manager). *Success* means, well, that the installation has completed successfully, *Pending* means that the job has not yet begun, and *Failure* means that Installation Manager tried to complete the job but was unable to do so for some reason.

After you've successfully applied a job to a MetaFrame server, the job will appear on an Applied Packages tab when you select the server's icon in the Citrix Management Console.

Troubleshooting Installation Jobs

If a job doesn't take, then check the following:

- The user account you specified to connect to the installation package files must have permission to read the network directory where the packages are stored.
- The network path to the installation packages must, obviously, be accurate and accessible to the target server.
- If you're deploying MSI files, try running them on a server locally. If they don't install, the file may be corrupt and you'll need to make another one. Sadly, this troubleshooting method doesn't work for ADF files.
- Make sure that you installed the agent on all target MetaFrame servers.

You can get some details about the process from the Installation Manager and more details from the Application Log in the Event Viewer on the target server. For example, if you select a failed job involving an MSI package and turn to the Job Results tab in its Properties sheet, you'll see a dialog box like the one in Figure 7.47, listing the servers you intended to install the package on and displaying the events that took place during the attempted installation. (These events aren't very illuminating. All they tell you is that Installation Manager stopped the server from accepting connections, began the installation, ended the installation, and then enabled server logon again—but at least they tell you that much.)

Now, if you were installing an application or change set from an ADF file, that would be all the information you could get from this location. However, this is an MSI package, so we can get a few more details by clicking the Job Details button. I'm not going to walk through the entire installation log here because it's mostly a litany of actions started and ended, but what you're looking for are potential errors to tell you what happened during the installation. (You can also be comforted by the entries that tell you that failed installations are rolled back, so that your MetaFrame servers won't have half-installed applications on them.) Those errors should give you a key to what went wrong with the installations.

ADF package users aren't left entirely out in the cold when it comes to installation troubleshooting—they'll just have to work a little harder to get the information. If you turn to the Application log in the Windows 2000 Event Viewer, you'll see a list of alert, warning, and/or information entries with their date, time, source, and other relevant information. The entries you need for ADF troubleshooting are from the Gemini Installer. By clicking on the entry and opening a dialog box like the one in Figure 7.48, you can find out what the problem was—failed permissions, files not found, or whatever. (Successful jobs will also appear, but with an Information icon instead of an Alert icon.) Jobs using MSI-based packages will have Event Viewer entries with a source of MSI Installer.

338   Chapter 7   Installing and Tuning Applications on an Application Server

Figure 7.47   The Job Results tab tells you very little about the installation.

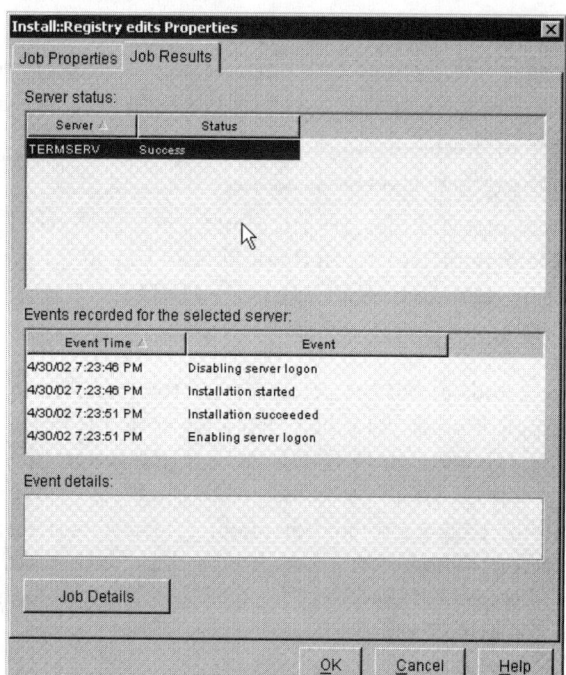

Figure 7.48   Event Viewer entry for a failed package installation

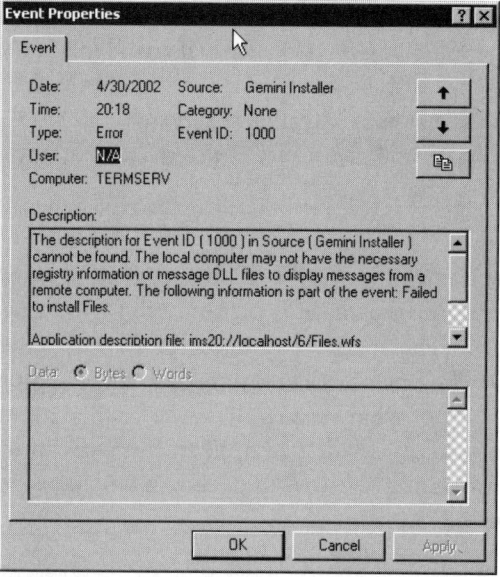

Summary

As you've seen, there's more to installing applications on an application server than just running SETUP.EXE. In this chapter, you've learned how the installation process works on a multiuser server, why you might need to tune applications post-installation and how you'll do it, and how to make applications available using Windows 2000 Terminal Services and the extras in MetaFrame XP. Now that people can run applications, let's talk about printing.

Supporting Printing in a Multiuser Environment

Although most of us probably would like to forget that printers exist, the paperless office never really happened and we're stuck with them. Printing in a single-user environment can be complex enough, but printing from applications running on an application server adds an entirely new element to the process. Therefore, we'll talk about those new elements in this chapter. We'll discuss how to map client-side printers to terminal sessions, how you can distribute printer drivers to application servers, and how you can reduce the amount of bandwidth print jobs need.

How Windows 2000 Printing Works

Before we can talk about how printing works specifically from an application server, I'd like to be sure that everyone is clear on how it works on a single-user computer. The Windows 2000 printing model has a lot to do with the problems associated with printing from applications running from a shared computer. (I don't mean to imply that it's a bad model, but, as you'll see, life can get interesting when you apply it to printing from terminal sessions.)

Printing Pieces

The Windows 2000 model uses several components to render application data for graphical output, get the data to a printer, and then help the printer manage multiple print jobs. The main chunks of Windows 2000 printing are the Graphics Device Interface (GDI), the printer driver, and the print spooler.

The Graphics Device Interface

The Graphics Device Interface (GDI) begins the process of producing visual output on a Windows 2000 computer, whether that output is to the screen or to the printer. Without the GDI, WYSIWYG output would be impossible. To produce screen output, the GDI calls the video driver; to produce printed output, the GDI calls the printer driver, providing information about the print device needed and the type of data used.

The Printer Driver

Windows 2000 is not designed to communicate directly with printers—if it were, Microsoft would have had to build into the OS support for every printer imaginable and apply patches every time a new printer was released. Rather, *printer drivers* play the role of middleman between OS and printer. They're incompatible across operating systems. Although any Win32 operating system can print to a Win2K Server print server without requiring you to first manually install a local printer driver—the OS will just download the correct driver from the print server—you'll have to make sure the drivers are available for the clients that will be using the printer. For example, if the print server (the computer to which the printer is physically attached) and the computer running an application from which you're printing are running different operating systems, you'll need printer drivers for both operating systems—one for the print server, and one for the computer where the application is running—so that the application can initiate the print job. Win2K printer drivers are composed of three subdrivers that work together as a unit: a printer graphics driver, a printer interface driver, and a characterization data file. The *printer graphics driver* renders the GDI commands into Device Driver Interface (DDI) commands that can be sent to the printer. The *printer interface driver* interacts with and configures the printer, and acts as the intermediary to the *characterization data file*, providing the information you see in a printer's properties pages. The characterization data file provides information about the make and model of a specific type of print device, including what it can do: print on both sides of a piece of paper, print at various resolutions, and accept certain paper sizes.

The Print Spooler

The print spooler (SPOOLSS.DLL, in *%systemroot%*\system32) is a collection of dynamic link libraries (DLLs) and device drivers that receive, process, schedule, and distribute print jobs. It is implemented with the Spooler service, which is required for printing, and is composed a print router, a local print provider, a remote print provider, print processors, and a print monitor.

The Print Router When a Win2K client computer connects to a Win2K print server, the client's print router (WINSPOOL.DRV) talks to the server's print router (SPOOLSS.DLL) through remote procedure calls. At this point, the server's print router passes the print request to the appropriate print provider (the local print provider if it's a local job, and the remote print provider if sent over the network).

The Print Provider To find the right print provider, the print router polls the Windows print provider. This provider then finds the connection that recognizes the printer name and sends a remote procedure call to the print router on the print server. That local print provider then writes the contents of the print job to a spool file (which will have the extension .spl) and tracks administration information for that print job. The spool file, because it contains routing and formatting information about the printer the print job is going to, is larger than the file being printed—perhaps quite a bit larger.

> **NOTE** Because spool files exist only to keep a print job from being lost during a power failure to the print server, Win2K normally deletes them after the print job they apply to is completed. If you want to keep track of data such as the amount of disk space required by spool files and what printer traffic is like, you can enable spooler event logging.

The Print Processor The data type for a print job tells the print spooler whether and how to modify the print job to print properly. This is necessary because methods of print job creation aren't standardized; for example, a Win2K client won't create a job the same way a Linux client does. Therefore, a variety of print server services exist to receive print jobs and prepare them for printing. Some of these print services assign no data type (in which case Win2K uses the default data type in the Print Processor dialog box), and some assign a data type. A print processor works with the printer driver to "despool" spool files during playback, making any necessary changes to the spool file based on its data type.

The spool file can accept data from the print provider in one of two forms: Enhanced Metafile (EMF) or RAW. EMF spool files are device-independent files used to reduce the amount of time spent processing a print job; all GDI calls needed to produce the print job are included in the file. Once the EMF file is rendered, you can continue using the application from which you were printing—all the rest of the print processing will take place in the background. Unlike EMF spool files, which still require some rendering once it's determined which printer they'll be spooled to, RAW spool files are fully rendered when created. Modern NT-based operating systems (such as Win2K and NT 4) use RAW spool files for local print jobs, for Encapsulated PostScript print jobs, or when otherwise specified by the user. Windows 9*x* uses EMF files for local printing but sends RAW data to a networked print server. Windows NT 4 uses EMF files for both local and networked printing, and NT 3.*x* uses RAW whether printing locally or to a network printer.

> **NOTE** All else being equal, EMF spool files are normally smaller than RAW spool files because they are instructions for rendering, not complete renderings.

The default data type is RAW, supported by all Windows clients. Although you can make it EMF, don't change the data type on a Windows 2000 print server unless you're *sure* it's a good idea. If a print client can use EMF files, it will do so even if the default data type is RAW, so you're not losing anything by making RAW the default.

The Print Monitor The print monitor, the final link in the chain getting the print job from the client application to the print device, is actually two monitors: a language monitor and a port monitor.

The *language monitor*, created when you install a printer driver if a language monitor is associated with the driver, comes into play only if the print device is bidirectional. A bidirectional print device can send meaningful messages about print job status to the computer. In this case, the language monitor sets up the communication with the printer and then passes control to the port monitor. The language monitor supplied with Win2K uses the Printer Job Language. If a manufacturer created a printer that spoke a different language, it would need to create another language monitor, as the computer and print device must speak the same language for the communication to work.

The *port monitor's* job is to transmit the print job either to the print device or to another server. It controls the flow of information to the I/O port to which the print device is connected (a serial, parallel, network, or SCSI port). The local port monitor supplied with Win2K controls parallel and serial ports; if you want to connect a print device to a SCSI port or network port, you must use a port monitor supplied by the vendor. Regardless of type, however, port monitors interface with ports, not printers, and are, in fact, unaware of the type of print device to which they're connected. The print job was already configured by the print processor.

The Printing Process (and Why Printing Can Be Problematic)

Those are the parts of the printing process. Here's how they fit together when printing from a Win2K client:

1. The user chooses to print from an application, causing the application to call the GDI. The GDI, in turn, calls the printer driver associated with the target print device. Using the document information from the application and the printer information from the printer driver, the GDI renders the print job.

2. Now rendered, the print job goes to the spooler. The client side of the spooler makes a remote procedure call to the server side, which then calls the print router component of the server.

3. The print router passes the job to the local print provider, which spools the job to disk.

4. The local print provider polls the print processors, passing the print job to the one that recognizes the selected printer. Based on the data type (EMF or RAW) used in the spool file, any necessary changes are made to the spool file in order to make it printable on the selected print device.

5. If you've enabled separator pages, the separator page processor adds a separator page to the print job.

6. The print job is despooled to the print monitor. If the printer device is bidirectional, the language monitor sets up communications. If not, or once the language monitor is done, the job is passed to the port monitor, which handles the task of getting the print job to the port to which the print device is connected.

7. The print job arrives at the print device and prints.

That's how the process works when you're printing from an application running on a single-user computer. It is much the same when the print job is initiated from an application running in a terminal session. From the user's perspective, once a printer is available, printing from an ICA or RDP session is usually no different than printing from an application running on the local computer, whether the client is printing to a network printer, a local printer directly attached to the MetaFrame server, or a client printer attached directly or via network to the client computer and automatically mapped to the ICA session. Print jobs sent to a client's network printer have an extra stop along the way to the printer, that's all.

Transparent from the user's perspective, perhaps, but the machine perspective may be a little different if you're printing to a mapped printer. In the first version of RDP—the one that came with TSE—RDP did not support mapped client printers. If you wanted to print from a terminal session to a printer attached to a client computer, you had to share that printer with the network and then connect to that share from the terminal session. Current versions of both

ICA and RDP automatically map both locally attached and network-accessible Win32 client printers to virtual ports associated with terminal sessions, so that the printers are only available to the sessions they're associated with (see Figures 8.1 and 8.2).

Figure 8.1 Client printer mapped to an RDP session

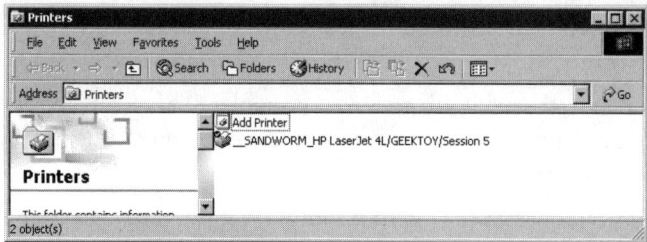

Figure 8.2 Client printer mapped to an ICA terminal session

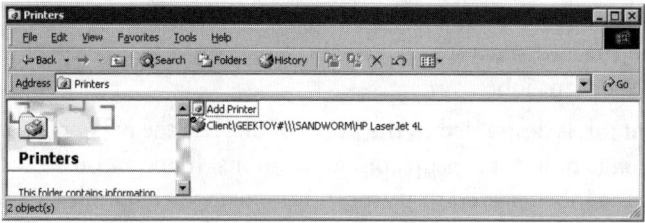

NOTE Notice that network printer connections on client computers map to terminal sessions, not just to locally attached printers. The print job can be managed from the client computer.

You can see port assignments if you check the properties of an assigned printer on the application server, as in Figure 8.3. RDP virtual ports look like TS001, TS002, and so forth. Virtual ports mapped to ICA sessions look like CLIENT*computername**printer name* or CLIENT*computername**shared printer name*. Both locally attached and network-accessible client printers can be mapped to terminal sessions using either display protocol. Do not change the mappings manually, or you'll misroute print jobs and confuse everybody.

Figure 8.3 Port mappings to terminal sessions

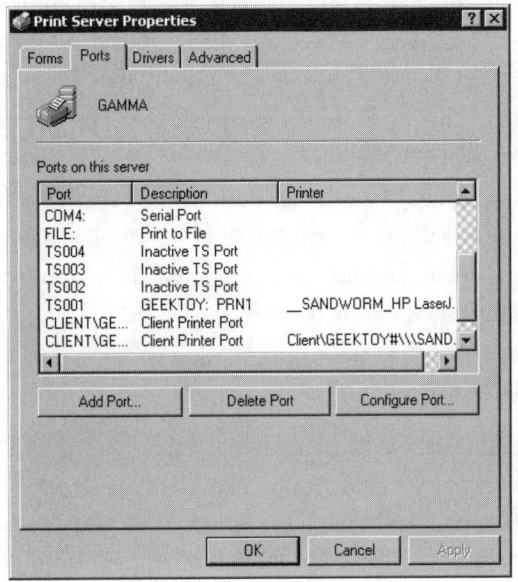

Printing to network printers from a terminal session doesn't raise any new problems. Printing to a mapped client printer, however, is an open can of worms of a different color. Consider the following potential wigglers:

- If you print from an application, the printer driver must be installed on the computer where the application is running. For those using MetaFrame XP, these printer drivers are stored in the data store for the farm.
- When an NT-based computer such as a Windows 2000 application server attaches to a printer, it automatically installs drivers for that printer if they're not already present and drivers are available. It does not ask first, nor does it ask which version of a driver you'd like to install.
- Unlike user applications, printer drivers run in Kernel mode—the areas of memory common to all low-level functions on a computer. A crashed application usually just terminates. A crashing driver can crash the entire operating system.
- Print spool files sent to a client printer mapped to a terminal session travel through an RDP or ICA channel.
- Print jobs sent to a mapped client printer act like local print jobs. The name of the printer driver on the client (the application server initiating the print job) and the print server (the client printer to which the printer is attached) must match.

So? What does all this mean? It means that:

- We'd like some way of controlling which drivers get installed, to make sure that the latest and least buggy versions are installed, not the two-year-old drivers that come with Windows 2000 (not buggy, but decidedly dated).
- We'd like to map client printer drivers to the ones on the application server, if the two don't have the same name.
- We'd like to keep spool files—larger than the files they're printing, remember—from interfering with session activity more than we can help.
- We'd also like control over how client printers are mapped to terminal sessions and whether those printers are the default.

Conveniently, the rest of the chapter explains how Windows 2000 and/or MetaFrame XP let you fulfill this wish list.

> **NOTE** Depending on whether you're using MetaFrame XP or not, (and for MetaFrame XP users, whether you're using FR1 or not), some of the options in this chapter may or may not be available to you.

Controlling Driver Distribution

Because a crashed application server inconveniences not one but perhaps dozens of people, the first order of the day is ensuring that the drivers getting installed on application servers aren't going to crash them. To ensure this, you'll need to test drivers before putting them into production, but you'll also need to create a launching point for those drivers. MetaFrame XP has a driver distribution method.

> **NOTE** Sadly, Windows 2000 doesn't seem to have a way to accomplish this. Although a couple of Knowledge Base articles describe ways of making an NT4 or a TSE computer only install drivers from a trusted source, neither method actually forces a Windows 2000 terminal server to install drivers from a trusted source and location. Sorry.

The Universal Printer Driver

The problem of letting people print from terminal sessions without installing printer drivers willy-nilly on the application servers isn't a new one. FutureLink (and a couple of other companies) addressed this problem with a printing tool that sent all print output to an Adobe Acrobat file, which was then printed from the client's computer using their local drivers. TriCerat's printing solution intercepts the EMF file generated on the application server, compresses it, and then sends it to the client computer to be made into a spool file there—thereby both reducing the amount of bandwidth required to get the print job to the client (since it's sending a compressed text file, not a spool file) and using the client's printer settings. Now, MetaFrame XP with FR1 installed has a universal printer driver (UPD) that acts as a generic driver for print jobs generated from terminal sessions.

The UPD approach to resolving driver compatibility problems differs from the other two approaches I already mentioned. It's a Printer Control Language (PCL) driver installed on the printer. After this driver creates the print job, it goes to the client's printer as described earlier. It doesn't need a separate driver installed for the client printers and therefore limits an application server's exposure to buggy printer drivers and reduces the amount of space needed to record those drivers in the data store. If the client's printer isn't PCL, the print job may be smaller than it would be otherwise, thereby reducing the amount of bandwidth required to get the job to the client for final processing. (It doesn't reduce the processing power required on the client to make the print job, but frankly that's less of a worry than the bandwidth required to transport the print job at all.) If you've read anything previously about the UPD and wondered where the "up to 50 percent reduction in bandwidth requirements" part was coming from, that's where. These bandwidth reductions don't apply to clients already using PCL printers.

Installing the UPD is simple. If you install and license FR1 on a MetaFrame XP application server, you've installed the driver. MetaFrame XP application servers without FR1 or later can't use it at all.

To make the UPD the default printer driver—or the default if the native printer driver isn't available—open the Citrix Management Console and right-click the Printer Management icon in the left-hand pane. Open the Properties sheet from the context menu that appears, and you'll see the Client Printers tab shown in Figure 8.4.

This tab has two sections. The section we want right now is Printer Drivers. As you can see, you have four options here:

- Always use the native driver.
- Always use the UPD.
- Create one instance of the printer using the native driver and one using the UPD. (This one sounds potentially confusing to users and sounds like one to avoid in most cases.)
- Use the UPD only if the native driver isn't already installed on the MetaFrame XP server.

Pick the option you want, and click OK. These settings apply to the entire server farm.

Figure 8.4 You can assign drivers to printer connections in a MetaFrame XP farm.

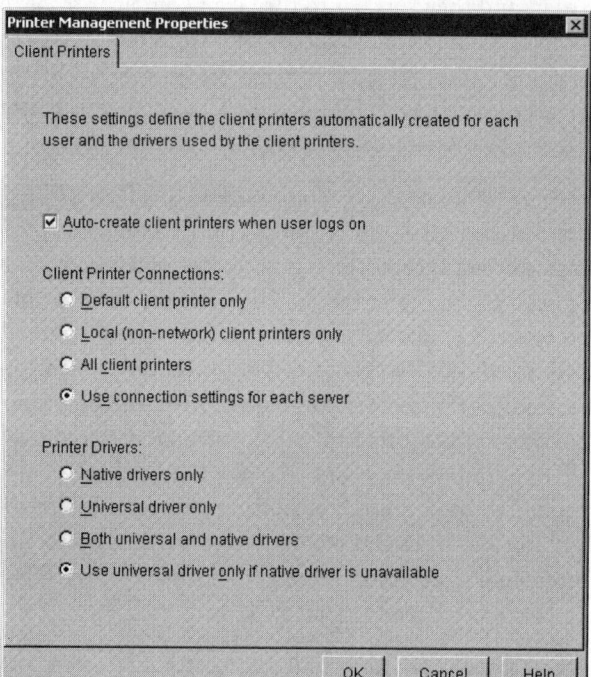

> **TIP** Even though these settings apply to the entire farm, you can force discrete usage of the UPD by selectively replicating printer drivers to servers in the farm, restricting the drivers that a server can install (explained in the following section), and opting to use the UPD only if the native driver is unavailable. The servers that have the native drivers will use them; the ones that don't will use the UDP.

The UPD isn't a universal replacement for standard printer drivers. Those who are everything to everyone have to sacrifice some individuality, and printer drivers are no exception. Print jobs created with the UPD can only be in black and white and up to 300dpi. In other words, the UPD is a good solution for draft output or memos (and older printers that print in black and white and 300dpi with their own drivers), but you're not need a standard driver to print your color slides. Having the UPD handy doesn't do a lot for preventing new drivers from being added to the server farm's data store, either. Therefore, for those who don't have FR1 and those who do but still want to control printer driver generation, there's MetaFrame XP's printer driver distribution system.

Using MetaFrame XP's Printer Driver Distribution System

The UPD is only one example of the way in which Citrix is trying to get serious about the problems of printer management for application servers. Another is the printer driver distribution system that comes with all versions of MetaFrame XP... and which does *not* require FR1. Using this system, you can install trusted print drivers on a single MetaFrame XP applications server, and then replicate those drivers to all MetaFrame servers in a farm or selected ones. Not only can you install print drivers to other servers, but you can later update the same drivers on those servers.

Setting Up Driver Replication

First, install the drivers that you'll use in the server farm (including the drivers used by client-mapped printers, if possible) on one particular MetaFrame server. Test the drivers *now* to make sure that they won't crash the server—the last thing you want to do is replicate buggy drivers. When you've finished installing the good drivers on one server, turn to the Printer Management section of the Citrix Management Console and right-click the Drivers icon subordinate to Printer Management. When you choose Auto-Replication from the context menu, you'll see a dialog box like the one in Figure 8.5.

Figure 8.5 Starting to auto-replicate installed printer drivers

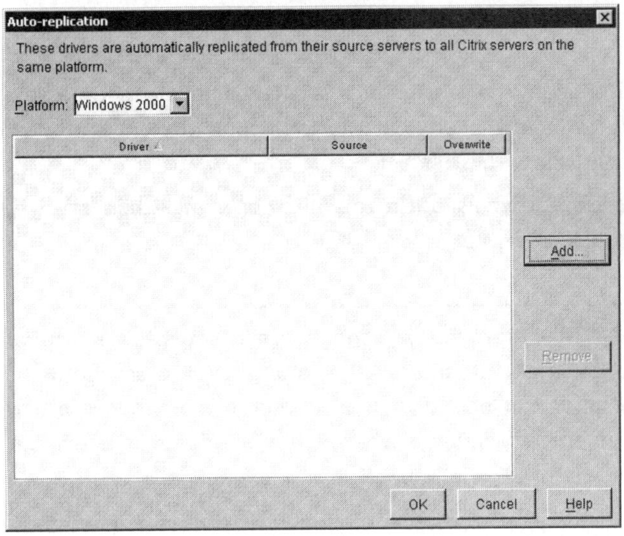

The first step here is to pick the platform from the drop-down list at the top of the dialog box—Windows 2000 in this case. Only the operating systems found in the server farm will be listed—so if you're running nothing but Windows 2000–based application

servers, you needn't worry about this step. Having picked the OS, you can now pick the drivers and replication sources by clicking Add to open the dialog box in Figure 8.6.

Figure 8.6 Choosing new drivers to replicate

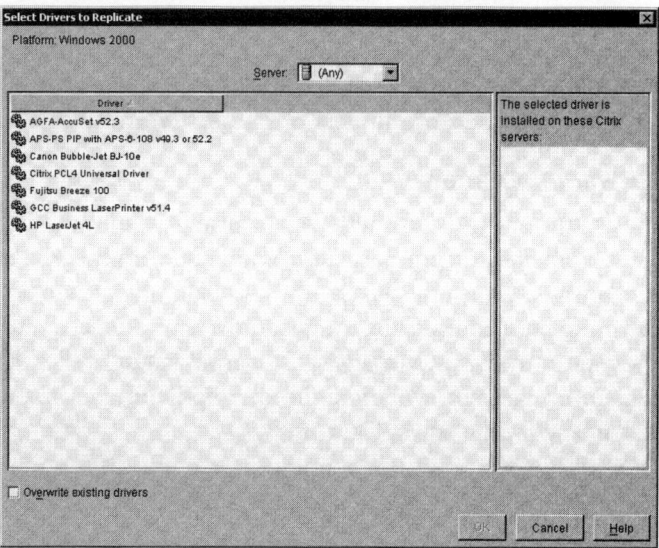

From here, you're going to choose the drivers to replicate, choose the servers you want to replicate them from, and specify whether replicated drivers should overwrite ones of the same name. Just follow these steps:

1. From the drop-down list at the top of the box, pick the server you want to use as the source for driver replication.

WARNING Make sure that you choose a server to replicate drivers from, rather than sticking with the default of Any. Letting just any server be the source of driver replication can lead to version problems and unnecessary traffic. The only reason to choose Any server is when the same drivers are available on more than one server.

2. When you opened the dialog box, all drivers installed in the server farm were visible; now that you've chosen a replication server, only those installed on that server will appear in the left-hand pane. Select the drivers that you want to replicate so that the server(s) it's installed on appear in the right-hand pane. If you want this driver to

replace any drivers by the same name that might already be on farm servers, check the Overwrite Existing Drivers box at the bottom of the screen. Click OK to return to the original dialog box.

TIP Ctrl+click to select more than one driver for replication. Don't bother replicating the UPD, though. If FR1 is installed on a server, the driver is installed; if it isn't installed, the server can't use the driver.

3. At this point, the Auto-Replication dialog box will show the drivers you picked, as in Figure 8.7. Check the settings here to make sure that you've got the right driver, source server, and overwrite options, and click OK. When you do so, you'll see a dialog box telling you that the drivers will be updated as bandwidth allows.

Figure 8.7 Drivers configured for replication

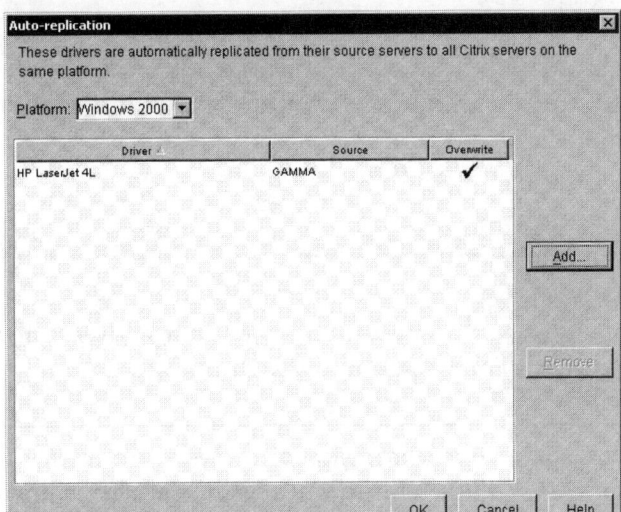

At this point, the drivers are configured to go to *all* servers in the farm. That may not be what you want—we'll discuss why in a moment—so let's see how to limit driver distribution when you're setting up replication. Turn to the Drivers section of Printer Management, so you can see all the currently installed drivers in the farm. (As in the previous example, when you select a farm in the list, the server that the driver is copied to will be listed in the right-hand pane.) Choose a server for a replication source, then right-click on a driver you want to replicate, and choose Replicate Driver from the context menu to open the dialog box in Figure 8.8.

354   Chapter 8   Supporting Printing in a Multiuser Environment

> **TIP** Again, you can Ctrl+click to select more than one driver before opening its replication settings. Just be careful that you've picked the right ones, since the replication settings dialog box will not name the drivers if you're configuring more than one.

Figure 8.8   You don't have to replicate drivers to every server in the farm.

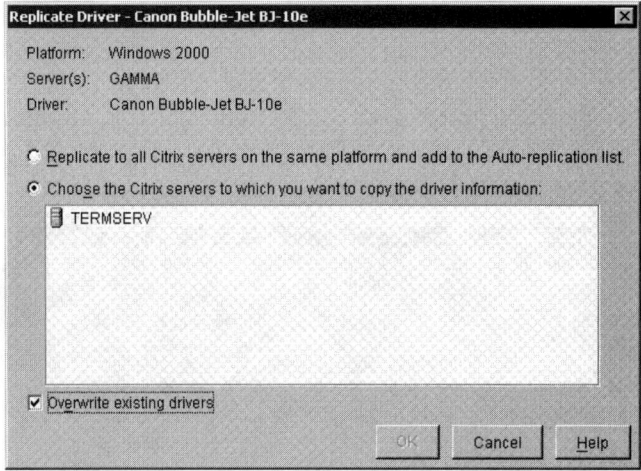

Choose the option you want—either to copy the selected driver to all servers in the farm or to pick servers to replicate it to—and click OK.

> **TIP** Are you curious to see the replication process? A utility called `qprinter` on the MetaFrame XP FR1 CD-ROM lets you monitor replication from the command line with the `/replica` switch.

Replication Considerations

That's *how* you set up drivers for replication. Which servers you should replicate drivers to and when you should perform this replication is another matter.

First, consider the size of the data store. The data store for a MetaFrame XP server farm contains entries for all objects in the farm. Printers, printer drivers, and servers associated with a printer are separate objects. Add a new printer and printer driver to a farm, and you're adding three new entries for each server that printer is set up on. In a large server farm, this could add up. The larger the data store, the longer it takes the IMA Service to start up, and, therefore, the more time it takes for MetaFrame servers to boot. While it would be silly to cripple your server farm in an effort to keep the data store as tiny as possible, there's no reason to cripple it by making the data store larger than it needs to be either.

Second, there is likely no reason to replicate all drivers to all servers, particularly in a geographically distributed server farm. The people in the Washington D.C. office probably won't often use the printers located in the Boston office.

Finally, if you have FR1 installed on your server farm, use the UPD as much as you can. As I said earlier, it probably won't replace native printer drivers in all cases. However, it's a good basic print driver for black-and-white low-resolution printing, and having it around may enable you to lighten the printer driver load in the farm data store, particularly when it comes to supporting client-side printers automatically mapped to ICA sessions.

Authorizing Driver Installation

Getting good drivers to application servers is important; equally important, however, is keeping bad drivers *off* the servers. If you're using MetaFrame XP, you can configure a server farm either to accept new drivers only from a preset list or to accept any drivers *except* those on a preset blacklist. From inside Printer Management in the Citrix Management Console, right-click the Drivers icon, and select Compatibility from the context menu to open the dialog box in Figure 8.9.

Figure 8.9 You can create a list of authorized or unauthorized printer drivers.

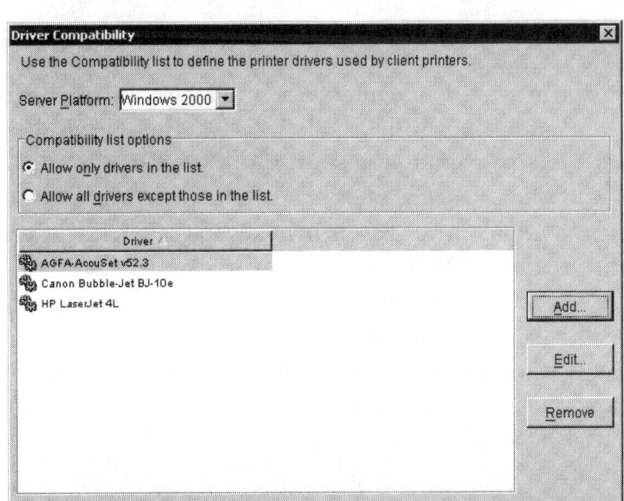

From here, just pick the option you want—either to specifically permit the installation only of the drivers listed here or to allow the installation of any drivers *except* those listed here. (For obvious reasons, you need to be careful to pick the right one or your driver restriction list will be backward.) Then click Add to add a new driver to the list with the dialog box in Figure 8.10.

Figure 8.10 Type the names of drivers that go on the blacklist or choose already installed drivers from the list.

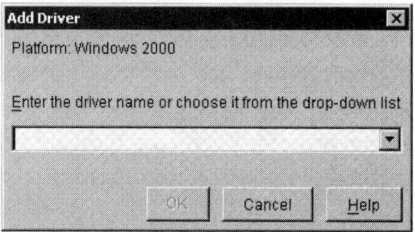

NOTE Although you can also choose drivers from the drop-down list, the only drivers listed here are those already installed. The drop-down list is useful only if you're creating a list of drivers that *must* be used, not a list of drivers that must not.

When you've picked a driver, click OK. You'll need to reopen the Add Driver dialog box for each driver in the list.

Uninstalling Old Drivers

Drivers installed when a client computer with an attached printer connects to an applications server are not automatically uninstalled when that user ends their terminal session. Even though the printers won't appear in the list of printers in the Control Panel, their printer drivers will still be installed on the server. If you'll need those drivers again, this is fine. However, each printer driver has its own key in the HKLM\System\ControlSet001\Control\Print\Environments\Windows NT x86\Drivers\Version-3, so unneeded but still-installed printer drivers can lead to Registry bloat. To uninstall drivers you won't need again, open the Printers section of the Control Panel and right-click anywhere to open the Print Server Properties dialog box. Turn to the Drivers tab shown in Figure 8.11, and use the Delete button to remove each entry you don't need anymore. Deleting the entries here will delete the Registry keys as well.

Figure 8.11 Uninstall drivers you no longer need.

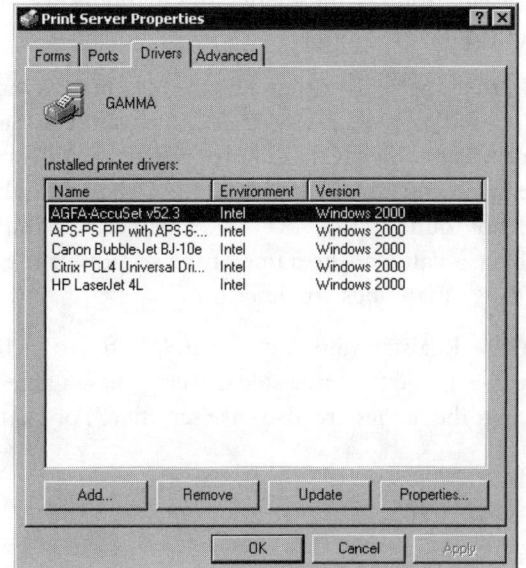

Correcting Driver Name Mismatches

Being unable to find the driver name isn't an entirely out-of-the-way problem. For example, Hewlett-Packard supplies Windows 98 and NT 4 drivers for the DeskJet 722C printer. This driver is called HP DeskJet 720C Series v10.3. The Windows 2000 version of the same driver is called HP DeskJet 722C. Because a print job created on an application server is essentially a local print job for the client computer, the names of drivers used on an application server and a client computer must match. Driver name mismatch means no working printer. Both Windows 2000 and MetaFrame XP have methods of getting around this difficulty, in effect telling an application server, "Now, when I say *this* driver name I really mean *that* one."

Windows 2000 Terminal Servers

Before SP2 came out, Microsoft's recommended fix for this problem was editing `NTPRINT.INF`, which worked but broke the digital signature on the file, making the system display a pop-up warning every time you installed a new printer. After you apply SP2 to the Windows 2000 server, however, you can edit the Registry to point to a secondary INF file with the printer information, in case Windows 2000 can't find the driver it's looking for in `NTPRINT.INF`. The end result is automatic print mapping even for mismatched printer names *and* an unsullied `NTPRINT.INF`.

To make this work, first apply SP2 or later to the terminal server. When you've done so, open the Registry and go to `HKLM\SYSTEM\CurrentControlSet\Control\Terminal Server\Wds\rdpwd`. Add two new values. `PrinterMappingINFName`, data type REG_SZ, should contain the name and complete path of the INF file to which you want to send lookups for drivers not found in `NTPRINT.INF`. `PrinterMappingINFSection`, data type REG_SZ, should have a value of the name of the section of the INF file you created where the printer driver mappings are described.

After adding these new Registry values, create an INF file to include the user-defined mappings from the client-side to server-side drivers. These names must match exactly, with identical spacing; the names are also case sensitive. For example:

```
[Version]
Signature="$CHICAGO$"
[Printers]
"HP DeskJet 720C Series v10.3"  =  "HP DeskJet 722C"
```

Save this file with the name you specified in `PrinterMappingINFName` when editing the Registry, and be sure to name the section mapping old and new printer names with the name of the section you specified in `PrinterMappingINFSection`.

MetaFrame XP Servers

For client printer mapping to ICA sessions to work, the drivers used on the client and server need to have the same name. This requirement won't cause any problems if both client and server are running Win2K, but may if the client is running an operating system that is not NT-based, say, Win98. Those using RDP-based terminal services without MetaFrame will need to manually edit a printer information file. In MetaFrame XP, you need to do the same thing, but MetaFrame XP is set up to let you do it through the Citrix Management Console.

To map mismatched client and server driver names, go to the Drivers section of Printer Management in the Citrix Management Console. On the Drivers tab, right-click any installed driver, and select Mapping from the context menu to open the dialog box in Figure 8.12.

Figure 8.12 MetaFrame XP has a graphical driver mapping tool.

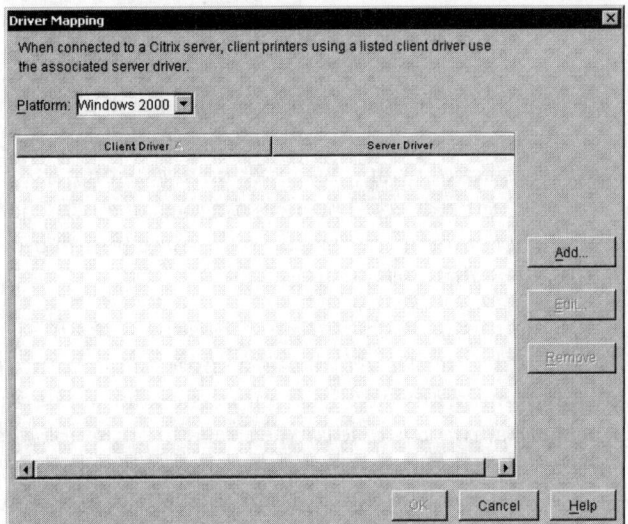

Click Add to open the dialog box in Figure 8.13, and type the name of the client and server drivers you're mapping. (You can choose drivers already installed on the server from a drop-down list.) Type the driver names carefully or the mapping won't work.

Figure 8.13 Choose client and server printer mappings.

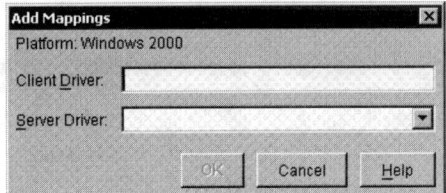

When you're done with each mapping, click OK in the Add Mappings dialog box to return to the Driver Mapping dialog box. The drive mappings you've created will appear in the list.

Controlling Bandwidth Requirements

In addition to driver distribution tools and the UPD, MetaFrame XP also tries to make printing from terminal sessions work better by controlling the amount of bandwidth that a print job can use while traveling to its printer. Controlling bandwidth may not make the print job print any more quickly over slow links—quite the opposite, probably—but it may help reduce the impact of print jobs on terminal session performance. Remember that print jobs sent to client redirected printers use the same ICA channels that all other application server-client communications do, so the more information traveling in those channels, the more slowly the screen will update.

One way to get around this problem is to compress the spool file itself, and that's the approach the Universal Printer Driver takes—compressed in comparison to print jobs created for non-PCL printers, anyway. The compression doesn't do anything for jobs for PCL printers. Another approach is to leave the size of the print job alone, but restrict the amount of bandwidth allocated to it. That's MetaFrame XP's other approach: restricting the amount of bandwidth that print jobs using ICA channels can use. With the bandwidth restricted, the print job may take a while, but it won't interfere with the ICA session using the same network path as much as it would otherwise.

To restrict the amount of bandwidth that print jobs can use, turn to the Bandwidth tab of Printer Management. Initially, the screen will look like the one in Figure 8.14—normally, all MetaFrame XP servers permit print jobs to client printers to use as much bandwidth as they need.

Figure 8.14 Print jobs normally get unlimited bandwidth.

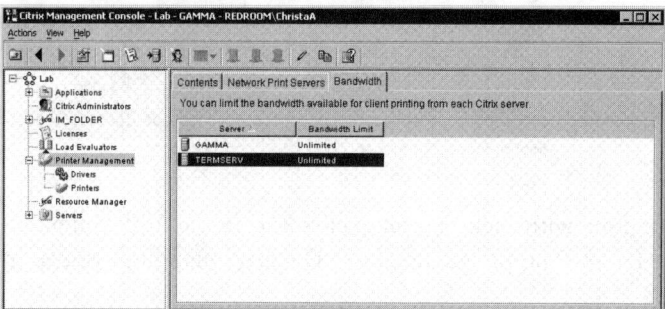

To reduce the amount of bandwidth for a specific printer (perhaps the one reserved for the people connecting to the farm via a 56Kbps dial-up connection), right-click the server's icon and select Edit (no, the menu item's name isn't very intuitive) from the context menu to open the dialog box in Figure 8.15. As you can see, you will need to know how much bandwidth you're willing to allocate to print jobs using ICA channels. The restrictions are not percentage-based; they are absolute. You will need to do your homework ahead of time so that you know how much bandwidth a given server has to work with. When you click OK, you'll be back at the Bandwidth tab. The space permitted to print jobs will be listed in the Bandwidth Limit column.

Figure 8.15 Choose the amount of bandwidth for print jobs sent to mapped printers.

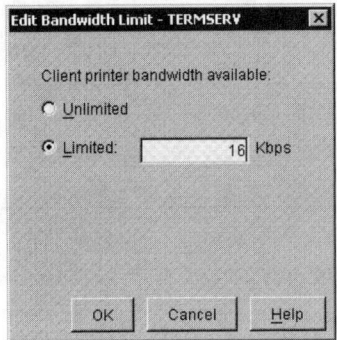

TIP The amount of bandwidth you pick may require some tweaking later. Too much bandwidth may cause print jobs to slow ICA sessions. Too little, and print jobs will take forever. The fewer ICA channels that sessions are using, the more you can allocate to printing. An ICA session not using mapped drives or sound requires less bandwidth than one going whole hog on ICA client features.

While the absolute use of bandwidth instead of percentages makes copying the settings a dicey business for servers not completely identical, copying bandwidth settings is an option. Right-click the server you've restricted, and select Copy from the context menu. From the dialog box that appears, choose the server to which you want to copy the bandwidth restrictions, and click OK.

If you have FR2 installed, you can have more discretion over limiting printer bandwidth. From the Policies section in the Citrix Management Console, create a new policy or edit an existing one from the Properties option in its context menu. Within the Resource Limits folder is the Limit the Client Printer Bandwidth policy. Enable it, set a Kbps limit, and then apply that policy to the group or individual accounts whose printer bandwidth you want to restrict.

Another way to control how much bandwidth ICA is using for print jobs is to use the `cltprint` command-line tool to adjust the number of pipes allocated to send print jobs from terminal sessions to mapped client printers. The tool's syntax looks like this:

```
cltprint /pipes:nn
```

where *nn* is the number of pipes from 10 to 63. You can also query the current value with cltprint /q, but the tool won't return any value unless you've already edited the pipes value. The default settings don't make it into the Registry.

Normally, ICA has ten pipes enabled, which means that people running ICA sessions can send up to ten print jobs to client printers at a time. You can't decrease this number, but you can add more pipes up to 63. Generally speaking, you probably won't want to enable more pipes than the default, because more print jobs traveling through ICA channels means more degradation of other ICA virtual channels battling for bandwidth.

> **NOTE** Because the minimum number of pipes is 10, you can't use `cltprint` to turn off ICA client printing altogether.

Controlling Client Printer Usage

So far, we've concentrated more on the server side of printer management, but we can't neglect the user component. Let's take a look at how you can control client printer mappings for Windows 2000 and MetaFrame XP terminal sessions, assign printers to users or groups, and make DOS and WinCE printers available to terminal sessions.

Printer Settings for RDP and ICA Users

Windows 2000 has per-user and per-connection settings for client printer mapping to terminal sessions. If you leave these settings alone, people logging onto an application server will have any network or locally attached printers mapped to their terminal sessions. This may be the way you want to leave things, because the printer that's convenient to use from locally running applications is also the one that's convenient to use from applications running in a terminal session. If it's not, you'll want to edit the settings either for individual users. Sorry, this doesn't work for either organizational units or user groups—or for everyone using a particular display protocol.

Per-User Settings

To edit printer settings for individuals, open Active Directory Users and Computers from the Administrative Tools program group on a domain controller. Right-click on user accounts to open their Properties sheets from the context menu, and turn to the Environment tab shown in Figure 8.16.

Figure 8.16 User account properties include printer mapping settings.

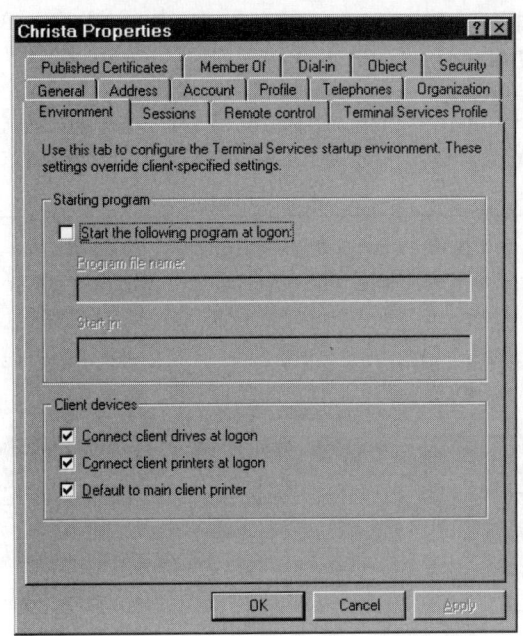

The first option—Connect Client Drives at Logon—applies only to people connecting to the application server via ICA, because the RDP server component on Windows 2000 terminal servers does not support client drive mapping. (This setting *will* apply to .NET Server RDP sessions using Remote Desktop.) The other two options here apply to mapping printers. If you don't want people to use their client mapped printers at all, uncheck Connect Client Printers at Logon. If you'd like them to have the option of using their client printers, but don't want their default printer to be the default for terminal sessions, uncheck Default to Main Client Printer.

For those maintaining user accounts for individual application servers, the same settings are on the Environment tab in local user accounts.

TIP To add Terminal Services–specific extensions to Local Users and Groups on a Windows 2000 server that does not have Terminal Services enabled, create a new MMC environment, add Local Users and Groups with the Add/Remove Snap-In option, and then turn to the Extensions tab and check the boxes for Terminal Services Extensions. All Terminal Services–related extensions are installed by default on Windows 2000 servers with Terminal Services installed and domain controllers.

Per-Protocol Settings

You can edit the same settings for everyone using the RDP or ICA protocol from the Terminal Services Configuration tool in Administrative tools on a Windows 2000 application server. If you look in the Connections folder in this tool (see Figure 8.17) you'll see entries for all the installed display protocols—RDP definitely, and ICA for every network protocol and separate network card for which you've installed ICA support.

> **NOTE** If you edit display protocol settings while people are using that display protocol, the settings won't apply to them until they log off and log back on.

Figure 8.17 Terminal Services Configuration manages settings that apply to all users of a display protocol.

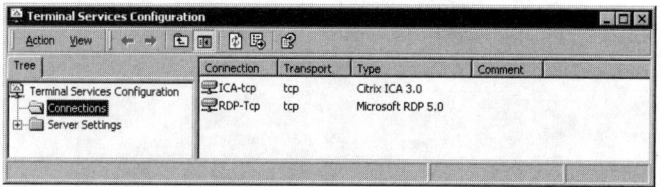

To edit the settings that apply to everyone using a display protocol, double-click on the protocol's entry to open its Properties sheet and turn to the Client Settings tab in Figure 8.18. The name of the protocol you're editing appears on the title bar for the Properties sheet. Normally, the client-configured settings control, but you can override that here by unchecking the Use Connection Settings from User Settings box and checking or unchecking the options you want. The settings in the bottom of the dialog box—those for mapping LPT and COM ports and the like—don't have any per-user equivalent, so you can either turn on the ability to map printers connected to parallel (LPT) ports for everyone using a display protocol or you turn it off.

As you can see here, the options for ICA and RDP aren't identical—that is, the dialog boxes are identical, but you can't edit the settings in the same way. All the printer-related settings apply to both protocols, but other options, such as audio mapping, apply only to ICA—again, because the RDP server component that comes with Windows 2000 doesn't support all those capabilities. The disabled options here will apply to .NET Server RDP sessions where the client computer is running Remote Desktop.

ICA also has a separate printer setting in addition to the ones it shares with RDP. If you turn to the ICA Settings tab in Figure 8.19, you'll see a difficult-to-find setting for connecting only the user's default printer.

Figure 8.18 ICA and RDP per-protocol options differ.

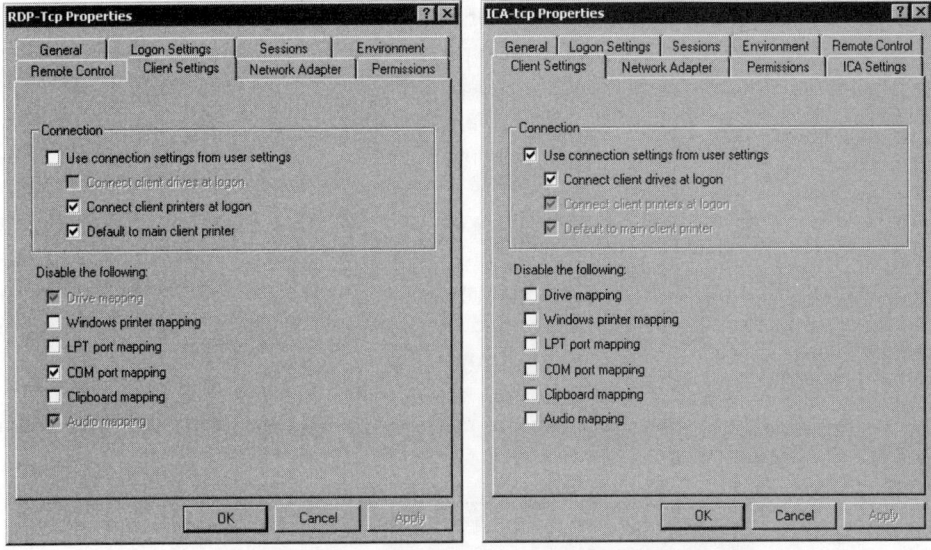

Figure 8.19 Turn to another tab to make ICA sessions map only the default client printer.

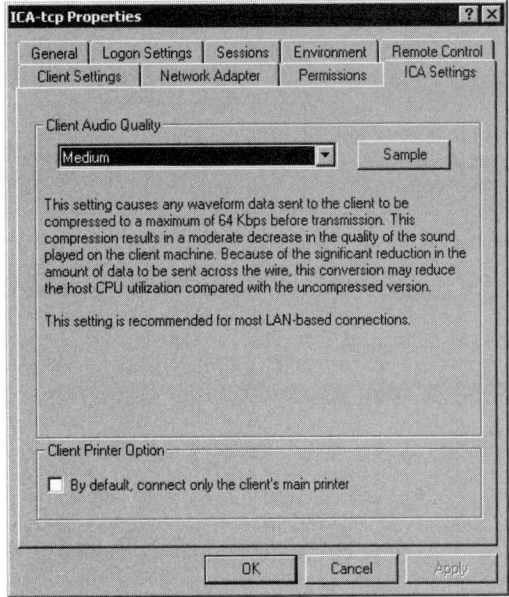

WARNING If you edit display printer mapping settings on a per-protocol basis, be sure to copy those settings to all application servers, or you'll confuse people by having different printing settings depending on which server they connect to. Per-user settings don't have this problem, because they apply to that user regardless of the application server she's using.

If you're using MetaFrame XP, you may want to use the Citrix Connection Configuration tool rather than Terminal Services Configuration to do all protocol-wide settings, mainly because Citrix Connection Configuration puts all the settings in one place. Same settings, better organization. From the MetaFrame XP section in the Citrix program group, choose Citrix Connection Configuration to open the dialog box in Figure 8.20.

Figure 8.20 MetaFrame XP users can edit per-protocol settings from Citrix Connection Configuration.

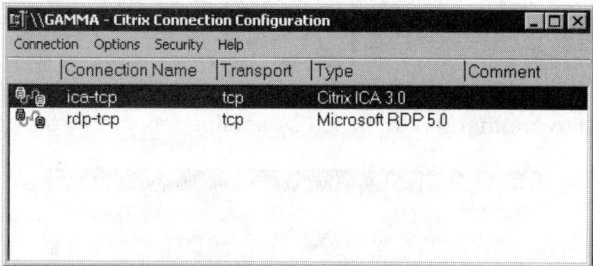

Double-click on a display protocol's icon, and click the Client Settings button visible on the dialog box that opens. You'll get the dialog box in Figure 8.21, which keeps all printer settings in one place. Again, the options here will depend on the display protocol you're editing, because RDP 5 is less capable than ICA.

Figure 8.21 Client printer mapping settings

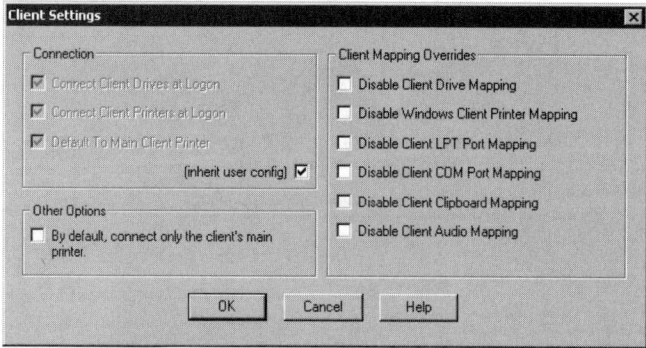

Per-Farm Settings

Although the Windows 2000 tools let you edit client printer mapping for both ICA and RPD settings, the tools in the Citrix Management Console give you some options not available with the Windows 2000 tools. They let you configure printing options not just for individual MetaFrame XP servers, but for the entire farm. From within the Citrix Management Console, right-click Printer Management to open the dialog box in Figure 8.22.

Figure 8.22 You can edit the client printer mapping settings for all the servers in a farm.

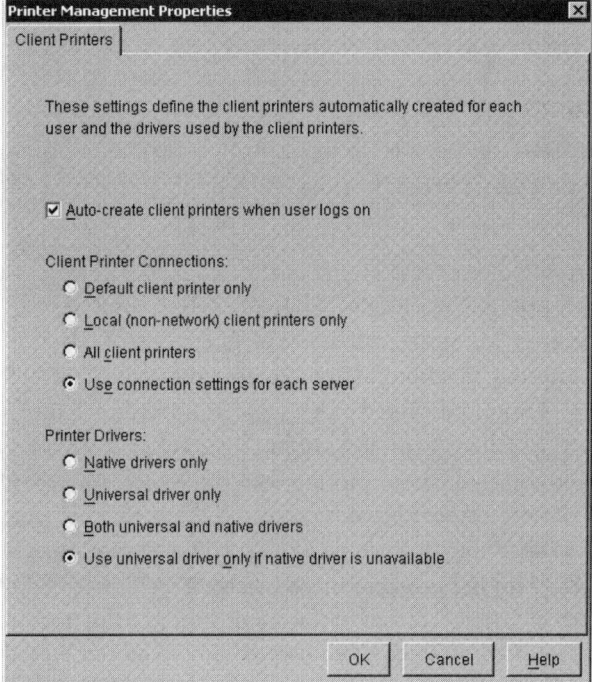

We've already discussed the driver settings in our discussion of the UPD, but the ones to pay attention to now are the ones for client printer mapping. As you can see here, from this tab you can disable client printer mapping entirely (meaning that you can forget about this chapter) or you can pick one of four options determining how client printers are mapped. Default Client Printer Only maps only the client's default printer to their terminal session, instead of all supported printers. The Local (Non-Network) Printers option maps only printers directly installed on client computers, instead of those attached to a printer server and to which the client has a network connection. The All Client Printers option, of course, maps all client-side printers to a terminal session and Use Connection Settings For Each Server puts the connection settings back on a per-server basis.

> **TIP** If the only printers a client is using are network printers, then consider unmapping them from terminal sessions and creating a network connection from within the terminal session. Doing so will keep the print job from having to make as many stops as it normally would, and it will prevent print jobs from taking up ICA bandwidth. It will also allow you to configure printer settings differently for terminal sessions than for applications running on the client printer, if that's desirable. (You could do this from the client computer by creating two instances of the same printer and configuring them differently, but that could lead to confusion.)

Per-Group Settings

Those using FR2 have another option for controlling printer mappings: policies. (Bet you expected that, didn't you?) From the Policies section in the Citrix Management Console, create a new policy or edit an existing one from the Properties option in its context menu.

The Client Printers folder accessible from the Properties sheet contains three policies: Client Printer Mapping, Connect to Client Printers, and Default to Client's Main Printer. Client Printer Mapping, when enabled, is controlled with a simple Turn Off Client Printer Mapping checkbox. If you enable this policy and check the box, client printer mapping is entirely disabled. Although Connect to Client Printers sounds like it might be identical to Client Printer Mapping, it's actually a way of controlling *which* client printers get mapped to a terminal session: the default client printer only, only locally attached (non-network) printers, or all client printers regardless of location. You can also use this policy to disable client printer mapping--it's really a superset of the Client Printer Mapping policy. Finally, Default to Client's Main Printer is a toggle between (you guessed it) defaulting to the client's main printer or not doing so. The policy is on a toggle in case you've applied more than one policy to the same group or user account and need to override a setting in another policy. Higher-priority policies override lower-priority polices.

> **TIP** To set any policy's priority, right-click on its icon in the Policies menu, and choose Priority from the context menu. You'll see a submenu allowing you to increase or decrease priorities or instantly make a policy have the highest or lowest priority of all policies.

Assigning Printers to User Accounts

MetaFrame XP lets you associate farm printers with user accounts, so that a user will print to the same printer regardless of the printers installed on the computer they're using to connect to the MetaFrame XP server and which application server they're connected to, and without mapping a client printer to their session.

> **NOTE** I'm not convinced that assigning printers to user accounts is a great idea. Your choice of printer often has more to do with *where* you are than with *who* you are. Someone connecting via ICA connection may be using the MetaFrame server from more than one computer depending on when they're using it—or even more than one building or more than one city. At the very least, I'd like the option of associating printers with client computer identity instead of just user identity.

To associate printers with user accounts, go to the Printers tab of the Printer Management section of the Citrix Management Console. Right-click an installed printer, and select Auto-Creation from the context menu to open the dialog box in Figure 8.23. (The Add List Of Names button is visible only if you have FR1 installed, and the same goes for NDS domains in the Look In drop-down list.)

Figure 8.23 Choose users or groups from any trusted account authority.

To add a printer for the use of a group in a domain or on a server, double-click the icon for the domain or server to display all the groups. To show individuals within groups, select the Show Users check box. You must add individuals or groups to the Configured

Accounts text box; to do so, just click Add, which is enabled when you select a group or individual account from the list. The added users or groups will appear in the Configured Accounts box.

For the FR1-using folk intrigued by the Add List Of Names button, it's for adding individuals without having to know which group they're in. When you click the button, you'll open a dialog box like the one in Figure 8.24. Type the name in an acceptable format (***domainname\username*** for NT 4-style domains; ***username@domainname.com*** for Win2K-style account names; and ***ndstree\account*** for NDS account names). To be sure that you typed the account names correctly, click Check Names. The Citrix Management Console will make sure that you formatted the account name correctly, then it will check with the security database for the domain or directory tree and either tell you that the names checked out or that they did not.

Figure 8.24 To quickly add users from multiple domains without enumerating user and group information, those with FR1 can enter accounts individually.

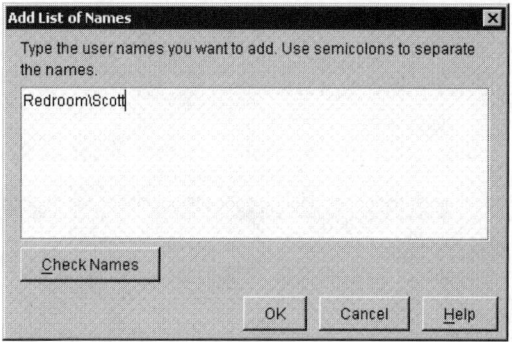

When you're done, click OK to return to the Auto-Creation Settings dialog box for the selected printer. The usernames you added will be in the Add List Of Names dialog box. When you click OK, the printer will be assigned to the users and groups you chose.

NOTE You can add users both from the drop-down list and from the Add List Of Names dialog box—the two won't cancel each other out.

If you want the users and groups you've got using one printer to get support for another one, you don't have to start from scratch. Rather, you can copy the Auto-Creation settings from one printer to another. From the Printers tab we started at, right-click the printer you just configured, and select Copy Auto-Creation Settings from the context menu. From the dialog box that opens, pick the printers to which you want to copy the settings, and then click OK.

Editing Printer Mappings During ICA Sessions

You can edit the client printer settings while an ICA session is live. Start an ICA session on the same application server that the terminal session whose printer settings you want to edit is connected to, and run the ICA Client Printer Configuration tool to open the dialog box in Figure 8.25. (This tool won't run outside an ICA session.) These settings apply only to printers mapped to ICA terminal sessions.

Figure 8.25   Editing client printer mappings

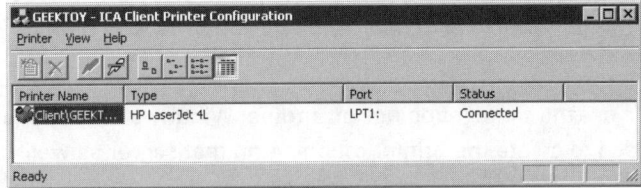

There aren't a whole lot of options here, but by right-clicking on a printer, you can choose to disconnect it (making it unavailable to the session) or change the default printer. Printers are identified by the name of the client computer to which they're connected.

Manually Mapping Printers to Terminal Sessions

As you've seen, you don't have to do anything special to map Win32 client printers to terminal sessions—the tweaking comes in when you *don't* want to do it. Older operating systems, and WinCE-based Windows terminals, however, don't automatically map client printers. If you'd like to user locally attached client printers in terminal sessions initiated from these devices, you'll need to set them up by hand. The good news is that those mappings will persist once you've got them enabled.

> **NOTE**   To map a client printer to a terminal session, clients must be running RDP 5 or ICA. If you're using an older Windows terminal, then make sure that you have the latest version of the RDP client installed.

Windows 2000 Manual Client Printer Mapping

To manually redirect a printer for a terminal services client, follow these steps:

1. Get the name of the client device, and start a terminal session from that client machine.
2. Start the process of manually adding a locally connected printer to the application server, as though you were installing the client's printer onto the application server.

3. In the part of the wizard where you're choosing the port the printer is connected to, scroll down in the list until you see the name or IP address of the client computer with the printer attached, like this:

    Ts002 CLIENTPC LPT1

4. Choose that port to attach the printer to, and install the printer normally.

When a client disconnects or logs off a session, the printer queue is deleted and any incomplete or waiting print jobs are deleted. Once you have manually redirected a printer for a terminal session, that redirection will take place automatically thereafter, and the print queue will be automatically created from the information stored on the client.

NOTE To use the same mappings on another Windows 2000 application server, you will need to create the printer mapping on that server as well.

MetaFrame XP Manual Client Printer Mapping

Using Windows 2000 manual printer mapping, you can map a legacy client printer to a port on a specific application server. If you're using MetaFrame XP, you can map the legacy client printers to a server farm, so that the application server to which the clients connect doesn't matter. To auto-create client printers from the Citrix Management Console, right-click Printers in the Citrix Management Console, and select Client Printers from the context menu to open the dialog box in Figure 8.26.

Figure 8.26 You'll need to manually map DOS and WinCE client printers with a server farm.

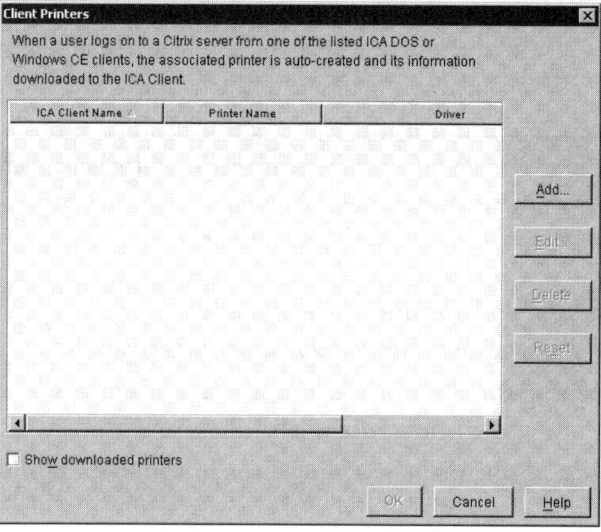

As you can see, by default, there are no manual client printer mappings. To create one, click Add to open the dialog box in Figure 8.27, in which you'll name the client device and its printer and—more important—pick the driver and any necessary driver mappings to use. (Given that you're trying to match DOS or WinCE drivers with Win2K drivers, I'll be very surprised if you don't need to map the drivers to get them to work.) Also, DOS and WinCE printing require an explicit port assignment, so choose that as well. When you're done, click OK to return to the Client Printers dialog box. The next time a user using the client you named initiates an ICA session, the user's client printer will be mapped to his or her session.

Figure 8.27 Mapping client printer driver names to Windows 2000 driver names

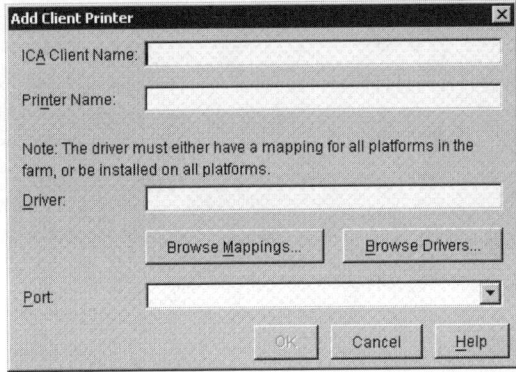

Summary

As you've seen, most of the concerns associated with printing from applications running on application servers has to do with supporting client printers mapped to terminal sessions. Print jobs sent to mapped printers can degrade session performance. Automatically installing printer drivers can be potentially dangerous to the application servers, and the default settings for client printer mapping may not be the best ones for your situation. In this chapter, you've learned how to address these problems and, hopefully, make printing from terminal sessions a bit less sticky.

9

Ongoing Server Management

By this point, you should have a working application server environment and a bunch of users able to happily type away from wherever they need to be. To wrap up, I'd like to take a look at some management issues that didn't exactly fit into the process of getting the application servers up and running. Even after our server is launched, you'll need to secure the settings, perform inventories, and perform ongoing resource management. These topics and are important to your server's long-term health.

Securing Application Servers

Securing a Windows 2000–based application server is complicated by the way that people use application servers. Most Windows 2000 servers don't allow normal humans to log on locally, but application servers *must* log on locally to work. Therefore, you'll need to consider how to secure the Windows 2000 server not only from "normal" attacks but also from the kind of attacks available to someone who has local access to a server, even if they don't have an administrator account. Application server security is complicated by the fact that users logged on locally to the server aren't actually sitting at the server, typing away. They are sending all their input across the network. Security-wise, I don't think it gets much worse than this—particularly if you're making the application server available to people via the Internet.

To effectively secure a Windows 2000–based application server, therefore, you'll need to secure three areas: the server, the network, and the client.

Server Security

Locking down the server while still keeping it usable can be a bit of a trick, but it can be done. Doing so is a matter of planning for security when installing Windows 2000, choosing the right security mode when installing Terminal Services, hiding system drives, sometimes editing file and folder permissions, and preventing people from running applications that (as users) they would normally be able to run but (as people sharing a server) you'd prefer that they didn't. You will also need to keep on top of post- Service Pack hotfixes, and you will need to be familiar with Windows 2000 group policies. As you'll see, they're quite useful when it comes to tuning the user environment.

> **TIP** Keep a personal user account that you can use for testing while you're experimenting with security settings. You can't really check security settings when logged on with administrative privileges.

Group Policies in Windows 2000

Using group policies effectively can be tricky. Finding the policy you want is not always easy. Although to help you with this, I've pointed you directly to some of the group policies that I think you'll find useful. Precedence also gets interesting, because conflicting policies applied at varying domain and organizational unit levels also follow what can be a complicated order of precedence. The policy closest to the individual always wins. That is, if you've applied one group policy at the domain level and one at the OU level, and the policies conflict, then the policy applied to the OU controls the policies applied to the people or computers in that OU. However, if a policy applies to both users and computers and the policies conflict, the computer policy wins—in all the policies I've personally checked, anyway.

Policies are applied to Active Directory structure such as domains or organizational units (OUs), rather than to user or group accounts. You can simplify things by creating a Terminal Services Users OU, creating a local group inside that OU, and then putting the domain Users group (or wherever you've put everybody) inside it. You can also create an OU for application severs and edit the group policies applied to those computers, because their policies will work even if the computers connecting to the MetaFrame servers are running operating systems that don't support group policies.

> **Group Policies in Windows 2000** *(continued)*
>
> To apply a group policy, go to a domain controller, right-click the OU or domain for which you want to set the policy, and choose Properties from the context menu. From the Group Policy tab, click the New button to create a new entry, and then Edit to edit the policies included in that GPO, choosing them from the Group Policy Editor that opens. When you're done, apply the policy. By default, policies refresh about every 90 minutes, but you can edit this value (with, unsurprisingly, another policy) or just reboot the server to make it refresh. You can also refresh group policy settings immediately with the `secedit` command. To refresh a group policy for the currently logged-in user, type `secedit /refreshpolicy user_policy`. To refresh group policies applied to a computer, type `secedit /refreshpolicy machine_policy`. To reapply group policies even if there haven't been any changes, add the `/enforce` switch to either command.

Planning a Secure Installation

When you're installing servers, consider partitioning server drives so that system data is separate from user data. As we'll discuss in a minute, you can hide logical drives or prevent people from browsing them—not the same thing. If all the system data that normal humans never need to look at is on one drive and user data is somewhere else, that simplifies security.

Another part of a secure Windows 2000 installation lies with keeping up with security fixes. The post-SP2 security rollup is completely incorporated in SP3.

Application servers open to Internet use are particularly vulnerable to DOS attacks, because they need to maintain an open port for incoming connections. Setting up the application server behind a firewall is an excellent idea. If you do put application servers into a DMZ, you'll need to leave ports 3389 (for RDP) and/or 1494 (for ICA) open, or 80 for Web access.

Tuning Terminal Services Security

Keeping a secure application server also depends on the way you configure the service. The default options work moderately well for security (and resource) purposes. All these settings are accessible through the Server Settings section of the Terminal Services Configuration tool.

When you're installing Terminal Services, you should use the default option of Windows 2000–compatible security, changing to the legacy security settings only if you need to support applications that will not work otherwise. As I mentioned already in Chapter 7, "Installing and Tuning Applications on an Application Server," the legacy settings work by giving applications permission to write to files in system directories. Because applications run in the security context of the people who start them, users can write to (or delete) files in system directories. You can hide these directories, or hope that people don't mess around with them, but the preferred tack is to just avoid the problem in the first place and keep normal humans out of the system files. If the applications simply will not work when you've got Windows 2000 security settings, you can always use the Terminal Services Configuration tool (located in Administrative Tools on any application server) to change the security settings.

Users should have their own temporary directories, and those temporary directories should be deleted when they log off the application server. Shared temporary directories not only give users access to each other's temporary files, they open the possibility of users overwriting each other's temporary files. Both of these options are secure by default—users have private temporary directories and those directories are deleted when they log off the server.

Active Desktop is normally on for remote sessions. Turn it off for each application server. Not only does enabling Active Desktop allow users to put bandwidth-hogging tools like news tickers on their Desktops, but enabling Active Desktop makes it possible to run scripts in web pages without meaning to run them.

Securing MetaFrame Tools and Communications

The Windows 2000 Terminal Services tools are available to any administrator who logs onto a server with the service installed in either Application Server or Remote Administration mode. The MetaFrame XP management tools, and the database used to back the server farm, are not. As you saw when installing MetaFrame XP in Chapter 4, you have to assign someone to be a MetaFrame administrator, and other user or group accounts are added to the list

Although authorized MetaFrame administrators can use the Citrix Management Console to manage MetaFrame XP farms from any computer that will run the Java application, Citrix doesn't recommend that you necessarily do this. If the computer you're using is accessing the MetaFrame servers via a network connection, the connection could be sniffed. However, don't go overboard. Although Citrix recommends running the Citrix Management Console through a secure ICA session for better security, doing so means that you're running a memory-intensive Java application on a MetaFrame server—not really an ideal solution unless you can arrange to run the tool only when no one else is using the MetaFrame server. Instead, I'd suggest running the Citrix Management Console from a separate computer, but make sure that the computer where you're running the CMC is located on a secure network where you can control the physical medium more easily. If you must run the Citrix Management Console from a remote site accessible only via a public network and don't want to expose yourself to packet sniffing, you could install the Citrix Management Console on a Windows 2000 server on the network—say, a file server. Install Terminal Services in Remote Administration mode on that server and then connect to that server through an encrypted RDP session. That way, you won't lose any licenses to server administration and won't be so exposed.

As discussed in Chapter 6, those with FR2 installed also have the option of assigning discretionary administrative access to a MetaFrame application server. If this option is available to you, taking it could widen the field of people who can do basic work from the console—or just checking the status of certain readings and reporting back to you—while keeping them from doing any accidental damage.

Auditing User Access to the MetaFrame Server

MetaFrame XP has an `auditlog` utility that you can use to keep track of user logons and logoffs on MetaFrame servers. You can track all sessions or look for specific users or session IDs, and dates for the auditing. The `auditlog` utility is not a complex tool, but it does give you some basic monitoring tools for RDP and ICA sessions. You'll also be able to check up on *failed* attempts to connect to the MetaFrame server.

Enabling Windows 2000 Auditing   `Auditlog` depends on the Security log visible from the Windows 2000 Event Viewer. (Actually, it's the same log, with a few bells and whistles that you can use to control how the data in the log are presented.) Therefore, before you can use `auditlog`, you'll need to enable Windows 2000 security auditing, controlled through a group policy. To enable auditing for the application server OU, go to Active Directory Users And Computers on a domain controller and right-click the OU. Choose Properties from the context menu and go to the Group Policy tab. Add a new GPO, and call it "Auditing," as I've done in Figure 9.1.

Now that you have a GPO you can add policies to it. Click the Edit button to open the Group Policy Editor, and browse to the Auditing policy section, as in Figure 9.2.

When you double-click a policy to define its settings, you'll see the options in Figure 9.3. Although normally you might not choose to run a success audit for security logging, you'll need to do so in this case, so that you can keep track of user sessions. Check the boxes, click OK, exit the Group Policy Editor, and refresh the policies applied to the MetaFrame OU.

Figure 9.1 Creating a new auditing policy for the application servers' OU

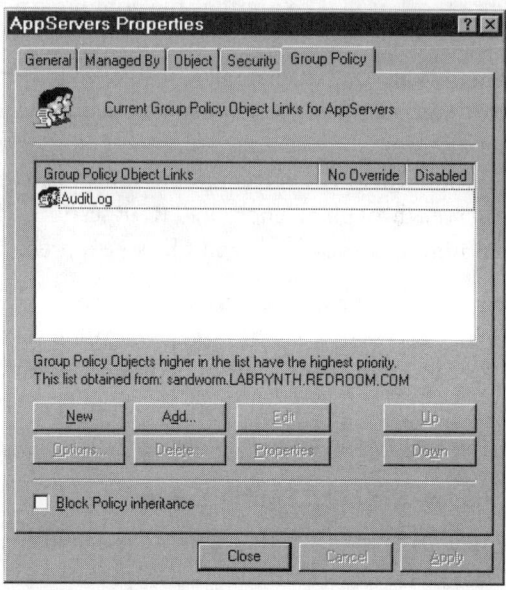

Figure 9.2 Available auditing policies

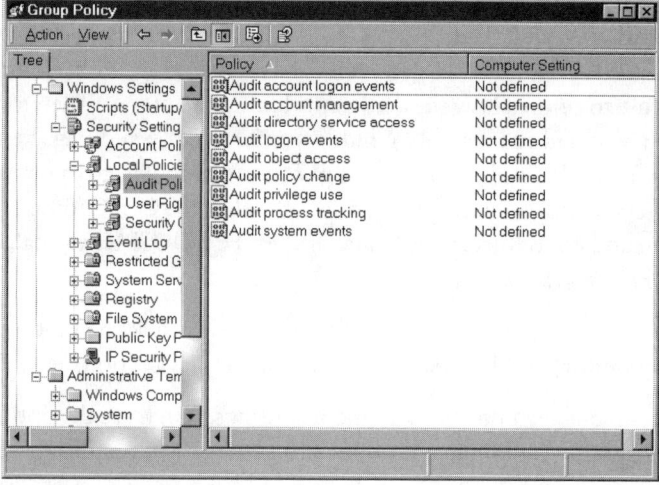

Figure 9.3 Enable both success and failure auditing to get a complete view of how people use application servers.

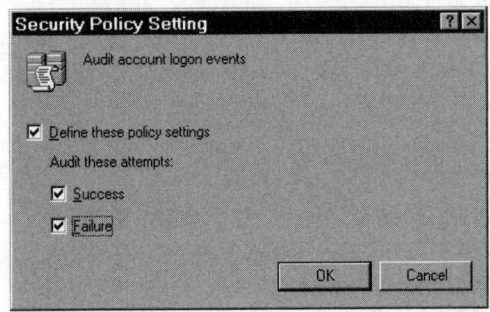

If you're not using a Windows 2000 domain, you can still enable auditing on application servers—you'll just have to do it one at a time rather than applying the policy once to the application server OU. From the Administrative Tools applet in the Control Panel, open Local Computer Policy and find the Audit Policy section of Local Policies. From here, you'll enable account logon events as you would for an OU's GPO.

Using *Auditlog* Now that auditing is set up, you're able to use `auditlog`. We'll start with a complete list of all application server logon activity starting from the time we enabled auditing by typing **auditlog** without any arguments.

```
DOMAIN\USERNAME              EVENT          TIME
REDROOM\Administrator        Logon OK       4/8/2002 12:43
REDROOM\Scott                Logon OK       4/8/2002 12:41
REDROOM\Bill                 Logon Fail     4/8/2002 12:41
   Reason: Unknown user name or bad password
REDROOM\Administrator        Logoff         4/8/2002 12:40
REDROOM\Administrator        Logon OK       4/8/2002 12:38
REDROOM\ChristaA             Logon OK       4/8/2002 12:37
REDROOM\ChristaA             Logoff         3/29/2002 17:56
REDROOM\ChristaA             Logon OK       3/29/2002 17:56
REDROOM\Administrator        Logoff         3/29/2002 17:48
REDROOM\Administrator        Logon OK       3/29/2002 17:47
REDROOM\ChristaA             Logoff         3/27/2002 20:54
REDROOM\ChristaA             Logon OK       3/27/2002 20:54
```

As you can see here, running `auditlog` on its own gives you a dump of all the connections to and disconnections from the application server, and their success or failure. (I use the term "disconnections" advisedly; in this mode, `auditlog` does not distinguish between logoffs and disconnects—both show up here as logoffs.) For only a few entries, this is acceptable, but months of audits on a heavily used MetaFrame server would produce a log too long to browse quickly, and the log information isn't visually organized very well for reading more than a few entries. The tool has some switches you can use to filter or enhance the log entries, so let's take a look at how to use them. Table 9.1 lists the switches; the following sections show you how to use them. You can make `auditlog` provide more detail. Just be careful what you wish for, because you may get it.

Table 9.1 Auditlog Filtering Switches

Switch	Description
/AFTER:*mm/dd/yy*	Normally, `auditlog` will give you all entries, starting from the time you enabled auditing on the MetaFrame server. If you use this switch with the appropriate parameters, it will report on activity only after the date you specify.
/ALL	Lists logon/logoff activity and type of connection for all accounts. Not used with /fail.
/BEFORE:*mm/dd/yy*	This works like the /after switch, except that it trims the audit to report on activity only after the date you specify.
/CLEAR:*filename*	Deletes the event log and saves the old log to the filename you provide as an argument.
/DETAIL	Detailed report of all activity. Not used with /time.
/EVENTLOG:*filename*	Use filename as input to AUDITLOG.
/FAIL	Reports only failed logons, and the reason for the failure (e.g., a nonexistent user account).
/TIME	Breaks down audit entries by user and reports the logon and logoff times, as well as the total amount of time each user spent connected to the MetaFrame server. Not used with /fail or /detail.

Table 9.1 Auditlog Filtering Switches *(continued)*

Switch	Description
/WRITE:filename	Send output to a text file whose name and path you specify. Both UNC names and mapped drives are acceptable file locations for saved files.
session	Supposedly, you can use this argument to make auditlog report on a per-session basis, but I have not found a session identifier that works for this tool. Neither the session ID nor the session name produces any output.
username	Specifies a user (identified by their logon name) for which to produce a report, and reports all sessions for that user. Works for both successful and failed logons.

> **NOTE** You can combine many of the filtering arguments and switches. For example, to get a time report for a specific user, type **auditlog /time** *username*.

The /all switch makes auditlog list *all* connections to the application server, including nonuser accounts such as NT AUTHORITY. You won't need most of these. The NT Authority\Anonymous Logon events may look like someone trying to break in, but they're just recording successful logons (Event ID 540 in the Event Viewer) and logoffs (Event ID 538). However, /all also lists the type of connection and disconnection that accounts are doing, so you can use this setting to collect detailed information about how accounts are connecting to and disconnecting from the application server.

Filtering Audit Information by Amount of Time Logged On Frankly, though, /all looks like overkill for most situations. What are you really interested in? How about the amount of time that people are spending logged onto the MetaFrame server (and, not incidentally, using up a per-connection license)? To find that out, use the /time switch, like this: auditlog /time. You'll get output that looks like this:

```
User: ChristaA
    Logon: 3/27/2002 20:54    Logoff: 3/27/2002 20:54    Total: 00:00:02
    Logon: 3/29/2002 17:56    Logoff: 3/29/2002 17:56    Total: 00:00:00
```

```
    Logon:  4/8/2002 12:37    CurTm:  4/9/2002 10:20    Total: 21:42:39
    Logon:  4/8/2002 14:37    CurTm:  4/9/2002 10:20    Total: 19:42:34
    Total logon time: 41:25:15

User: Administrator
    Logon:  3/29/2002 17:47   Logoff: 3/29/2002 17:48   Total: 00:01:08
    Logon:  4/8/2002 12:38    Logoff: 4/8/2002 12:40    Total: 00:01:16
    Logon:  4/8/2002 12:43    Logoff: 4/8/2002 12:44    Total: 00:01:17
    Logon:  4/8/2002 14:33    Logoff: 4/8/2002 14:35    Total: 00:02:04
    Total logon time: 00:05:45

User: Scott
    Logon:  4/8/2002 12:41    Logoff: 4/8/2002 12:44    Total: 00:03:19
    Total logon time: 00:03:19
```

The /time switch works fine with usernames (as discussed below), so you can collect time-specific information for only specific usernames if you prefer. The order doesn't matter—auditlog /time *username* provides the same output as auditlog *username* /time.

Filtering Audit Information by User Account If you'd like to gather information about a specific person's logon habits, you can supply that person's username as an argument to auditlog, like this: `auditlog christaa` to get logon activity information for the account christaa. This command nets exactly the same information as typing **auditlog** without arguments, but shows only the account activity for that particular user, like this:

```
DOMAIN\USERNAME         EVENT        TIME
REDROOM\ChristaA        Logon OK     4/8/2002 14:37
REDROOM\ChristaA        Logon OK     4/8/2002 12:37
REDROOM\ChristaA        Logoff       3/29/2002 17:56
REDROOM\ChristaA        Logon OK     3/29/2002 17:56
REDROOM\ChristaA        Logoff       3/27/2002 20:54
REDROOM\ChristaA        Logon OK     3/27/2002 20:54
```

Filtering Audit Information by Date Auditlog displays all information, starting from the time you enabled auditing on the MetaFrame server. (This is true unless you use the /clear switch discussed a little later. In that case, the log starts at the time you cleared the log.) If you enabled auditing in December and it's now May, you probably don't need to—or want to—review *all* that logon data each time you're checking the audit logs. Instead, you can tune the audits to only list information before or after a specific date.

> **TIP** The /before switch is not inclusive. That is, if you want to gather audit information for June 8 and before, you'll need to supply **06/09/02** as the argument to the /before switch, not 06/08/02. However, the /after switch *is* inclusive, so if you want to gather information for June 8 and after, type **06/08/02**.

The syntax for this is pretty simple. To create a log that includes data only before a specific date (in this example, April 8, 2002), type **auditlog /before:04/08/02**. To create a log including logon data only from April 8 on, type **auditlog /after:04/08/02**.

Again, you can combine the /before and /after switches with username information to create an audit log filtered for both username and date. As with /time, the order of the switches doesn't change the output.

Logging for Successes or Failures Sometimes, you want to know not who's legitimately able to get into the MetaFrame server, but who's trying to do so. Auditlog normally shows both successes and failures, but if you'd like to display only failed attempts to log on, you can use the /fail switch, like this: **auditlog /fail**. This will create a report of all failed connections and the reason why they failed, as in this example:

```
DOMAIN\USERNAME           EVENT       TIME
REDROOM\Bill              Logon Fail  4/8/2002 12:41
   Reason: Unknown user name or bad password
```

> **NOTE** Logging for failed logons is only marginally helpful when it comes to troubleshooting failed connections. Only those attempts that get as far as a domain logon screen will create an entry. If someone can't log on because they don't have interactive privileges, then you'll know it; however, if someone can't log on because they can't create a connection to the MetaFrame server, auditlog won't catch it.

Saving Audit Output to a File If you'd like to save the `auditlog` reports for later perusal, you can save the logs to a file. Auditlog supports a couple of different ways to do this.

To just save the auditing logs, use the /write switch like this: `auditlog /write: \path and filename,` where the path is a UNC name or mapped drive letter for the file location. (Don't forget to give the file a .txt extension—it's a text file.) Be careful to save the file to the right location and use the right syntax. If you forget part of the path, for example, `auditlog` won't warn you that it did not successfully save the log. The file you save will look like this (although it won't be wrapped):

```
User, Logon Type, Logon Date, Logon Time, Logoff Type, Logoff Date,
Logoff Time, Connection Time

Administrator: Logon, 3/29/2002 17:47 , Logoff, 3/29/2002 17:48 ,
00:01:08

Administrator: Logon, 4/8/2002 12:38 , Logoff, 4/8/2002 12:40 ,
00:01:16

Administrator: Logon, 4/8/2002 12:43 , Logoff, 4/8/2002 12:44 ,
00:01:17


Scott: Logon, 4/8/2002 12:41 , Logoff, 4/8/2002 12:44 , 00:03:19


ChristaA: Logon, 3/27/2002 20:54 , Logoff, 3/27/2002 20:54 , 00:00:02

ChristaA: Logon, 3/29/2002 17:56 , Logoff, 3/29/2002 17:56 , 00:00:00

ChristaA: Logon, 4/8/2002 12:37 ,  CurTm, 4/8/2002 13:26 , 00:49:26
```

If you're willing to hand-edit the file, you can make it into a comma-delimited file that you can import into Excel. (You'll need to add commas in a few key places to make the columns break out properly.) What you *can't* do is create reports that use the filters such as /time or username, so the logs you save will list all user connections, using the format you see here.

If you want to filter the saved event log, you can do this with the /eventlog switch, but you'll need to save the log file with the /clear switch. (Auditlog cannot open a saved log file unless you save the file with /clear–perhaps because the Security log file it depends on is still technically "open" when you use the /write switch.) To clear the current auditlog file and save it to a file, type the command like this: **auditlog /clear:*path and filename*.** This will create a log that looks just like the one you created with the /write switch, but it is one you can load and filter.

> **WARNING** Although you don't *have* to save the log to a file when you use the /clear switch, I strongly recommend that you do. Once you clear the auditlog file, it's gone—there is no way to get it back, and the Security log that auditlog gets its information from is cleared too. Therefore, once you clear the log you won't be able to do any historical analysis of log events without using the /eventlog switch to load a saved file. Because the log is saved as text, it takes up little space on disk.

To load that saved file and apply filters to it, use the /eventlog switch, supplying the name of the saved log file as an argument like this: auditlog /eventlog:*path and filename*. Now, however, you can apply content filters to the log contents, just as you could when using auditlog not from saved information—just add the filter switches after you load the file.

> **TIP** You can automatically generate audit logs with the Windows 2000 at command. To get the syntax for scheduling audits, type **at /?** at the command prompt, and then use the command to write temporary backup logs or clear the security log and write the contents to a file, as appropriate.

Controlling Drive Access

Normally, when a user logs onto an application server's Desktop, they'll see everything that users are allowed to see on the desktop: My Computer, My Network Neighborhood, the Recycle Bin, and so on. You can leave this situation as-is, or, since this computer is the working environment of a bunch of people and you'd rather that one person didn't mess it up, you can change what they can see and how they can browse the application server and the network. The latter approach means either hiding parts of the OS or making sure that people can't touch them.

Hiding Important Files and Folders Although users don't have the right to delete, create, or modify files in the system directories (if they try, they'll get an error), they can still browse those directories. However, system files can be hidden—as you know from trying to browse these folders yourself and having to click that blue Show Files link every time you want to look at something. (As you might guess, I feel that administrators shouldn't have to go through this.) One way to keep people out of the system directories—or other directories they have no business in—is to hide them. If they can't see them, they may assume that they aren't there. (This works best when you're worried more about people inadvertently screwing something up than you are about a deliberate effort to bring the application server down.)

With group policies, you can take a couple of different approaches. First, you can hide specified drives in My Computer. Doing so won't prevent people from *using* these drives, or even from browsing them from the command line. It will, however, help to keep out the idle curious wandering through My Computer and wondering "What does this do?" Another approach is to tune the file display settings (to show or not show extensions, or to hide or not hide system files) and then keep people from editing those settings ever again by using a group policy to remove the Folder Options menu item from the Tools menu in Explorer windows. Again, this doesn't affect the way that people can use those files, but it does affect the way that they see them—when they're using Explorer, anyway.

If you're serious about keeping out the idle curious, then another approach is to prevent people from accessing drives. This isn't the same thing as hiding them, although you could apply both policies to get a double whammy. Preventing people from accessing drives doesn't hide the drives in My Computer, but it does prevent them from browsing the drives using any tools at all. Neither hiding nor preventing people from browsing drives keeps people from accessing those drives through applications.

Table 9.2 lists the group policies I've mentioned here and shows you where to find them in the Group Policy Editor.

Table 9.2 Group Policies Allowing You to Hide Drives or Files

Policy Name	Location	Explanation
Hide All Icons on Desktop	User Configuration\Administrative Templates\Desktop	Removes all default and user-defined shortcuts from the Desktop, although it does not prevent people from accessing these locations through other means.
Hide These Specified Drives in My Computer	User Configuration\Administrative Templates\Windows Explorer	This policy hides selected drives in My Computer, but it does not prevent people from listing the contents of those drives from the command line (with a DIR command) or from the Run tool.

Table 9.2 Group Policies Allowing You to Hide Drives or Files *(continued)*

Policy Name	Location	Explanation
Prevent Access to Drives from My Computer	User Configuration\Administrative Templates\Windows Explorer	The drive icons will still appear in My Computer, but users to whom this policy applies won't be able to browse them.
Removes the Folder Options Menu Item from the Tools Menu	User Configuration\Administrative Templates\Windows Explorer	Without this menu item, users cannot open this dialog box, which controls the way that Explorer windows are presented, file extensions, and whether hidden and/or system files are visible.

Setting File Permissions If you're using NTFS from the beginning as I advised earlier, this one should be less of a problem so long as you're not concerned about users being able to *see* files they shouldn't be accessing. Normal users are allowed to browse system folders and the contents of Program Files (where Win32 files will install themselves if you follow the defaults), but they can't even browse profile folders belonging to other people. If you have files in nonstandard folders, however, you may need to edit the permissions by hand. You can't just lock people out entirely; you will need to edit the permission set so that average users can't hurt program files but can still use them.

For people to be able to browse directories but not change or delete their contents, they need permission to Read and Execute, List Folder Contents, and Read. Give this permission to the Users group (or whatever group you use for average people using a terminal server), and people in that group should be able to run applications without problems. If you must, add Modify to allow them to change configuration files—but in that case, you'd be better off copying the program configuration files to their home directories as discussed in Chapter 7 on application tuning. If you have individual folders that only certain people should be able to browse (like home directories), give those individuals full control over the contents and do not set permissions for anyone else.

> **NOTE** The System account and the Administrator group should always have full control over folders.

Restricting Application Usage

Another way to protect application servers is to control the applications that people are allowed to run on them. How you go about doing this depends on how serious you are about people not doing anything you don't permit them to do. You can present people with single applications and no back doors to run more, or you can explicitly permit or deny people the right to use certain applications.

Presenting Single Applications If you're using the RDP client, you can create user connections that run only a single application, terminating the connection when the user closes the application window. For applications that don't offer any way to initiate another application (i.e., no Run command), this works pretty well. The main disadvantages to this technique are that you have to create explicit connections for running a single application, and that it's very difficult to tweak permissions to allow everyone to list files in a particular directory while allowing only certain individuals to execute applications there.

If you have MetaFrame, it's much easier to give people selective access to individual applications. First of all, you can publish applications to automatically create connections in a user's Program Neighborhood (or on their desktop) or even in a web browser if you're using NFuse. Second, and more important from a security perspective, you can publish applications to be available only to particular users or groups. If you don't allow people to log onto server desktops, then you can present people with a selected group of applications allocated to them based on their user identity.

Controlling User Application Access and Startup Present an entire Desktop, however, or applications such as IE that have convenient back doors into other applications, and control becomes more difficult. At that point, it's time to drag out group policies again.

Start with preventing people from using tools that allow them to run other applications. Sadly, there's no single group policy to do this. However, you can lock down Windows 2000 reasonably effectively with Remove Run From Start Menu, which removes the Run command from the Start menu and from the Task Manager, and also by using Don't Run Specified Windows Applications to disable the command shell. If you *really* want to lock down the Desktop, apply the Run Only Allowed Windows Applications policy... and then also protect drives to make sure that users can't change executable names to evade the policy. I've listed these policies and their locations in Table 9.3.

Table 9.3 Group Policies for Controlling Which Executables Users Can Run

Policy Name	Location	Explanation
Disable Task Manager	User Configuration\Administrative Templates\Logon/Logoff	Disables the Task Manager so that it cannot be used to start new processes or stop running ones. Removing the Run command will prevent people from running new programs from the Task Manager without disabling the tool altogether, however.
Don't Run Specified Windows Applications	User Configuration\Administrative Templates\System	Creates a list of image names that users cannot initiate (e.g., `cmd.exe` or `regedt32.exe`). Applications on this list won't run, but if the image name is different from the one you enter, then the policy won't apply to it.
Remove Run from Start Menu	User Configuration\Administrative Templates\Start Menu and Taskbar	Disables the Run command on the Start menu and in the Taskbar, so that people cannot use it to launch new applications.
Run Only Allowed Windows Applications	User Configuration\Administrative Templates\System	Creates a list of image names that users *are* allowed to run (e.g., `mspaint.exe`). Applications not on this list won't work. Again, this depends on the name of the executable, not on the function of the application.

That covers the server. What about the network?

Network Security

When applications are installed on a workstation, then the user logs onto the console and provides all input through the keyboard and mouse. For everything outside ultra-secret environments that have to worry about keyboard input being picked up by electronic surveillance, this is pretty secure. As long as no one is standing behind you or running keyboard-monitoring tools, no one can tell what you're typing.

If the applications are running on an application server and being displayed on a computer accessing them across the network, the story changes. Both user input and output travel across the network, so they're vulnerable to network tapping. (They're also vulnerable to downed network connections, but aside from redundancy there isn't a lot to be done about that problem and at least disconnected sessions will remain in memory on the server until the client reconnects.)

Encrypting Remote Connections

One way to make network communications more secure is to encrypt the data being sent. Both RDP and ICA support encryption of various levels. RDP divides encryption levels into Low, Medium, and High. For Low encryption, data sent from the client to the server is encrypted with a 56-bit key, but data sent from the server to the client is not. Not only does Low encryption use a key that's relatively easy to break (current standards advise 128-bit encryption at a minimum) but having the data in cleartext, even if it's the half that's harder to interpret if intercepted, is not secure. The only advantage to Low encryption is that it will provide the fastest connection for people using RDP. Encrypting and decrypting data takes time. Medium encryption also uses a 56-bit key, but it encrypts the data stream in both directions. High encryption encrypts the data stream in both directions and uses a 128-bit key. For ICA, Basic encryption, the default setting, does not secure ICA sessions from network sniffing attack, and RC5 (128-bit) only secures the logon, not the rest of the session. To encrypt all session information, you'll need to use RC5 (40-bit) encryption or higher in both directions.

If you require a certain degree of encryption on the server end, then clients will have to meet that requirement to connect to the application servers. To force ICA connections to use a minimum level of encryption, you'll need to edit the ICA settings. From the Citrix Connection Configuration tool, double-click the ICA protocol to open the dialog box in Figure 9.4.

From here, click the Advanced button to open the dialog box in Figure 9.5.

Figure 9.4 Properties for the ICA protocol

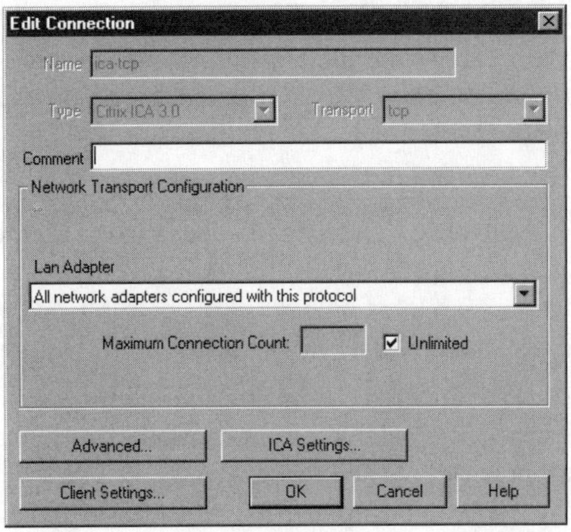

Figure 9.5 Editing advanced properties for the ICA client

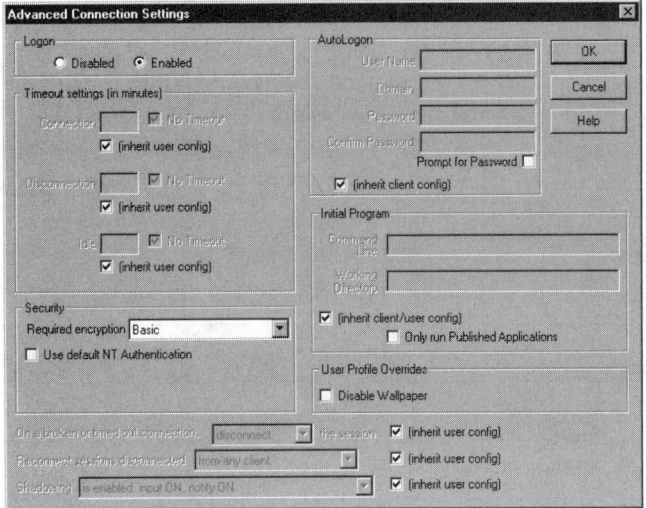

As you can see, this dialog box allows you to configure protocol-wide settings for ICA, instead of relying on the settings in each user account's Properties sheet. The Security section we want, however, may be configured only on a per-protocol level. Choose the

required level of encryption from the list, and ICA Client connections will be forced to use at least that level of encryption.

You don't need to worry about the Use Default NT Authentication check box in this section unless you have a third-party GINA installed. If you do, ICA clients will use that GINA unless you check this box.

> **NOTE** If you've enabled ICA for more than one network protocol, you'll need to edit the encryption settings separately for each one.

Protecting the Server from Network Attacks

Another aspect of securing the network lies in protecting the server from denial of service (DoS) attacks. DoS attacks make servers unavailable by saturating server ports with junk packets, preventing user packets from getting through to the server or even crashing it. One obvious way to reduce your exposure to DoS attacks is to block ports for services that you're not using—for example, a MetaFrame server that is not also acting as an IIS server does not need to keep port 80 open. In addition to blocking unused ports, Microsoft recommends that you edit the TCP/IP stack's Registry settings in Table 9.4 to make the server less vulnerable. These keys are mostly located in HKLM\System\CurrentControlSet\Services\Tcpip\Parameters, but NoNameRelease On Demand belongs in Services\Netbt\Parameters. I'd include the descriptions of the keys, but frankly, unless you're a serious TCP/IP geek, most of them won't make any sense with the exception of NoNameReleaseOnDemand, which prevents an application server from giving up its NetBIOS name to just anyone and thus becoming vulnerable to anonymous attacks. These are, however, the values that Microsoft recommends for these Registry entries in order to secure your servers.

Table 9.4 Recommended Registry Edits for the TCP/IP Stack

Registry Entry	Default Value	Recommended Value
Enable PMTUDiscovery	1 (True)	0 (False)
EnableDeadGWDetect	1 (True)	0 (False)
EnableICMPRedirects	1 (True)	0 (False)
KeepAliveTime	7,200,000 (two hours)	300,000
NoNameRelease On Demand	0 (False)	1 (True)

Table 9.4 Recommended Registry Edits for the TCP/IP Stack *(continued)*

Registry Entry	Default Value	Recommended Value
PerformRouterDiscovery	2 (DHCP-controlled but off by default)	0 (disabled)
SynAttackProtect	0	2
TcpMaxHalfOpen	100 for Windows 2000 Server, 500 for Advanced Server	Default
TcpMaxHalfOpenRetried	80 for Windows 2000 Server, 400 for Advanced Server	Default

In addition to editing application server TCP/IP settings, you'll also find it useful to put the servers behind a firewall. To use a firewall but still permit people in the outside world to use the application server, you can use Network Address Translation (NAT), a method of presenting a public IP address to the world and a private (and, critically, nonroutable) IP address internally, one with a 192, 172, or 10 prefix in one of these ranges:

10.0.0.0-10.254.254.254

172.16.0.0-172.31.254.254

192.168.0.0-192.168.254.254

To use NAT, you'll need a router or firewall that supports it and you'll need to configure the router to forward packets sent to the public address. (Make sure that you configure the router to only forward packets sent to the ICA port, to reduce the security risk. Indiscriminate port forwarding from public to private IP addresses is a way of saving on public IP addresses—which cost money—not a security measure.) You'll also need to tell the application server which IP addresses belong to it. MetaFrame doesn't come with a graphical utility for this; you'll use a command-line tool called `altaddr` to map the public IP addresses to the private ones on each server.

> **NOTE** ICA files support NAT, so if you're supplying a specific IP address for a connection, use the public one. For clients using NFuse, edit the `NFUSE.CONF` File to set `AlternateAddress=Off`, or turn on Alternate Address in the ICA file.

The router maintains a translation table, recording the source IP address, protocol type, and port from which packets were sent, and the destination IP address, protocol type, and port number. When the packet passes through the translation table, the router replaces the source IP address with the router's WAN port address, maintains the protocol type, and changes the port address. The port number used in the source information is the table "key" for finding the proper mapping when a response is received. Each connection gets its own port number for mapping purposes.

Every time the IMA service on a MetaFrame server starts, the service reads the `altaddr` settings to find out the server's external IP address (or addresses, if the server has more than one NIC). If there are no mappings, things proceed as normal. If there are, the MetaFrame server knows that it needs to accept packets directed for the public IP address that people are using. IMA only checks the address mapping settings when the service is first starting up, so you'll need to reboot the server or otherwise restart the server after creating the mappings.

To map a public IP address to a private one, get the public address. From the command prompt (you don't need to be a Citrix administrator to do this) type **altaddr /set *nnn.nnn.nnn.nnn***, where *nnn* is the publicly presented IP address. If a server has more than one NIC, you'll need to specify which NIC you're assigning the public address to, like this: `altaddr /set xxx.xxx.xxx.xxx nnn.nnn.nnn.nnn`, where *xxx* is the private IP address and *nnn* is the public one. To stop using NAT on a server, just delete the mapping like this: `altaddr /delete`. If the MetaFrame server has more than one NIC you'll need to provide the private IP address of the NIC whose address translation entry you want to delete.

You'll need to edit the IP mappings on each MetaFrame server using NAT. So you don't have to walk around to each console, `altaddr` lets you specify the server on which you want to run the command, like this: `altaddr /server:servername /set nnn.nnn.nnn.nnn`. You'll still need to reboot the remote servers, but you can do this from the command line with the `tsshutdn /server:servername /reboot` command, where *servername* is (as you'd guess) the name of the server you want to reboot.

Client Security

Finally, you can set up security on the client. Mostly, that's a matter of making sure that only the people supposed to be using the application servers actually are. You'll do that by requiring people to log on to use application servers explicitly. Obviously, you don't *have* to take these measures—you'll just have a more secure client environment if you do.

It is possible to create ICA or RDP connections to an application server that have the username and password information already built into them, either included in the connection setup information or (in the case of MetaFrame XP) using pass-through authentication, where the ICA connection picks up on the credentials of the person currently logged on and gives them to the application server for authentication. Obviously, this speeds up connection time and makes it easier for people to use application servers, but it's a security hole since it permits automatic logon to domain resources. Granted, this automatic logon is only possible for someone who's already got some degree of domain access, but some applications or data could be available from a application server that are not available through a standard domain logon.

In addition to the obvious security issues associated with pass-through authentication is another issue that is not so obvious. When Pass-Through Authentication is enabled, the Ssonsvr.exe process starts at logon time and collects the current user's username, domain, and password. Connections tuned to use pass-through authentication (recall, this is an option, not an automatic setting if pass-through authentication is enabled for ICA) get the logon information from the service. User accounts that have the Debug Programs right (an advanced right) can use a debugger to view this information in cleartext. So long as people are careful about logging out when leaving their computers, this isn't terrible, but it's never a good idea to have password information stored in cleartext in an unprotected file. If this potential vulnerability is an issue for you, you may want to permanently disable pass-through authentication.

If you want to permanently disable pass-through authentication for an ICA Client, open the Program Neighborhood and choose ICA Settings from the Tools menu. From the General tab visible in Figure 9.6, make sure that the box for Pass-Through Authentication is unchecked.

Figure 9.6 Disable pass-through authentication for greater client-side security.

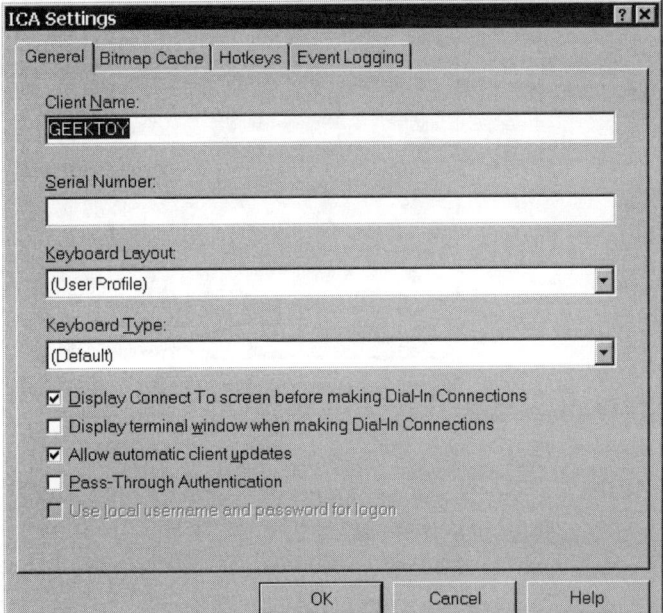

Great—but what happens when someone just goes back into this setting and reenables the option? You can permanently disable the setting by browsing to Program Files\Citrix\ICA Client and deleting `Ssoncom.exe`, `Ssonstub.dll`, and `Ssonsvr.exe`. Without these files, pass-through authentication won't work.

Checking Resource Usage

We talked about evaluating server performance while capacity-planning application servers, but capacity planning isn't the end of it. No matter how carefully you size your application servers, it's wise to keep tabs on them so you can make sure that they're able to keep up with the demands on them. Anyone can use Windows 2000's system monitoring tools to do this, and MetaFrame XPe (not XPs or XPa, I'm afraid) administrators can use Resource Manager.

Windows 2000 System Monitor

Because they're available to everybody, let's start with the System Monitor tools, which is available from Computer Management or by typing **perfmon** from the Run command. Whichever method you use, you'll open the System Monitor shown in Figure 9.7.

Figure 9.7 Windows 2000 System Monitor

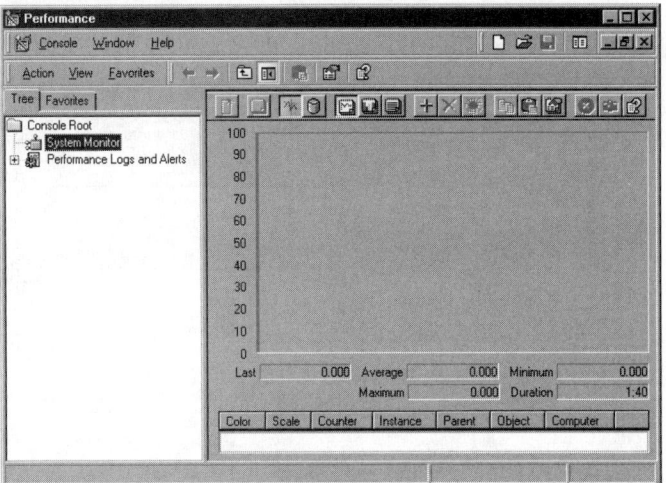

This isn't really the place for doing a complete write-up on the System Monitor; instead, let's concentrate on using it to gather application server-specific information. Of the basic performance counters, you'll probably spend the most time monitoring memory usage, processor time, and network performance, particularly the first. The memory-related counters in Table 9.5 are the most useful overall when it comes to tuning application server performance.

Table 9.5 Helpful Memory-Related Performance Counters

Counter	Description	What This Tells You
Memory: Available Bytes	Records the memory currently available on the server.	A low value may indicate that your server is low on memory or that one of the programs is experiencing memory leaks (especially if the number keeps decreasing).
Memory: Commit Limit	Records the amount of memory that can be committed without extending the paging file. You can increase the paging file up to the limit of available space on the volume.	Extending the paging file is an expensive procedure (and requires processor time), so it's a good idea to do this as little as possible. Make the paging file as large as you think you'll need—at least 2.5 times the size of RAM you have installed.
Memory: Committed Bytes	Records the amount of memory committed to processes running on the server.	Records the amount of used RAM that requires space in the paging file in case the data must be paged to disk. Therefore, this is memory in use and unavailable to other processes, not just reserved in case a process needs it.
Memory: Pages Input/sec	Records the rate at which pages of data are written to RAM from the paging file to resolve page faults.	This value describes hard page faults (the Page Faults counter includes soft page faults, which pull data from another area of memory and don't incur much of a hit), so it's a good measure of how often you're having to pull data back from disk.

Table 9.5 Helpful Memory-Related Performance Counters *(continued)*

Counter	Description	What This Tells You
Memory: Pages Output/sec	Records the rate at which pages of data are written to the paging file to free RAM.	If the server seems to be running more slowly than it used to, monitor this counter. A high rate may indicate that the server doesn't have enough RAM to support all the data that the running applications need to keep handy.
Memory: Pages/sec	Records the current rate at which pages (4KB chunks of data on an x86 system are read from disk back into physical memory to satisfy a page fault or are written to disk to free RAM.	A value of more than 20 pages per second implies a lot of paging and suggests that your server needs more memory.
Paging File: % Usage	Records the percentage of the paging file currently in use.	If this value approaches 100%, then you need to enlarge the paging file or add more RAM. Although Win2K will make the paging file larger if need be, it's better if you do this manually so that Win2K doesn't need to use up CPU cycles to grow the paging file as needed.
Paging File: Usage Peak	Records the peak size of the paging file.	If this value is close to the maximum size of the paging file, you need to either enlarge the paging file or add more RAM. A high value implies that the paging file isn't big enough to hold all the data it must.

Table 9.5 Helpful Memory-Related Performance Counters *(continued)*

Counter	Description	What This Tells You
Physical Disk: % Disk Time	Records the percentage of time the disk spends servicing read or write requests.	Monitor this value for the physical disk that the paging file is located on. If this amount seems to be increasing, check paging file usage and consider adding more memory.
Physical Disk: Avg Disk Queue Length	Records the average number of read and write requests waiting for the disk during the selected interval.	If this number is increasing at the same time the number of Memory: Page Reads/sec is increasing, that indicates that a lot of paging is going on. Monitor this value for the physical disk that the paging file(s) are located on.
Physical Disk: Avg Disk sec/ Transfer	Records the length of time it takes the disk to transfer data to or from disk.	Monitor this value for the physical disk that the paging file(s) are located on to find out how responsive those disks are. This information may encourage you to move the paging file to a faster disk.
Process: Private Bytes	Records the virtual memory committed to that process.	This counter shows you how much memory a process (for all practical purposes, an application) is using. Especially if you're monitoring a terminal server, consider moving demanding applications to the client side or a different server to prevent other processes from being starved for memory.

Table 9.5 Helpful Memory-Related Performance Counters *(continued)*

Counter	Description	What This Tells You
Process: Working Set	Records the amount of RAM that the process is using to store data. The larger the working set, the more memory the process is consuming.	If a process's working set increases over time when you're not doing anything with it (like over a weekend), the process may be experiencing a memory leak.
Server: Pool Nonpaged Failures	Reports the number of errors the server is reporting as it tries to allocate nonpaged pool.	Lots of errors means that the server is running low of RAM and you'll need to add more.

Although you can't really do serious network monitoring with System Monitor, you might find the counters in Table 9.6 useful.

Table 9.6 Helpful Network Monitoring Counters

Counter	Description	What This Counter Tells You
Server: Bytes Total/sec	Reports the rate at which the server is sending and receiving network data.	The total of bytes going in and out of the server per second gives you a pretty good indication of how busy the server is. If you do something to change the server load, like adding another server of that kind or added load balancing to the network, you can monitor this value to see whether the change actually did any good.
Network Interface: Bytes Total/sec	Reports the rate at which the network card is sending and receiving network data.	If this rate is significantly lower than what you'd expect, given the speed of your network and network card, it's time to do a little investigating to see whether something's wrong with the card.

Not all the Processor counters are especially helpful for monitoring application servers—but if you're performance tuning, keep an eye on the ones in Table 9.7. These counters should help you determine how busy the server processor(s) are and how much time they're spending processing interrupts.

Table 9.7 Helpful Processor-Monitoring Counters

Counter	Description	What This Counter Tells You
Processor: % Processor Time	Indicates percentage of time that the selected processor is doing something other than executing its "marking time" thread—the system Idle thread.	Ideally, the processor is supposed to spend most of is time executing the Idle thread—because if that's the case, then the processor is available when it's needed. If Processor: % Processor Time rises above 75 percent on average, then that processor is working pretty hard and the server might benefit from a faster processor or an additional processor.
Interrupts/sec and % Interrupt Time	Tell you how much time the processor is spending interrupting itself to handle requests from its hardware (network cards, video cards, keyboards, and so forth).	If the value of Interrupts/sec exceeds 3,500, then something's probably going wrong, either a buggy program or a board spewing out spurious interrupts.

> **NOTE** I'd like to tell you that there's a System Monitor counter that lets you track interrupts/second on a program-by-program basis, but there isn't—much of this is just trial and error.

In addition to the performance counters in the previous tables, when you enable Terminal Services on a Windows 2000 Server computer, you'll add a couple of additional System Monitor objects that are worth examining. First, there's the Terminal Services object. This object has counters representing the number of active sessions (sessions where the user has connected to the terminal server and successfully logged on), inactive sessions (where the user is still logged onto the terminal server but has stopped using the session), and the total combined. This object is useful mostly for keeping track of how many sessions a terminal server is having to support. It won't *stop* people from using the terminal server, but it does give you an idea of what the connection load looks like.

Although you can get some session-level information from the Terminal Services Manager, a performance object called Terminal Services Session provides quite a bit more. Use the Terminal Services Manager to find the session you want to monitor (since they're identified in System Monitor by their session numbers, not user logon name) and then add counters to monitor for that session. Each session object has processor and memory counters that should look familiar to anyone who's used System Monitor, but it's also got session-specific counters such as the ones in Table 9.8. I haven't included all the counters here, just the ones to show you the kind of information that's available.

> **NOTE** If you're using both RDP and ICA sessions to connect to an application server for some reason, the ICA sessions will be identified by their display protocol (e.g., ica-tcp 2). RDP sessions are the ones with no recorded display protocol.

Table 9.8 Key Terminal Services Session System Monitor Counters

Counter	Description	See Also
% Processor Time	Percentage of time that all of the threads in the session used the processor to execute instructions. On multiprocessor machines, the maximum value of the counter is 100% times the number of processors.	N/A
Total Bytes	Total number of bytes sent to and from this session, including all protocol overhead.	Input Bytes, Output Bytes

Table 9.8 Key Terminal Services Session System Monitor Counters *(continued)*

Counter	Description	See Also
Total Compressed Bytes	Total number of bytes after compression. Total Compressed Bytes compared with Total Bytes is the compression ratio.	Total Compression Ratio
Total Protocol Cache Hit Ratio	Total hits in all protocol caches holding Windows objects likely to be reused. Hits in the cache represent objects that did not need to be resent, so a higher hit ratio implies more cache reuse and possibly a more responsive session.	Protocol Save Screen Bitmap Cache Hit Ratio, Protocol Glyph Cache Hit Ratio, Protocol Brush Cache Hit Ratio
Working Set	Current number of bytes in the Working Set of this session.	N/A
Virtual Bytes	The current size of the virtual address space (RAM and/or paging file) the session is using.	Page Faults/Sec

Adding MetaFrame XP to a server also adds a new performance object to System Monitor. ICA Session has three counters. Average Client Latency represents the average amount of time it takes for information to make a round trip for a particular session—it is a measure of how responsive a session is on average. Last Client Latency represents the most recently recorded response time, so you can tell how responsive a session is being now. Round Trip Deviation represents the difference between the least and the most recorded latency for that session, so you can tell how much difference there has been. Helpfully, the instances for ICA Session are identified by both Session ID and username, so it's easy to find the session you'd like to monitor.

NOTE For those wondering why I didn't include the Process object and its counters in this list, it's because the instance labeling system (e.g. explorer #3) makes it very hard to determine which instance of a process is associated with which session identifier (e.g. Tcp 1). The numbers in the two identifiers for a single process might correspond, or they might not, and the process' Process ID has nothing to do with either of these. If you can monitor process creation from within the System Monitor and figure out which session spawned which process, you could theoretically keep tabs on its user time, process time, and the other information available from the Process object, but generally speaking I suspect that you'll find this to be too much trouble to be useful.

Viewing Real-Time Statistics

To add a counter to the chart in System Monitor, click the button with a plus sign on it. From the dialog box that opens, choose the object, counter, and specific instance (if applicable) that you want to monitor. The only thing that really needs to be said about this is that the Performance Monitor *itself* consumes resources. You should never run the System Monitor on an application server, first because it will hurt local performance and second, because it will skew the results. The only time when it's to your benefit to run Performance Monitor locally is when you're monitoring counters related to network traffic. Monitoring remotely will increase network traffic and skew the results.

Setting up remote performance monitoring is quite simple. When you're adding a counter to the monitor, you can choose between adding the counter for the local machine or another one. You can monitor any generation of NT computer, so having a mixed environment doesn't matter. You can also use Win2K Professional computers to do the monitoring, so you don't have to tie up a server for this task.

Make sure you've selected Select Counters from Computer, and type in the name of the computer you want to monitor with two preceding backslashes, like this: **\\Gamma**. (There's no Browse feature, so you have to know the name of the server you want to monitor. Annoyingly, Performance Monitor doesn't consistently "remember" the names of remote servers that it has monitored previously. Sometimes it does, and sometimes it develops amnesia.) Type server names carefully. If you mistype, the System Monitor takes a while to discover that the name you've specified does not exist on the network.

TIP One of the cool things about doing remote performance monitoring is that it lets you compare server stress easily. Just select the same performance counter on two different servers.

Resource Logging

Real-time data is helpful to a point, but you may want to consider logging performance data if you don't plan to hover over the System Monitor. The System Monitor supports three types of logs: counter logs, trace logs, and alert logs. *Counter logs* record data from local or remote computers about hardware usage and system service activity. *Trace logs* are event driven, recording monitored data such as disk I/O or page faults. When a traced event occurs, it's recorded in the log. *Alert logs* take trace logs one step further. They monitor counters and wait for them to exceed user-defined tolerances. When this happens, the event is logged. You can also set up an alert log to *do* something when the event happens (for example, send a message or run an application). I find counter logs and alert logs to be most useful for application servers.

> **NOTE** You can either set up perpetual logging or log only for a preset period of time, so you aren't overwhelmed with data.

Creating Logs To create a log, turn to the Performance Logs and Alerts section of the System Monitor. Open the folder for the type of log you want, so that its contents (or lack thereof) are displayed in the right details window. Right-click the background in the Details window and choose an option for creating a new log from the shortcut menu that appears.

What happens from here depends on the type of log you're creating: a *counter log* or an *alert log*. Counter logs record system counters, like static versions of the performance logs we've discussed so far in this chapter. Alert logs take counter logs one step further. Counter logs just collect data. Alert logs collect performance object data for selected counters (using the same UI used for monitoring performance objects), and they assess those counters against tolerances that you set when creating the log. In other words, with an alert log you don't collect *all* the data for the selected counters, just for the times when the performance data falls outside the acceptable range.

> **TIP** You could use counter logs to find out what's normal, and then use alert logs to record aberrations from the norm.

If you're starting from scratch, choose the New Log Settings option. Provide a unique descriptive name for the log in the box provided. Click OK, and you'll see the General tab of the log property sheet as shown in Figure 9.8.

Figure 9.8 When you create a new log, it will contain no counters to monitor.

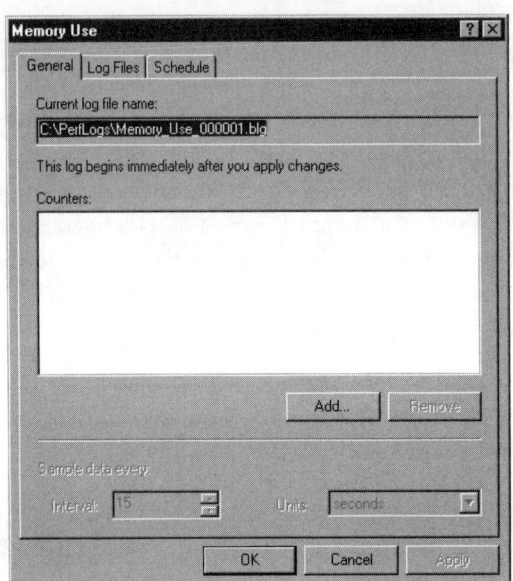

You aren't monitoring anything yet. To begin, click the Add button. You'll open the same Select Counters dialog box you used to add counters to a Performance Monitor chart (see Figure 9.9). Make sure you've selected the computer that you want to log. As with charting, logging takes up resources, so consider running logs remotely.

Figure 9.9 Adding counters to a log

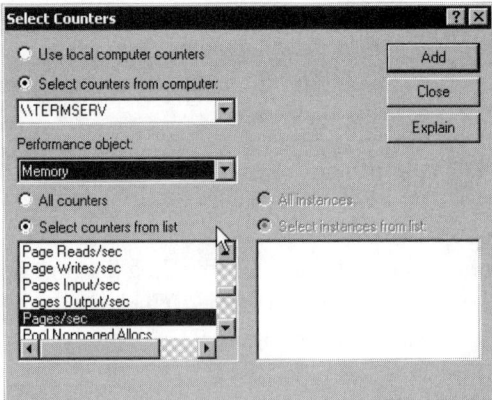

Click the Add button to add counters—you can add more than one from this window; just keep pushing the Add button—and click the Close button when you're done. The counters you selected will now be added to the Counters list on the General tab.

Back in the General tab, you can edit the sampling interval from its default of 15 seconds. The Sample Data Every box accepts an integer between 1 and 10,000, and the drop-down list of time units supports seconds, minutes, hours, or days. Pick an interval based on the duration of your expected logging time—the longer the period you're logging for, the wider you'll probably want the interval to be so you can see trends.

Turn to the Log Files tab to edit file settings for the log. Most of these options are fairly self-explanatory, but let's take a quick tour:

- By default, logs are stored in a Perflogs folder on your Win2K server's boot partition. Unless you regularly back up this location, you might want to put the logs somewhere else for safekeeping.

- The name of the log is the filename. It must conform to the naming convention of the filesystem where you're storing the log.

- The auto filename suffix is an extension to the log filename that allows you to identify logs by their names, if you maintain more than one log with the same filename. The *nnnnnn* naming means that the files will be numbered in order (the first serial number determines the first number that will be used). Other options identify the file by the date it was created—whether by year, month-day-hour or some other mechanism. Open the drop-down list to find the naming convention that works best for you.

- The log file comment will appear next to the list of log names in the folder, so add a comment if the log file requires further description.

- Unless you specify otherwise, the file is a binary file, but you can also save the data as a binary circular file, comma-delimited file (.CSV), or tab-delimited file (.TSV). CSVs and TSVs can both be opened in analysis applications such as Microsoft Excel. The only limitation to CSV and TSV logs is that they must log all at once—they can't accommodate logs that start and stop. Binary and binary circular files (both of which have .BLG extensions) are for recording data intermittently, when data collection may stop and then resume while the log is recording data. The binary files create sequential lists of all events, while the binary circular files record data continuously to the same log file so that previously written records are overwritten when new data is available.

- Choose whether to limit the log file size. If you're planning to log for only a certain period of time (specified on the Schedule tab), then you may not want to limit the log's size, so you don't lose any of the data you choose to save. However, if you don't plan to choose an automatic ending time, it might not be a bad idea to limit the log size so you don't get more data than you can usefully examine.

When you've edited all the file settings, turn to the Schedule tab to finish creating the counter log file. Normally, the log is set to start as soon as you finish—that is, it's set to start automatically at the time you started creating the log, which means it will begin logging as soon as you finish setting up options. You may not want to begin auditing the server as soon as you create the file if you're trying to gather information about server information under circumstances that you know will apply at a specific time. To manually start the log, choose that option here. Alternatively, you can specify a specific date and time the log should start.

Unless you specify otherwise, the log will keep collecting data until you shut it off manually. To schedule a stopping time or logging duration, click the After button and specify the time or period for which you want to log. In this same dialog box, you can also tell the System Monitor to restart the log when the preset period is ended (as you might do if you wanted to compare data from several different times of day) and name an application to run when the log is completed.

Click OK, and the new log will appear in the Details side of the Counter Logs folder. Its icon will be red until the log starts collecting data, either at the time you specified on the Schedule tab or when you right-click the log object and choose Start from the shortcut menu.

The initial stages of creating an alert log are much like those of creating a trace or counter log. Open the Alert Logs folder so that its contents are displayed on the right side of the System Monitor tool. Right-click anywhere in the blank area on the right of the display. Choose New Alert Settings to define new counters to log or New Alert Settings From to open a saved Performance Monitor file and use its counters. Choose a name for the new alert, and then click OK to open the alert log's property sheet. Assuming you're creating this log from new data, you'll need to add counters to the log as you did for a counter log. Click the Add button, and choose the application server and performance counters you want to monitor. When you're done making selections (remember, you can add as many counters as you like by clicking the Add button), click Close to return to the General tab. The counters will show up in the list.

Below the list of added counters, you'll need to specify tolerances for each counter you choose. When the counter exceeds those tolerances, the alert log will add an entry to the file. This is why you need to make a counter log before you do alert logging—or at least use System Monitor to find out what's normal for your application servers. Otherwise, you won't know when to tell Windows 2000 to start logging alerts and you'll either gather more information than you need or miss important events. Notice that the default sampling interval for alerts (five seconds) is much shorter than the one for counters. This is because of the different nature of the log—it's assumed that you're a little more concerned about the contents of this one. If you need to, use the drop-down lists to edit the sampling intervals.

TIP Tune alert logs carefully. The shorter interval and extra processing required to manage alerts will impact a server.

The scheduling tab for alert logs works just like the one you used to configure counter and trace logs, but the Action tab (see Figure 9.10) is something new. From this tab, you'll need to tell the System Monitor what you want it to do when it generates an alert.

Figure 9.10 Edit the alert settings.

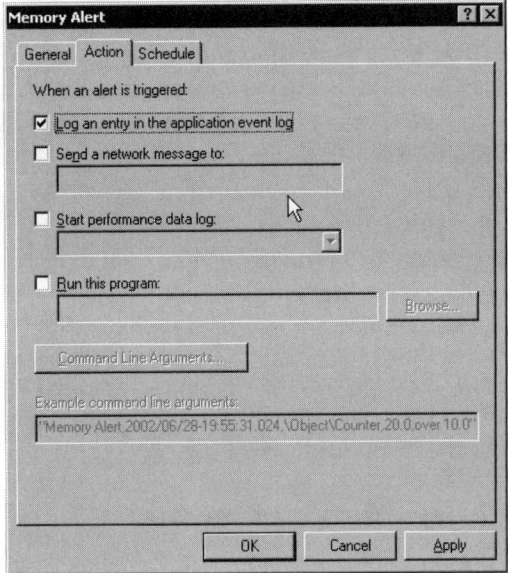

Normally, System Monitor just adds an entry to the Event Viewer's application event log. If the alert isn't something that you need to know about right away, you can leave it at that. More important alerts, however, like those generated by network errors or a severe shortage of memory, may require immediate action. From the Alert menu, you can tell System Monitor to send you (or someone else) a message when writing an entry in the alert log or even to have it run a specific application that you can use to resolve the problem. Use this tab to send arguments to the application.

Once again, when you're done editing the alert log's properties, click OK to add it to the Alert Logs folder. When it's running, its icon will be green.

Viewing Log Data Setting up the log data is the easy part, once you know what you want to monitor. Reading and interpreting that data is harder. The method of viewing log output depends on the file type in which you've saved the log.

Recall that when you're creating counter logs, you can choose how to present the data. The default option is to save the data in a binary log file (.BLG) that you can examine from System Monitor. To see this data, click the icon on the System Monitor that has the database symbol (a cylinder) on it and browse to the location where you saved the log file when setting it up. This will open the contents of the log like a static performance monitoring chart, so you can see what performance was like at a given time without having to be on the spot at that moment.

Charts are nice, but there will also be times when you want to view the information in a spreadsheet so you can manipulate the way it's presented. To do so, you'll save the log data in a tab-delimited (.TSV) or comma-delimited file (.CSV) that you can open with a spreadsheet application such as Microsoft Excel. To view the data, just open the file with Excel. If the log is still active, you'll see an error message telling you that another user or application is using the data. However, you can open it as a read-only document or click the Notify option to open the file—you just can't save it to its current name while the log is still writing to the file. From there, you can use Excel's charting tools to massage the data to make a good presentation.

Alert logs don't go into a regular file; they go directly to the Event Viewer's Application log. When the counters exceed the tolerances you've set up, Windows 2000 will add an Information record to the Application event log.

Resource Manager (MetaFrame XPe)

For those using MetaFrame XPe, there's an additional option: the Resource Manager. The Resource Manager gets its information from the same place as Windows 2000's System Monitor, but easy reporting tools give it a leg up on the standard tools. (I'd use both, personally. Resource Manager's real-time tools are good for a visual snapshot, but they don't really do long-term charting.)

Although it comes with MetaFrame XPe, Resource Manager is not installed by default. To install it, just get the CD from the MetaFrame XPe kit, choose to install the product, and let the setup routine copy the files. That's it. Once you've done so, you'll see a new entry in the Citrix Management Console called Resource Manager, as in Figure 9.11. You'll also notice that the Servers and Applications entries in the Citrix Management Console have some new tabs for resource management.

Figure 9.11 Installing Resource Manager adds new information to the Citrix Management Console.

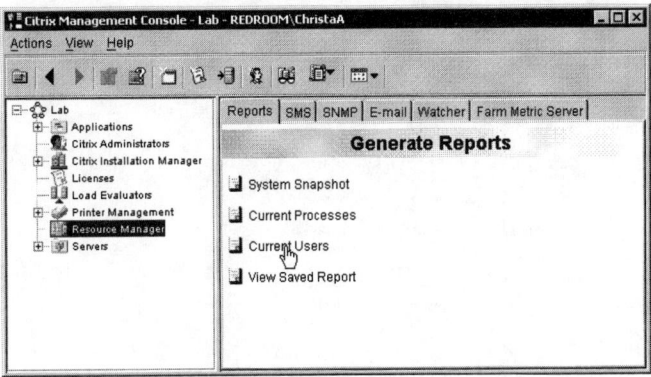

This new section has several tabs. The Reports tab visible in Figure 9.11 has links to help you create different kinds of reports. (We'll go into *how* to create those reports in a minute.) Watcher has links to real-time server monitoring, the kind of stuff you can get from using System Monitor. You'll use the Farm Metric Server tab to pick the server used to gather application metrics for published applications, and the SMS, SNMP, and E-Mail tabs are all for configuring the Resource Manager to contact you or someone else when a server meets or exceeds an acceptable strain.

Viewing Real-Time Statistics for Servers and Applications

Resource Manager can supply either real-time information or reports. If you're interested in seeing how a particular server or application is doing right this minute, then you'll actually find that out from the Resource Manager for that server or application. (Monitored servers appear on the Watcher tab in Resource Manager; but if you click on them, you'll move to the other section of the Citrix Management Console.) The server monitoring metrics use a relative color-coded scheme of red, yellow, and green, as shown in Figure 9.12.

From this information, I can deduce that the currently selected MetaFrame server is fine on most counts, but it is using the paging file too often and may need more virtual memory so that it'll stop using the paging file so much. Were a circle yellow, perhaps for memory usage, then I'd know that I needed to watch memory usage and a pattern of memory overuse could indicate that I needed to add more memory to the MetaFrame server. As it is, I should probably think about adding more memory anyway, because my paging file is being used far too often. Double-clicking on the Paging File's red circle displays the graph in Figure 9.13, which confirms that the paging file is getting way too much use to be healthy.

Figure 9.12 Real-time MetaFrame XPe server statistics

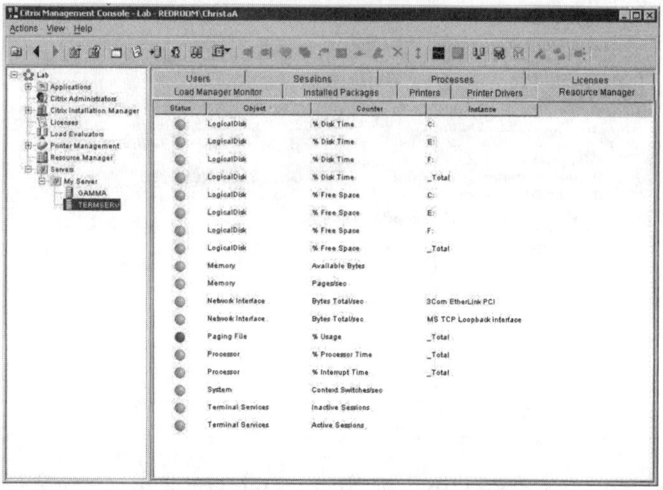

Figure 9.13 Current paging file usage scored against suggested thresholds

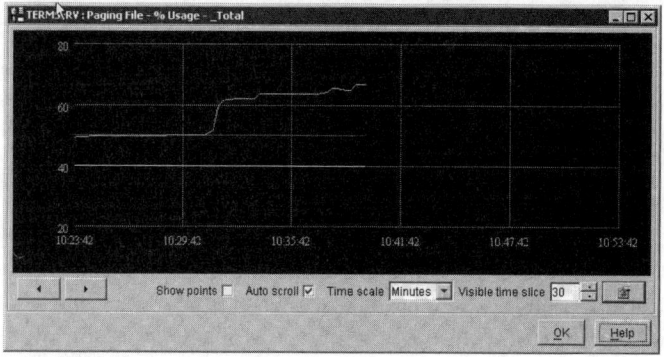

The yellow and red lines in this graph indicate the "worry" points, if you will—yellow means that my paging file is bursting at the seams, and red that paging file usage is definitely too high for optimal performance. Because the green line representing usage is way above the red line, I know that it's well past time to add more memory to this server so I can stop using the paging file so much.

> **NOTE** To close a graph, just click OK, but you can keep running a graph in the background by minimizing its window.

Reading the performance graphs is not difficult if you're familiar with server resource needs, but you should pay attention to how the information in the graphs is displayed. For example, the paging file graph in Figure 9.13 arranges its data so that, the higher on the chart the green usage line is, the worse the news. But the graph in Figure 9.14, showing free space on logical disks, also has a green line far above the red and yellow lines. In this case, though, that's *good* news because we're measuring free space on a logical disk and we want that number to be high.

Figure 9.14 The layout of "danger zones" will vary depending on the metric the graph is displaying.

Monitoring applications works similarly to monitoring servers, but the color coding and information available is different, and you'll need to set up the application monitoring explicitly. To get real-time application statistics, go to the Applications section of the Citrix Management Console and click the Resource Manager tab that was added when you installed the Resource Manager. As you can see in Figure 9.15, all individually published applications on managed servers are metered.

Figure 9.15 Resource Manager manages published applications.

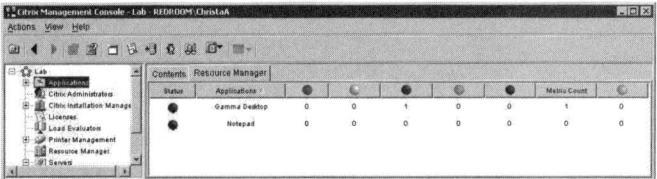

Unlike the red-yellow-green scheme used for real-time server monitoring, the application color coding requires a little more interpretation. Some parts will be familiar. Green means that the application metering is within acceptable thresholds, yellow means that the application metering is in the danger zone, and red means that it's exceeded acceptable tolerances—in the case of applications, instance count. Other colors are less obvious. A blue counter means that I haven't yet configured the applications. A gray counter indicates that I'm "snoozing" metering the application—that I'm not metering the application for a defined period. A black counter means that I've shut off metering for some undefined period. In Figure 9.15, the 1 count in the blue column means that there is one instance of an unconfigured application running.

NOTE You cannot snooze or sleep metering on an application until you've configured it in the first place. This makes sense—if you haven't yet started metering application usage, you don't need to *stop* metering.

Configuring application metering is simple: double-click on the application's icon until you see its name next to a Counters metric, then right-click on it and choose Properties. From the dialog box that appears, you can specify the circumstances under which you want to be notified of application metrics. For example, monitoring application count gives you an easy way to keep tabs on application licensing. If you have 30 licenses for an application, you could set a yellow threshold of 25, telling you that you're almost out of licenses, and a red threshold of 30. You could also configure Resource Manager to e-mail you when the yellow threshold had been reached. To configure time or instance information, double-click in the appropriate box in the dialog box shown in Figure 9.16 and enter the properties there.

Figure 9.16 Editing the Yellow Limit to five instances of the published application Gamma Desktop

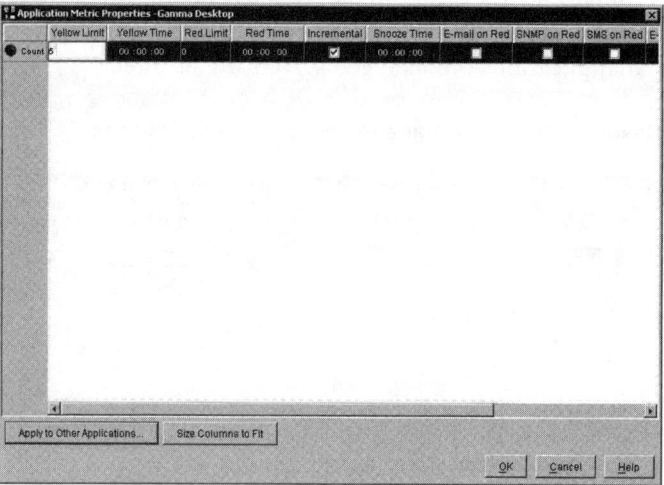

TIP Tune your notification thresholds carefully, or else you'll either get swamped with e-mails and miss the crucial ones in the flood or you won't hear about problems until it's too late. Generally speaking, don't bother monitoring "Green" status unless you really need to know that the MetaFrame servers are working as expected.

By default, you can monitor all published applications, but ones resident on the MetaFrame servers but not yet published are not monitored. You can add them, though. Right-click the Applications icon in the Citrix Management Console and choose New Resource Manager Application to begin the wizard. You'll need to name and describe the application, as though you were creating a published application, and then supply the path for the application on the appropriate server. Next, as in Figure 9.17, choose the servers on which you want to monitor the application and change any server path information as appropriate—again, as though you were publishing an application that was not necessarily located in the same folder on all MetaFrame servers. When you click the Finish button, the application will show up on the Resource Manager tab alongside the published applications. Although it will also appear in the list of published applications, it won't show up in user Program Neighborhoods unless you explicitly publish it.

Figure 9.17 Pick the servers hosting the application that you want to monitor.

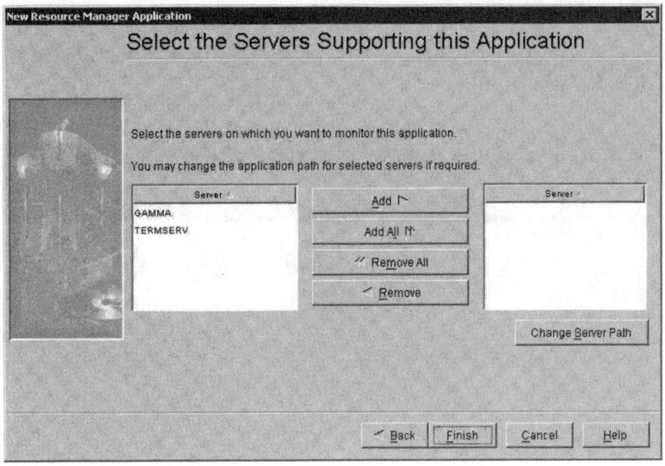

Once you've added an application to the list, you can set up its metering as you did for a published application.

Generating Server Reports

Real-time metering is good for finding out what's happening right this minute, but not so useful when you're trying to find out how the servers were doing at a certain time—say, at 8 A.M. while everyone was logging on or at 12:30 when most people were at lunch. With Resource Manager, you'll gather this information by creating reports, which you can then save either as HTML files that you can display in a browser or open again from Resource Manager, or as comma-delimited files that you can open in a spreadsheet package like Excel.

To create a report, turn to the Reports tab in the Resource Manager section of the Citrix Management Console. You can create three kinds of reports here:

- System Snapshots
- Current Processes
- Current Users

System Snapshot gives you resource usage metrics for the time period you specify. Current Processes displays system statistics related to the running of processes on the selected MetaFrame server, either as a total or for a particular user. Current Users shows you the logon times and processes being used by a particular user. There's a fair amount of overlap in terms of the type of information being displayed, but the emphasis of each report type is slightly different.

To create a System Snapshot, click on that icon on the Reports tab to open the System Snapshot dialog box in Figure 9.18.

Figure 9.18 Creating a system snapshot report

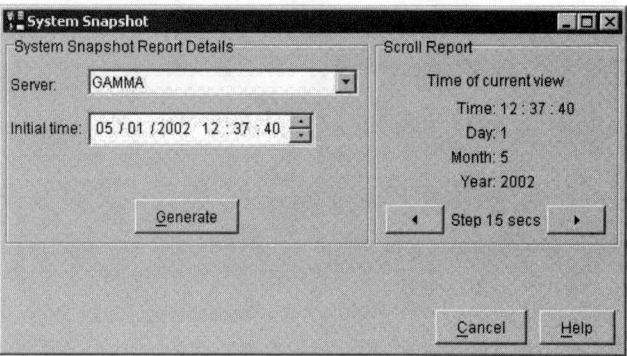

From this dialog box, you'll need to choose the server you want to take a snapshot of and choose the time and date for which you want the information. The initial time here won't give you a report from the specified time until the present, but just for that specific date and time. To create the report, click Generate. In a few seconds you'll see output listing the people logged onto the selected MetaFrame server at that time, the processes they were running, and the server resource statistics shown in Table 9.9 as an example of the kind of information available.

> **NOTE** In addition to the columns shown here, the report will also include specific instances of the objects, the time the snapshot applies to, and the value reported.

Table 9.9 Information Generated by a System Snapshot Report

Object	Counter	Description
LogicalDisk	% Disk Time	Record of how busy that instance of a logical disk (disk with a drive letter name) was. Reported as a percentage.
LogicalDisk	% Free Space	Record of how full that instance of a logical disk was.
Memory	Available Bytes	Record of how much physical memory was available at the time of the snapshot. This total does not include virtual memory, which would include space in the paging file.
Memory	Pages/sec	Rate at which data was read from or written to disk to resolve hard page faults (page faults, recall, being times when data must be read from or written to the paging file instead of physical memory). Reported as a rate.
Network Interface	Bytes Total/sec	Rate at which the network interface was passing data between the server and the network. There will be one instance for each NIC and another for the loopback interface.
Paging File	% Usage	Percentage of the paging file in use at the time of the snapshot. Although Windows 2000 is designed to use the paging file to supplement physical memory, overuse of the paging file may indicate that a server is low on memory—a common condition among MetaFrame servers.

Table 9.9 Information Generated by a System Snapshot Report *(continued)*

Object	Counter	Description
Processor	% Interrupt Time	Percentage of time that a particular processor instance was handling interrupts from hardware devices. This percentage will indicate hardware device activity.
Processor	% Processor Time	Percentage of time that an instance of the processor was busy doing something other than processing the Idle thread used to twiddle the processor's thumbs.
System	Context Switches/sec	Rate at which the processors in the selected server are performing context switches—that is, are swapping out data used with one process so that they can start performing calculations for another process, or switches between user mode and kernel mode. The more context switches the system is performing, the busier it is.
Terminal Services	Active Sessions	Active sessions running on the selected MetaFrame server. Includes both RDP and ICA sessions, if applicable.
Terminal Services	Inactive Sessions	Inactive sessions running on the selected MetaFrame server. Again, this total may include both RDP and ICA sessions.

To create a Current Process report, click on the appropriate link to open the Current Processes dialog box in Figure 9.19. From here, you'll need to choose the server to monitor, and the processes and users to be tracked. The default is All, meaning that you'll get a report of all the processes for all current users and the amount of memory and processor time those processes are using. However, you may want a more directed view of the system that tells you that *this* instance of the process that *this* person is using is consuming X amount of server resources.

Figure 9.19 Creating a report for a particular process

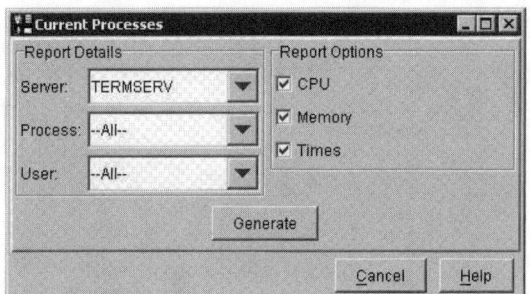

Be warned: A full process report generates a *lot* of information. For every process running on the selected MetaFrame server, you'll get the image name, the path, the date it was installed, the version information, the time and date the process started, the percentage of time that it's been active (instead of just open but not being used), and the person running it. On a busy server, this could be quite a list. In addition, you'll also generate statistics showing how much processing time and virtual and physical memory the selected MetaFrame server used to support the selected processes. Rather than using the Current Processes report like a version of System State, try using it to find out how a particular person or process—or a particular person using a particular process—is impacting the MetaFrame server.

NOTE Even if you select only a single process, don't be surprised if the report lists more than one. The list in the Current Processes dialog box actually represents *images*, not processes, and some images are supported by more than one process.

The Current Users report is the simplest of the bunch. When you click Generate after choosing a server and user accounts to monitor from the dialog box in Figure 9.20, you'll create a report of the people currently logged onto the MetaFrame server, along with their session identifier and the processes they're running.

You can save any report generated with Resource Manager. At the bottom of each report page are links to save the reports as HTML or comma-delimited files. Choose the format you want to use—recalling that you can only load HTML files back into Resource Manager—and browse to the location where you want to store it. To load a saved report, just click that button on the Reports tab and browse to the location where you saved the report as an HTML file.

Figure 9.20 Creating a user report for a specific server

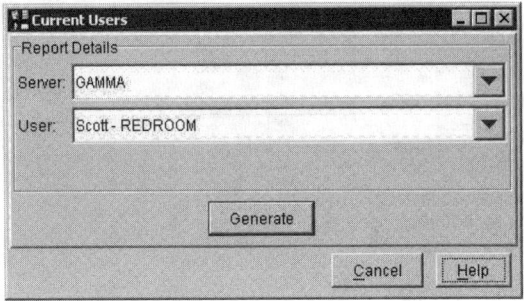

Changing the Farm Metric Server

One server in the farm is normally responsible for collecting performance statistics—normally, the first server on which you installed Resource Manager—with a backup in case the main metric server is unavailable. Most of the time, you won't need to worry about this. However, if you take a MetaFrame server offline for an extended period of time or move it to a new farm, you should change the farm metric server before you do. To do so, just go to the Farm Metric Server tab in Resource Manager in Figure 9.21. The current metric server information will be visible here.

Figure 9.21 Check the farm metric server before removing a server from the farm.

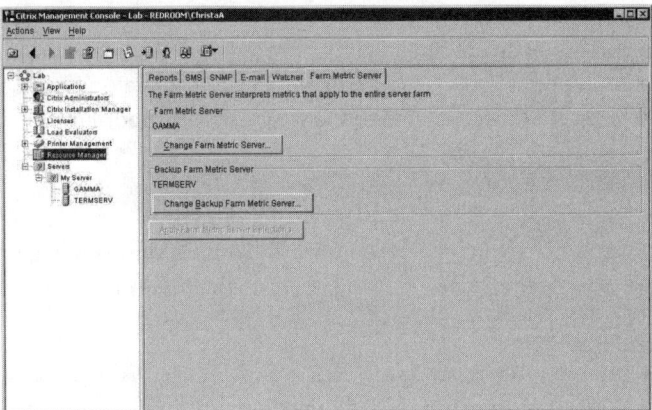

Click the appropriate button to change the server, then use the arrows to put the server you want to take the specified role at the top. Close the window, and then click the button on the Farm Metric Server tab to apply the changes. The main and backup metric servers cannot be the same ones.

Summary

That about wraps it up. It's been quite a ride. At this point, you should be comfortable with the basics of application server administration, including planning, installation, installing applications, printer and session management, and system monitoring and security. Thanks for reading, and be sure to sign up for the newsletter discussed in the introduction so that we can continue the conversation!

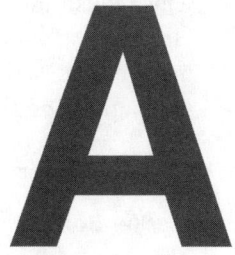

Scripting Application Server Management

In Chapter 6, "Managing Terminal Sessions," we talked about the session and server-management graphical and command-line tools that come with Windows 2000 and MetaFrame XP. These tools aren't your only options, however. Anyone using MetaFrame XP (sorry, this doesn't apply to people using previous versions of MetaFrame) can do some administrative scripting through the MetaFrame COM Server, an object representing all the objects in a MetaFrame XP server farm. Using VBScript, you can perform many of the same tasks that you can do with the Citrix Management Console. Although I don't have room for a complete scripting guide in this appendix, I'd like to show you the basics of VBScript, the scripting interface for MetaFrame XP, and walk you through an example of a script using this interface.

Basic Administrative Scripting Concepts

Obviously, administrative scripting is a bigger topic than I can cover in an appendix of a book about something else. What I'd like to do here is show you some ways you can manage MetaFrame XP servers with VBScript. If you're interested in learning more about scripting application server management (or any other kind of server management), you might be interested in another book of mine from Sybex, *Windows 2000 Automated Deployment and Remote Management*, which discusses administrative scripting with VBScript. I also write the *Windows and .NET Magazine* "Scripting Solutions" column, which illustrates ways of using VBScript to accomplish common administrative tasks. However, to understand the following discussion, you'll need to know some basic scripting concepts: scripting hosts, statements, data types, procedures, such as functions and subroutines, and objects, properties, and methods.

> **Why Script?**
>
> Given the plethora of utilities that comes with Windows 2000 Terminal Services and MetaFrame XP, you might wonder why you'd bother writing your own. One reason, for those not using FR2, is to avoid loading the Java-based console on an application server that needs all the memory it can get. Another is avoiding repetition. If you find yourself performing the same kinds of tasks repeatedly—and you will—you'll eventually want some way of automating at least some of that work. One way to do this is to create batch files using the command-line utilities discussed in Chapter 6, but batch files have their limitations. It's not always easy or possible to build in variables, and the command-line tools sometimes can't access the information you need. Finally, the syntax for command-line tools varies. VBScript is more complicated than a command-line utility, but the syntax is consistent. This isn't necessarily the case with command-line utilities. Developing scripts takes time, and if you're new to VBScript or the MetaFrame XP scripting interface (or both), it takes more time. For tasks that you'll perform only once, you're probably better off using the standard tools. But for tasks that you'll perform many times, need to perform consistently for tracking purposes, or both, scripting can simplify your job.

Scripting Hosts and Script Engines

Windows doesn't understand VBScript. Type a line of VBScript code at a command prompt and press Enter, and all you'll get for your trouble is an error message. To execute VBScript, Windows needs a *scripting host*, an interface that *does* understand VBScript. When Windows encounters a file with a recognized scripting extension, it passes the script to the scripting host for interpretation. The scripting host interprets the script, and then passes the script's message (e.g., a request for published application data) to Windows for execution. Windows supports two scripting hosts: Microsoft Internet Explorer (IE) and Windows Script Host (WSH). The scripting host you use affects the options available to you in building your scripts. If you use WSH as the scripting host, you can use the objects WSH supports but not the ones that IE supports, and vice versa. You don't have to do anything special to use a particular scripting host; it's mostly a matter of where you run the script. Run a script from within a web page displayed in IE, and you'll use the IE scripting host. Run the script from the command prompt, and you'll use WSH.

A scripting host doesn't understand all scripts; it understands only the ones written in languages—*script engines*—that the host supports. Both WSH and IE natively support the VBScript and JScript script engines.

Statements and Comments

The basic structure of a script is straightforward: Each executable line is a *statement* that tells the computer what to do next. Statements usually have a simple verb-object form, expressing the action and what to perform the action against. In addition to their executable components, scripts usually have nonexecutable lines called *comments* that you'll use to document what the script or portion thereof is supposed to do. Because you mark comments in a script by prefacing a line or part of a line with a REM or an apostrophe, you can also use comments for debugging by selectively disabling executable parts of the script.

VBScript Data Types

VBScript recognizes four types of data: numbers, strings, dates and times, and Boolean statements. Numbers are numbers such as 2 or 9458. Strings are any combination of characters or spaces enclosed within quotation marks, such as "fish" and "This is a string %@#^>". Date and time information must be within octothorps, or pound sign (#) characters, and it must follow VBScript's idea of what dates and times should look like; #1/01/02 11:45 PM# and #16 January 1968# are both valid VBScript date or time values. Boolean statements are either TRUE or FALSE, as in $x<x+1$ = TRUE. (They don't have to be capitalized, but I find it easier to see them if they are.) You'll often use Boolean statements when testing the validity of statements. VBScript sees all four of these data types as subsets of a larger data type, type *variant*, which can contain any kind of data. Therefore, you don't have to tell VBScript what type of data you're feeding it, nor can you perform some tasks possible with languages such as Visual Basic (VB), which treat these four data types differently. (Don't worry too much about any such limitations—you might never run into them.) Groups of like data treated together are called *arrays*. To simplify data manipulation, VBScript supports two other data types that have no starting value but are assigned one in the course of a script: *variables* and *constants*. Variables can (and frequently do) change values in the course of the script while retaining the same name. Constants have one value for the duration of the script and can't be changed.

You can make data available to scripts in several ways. First, you can hard-code the data in the script. For example, "\\bigserver\sharedfolder" is a valid way of including path information in a script. Another option is to have the person running the script provide the information directly or indirectly, either explicitly providing the data or providing input that, to the script, means that it should use certain data. Many scripts include reader instructions such as "Please provide a valid account name" to prompt the person running the script for the necessary information. The script can then store that information in a variable, accepting it as a string or converting it to the necessary data type. The script can also gather its own data, perhaps by calculating the date two weeks from today's date and working with the result, or by reading the value of an object's property (which will be explained in "Objects, Properties, and Methods").

Operators

One way to manipulate data is with *operators*, symbols typically used to represent mathematical functions. Some operators take precedence over others, so although VBScript typically reads lines in a script from left to right, operator precedence affects the order in which the operators are interpreted. An *expression* is a calculation that might contain any combination of numbers, variables, strings, or constants to get some result. Expressions can include operators. For example, the expression *dInputDate* + 2 = *dNewDate* increments the variable *dInputDate* by 2, and then assigns the new value to the variable *dNewDate*.

Procedures

VBScript supports two kinds of *procedures*, a kind of condensed form of instructions that you can refer to many times within the course of a script to save repeating yourself or, in the case of built-in functions, to keep from typing the complete instructions at all. *Functions* let you perform certain operations without having to spell those operations out in expressions. With these built-in functions, you can manipulate numbers, strings, dates and times, and arrays, or you can convert any data type to another. Subroutines are mini-scripts that exist within the body of the main script, and which you can call upon if necessary. Again, they're a way to avoid repeating yourself if your script will need to perform the same set of instructions more than once.

Objects, Properties, and Methods

Objects represent physical or logical parts of the computing environment, such as disk drives, files, or user account names. You can do simple scripting without resorting to objects, but most administrative scripts—and all the ones you'll create for MetaFrame sever management—use them. To use the proper jargon, MFCOM objects *expose* parts of MetaFrame XP and unless a part is exposed, it's inaccessible to a script. For example, a reader recently asked me how to use WMI and VBScript to find out the remaining free space on a physical disk. That information is not accessible through WMI because there is no `FreeSpace` (or equivalent) property for the WMI object representing the physical disk. It potentially could exist, and might in later versions, but it doesn't now.

So what objects do you have? If you're using WSH for the scripting environment, VBScript can use objects native to WSH. VBScript also supports Windows Management Instrumentation (WMI) and Active Directory Service Interfaces (ADSI) objects. WMI objects represent physical and logical parts of the computing system, such as IP addresses, file systems, and network cards. ADSI objects represent resources stored in a directory service such as Active Directory (AD) or other supported directories, such as the Windows NT 4 SAM. MetaFrame COM objects, as we'll see, represent parts of the server farm. If you run into questions you'd like to ask an application server but can't because MFCOM doesn't expose the objects, properties, or methods you need to do the asking, then you can try using WSH or ADSI or WMI. You can use more than one object source in the same script.

Objects have properties and methods. Properties have values describing the object they relate to (e.g., IP Address could be a property of the Network Card object, with 12.4.21.197 the value of that property). Properties may be read/write (meaning that you can change them) or read-only. *Methods* are actions you can take against an object (e.g., Copy could be a method of the File object). Not all objects have methods.

> **NOTE** One method for all MetaFrame objects is Initialize, the act of assigning an object to a variable (e.g., you could initialize the farm object by assigning its value to the variable *oFarm*). You must initialize an object before you can address its properties or methods. (The term *instantiate* refers to the act of creating an object that does not already exist.)

Groups of like objects are normally called *collections* or, if user-defined, *dictionaries*. Static groups of objects of the same ilk are known as *classes*.

Useful VBScript Statements for MetaFrame Scripting

These are some of the statements and functions that you might use when creating administrative scripts for MetaFrame XP servers.

Declaring Variables

Every administrative script you ever write is almost certain to include variables—and I say "almost" only to forestall the person who will point out that a script consisting only of `Wscript.Echo 2+2` does not. Although VBScript does not require you to state ahead of time (*declare*, to use the jargon) the variables you intend to use, it's good programming practice to do so. Declaring variables ahead of time and telling VBScript not to accept any variables that you didn't declare will keep you from mistyping variable names and thereby creating new variables, thus leading to weird errors that can be hard to debug. To do so, start all your scripts like this, where *variable1* and so forth are the names of your real variables:

```
Option Explicit
Dim variable1, variable 2, variable 3
```

If you do this and then introduce a new variable not in this list, the script will halt with an error when it encounters the new variable, making it easy to tell where you went wrong.

Conditional Statements

Conditional statements are for telling VBScript what you want to do in a specific set of circumstances. For example, before you run a script you'd like to test for whether the person running it is a Citrix Administrator. If they are, then you'll do one set of actions (finish the script), and if they aren't, you'll do another (tell them that they can't run the script). In such a situation, you'd use an If...Then...Else statement, which essentially says, "If X is true, then I want you do *this*. Otherwise, I want you to do *that*." The Select Case statement works similarly, except that it allows the script to choose among several options, instead of just an "either-or" situation.

VBScript also supports two other conditional statements you can use either to make a command apply to all objects in a collection (For Each) and to run through a set of statements so long as the condition you name is true (Do While), or until it becomes true (Do Until).

Functions

VBScript and WSH support a lot of functions, but two you'll definitely need are CreateObject (used to instantiate an object) and Now, which reports the current date and time.

Creating Output

Although you don't always need to create output, doing so provides some visual feedback for the script's success. The simplest way to print script output is to use the Echo method to Wscript, the object representing the WSH environment. Wscript.Echo prints text or variable contents to the screen, so it's possible to make the output as explanatory as you like. For example, say that you'd like to show the working directory for a published application that you've initialized as *WinApplication*. The working directory is represented by the property DefaultWorkDir. To create this output and make it clear what you were talking about, you could include a line in your script like this:

```
WScript.Echo "Working Directory: " & aWinApplication.DefaultWorkDir
```

For a published application whose working directory is \AppDir, the output for this line would look like this:

```
Working Directory: C:\AppDir
```

> **TIP** By default, WSH uses the graphical interface, which means that each line of script output is sent to a separate dialog box with an OK button that you'll need to click to close it. Not only will this keep you from seeing all script output in a single lump, the script will pause while waiting for you to click OK to close each dialog box. Before you run any scripts at all, I strongly recommend that you set the scripting environment to the command line by typing **wscript /h:cscript //nologo /s** at the command prompt. This will set the execution environment to the command line, turn off the logo information for the scripting environment, and make those settings the default for the current user.

MetaFrame Scripting

Now that you've seen the basics of scripting in general, let's take a look at some specifics of MetaFrame scripting.

Preparing to Develop (and Run) MetaFrame Scripts

The first thing you'll need is the Software Development Kit (SDK), which has not only the complete object documentation (listing all the objects and telling you the available properties and methods for each) but also a utility for making MetaFrame scripting work. You can currently download the SDK from the Citrix Developer Network site at http://apps.citrix.com/CDN/SDK/server_sdk.asp. (You need to register before you can do this, but it's a free register.) When you've downloaded the 8MB file that is CSSDK.EXE, run the file on a computer where you plan to do your developing. This computer needs MetaFrame XP (so you can test scripts). Although it will need to be in a farm (at least in a development farm) so that it can query the farm's database, it should *not* be a production server for what are probably obvious reasons.

> **TIP** On another "prepping" note, make sure that the development server in the farm can get to the database either directly or indirectly, because that's where farm-level information originates. If it can't, because of a firewall or other reason, then your scripts will fail.

You'll go through most of the Installation Wizard in a straightforward manner until you get to the part where you choose components to install. Although all three components are selected by default, there is no point in installing any component other than MFCOM if you're planning to use VBScript as your development tool—you can't talk to the other two pieces with VBScript. Uncheck any components you don't want to install, and click the Install Selected Components button. Having done that, you'll just need to choose whether or not to read the README and click the Finish button. In the location where you chose to install the SDK, there is now a folder called \Mfcom that contains several folders. For our purposes here, the two you care about are \Docs, which holds the documentation, and \Scripts, which contains some sample scripts that you can peek into by right-clicking on their icons and choosing Edit from the context menu.

Before you can run scripts using the MFCOM interface, you'll need to register the COM Server with MetaFrame. If it's not registered, when you run MetaFrame administration scripts you'll see the following error:

```
Can't create MetaFrameFarm object
(429) ActiveX component can't create object
```

Anyone who's already installed SP1 or later doesn't need to worry about this, since installing FR1 registers the COM Server automatically. Unfortunately, SP1 seems to be a requirement. Supposedly, you can register the COM server with the mfreg.exe utility in the \Utils folder (copy it to \System32 first) by typing **mfreg /regserver** from the command prompt to make the scripts work with MetaFrame XP servers without FR1 installed. However, this doesn't work for me. Installing SP1 seems to be the best bet for registering the component and getting MetaFrame scripting to work.

MetaFrame Management Object Architecture

We talked about objects earlier. Just about all the parts of a MetaFrame XP farm—and the farm itself—are represented with the objects listed in Table A.1. I haven't listed all of the available properties and methods in this table—only enough to give you an idea of the kinds of properties and methods supported for each object so you can see what you can *do* with these objects. For a complete list of the properties and methods for each object, see the documentation in the SDK.

Table A.1 Farm Objects Supported with MetaFrame XP Scripting

Object	Description	Sample Properties	Sample Methods
Account Authority	Represents the account authority (domain or server; NDS isn't supported through scripting, even with FR1) for the farm.	Account authority type and name	Initialize

Table A.1 Farm Objects Supported with MetaFrame XP Scripting *(continued)*

Object	Description	Sample Properties	Sample Methods
Application	Represents a published application in the farm.	Application name, default encryption level, working directory, application window settings	Add or remove a server, add or remove a user, read application icon from a file
Farm	Represents the entire MetaFrame XP farm. Settings here will apply to all objects in the farm.	Farm name, use of local time for clients, license strings for installed licenses	Add a new license, publish a new application
Folder	Represents a folder in the Citrix Management Console, containing servers or applications.	Folder type and name	Move, delete, create subfolder, move contents to another folder
Group	Represents the groups to which user accounts belong.	Group name and type; account authority name and type	Initialize
License	Represents a connection or product license for the farm.	License type, license number, grace days before activation, count in use, assigned license count	Activate or remove licenses
Process	Represents a process running in the farm.	Process name, ID, name of the server it's running on, name of person running it, process resource statistics (page count, kernel time, memory used, etc.)	Initialize, or terminate process

Table A.1 Farm Objects Supported with MetaFrame XP Scripting *(continued)*

Object	Description	Sample Properties	Sample Methods
Server	Represents MetaFrame XP servers in the farm.	Server name, network address, product code, enable logons to server	Initialize server object
Session	Represents an ICA session to a server in the farm.	Name of person using the session, name of server they're connected to, client computer name, client caching information, session name and ID	Disconnect session, logoff session, send a message to session
User	Represents an account using the server farm.	Username and type; account authority name and type	Initialize
Virtual Channel	Represents a virtual channel (route for passing one type of session data between client and server) in a particular session.	Virtual channel name and Session ID	Read client data, read (or write) virtual channel data
Zone	Represents a zone in the server farm.	Zone name, zone data collector	Initialize zone object

Except for the farm object, all of these objects are collection objects—that is, they're general categories that contain individual instances of themselves. For example, if you *enumerated*—listed—the Application object, you'd get a list of published applications in the farm, each with its own Application object. This is important because sometimes you'll want to do something that applies to a single instance of an object (such as activate a single license), and sometimes you'll want to do something with all the objects in that collection (such as list all the licenses installed in the farm).

For an example, I'll walk you through a short script that prints the name of the MetaFrame XP farm and displays some general information about it. The numbers in the script correspond to the callouts below.

```
Const MetaFrameWinFarmObject = 1
On Error Resume Next
' 1
Option Explicit
Dim MyFarm, WinFarm
' 2
' Create MetaFrameFarm object
Set MyFarm = CreateObject("MetaFrameCOM.MetaFrameFarm")
' 3
' Initialize the new farm object
MyFarm.Initialize(MetaFrameWinFarmObject)
' Represent the Windows farm object with a variable
Set WinFarm = MyFarm.WinFarmObject
'Confirm that the person running the script is a Citrix admin
if WinFarm.IsCitrixAdministrator = 0 then
    WScript.Echo "You must be a Citrix administrator to run this application."
    WScript.Echo "This script will now end."
    WScript.Quit
End If
' 5
' Print out the farm name and some properties of that farm
WScript.Echo "MetaFrame Farm Name: " & MyFarm.FarmName
WScript.Echo "MetaFrame WinFarm object properties"
WScript.Echo "Alternate Caching Method : " & WinFarm.AlternateCachingMethod
WScript.Echo "FarmRespondToClientBroadcast: " & WinFarm.FarmRespondToClientBroadcast
```

In order, this script accomplishes the following:

1. Tells the script to use only explicitly defined variables, and then defines the ones to use.
2. Creates an object representing a generic "farm" object, and assigns it to a variable to make working with it easier.
3. Initializes the created object so the script can address it, and then assigns a specific instance and type of that object (WinFarm) to a variable to make working with it easier.
4. Makes sure that the person running the script is a Citrix Administrator, and then ends the script with an error if they are not.
5. Prints the name of the farm and some properties of the farm, using strings to identify the property values being printed.

Index

Note to the Reader: Throughout this index **boldfaced** page numbers indicate primary discussions of a topic. *Italicized* page numbers indicate illustrations.

A

AcceptLicense key, 163
access
    auditing. *See* auditlog utility
    to drives, **387–389**
    licensing, **66–70**
    problems in, **276–277**
    to published applications, **297–298**, *297–298*
Access application, 278
Access Control Settings dialog box, 274–275, *275*
access time, memory, 82
Account Authority object, 432
account-level RDP settings, **218**
accounts. *See* users and user accounts
ACINIUPD utility, 283
ACREGL utility, 282
ACSR utility, 282
Action tab, 411, *411*
action tags, **143–146**
activating Terminal Services Licensing, 118–119
Activation Wizard, 118
Active Desktop
    in RDP, 229
    in Server Settings folder, 48
Active Directory
    for MetaFrame, **95–96**
    policies in, 376
Active Directory Service Interfaces (ADSI) objects, 428–429
Active Directory Users and Computers tool
    for printers, 362
    for profiles, 224
    for RDP, 218
Active Sessions counter, 420
active sessions in RDP, 220
Add Citrix Administrator dialog box, 240–241, *240*
Add Client Printer dialog box, 373, *373*
Add Driver dialog box, 356, *356*
Add IP Range dialog box, 312, *312*
Add Key dialog box, 288, *288*
Add List of Names dialog box, 241, *241*, 298, *298*, 370, *370*
Add Local Administrators option, 241
Add Mappings dialog box, 359, *359*
Add New ICA Connection dialog box, 206–207, *206–207*, 210–211, *210–212*
Add Package dialog box, 332–333, *332*
Add Recording option, 328
Add/Remove Programs applet
    for applications, 271–273
    for RIS installation, 139
    for Terminal Services, 110
Add/Remove Windows Components, 110, 114
Add Server Location Address dialog box, 208
addresses, memory, 34
ADF files, 314–315
    packaging for
        files to copy, **327–328**, *327*
        with Installation Management services, 64
        installation recording, **319–325**, *320–324*
        service packs and hotfixes for, **325–327**, *326*
        troubleshooting, 337, *338*
Administration tab, 213
administrative scripting, **425–426**
    comments in, **427**
    data types in, **427–428**
    objects, properties, and methods in, **428–429**
    operators in, **428**
    procedures in, **428**
    purpose of, **426**
    scripting hosts and script engines for, **426–427**
    statements in, **427**, **429–431**
administrators
    adding, **240–242**, *240–241*
    assigning tasks to, **242–244**
ADSI (Active Directory Service Interfaces) objects, 428–429
Advanced Connection Settings dialog box, 257–258, *258*, 392, *393*
Advanced load evaluators, 302, 305–306
Advanced tab, 227
.aep files, 330
/AFTER filtering switch, 382
Alert logs, 407, 411
Alert Logs folder, 410–411
All Client Printers option, 367
/ALL filtering switch, 382
All Jobs tab, 336
All Tasks/Disable Connection option, 260

Allow Logon to Terminal Server option, 224
AllowShadowing value, 166
altaddr tool, 62, 395–396
Anonymous logon option, 233
answer files, **126–130**
app tool, 62
application compatibility scripts, **278–280**
    for ADF files, 321–322, *321*
    built-in support for, **282–283**
    editing and creating, **281–282**
    flow of information in, 283
    working with, **280–281**
Application Compatibility Scripts dialog box, 322, *322*
Application Display tab, 233
Application Limits tab, 263–264, *264*
Application Log, 337
Application object, 433
Application Publishing Wizard, **292–299**, *292–294, 296–297*
Application Refresh tab, 236
Application Server mode, 6, 112
application servers, 37
    connections for, **39–40**
    disconnections from, **40–41**
    ICA display protocol for, 38
    installing applications on, **269–272**, *271*
        with Installation Manager. *See* Installation Manager
        process of, **269–272**, *271*
    load balancing on. *See* load balancing
    publishing applications on, **290–300**, *292–294, 296–298*
    RDP display protocol for, 37
    security for. *See* security
    session initialization on, **38–39**
    for shared environments, **266–269**
    tuning applications on, 272
        benefits of, **273–277**, *275*
        compatibility scripts for, **278–283**
        editing manually, **277–278**
        Registry settings for, **283–290**, *286, 288–289*
application service providers (ASPs), 2–3
Application User Load rule, 307, 310–311
applications
    on application servers. *See* application servers
    compatibility of. *See* application compatibility scripts
    DOS, 267–268, 289
    licensing, 75
    multithreaded, 79–80
    packaging. *See* packaging applications
    publishing, **290–291**
        content, 13, **299–300**
        desktops, 299
        packages, **331–333**, *331–333*
        to Program Neighborhood, **291–299**, *292–294, 296–298*
        for RDP connections, 190
        referencing usernames in, 290
        restricting usage of, **390–391**
        terminating, **251–252**
Applications folder, 291–292, 324
Applications key, 286, *286*, 288
Applied Packages tab, 336
applying
    load balancing evaluators, **303–304**, *303–305*
    service packs, 121–122
arrays, 427
ASPs (application service providers), 2–3
Assigned Rules list, 311
asterisks (*) in unattend.txt, 163
asynchronous DRAM, 81–82
attacks, protection from, **394–396**
Audio Mapping settings, 49
auditing
    for common paths, 274, *275*
    for user access. *See* auditlog utility
Auditing tab, 274, *275*
auditlog utility, 62, **381–383**
    enabling, **379–381**, *380–381*
    filtering audit information
        by amount of time logged on, 383–384
        by date, 385
        by user account, 384
    logging successes and failures, 385
    saving output from, 386–387
authentication
    pass-through, 397, *397*
    in RDP, 231
authorizing printer driver installation, **355–356**, *355–356*
Auto Client Reconnect feature, 12
Auto-Creation Settings dialog box, 369–370, *369*
Auto-replication dialog box, 351–353, *351, 353*
automatic Administrator logons for answer files, 129
automatic client deployment, **182**
Automatic license agreements for answer files, 129
Automatic Logon screen, 189, *189*
automatically deploying terminal services, **119–121**
    answer files for, **126–130**
    licensing servers for, **134**
    prep work for, **121**

Registry changes for, **122–125**
scripted installations for, **126**, **136**
system file updates for, **121–122**
terminal servers for, **130–134**
UDFs for, **134–136**
Available Bytes counter, **399**, **419**
Average Client Latency counter, 405
Avg Disk Queue Length counter, 401
Avg Disk sec/Transfer counter, 401

B

backing stores, 35
backing up data stores, **96–98**
Bad Applications, **286–289**
badly designed applications, 29
bandwidth requirements
    in printing, **360–362**, *360–361*
    in server side planning, **99**
Bandwidth tab, **360–361**, *360*
"Because of a network error, the session will be disconnected" message, 204
/BEFORE filtering switch, **382**, **385**
binary log (.BLG) files, 409, 412
bit-flipping, 83
Bitmap Cache tab, 231
bitmaps
    RDP support for, 37
    in shared environments, 268
.BLG (binary log) files, 409, 412
Boolean data types, 427
BOOTFILE variable, 146
[Branding] section, 133
Bring to This Computer option, 198
Browse for computers dialog box, **195**, *196*
browsers, installing clients via, **182–184**, *183*
build locations for ADF files, **322**, *322*
built-in load balancing evaluators, **302–303**
Bytes Total/sec counter, 402, 419

C

CA Unicenter TNG plug-in, 12
caches
    for farm information, **45–46**
    in terminal server sizing, **78–79**
calculating speed in terminal server sizing, **78–79**
Call command, 282
change client tool, 62, 235
Change Icon dialog box, **191**, *192*
change logon tool, 51, 261
change port tool, 51

change user tool, 51, **271–273**
character caching, 37
character repeat settings, 213
characterization data files, 342
chfarm tool, 62
CHOICE.OSC menu, **148–149**
Citrix, emergence of, **3–4**
Citrix Administrators task, 242
Citrix Connection Configuration tool
    for encryption, **392–394**
    for printer settings, **366**, *366*
Citrix Connection Information tool, **58**, *58*
Citrix Management Console tool, 14, **60–62**, *60*
    for administrators
        adding, **240–242**
        tasks for, **242–244**
    for concurrent sessions, 262
    for farm nodes, 173–174
    for IMA service, 45
    planning for, **98–99**
    for printers
        bandwidth, 361
        drivers, 355, 358
        mapping, 372
        settings, 367
        usage, 369–370
    for process information, 246
    for Resource Manager, 412
    for security, **378–379**
    for sending messages, 249, *249*
    for shadowing, **253–255**, *254–255*, 258
Citrix packager, **328–330**, *329*
Citrix Program Neighborhood. *See* Program Neighborhood
Citrix SSL Relay Configuration tool, **59–60**, *60*
Citrix XML Service, 159
[Citrix XML Service] section, 167
classes in VBScript, 429
/CLEAR filtering switch, **382**, **386**
clicense tool, 62
client computer names, 246
Client Connection Manager Wizard, **188–193**, *189–192*, **215–216**
client connections, **175–176**
    display protocol updates for, **217**
    on handheld PCs, **215–216**
    with ICA
        client-side, **205–211**, *206–207*, *210–212*
        server-side settings, **231–237**, *232*
    PC support for. *See* personal computers (PCs)
    with RDP. *See* RDP (Remote Desktop Protocol)
    on Windows terminals, **212–215**

"client could not connect to the terminal server"
    message, 205
Client Creator tool, 47
Client Disconnection and Reconnection Settings, 234
Client Drive and Printer Mapping setting, 233
[Client ID] section, 168
Client Printer Mapping policy, 368
Client Printers dialog box, 372–373, *372*
Client Printers folder, 368
Client Printers tab, 349, *350*
Client Settings dialog box, 366, *366*
Client Settings tab, 49, 364, *365*
clients
    connections for. *See* client connections
    path information for, 222–226, *224*
    printer usage
        mapping, 99, **372–373**, *372–373*
        per-farm settings, **367–368**, *367*
        per-group settings, 368
        per-protocol settings, **364–366**, *364–366*
        per-user settings, **362–363**, *363*
    security for, **396–398**, *397*
    types, **99**
        handheld PCs as, **106**
        personal computers as, **100–101**
        security for, **105**
        terminal hardware and device performance in, **104–105**
        terminal operating systems for, **103–104**
        windows terminals as, **101–102**
Clipboard
    in MetaFrame, 9
    in Windows .NET server, 8
Clipboard Mapping setting, 234
cloning servers, 120, **169–170**
cltprint tool, 62, 362
.cns files, 193
collections, 429
color
    bandwidth for, 99
    in ICA connections, 211
    in MetaFrame, 9, 22
    in published applications, 294
    in RDP, 223
    in Resource Manager, **413–416**, *416*
    in Windows .NET server, 7
    in Windows Terminal Services, 22
comma-delimited (.CSV) log files, 409, 412
command-line tools and options, **62–63**
    for installing clients, **185–186**
    for profile updates, **224–226**

for published applications, 292, *293*
for sending messages, **250–251**
for terminating applications, **251–252**
for user and process information, 247
for user sessions
    ending and preventing, **260–261**, *261*
    shadowing, **255–256**
    Windows 2000-specific, **50–52**
comments
    in administrative scripting, **427**
    in unattend.txt, 163
Commit Limit counter, 399
Committed Bytes counter, 399
committed memory, 35
common path problems, **274–276**, *275*
Communicator application, 280
compatibility scripts, **278–280**
    for ADF files, **321–322**, *321*
    built-in support for, **282–283**
    editing and creating, **281–282**
    flow of information in, **283**
    working with, **280–281**
[Components] section
    in answer files, 127
    in ristndrd.sif, 153
    for terminal servers, 130, **133–134**
Computer Management tool, 218
computer names in answer files, 128
concurrent sessions, **262–264**, *263–264*
conditional statements, 430
config.xml file, 235
Configure tab, 215
Configure User Shadowing option, 258
Configure Your Server dialog box, 114, 139
Connect Client Drives at Logon option, 226, 363
Connect Client Printers at Logon setting, 226
Connect to Client Printers policy, 368
Connection method, 117
Connection Options tab, 194, *194*
connections
    for application server sessions, **39–40**
    client. *See* client connections
    licenses for, 72
    in MetaFrame, 13
Connections folder, **230–231**, *230*, 364
Connections section, **48–49**
Consecutive Duplicates events, 329
console, applications running from, **276–277**
constants, 427
content publishing, 13, **299–300**
content redirection, 16

Contents tab, 305
context switches, 32
Context Switches rule, 307
Context Switches/sec counter, 420
Conversion Successful dialog box, 125
copy command, 282
copy-on-write technique, 27–28, 34
Copy The Current Computer option, 128
copying profile-path information, 226
Corel application, 278
costs, **26–27**
Counter logs, 407
Counter Logs folder, 410
cprofile tool, 51
CPU prioritization, 13
CPU Usage rule, 310
CPU Utilization rule, 302, 307
Create a Connection screen, 188, *189*
Create a Server Group dialog box, 333, *334*
Create Installation Disk(s) dialog box, 47, *47*, 56, *56*, 178–179, *178–179*
CreateFarm key, 163
cshadow command, 255–256
CSRSS.EXE process, 34, 39
CSSDK.EXE program, 431
.CSV (comma-delimited) log files, 409, 412
ctxxmlss tool, 63
Current Processes report, 418, 420–421, *421*
Current Users report, 418, 421, *422*
CUSTOM.OSC file, 149–150
customizing menus, 146–155

D

data collectors, 43–46
[Data] section
    in answer files, 127
    in ristndrd.sif, 139–140, 151–152
    for terminal servers, 131
[Data Store Configuration] section, 163–165
data stores, 45
    databases for, **96–98**
    in MetaFrame installation, **155–157**
    size of, 354
data types, **427–428**
databases
    for data stores, **96–98**
    UDFs, **134–136**
dates
    filtering audit information by, **385**
    in VBScript, 427
dbgtrace tool, 51

DDI (Device Driver Interface) commands, 342
deadlocks in unattended installations, 162
debugging, comments for, 427
declaring variables, **429–430**
DedicatedPortNumber key, 167
Default Client Printer Only option, 367
Default to Client's Main Printer policy, 368
Default to Main Client Printer option, 226, 234
defaults
    for client connections, 213
    load evaluators, 302, 305–306
    UDF values, 134
    zone names, 156
DefaultWorkDir property, 430
delegated administration, 16
Delete Temporary Folders on Exit setting, 48
deleting
    load evaluators, **314**
    packages, 333
    RDP connection information, **195**
    temporary folders on exit, 48, 229
    terminal services from Windows 2000 servers, **114**
denial of service (DoS) attacks, 377, 394
deploying terminal services. *See* automatically deploying terminal services
descriptions
    for load evaluators, 305
    for published applications, 292, *292*
desktops
    display settings for, 213
    publishing, **299**
/DETAIL filtering switch, 382
Device Driver Interface (DDI) commands, 342
device performance, **104–105**
DHCP
    for client connections, 213
    for RIS installation, 137–138
dictionaries, 429
[Direct Connect Settings] section, 164–165
direct mode, **45–46**, 98
directories
    deleting on exit, 48, 229
    hiding, 387
    permissions for, 378
    in RDP settings, **227–228**, *227*
Disable Connection option, 230
Disable Task Manager policy, 391
disabling shadowing, 158
disconnected RDP sessions, 220
disconnecting from application server sessions, **40–41**
Discover program, **123–125**

discovery with ICA connections, 208
Disk Data I/O rule, 307
disk duplexing, 87
disk mirroring, 87
Disk Operations rule, 308
disk striping with parity, 88
% Disk Time counter, 401, 419
disks, server, **85–93**
display protocols
    ICA, **38**
    RDP, **37**
    updating, **217**
display resolution
    of ICA connections, 211–212, *212*
    for terminal sessions, 190, *190*
[Display] section, 141, 153
Display tab
    for client connections, 213
    for RDP connections, 197–198, *198*
DNS servers, 137
Do Not Play option, 198
Do While statements, 430
domain controllers, 137
domain structure, **94**
Don't Run Specified Windows Applications policy, 390–391
DOS applications, **28–29**
    in shared environments, 267–268
    Tame tool for, **289**
DoS (denial of service) attacks, 377, 394
DOSKBD utility, 28–29, 289
DRAM (dynamic RAM), 79, 81–83
drive access, controlling, **387–389**
drive mapping
    bandwidth for, 99
    in MetaFrame installation, **159**
    in Windows .NET server, 8
    in Windows Terminal Services vs. MetaFrame, 22
Driver Compatibility dialog box, 355, *355*
Driver Mapping dialog box, 358–359, *359*
[DriveReassignment] section, 166–167
drivers
    for MetaFrame, 97
    for printing, 342, 348, 355
        authorizing installation of, **355–356**, *355–356*
        graphics, 342
        interface, 342
        name mismatches in, 357–359, *359*
        replication, **351–355**, *351–354*
        uninstalling, **356**, *357*
        universal, **348–350**, *350*
Drivers tab, 356, *357*, 358

dsmaint tool, 63
DSNFilePath key, 165
Duplicate Evaluator dialog box, 306, *306*, 311–313, *311–313*
Duplicate Load Evaluator option, 305
duration setting for log files, 410
DWORD Editor dialog box, 289, *289*
dynamic RAM (DRAM), 79, 81–83

E

ECC (error correcting code) memory, 83–84
Echo method, 430
Edit Bandwidth Limit dialog box, 361, *361*
Edit Connection dialog box, 257, 392, *393*
Edit Properties dialog box, 262–263, *263*
editing
    application settings, **277–278**
    compatibility scripts, **281–282**
    connection icons, 191, *192*
    CUSTOM.OSC, 150
    ICA settings, **231–237**, *232*
    INI files, 283
    IP mappings, 396
    load evaluators, **305–306**, *396*
    log files, 409
    OSC files, 143
    printer mappings, **371**, *371*
    published application settings, 298
    RDP connection information, **193–195**, *194–195*
    Registry, 284–286, 289
EDO (Extended Data Output) DRAM, 82
EIDE (Extended/Enhanced Integrated Drive Electronics), **85–86**
elections for data collectors, 44
EMF (Enhanced Metafile) format, 343–344, 349
Enable Account option, 244
Enable DeadGWDetect entry, 394
Enable ICMPRedirects entry, 394
Enable PMTUDiscovery entry, 394
Enable Terminal Services option, 110
enabling auditing, **379–381**, *380–381*
enclosures, RAID, 92
encryption
    for ICA connections, 210, *210*, 234
    for RDP sessions, 40, 230–231
    for remote connections, **392–394**, *393*
Encryption Level setting, 234
End Process option, 251
ending
    RDP sessions, **202**
    user sessions, **259–261**

Enhanced Metafile (EMF) format, 343–344, 349
Enhanced Registry Scan option, 124
Environment tab
    for printers, 362, *363*
    for sessions, 54, 226
Environment Variables dialog box, 224, *224*, 227, *227*
environments
    session, 54, **226**, 227
    shared, 265
        application installation in, **269–272**, *271*
        application suitability in, **266–269**
    suitability of, 25
error correcting code (ECC) memory, 83–84
Eudora application, 278
Evaluator Properties dialog box, 313
evaluators, load balancing. *See* load balancing evaluators
Event Logging tab, 231
Event Viewer, 337, *338*
/EVENTLOG filtering switch, 382, 387
Excel application, 278
Exchange application, 279
Executable Environment for Applications, 33
Execute operating mode, 270
Experience tab, 200, *201*
expressions, 428
Extended Data Output (EDO) DRAM, 82
Extended/Enhanced Integrated Drive Electronics (EIDE), **85–86**
extensions for published applications, 293, 298

F

factory default client connection settings, 213
/FAIL filtering switch, 382, 385
failures, logging, **385**
Farm Management task, 242
farm metric server, **422**, *422*
Farm Metric Server tab, 413, 422
Farm object, 433
[Farm Settings] section, 165–166
farms, **42–44**
    creating, **156**
    information for, **45–46**
    joining, 156–157
    mixed-mode, **173–174**
    in Windows Terminal Services vs. MetaFrame, 20
FAT file system, **92–93**
File Read Attributes events, 329
File Reads events, 329
file-specific problems, **274–276**, *275*
File System Changes folder, 324

file systems for server disks, **92–93**
FileErr.txt error log, 124
files
    answer, **126–130**
    hiding, **387–389**
    locations of, 277–278
    packaging, **327–328**, *327*
    permissions for, **389**
filtering audit information, 382–383
    by amount of time logged on, 383–384
    by date, **385**
    by user account, **384**
finding processes, **244–248**, *245*
Finish Admin Install dialog box, 271, *271*
FirstCountMsgQPeeksSleepBadApp value, 287
Flags key, 284, 287
flattemp tool, 51, 227–228
flow of information in compatibility scripts, **283**
Folder object, 433
folders
    deleting on exit, 48, 229
    hiding, 387
    permissions for, 378
    in RDP settings, **227–228**, *227*
For Each statements, 430
forcedefault attribute, 236–237
forests, **95–96**
<FORM> tag, 144
formatting tags in OSC files, 143
% Free Space counter, 419
Full Screen mode, 188
functions, 428, **430**

G

GDI (Graphics Device Interface)
    in shared environments, 268
    for Windows 2000 printing, **342**
GDI kernel, 39
General tab
    for client connections, 213
    for counters, 409
    for ICA, 232, *232*
    for logs, 407, *408*
    for pass-through authentication, 397, *397*
    for RDP, 194, *194*, 197, *197*, 230–231, *230*
global objects, 277
glyph caching, 37
Goto statement, 283
GPOs (Group Policy Objects), 177, **184–185**
graphical tools and support
    for RDP settings, 219

for sending messages, **248–250**, *249*
for terminal servers, 130
for terminating applications, **251**
for user and process information, **245–247**, *245*, *247*
for user sessions, **253–255**, *253–255*, **260**
Graphics Device Interface (GDI)
in shared environments, 268
for Windows 2000 printing, **342**
Group object, 433
group policies
for clients, **184–185**
for server security, **376–377**, 388
Group Policy Editor, 377, 379, *380*
Group Policy Objects (GPOs), 177, **184–185**
Group Policy tab, 377
groups
for published applications, **297–298**, *297–298*
server
for application deployment, **333–335**, *334*
for ICA clients, **208–209**
for network traffic reduction, **208–209**
GUID variable, 146
[GuiRunOnce] section, 133
[GUIUnattended] section
in answer files, 127
in ristndrd.sif, 140–141, 152–153
for terminal servers, 131

H

handheld PCs
as client types, **106**
setting up, **215–216**
support for, 66
hard errors, 83
hardware RAID systems vs. software, **91–92**
Hide All Icons on Desktop policy, 388
Hide These Specified Drives in My Computer policy, 388
hiding files and folders, **387–389**
High encryption, 232, 392
history of Windows Terminal Services, **2–3**
Citrix and Multi-Win in, **3–4**
Microsoft in, **4–5**
MetaFrame, **9–18**
Windows 2000 Server, **5–7**
Windows .NET server, **7–9**
HOBLinkJWT client, 18
host caches, **45–46**
hotfixes, **325–327**, *326*
Hotkeys tab, 231
hpcrdp.exe program, 216

I

Iacobucci, Ed, 3
ICA
clients in
connecting with, **205–211**, *206–207*, *210–212*
files for, 177
print settings for, **362**, **364**, *365*
server groups for, **208–209**
settings for, **231–233**, *232*
unexpected disconnects with, 205
connections for, **215**
as display protocol, **38**
installing, **180–182**, *180*
in MetaFrame installation, 157, **160–161**
server-side settings for, **233–237**
sessions in
monitoring, 14
printing in, **345–347**, *346*, **361**, **371**, *371*
starting, **300–302**
toolbar in, **55–56**, *55*
ICA Client Creator tool, **56**, *56*, **178**, *179*
ICA Client Distribution Wizard, **59**, **160–161**
ICA Client Update Configuration tool, **56**, *57*
[ICA Network Protocols] section, 166
ICA Options tab, 233
ICA Settings dialog box, **231–232**, *232*, **397**, *397*
ICA Settings tab, 364, *365*
ICA-Tcp Properties tab, 364, *365*
icaport tool, 63, 235
ICLs (Internet Connector Licenses), 66, **70–71**
.ico files, 191
icons
editing, 191, *192*
for packages, 333
IDE (Integrated Drive Interface) disks, 85
IdelWinStationPoolCount key, 39
identification of users, **269**
[Identification] section
in answer files, **126–127**
in ristndrd.sif, 141, 153
for terminal servers, 132
Idle Session Limits setting, 234
IDs
process, 246
SCSI, 85
IE (Internet Explorer), 426
If Exist statement, 283
If Not Exist statement, 283
If...Then...Else statements, 430
IMA (Independent Management Architecture) service, **41–43**
for farm information, **45–46**

for server communication, **43–44**
image names for processes, 246
Inactive Sessions counter, 420
Include Compatibility Script option, 320
Independent Management Architecture (IMA) service, **41–43**
    for farm information, **45–46**
    for server communication, **43–44**
[Indirect Connect Settings] section, 165
indirect mode, **45–46**, 97
IndirectServerName value, 165
IndirectServerPort value, 165
INI files, editing, 283
initializing sessions, **38–39**
Input tab, 213–214
<INPUT> tag, 144
Install operating mode, **270–271**
/install option in change user, 271–273
Installation Manager, 10, 243, **314–315**
    benefits of, **63–65**
    installing, 316–317, *316*
    for packaging applications and hotfixes, **319**
        files to copy, **327–328**, *327*
        installation recordings, **319–325**, *320–324*
        service packs and hotfixes, **325–327**, *326*
    for publishing packages, **331–333**, *331–333*
    for scheduling jobs, **335–336**, *335–336*
    for server groups, **333–335**, *334*
    for troubleshooting jobs, 337, *338*
Installation Recordings package, **319–325**, *320–324*
Installation Wizard, 216
installing
    applications
        with Installation Manager. *See* Installation Manager
        process of, **269–272**, *271*
    clients via browsers, **182–184**, *183*
    ICA, **180–182**, *180*
    Installation Manager, 316–317, *316*
    MetaFrame, **155**
        data store setup for, **155–157**
        drive letter mappings for, **159**
        ICA client rollout in, **161**
        ICA files and licensing for, **160**
        network connections and shadowing setup for, **157–158**
        preparing servers for cloning, **169–170**
        unattended installations, **161–168**
        updates for, **160–161**
        upgrading in, **170–174**
        web services for, **159**

RDP, **179–180**, 216
terminal services, **109–110**
    automatically deploying. *See* automatically deploying terminal services
    customizing menus for, **146–155**
    on existing servers, **110–119**, *111–113*, *115*, *117*, *119*
    RIS for, **136–146**
    Terminal Services Licensing, **114–119**, *115*, *117*, *119*
INSTALLPATH variable, 146
instances for published applications, 295
Integrated Drive Interface (IDE) disks, 85
interface drivers, 342
Internet Connector Licenses (ICLs), 66, **70–71**
Internet Connector licensing option, 48, 229
Internet Explorer (IE), 426
Interoperability tab, 173
Interrupt Time counter, 403, 420
Interrupts/sec counter, 403
inventory information settings, 214
Inventory tab, 213
IP Range rule, 308, 312

J

Job Results tab, 337, *338*
joining farms, 156–157

K

KeepAliveTime entry, 394
keyboard polling, **28–29**, 289
keyboard settings, 213
keyboard shortcuts, **201–202**
keys in answer files, 126
kill command, 252
killing applications, **251–252**

L

L1 caches, 79
L2 caches, 79
L3 caches, 79
language monitors, 344–345
LANGUAGE variable, 147
languages for ICA clients, 184
Last Client Latency counter, 405
Least Recently Used (LRU) algorithm, 37
Leave at Remote Computer option, 198
[License Agreement] section, 168
license numbers, 73

License object, 433
[License Serial Numbers] section, 167–168
License Server Activation screen, 117, *117*
License Thresholds rule, 308
[LicenseFilePrintData] section
    in answer files, 127
    in ristndrd.sif, 141, 153
    for terminal servers, 132
Licenses task, 243
licensing
    access, 66–70
    application, 75
    in automatic deployment, **134**
    ICA, **160**
    MetaFrame, 71–74, 160
    Terminal Services Licensing, **114–119**, *115*, *117*, *119*
    TSICL, 70–71
    in Windows 2000 Server, 6
Licensing Wizard, 116–119, *117*, *119*
Limit the Client Printer Bandwidth policy, 361
limitations, 27
    16-bit applications, 27
    badly designed applications, 29
    demanding clients, 27
    DOS applications, 28–29
Linux-based Windows terminals, 213
load balancing, 300
    with ICA connections, 208
    ICA session start in, 300–302
    in MetaFrame, 11, **21–22**, 96
    in Windows Terminal Services, **21–22**
load balancing evaluators, 300
    applying, **303–304**, *303–305*
    built-in, 302–303
    custom
        creating, 310–313, *311–313*
        editing, 305–306, *306*
        rules for, 307–311
    operation of, 302–303
    renaming and deleting, **314**
Load Manager, 243, 300–302
Local Computer Policy, 381
local host caches, **45–46**
Local (Non-Network) Printers option, 367
"local policy of this system does not allow you to log on interactively" message, 203
Local Resources tab, 198, *199*
Local Security Authority (LSA), 40
Local Users and Groups section, 218

Locate Server or Published Application dialog box, 207–208, *207*
Log Files tab, 409
logging off RDP sessions, **202**
LogicalDisk counters, 419
logoff tool, 51
logon time, obtaining, 246
logs
    for successes and failures, **385**
    in System Monitor
        creating, **407–411**, *408–411*
        viewing, **412**
Lotus Notes application, 278
Lotus Smart Suite application, 278
Low encryption, 231, 392
LRU (Least Recently Used) algorithm, 37
LSA (Local Security Authority), 40

M

MAC variable, 147
machine-specific Registry settings, **273–274**
MACHINEDOMAIN variable, 147
MACHINENAME variable, 147
MACHINEOU variable, 147
MACHINETYPE variable, 147
main memory in terminal server sizing, **80–81**
maintenance requirements, **23**
man files, 224
Manage Your Server screen, 114
management tools, 239
    application termination, **251–252**
    messages, **248–251**, *249*
    in MetaFrame. *See* MetaFrame XP
    server management, **240–244**, *240–241*
    server shutdown, **261–262**
    user and process information, **244–248**, *245*, *247*
    user connections, **262–264**, *263–264*
    user sessions, **252–261**, *253–255*, *257–258*, *261*
    in Windows 2000 Server. *See* Windows 2000 Server
mandatory profiles, 224
mapping
    drives
        bandwidth for, 99
        in MetaFrame installation, **159**
        in Windows .NET server, 8
        in Windows Terminal Services vs. MetaFrame, 22
    for MetaFrame installation, **159**
    printers
        client-side, 99

drivers for, 358–359, *359*
for RDP connections, 199
to terminal sessions, 346–347, *346–347*, 371–373, *372–373*
in Windows Terminal Services vs. MetaFrame, 22
public IP addresses to private addresses, 396
Medium encryption, 392
memory
for client connections, 213
in multiuser environments, 34–36
for PTEs, 36
reliability of, 83–84
in shared environments, 266–267
speed of, 81–83
in terminal server sizing, 80–81
Memory Alert dialog box, 411, *411*
Memory counters, 399–400, 419
memory leaks, 29, 267
Memory Manager, 38–39, 81
Memory Usage rule, 302–303, 308, 310
Memory Use dialog box, 407, *408*
menus, customizing, **146–155**
messages, sending, **248–251**, *249*
<META ACTION> tag, 144
<META KEY> tag, 144
<META SERVER ACTION> tag, 145
MetaFrame Settings tab, 262–263, *263*
MetaFrame XP, 41–42
Active Directory for, 95–96
auditing access to, 379–387
data store databases in, 96–98
domain structure for, 94
farm information for, 45–46
features in, 9–18
installing. *See* installing
licensing for, 71–74, 160
load balancing in, 11, **21–22**, 96
organizational model for, 42–43
OS requirements for, 94
for printers
driver distribution, 351–355, *351–354*
driver name mismatches in, 358–359, *359*
mapping, 372–373, *372–373*
publishing in, 290–291
content, 13, 299–300
desktops, 299
packages, 331–333, *331–333*
to Program Neighborhood, **291–299**, *292–294*, *296–298*
Resource Manager in, 11, 243, **412–413**, *413*
farm metric server for, **422**, *422*
server reports in, 418–421, *418*, *421–422*
viewing real-time statistics in, 413–417, *414–417*
scripting in, **431**
object architecture in, 432–436
preparing for, 431–432
statements in, 429–431
security for, 378–379
servers for
communication with, 43–44
memory for, 84
naming in, 94–95
structure of, 94
tools for
Citrix Connection Information, 58, *58*
Citrix Management Console, 60–62, *60*
Citrix SSL Relay Configuration, 59–60, *60*
command-line utilities, 62–63
ICA Client Creator, 56, *56*
ICA Client Distribution Wizard, 59
ICA Client Update Configuration, 56, *57*
ICA toolbar, 55–56, *55*
Installation Management services, 63–65
Resource Manager server, 65
Shadow Taskbar, 57, *57*
SpeedScreen Latency Reduction Manager, 58–59, *59*
vs. Windows Terminal Services, 18
load balancing, **21–22**
multiprotocol support, **19**
seamless client sessions, **19–20**
server farming, 20
support for non-windows clients, 18
[MetalFrame License Agreement] section, 163
[MetalFrame Product Code] section, 168
methods, **428–429**
mf20.dsn file, 170
MFCOM objects, 428, 432
mfreg.exe utility, 432
Microsoft, 4–5
MetaFrame, 9–18
Windows .NET server, 7–9
Windows 2000 Server, 5–7
Microsoft Installer (.msi) files and packages, 184–185, 314–315, 317
guidelines for, **125**
with Installation Management services, 64
Software Console for, 123
Microsoft License Pack (MLP), 67
Microsoft Open License program, 67
mirror sets, 87–88
misplaced Registry entries, 273–274

mixed mode in MetaFrame, 171–174
mkdir command, 282
MLP (Microsoft License Pack), 67
modifiable attribute, 236–237
monitors
    system. *See* System Monitor
    for Windows 2000 printing, **344**
Most Preferred servers, 44
mouse settings for client connections, 213
msg tool, 51, 250
MsgQBadAppSleepTimeInMillisec value, 287
MSI files and packages, 184–185, 314–315, 317
    guidelines for, **125**
    with Installation Management services, 64
    Software Console for, 123
msiexec command, 185–186
msrdpcli.exe program, 179
Multi-Win, emergence of, 3–4
multiple instances, **269**
multiple office support, **23–24**
multiprotocol support, **19**
multithreaded applications, 79–80
multiuser-enabled applications, **272**
multiuser environments, memory in, **34–36**

N

name mismatches, printer driver, **357–359**, *359*
named accounts for published applications, 298
names
    in answer files, 128
    applications, 191
    farms, 156
    ICA clients, 180
    load balancing evaluators, 305
    logs, 409
    projects, 328, *328*
    published applications, 292, *292*
    RDP connections, 188–189, *189*
    servers, **94–95**
    zones, 156
NAT (Network Address Translation), 395–396
native mode, **171–172**
Navigator application, 280
NETBIOSNAME variable, 147
[NetClients] section, 141, 154
[NetProtocols] section, 141, 153
Netscape applications, 280
[NetServices] section, 142, 154
Network Account dialog box, 332
Network Address Translation (NAT), 395–396
network interface cards (NICs), **93**
Network Interface counter, 402, 419
Network Load Balancing (NLB), 21
Network-Management Tools, 11
Network Protocol list, 208
Network tab, 213–214
[Networking] section
    in answer files, 127
    in ristndrd.sif, 141, 153
    for terminal servers, 133
networks and network settings
    for client connections, 213–214
    installation from, 121
    in MetaFrame installation, **157–158**
    protocols for
        for MetaFrame installation, 157
        in unattend.txt, 166
    security for, 392
        attack protection in, **394–396**
        encryption in, **392–394**, *393*
    traffic reduction in, for, **208–209**
New Load Evaluator option, 310
New Log Settings option, 407
New project dialog box, 328, *328*
NewDriveLetter key, 166
NFuse, 9
    for ICA clients, 181, 183
    for MetaFrame, 15, 17, 159
    for NAT, 395
NFUSE.CON file, 395
[NFuse] section, 167
NICs (network interface cards), **93**
NLB (Network Load Balancing), 21
non-parity memory, 83–84
NoNameRelease On Demand entry, 394
Notes application, 278
Novell NDS support, 15
NTFS file system, **92–93**
NthCountMsgQPeeksSleepBadApp value, 287
NTPRINT.INF file, 357–358
NTVDM.EXE process, 267
numbers, 427

O

Object Manager, 277
objects
    in MetaFrame scripting, **432–436**
    in VBScript, **428–429**
Obtain Client License Key Pack, 119
ODBC application, 279
ODBC drivers, 98
[ODBC] section, 162–163

Office application, 279
Offline Files, 228
operating systems
    for clients, **103–104**
    for MetaFrame, **94**
    for personal computers, 100
    for shared environments, 267
operators, **428**
<OPTION> tag, 145
optional terminal services, **146–155**
[Options] section, 168
OPTIONS variable, 147
Oracle with data stores, 97–98
organizational model for MetaFrame, **42–43**
organizational units (OUs), 376–377
OS/2 operating system, 3–4
OSC files, 142–143
    editing, 143
    tags in, **143–146**
[OSChooser] section, 142, 154
OUs (organizational units), 376–377
Outlook application, 279
output in VBScript, **430**
Overwrite Existing Drivers option, 353

P

Package an Installation Recording dialog box, 319–323, *321–323*
Package an Unattended Program dialog box, 325–326, *326*
Package Files dialog box, 327, *327*
Packager application, 324, *324*, 328
packaging applications, 13, **319**
    Citrix packager for, **328–330**, *329*
    files to copy in, **327–328**, *327*
    installation recordings in, **319–325**, *320–324*
    publishing packages in, **331–333**, *331–333*
    restoring packaging servers in, 330, *331*
    scheduling installation jobs, **335–336**, *335–336*
    server groups for application deployment in, **333–335**, *334*
    service packs and hotfixes in, **325–327**, *326*
    single-purpose servers for, **317–318**
    troubleshooting installation jobs, **337**, *338*
Packaging Files package, 319
Page Faults rule, 309
Page Swaps rule, 302, 309
page table entries (PTEs), 36
page tables, 35
paged in data, 80
paged out data, 80

pages, 35
Pages Input/sec counter, 399
Pages Output/sec counter, 400
Pages/sec counter, 400, 419
Paging File counters, 400, 419
paging files, 80–81
parameters for unattended packaging, 325–326, *326*
[params.MS_MSClient] section, 142, 154
[params.MS_Server] section, 142, 154
[params.MS_TCPIP] section, 141, 154
parity in disk striping, 88
parity memory, 83–84
pass-through authentication, 397
password-protected screensavers, **203**
*PASSWORD variable, 148
passwords
    in answer files, 128
    for ICA, 180, 233
    for RDP connections, 188–189
    for shadowing sessions, 254
paths
    to installation files, 320, *321*
    problems with, **274–276**, *275*
    in RDP settings, **222–226**, *224*
PCL (Printer Control Language), 349
Peachtree Complete Accounting application, 280
per connection licenses, **69**
per-farm settings, **367–368**, *367*
per-group settings, **368**
per-protocol settings, **364–366**, *364–366*
per-user information storage, **266–268**
per-user settings, **362–363**, *363*
Perflogs folder, 409
perform command, 398
performance in clients, **104–105**
PerformRouterDiscovery entry, 395
Permission Compatibility dialog box, 112–113, *113*
Permission Compatibility setting, 48
permissions
    for files, **389**
    for shadowing, **256–259**, *257–258*
    for system directories, 378
    for Terminal Services, 112–113, *113*
personal computers (PCs)
    for client connections, **176**
        automatic client deployment, 182
        client installation via browser, **182–184**, *183*
        command prompt for, **185–186**
        group policies in, **184–185**
        ICA connections in, **205–211**, *206–207, 210–212*

ICA installation, **180–182**, *180*
manual installation, **176**
RDP connections in. *See* RDP (Remote Desktop Protocol)
RDP installation, **179–180**
setup files for, **177–178**, *178–179*
as client types, **100–101**
support for, **65**
Phone and Modem Options applet, **157**
Physical Disk counters, 401
physical memory, 34
planning
server security, **377**
server side, **77**
bandwidth requirements in, **99**
Citrix Management Console, **98*-99**
client types in, **99–106**
MetaFrame for, **94–98**
server roles, **77–78**
terminal server sizing. *See* terminal servers
user training in, **106–107**
policies
for clients, **184–185**
for printer bandwidth, 361
for server security, **376–377**, 388
polling keyboard, **28–29**, 289
Pool Nonpaged Failures counter, 402
pooled licenses, 72
Port Mapping setting, 234
port monitors, 344
ports
ICA, **234–235**
printer, **346–347**, *347*
pound signs (#) in VBScript, 427
power costs, **26–27**
PowerBuilder application, 280
PowerPoint application, 279
Prevent Access to Drives from My Computer policy, 389
preventing user sessions, **259–261**, *261*
Print Server Properties dialog box, **356**, *357*
Printer Control Language (PCL), 349
printer installation setting, 214
Printer Job Language, 344
Printer Management, **355**, **360–361**, *360*
Printer Management Properties dialog box, 349, *350*, *367*, *367*
PrinterMappingINFName value, 358
PrinterMappingINFSection value, 358
Printers tab
for client connections, 213
for client printer usage, 369

printers and printing, 341, 367
bandwidth requirements in, **360–362**, *360–361*
client usage in
RDP and ICA settings for, **362–368**
user accounts for, **369–373**, *369–373*
drivers for. *See* drivers
GDI for, **342**
mapping
client-side, 99
drivers for, **358–359**, *359*
for RDP connections, 199
to terminal sessions, **346–347**, *346–347*, **371–373**, *372–373*
in Windows Terminal Services vs. MetaFrame, 22
monitors for, **344**
performance of, 14
process, **345–348**, *346–347*
processors for, **343–344**
providers for, **343**
routers for, **343**
spoolers for, **342–343**
Printers task, 243
priority
of processors, 295
of threads, **32–34**
private addresses, mapping to, 396
Private Bytes counter, 401
procedures, **428**
Process counters, **401–402**
Process object, 406, 433
processes, **32–34**
ids for, 246
information about, **244–248**, *245*, *247*
memory for, 35
Processes tab, 245, *245*, 251
Processor counters, 403, 420
% Processor Time counter, 403–404, 420
processors
print, 345
priority levels for, 295
in server-based computing model, **32–34**
in shared environments, 266
in terminal server sizing, **78–80**
for Windows 2000 printing, **343–344**
product codes, **72–73**, 160
product licenses, **71–72**
Profile tab, 223
profiles
command-line updates to, **224–226**
for RDP, **222–224**
Profiles folder, 222

Program Neighborhood, 11, 15, 20
	for ICA clients, 161, 181, 183–184, 186, 205–206, 231–232
	for MetaFrame installation, 159
	for pass-through authentication, 397
	publishing applications to, **291–299**, *292–294, 296–298*
Program tab, **195**, *195*
Programs tab, 199–200, *200*
Project application, 279
Project Wizard, 319–320, *320*, 327
properties in VBScript, **428–429**
protocols
	in MetaFrame installation, 157
	for sessions, 246
	for shadowing, 257
	in unattend.txt, 166
providers, print, 343
[Proxy] section, 133
PTEs (page table entries), 36
public IP addresses, mapping, 396
Publish Application dialog box, **292–299**, *292–294, 296–297*
published applications, 20
Published Applications task, 243
publishing, **290–291**
	content, 13, **299–300**
	desktops, **299**
	packages, **331–333**, *331–333*
	to Program Neighborhood, **291–299**, *292–294, 296–298*

Q

qprinter utility, 354
query farm tool, 63, 247
query process tool, 51, 248
query session tool, 51
query termserver tool, 51
query user tool, 51
quotation marks (") in VBScript, 427

R

RAID subsystems, 86–87
	hardware vs. software, **91–92**
	types of, **87–91**
RAM. *See* memory
RAW spool files, 343–344
RDP (Remote Desktop Protocol)
	accessibility of, 177
	for client connections, **187**
		creating, **188–193**, *189–192*, **214–216**
	editing and deleting information for, **193–195**, *194–195*
	limitations of, **200–203**
	with RDP5 client, **187–188**, *187*
	with Remote Desktop, **195–200**, *196–200*
	reusing, **193**
	as display protocol, 37
	installing, **179–180**, 216
	for printing settings, 364, *365*
	server management permissions in, 240
	server-side settings in
		account-level, **218**
		for all connections, **228**
		client path information, **222–226**, *224*
		Connections folder, **230–231**, *230*
		environment, **226**, *227*
		profile updates, **224–226**
		remote control, **218–220**, *219*
		Server Settings folder, **228–229**, *229*
		temporary directories location, **227–228**, *227*
		time-outs, **220–222**, *221*
	sessions in
		printing in, 345–347, *346*
		shadowing, **253–258**, *253–255*
RDP display driver (RDPDD), 39
.rdp files, 193
RDP-Tcp Properties dialog box
	for connections, 49, *49*, 230, *230*
	for protocols, 364, *365*
	for shadow permissions, 257, *257*
RDPDD (RDP display driver), 39
ReassignDriveLetters key, 166–167
[Reboot] section, 168
reconnecting from application server sessions, **40–41**
Recording dialog box, 323–324, *323*, 330
referencing usernames, 290
refreshing group policy settings, 377
register tool, 51, 277
Registry, 358
	for applications, **283–284**
		bad, **286–289**, *286, 288–289*
		installing, 269–270, 272
		purpose of, **273–274**
		sample values, **284–285**
	for deploying terminal services, **122–125**
	for printer drivers, 357–358
	searching in, 282
Registry Changes folder, 324
Registry Value Reads events, 329
reliability, memory, **83–84**
remapping, access problems with, 276
Remote Administration mode, 6, 114

Remote Administration mode licensing, **74**
remote connections, encrypting, **392–394**, *393*
Remote Control dialog box, **253**, *253*
remote control RDP settings, **218–220**, *219*
Remote Control tab, **54**, **218**, *219*, **256**, *257*
Remote Desktop Protocol. *See* RDP (Remote Desktop Protocol)
Remote Installation Services (RIS), **136–138**
    customizing menus in, **146–155**
    prep work for, **138–139**
    setting up, **139**
    for terminal server installation in, **139–146**
remote updates, **266**
[RemoteInstall] section, 142, 154
Remove Package option, 333
Remove Run From Start Menu policy, **390–391**
Removes the Folder Options Menu Item from the Tools Menu policy, 389
renaming load evaluators, 314
Replicate Driver dialog box, **353–354**, *354*
replication, driver, **351–355**, *351–354*
Report Full Load When setting, 306
reports in Resource Manager, **418–421**, *418*, *421–422*
Reports tab, 413, *413*, 418
reserving memory, 35
reset tool, 52
reset session tool, 260
resetting RDP sessions, 220
resolution
    of ICA connections, **211–212**, *212*
    for terminal sessions, **190**, *190*
resources, 398
    logging, 407
    Resource Manager for, 11, 65, 243, **412–413**, *413*
        farm metric server for, **422**, *422*
        real-time statistics in, **413–417**, *414–417*
        server reports in, **418–421**, *418*, *421–422*
    in shared environments, 266
    System Monitor for. *See* System Monitor
restoring
    packaging servers, **330**, *331*
    Registry keys, 284
restricting
    application usage, **390–391**
    shadowing, 158
RIS (Remote Installation Services), **136–138**
    customizing menus in, **146–155**
    prep work for, **138–139**
    setting up, **139**
    for terminal server installation in, **139–146**
ristndrd.sif file, **139–141**, **151–153**

roaming profiles, **222–223**
Rollback dialog box, **330**, *331*
rolling back changes, **330**, *331*
rootdrive.cmd file, 281
rootdrv2.cmd file, **280–281**
Round Trip Deviation counter, 405
routers, printer, **343**, **345**
Rule Disabled option, 258
Rule Enabled option, 258
Rule Not Configured option, 258
rules for load balancing, **300–303**, **307–311**
Run Only Allowed Windows Applications policy, **390–391**

S

Sample Data Every setting, 409
Save Key dialog box, **288**, *288*
saving
    audit output, **386–387**
    Registry keys, **288**, *288*
Schedule application, 279
Schedule Details dialog box, **335**, *336*
Schedule Install: Registry edits dialog box, **335**, *335–336*
Schedule tab, 410
scheduling
    audits, 387
    installation jobs, **335–336**, *335–336*
    log files, 410
Scheduling rule, 309
Scheduling Wizard, **335–336**
Screen Options screen, **190**, *190*
screensavers
    with client connections, 203
    for RDP, 223
    settings for, 213
scripting hosts and script engines, **426–427**
scripts, 425
    administrative. *See* administrative scripting
    application compatibility, **278–280**
        for ADF files, **321–322**, *321*
        built-in support for, **282–283**
        editing and creating, **281–282**
        flow of information in, 283
        working with, **280–281**
    for deploying terminal services, **126**, **136**
    for FR1 installation, 168
    MetaFrame, 431
        object architecture in, **432–436**
        preparing for, **431–432**
        statements in, **429–431**

for unattended installations, 162–168
SCSI (Small Computer Systems Interface) drives, 85–86
SDK (Software Development Kit), 431
SDRAM (synchronous DRAM), 81–83
seamless client sessions, 19–20
Seamless Windows
    in ICA connections, 211
    with published applications, 291
Secure Sockets Layer (SSL), 15, 59
security
    for application servers, 375–376
        auditing user access. *See* auditlog utility
        drive access, 387–389
        group policies for, 376–377
        for MetaFrame tools and communications, 378–379
        network, 392–396, *393*
        planning for, 377
        restricting application usage, 390–391
        Terminal Services for, 377–378
    for clients, **105**, 213–214, **396–398**, *397*
Security Policy Setting dialog box, 381, *381*
Security tab
    for client connections, 213
    for common paths, 274
Select Columns dialog box, 53, *53*
Select Components dialog box, 316, *316*
Select Counters dialog box, 408, *408*
Select Counters from Computer option, 406
Select Desired Features dialog box, 180, *180*
Select Drivers to Replicate dialog box, 352, *352*
<SELECT> tag, 146
semicolons (;) in unattend.txt, 163
Send Message dialog box, 249, *249*
sending messages, **248–251**, *249*
separator page processors, 345
serial numbers, 73, 160
server-based computing, 1, 3, **31–32**
    memory in, **34–36**
    processor allocation basics in, **32–34**
Server Configuration dialog box, 296, *297*
Server counter, 402
Server object, 434
Server Settings folder, 47–48, **228–229**, *229*
server-side session settings, **217**
    ICA, **231–237**, *232*
    RDP. *See* RDP (Remote Desktop Protocol)
Server tab, 233
Server User Load rule, 302, 309
SERVERDOMAIN variable, 147
SERVERNAME variable, 147

servers
    application. *See* application servers
    cloning, 120, **169–170**
    communication with, **43–44**
    disks for, **85–93**
    farms. *See* farms
    groups of
        for application deployment, 333–335, *334*
        for ICA clients, **208–209**
        for network traffic reduction, 208–209
    naming, **94–95**
    for packagers, 317–318, 330, *331*
    for published applications, 295, *296–297*
    resource reports for, **418–421**, *418*, *421–422*
    roles of, **77–78**
    security for. *See* security
    shutting down, **261–262**
    structure of, 94
    terminal. *See* terminal servers
Servers task, 243
service packs
    applying, 121–122
    packaging, **325–327**, *326*
[ServicesSection] section, 142
session data, 43
session ids
    for access, 277
    obtaining, 246
Session Manager, 38–39
Session object, 434
sessions, 31, 34, **226**, **227**, **252**
    command-line tools for, **255–256**
    concurrent, **262–264**, *263–264*
    ending and preventing, **259–261**, *261*
    graphical tools for, **253–255**, *253–255*
    idle time in, 246
    initializing, **38–39**
    managing. *See* management tools
    mapping printers to, **371–373**, *372–373*
    printing in, 345–347, *346*
    shadowing, 11, **253–259**, *253–255*, *257–258*
    starting, **300–302**
    status of, 246
    time-outs for, **220–222**, *221*
    in Windows Terminal Services vs. MetaFrame, 22
Sessions tab, 54, *54*, 245
Sessions task, 243
SessionSpace, 36, 38, 40
SetDefaultPage key, 167
setup files, **177–178**, *178–179*
Setup floppies, 178, *178*

SETUP keys, **286–288**
Setup Manager, 129–130
Setup Wizard, 271, 273
    for MetaFrame installation, 157–160
    for RDP, 180
    for Terminal Services Licensing, 114
[SetupData] section, 140, 152
[SetupMgr] section, 132
Shadow Session dialog box, 57, *57*, 255, *255*
Shadow Taskbar, **57**, *57*
shadow tool, 52, 255–256
shadowing
    in MetaFrame, 11, **157–158**
    sessions, **253–259**, *253–255*, *257–258*
    taskbar for, 57, *57*
    in unattend.txt, 166
[Shadowing Restrictions] section, 166
shared environments, **265**
    application installation in, **269–272**, *271*
    application suitability in, **266–269**
shared temporary directories, 378
Show Users option, 241, 369
shutting down servers, **261–262**
SIF files, 150–151
SIFFILE variable, 148
simultaneous connections, 6
single applications, presenting, **390**
single-purpose servers, **317–318**
single-threaded programs, 79
16-bit applications, 27
size
    data stores, 354
    ICA windows, 211–212, *212*
    log files, 409
    published application windows, 294
    terminal servers. *See* terminal servers
slipstreaming, 121
SLR (SpeedScreen Latency Reduction), **58–59**, *59*
Small Computer Systems Interface (SCSI) drives, **85–86**
Smart Suite application, 278
SNA Client application, 279
SNA Server application, 279
soft errors, 83
Software Console, 123
Software Development Kit (SDK), 431
software RAID systems vs. hardware, **91–92**
sound
    bandwidth for, 99
    for RDP connections, 198
    in Windows .NET server, 8
    in Windows Terminal Services vs. MetaFrame, 22

Specify Application Limits screen, 295, *296*
Specify Servers screen, 296, *296*
Specify Users screen, 297–298, *297*
Specify What to Publish screen, 292, *293*
speed, memory, **81–83**
SpeedScreen Latency Reduction (SLR), **58–59**, *59*
.spl files, 343
spoolers, **342–343**, 345
SPOOLSS.DLL file, 342–343
SQL Server, 97–98
SRAM (static RAM), 79
SSL (Secure Sockets Layer), 15, *59*
SSL Relay Configuration tool, *59*, *60*
Ssonsvr.exe process, 397–398
Start Recording dialog box, 329, *329*
Start Shadowing dialog box, 254, *254*
Starting a Program screen, 190, *191*
starting ICA sessions, **300–302**
Startup Program setting, 234
statements, **427**, **429–431**
static RAM (SRAM), 79
stopping time for log files, 410
strings in VBScript, 427
stripe sets, 88
SUBERROR variable, 148
successes, logging, **385**
supported client types, **65**
    handheld PCs, **66**
    personal computers, **65**
    Windows terminals, **66**
SWIADMLE.MSI program, 122
Symbols folder, 324
SynAttackProtect entry, 395
synchronous DRAM (SDRAM), 81–83
SysInfo tab, 213
system bus type, **93**
System counter, 420
system directories
    hiding, 387
    permissions for, 378
system file updates, **121–122**
system global objects, 277
System Monitor, 17
    counters in, **398–406**, *398*
    logs with, **407**
        creating, **407–411**, *408–411*
        viewing, 412
    real-time statistics with, **406**
System Monitor objects, 404
System Snapshot report, 418, *418*

T

tab-delimited (.TSV) log files, 409, 412
tags in OSC files, **143–146**
Tame tool, 29, **289**
TAPI (Telephony API) settings, 157
TCO (Total Cost of Ownership), 26
TCP/IP with ICA connections, 208–209
TcpMaxHalfOpen entry, 395
TcpMaxHalfOpenRetried entry, 395
Telephony API (TAPI) settings, 157
temporary directories, 378
    deleting on exit, 48, 229
    in RDP settings, **227–228**, 227
Terminal Server Advanced Client (TSAC) package, 7
Terminal Server Client, 216
Terminal Server Client Access Licenses (TSCALs), 61, **66–70**, 74, 114–116
Terminal Server Edition (TSE), 4–5, 109
    for DOS applications, 289
    tsprof with, 225
"Terminal server has exceeded the maximum number of allowed connections" message, 204
Terminal Server Mode setting, 48
"Terminal Server sessions disabled" message, 204
Terminal Server toolkit, **46**
    MetaFrame tools. *See* MetaFrame XP
    Windows 2000 tools. *See* Windows 2000 Server
terminal servers, 1
    in deploying terminal services, **130–134**
    hardware for, **104–105**
    name setting for, 214
    number of, **93–94**
    operating systems for, **103–104**
    sizing, 78
        cache vs. and calculating speed in, **78–79**
        main memory, **80–81**
        memory reliability in, **83–84**
        memory speed considerations in, **81–83**
        processors in, **78–80**
        server disks in, **85–93**
Terminal Services administrator, 290
Terminal Services Client, 187–188, *187*, 191
Terminal Services Client Configuration tool, **47**, *47*
Terminal Services Client Creator, 178
Terminal Services Configuration tool, **47–49**, *49*
    for client printing, 364, *364*
    for RDP, 228
    for server connections, 260
    for server security, **377–378**
    for shadow settings, 256
Terminal Services counter, 420

Terminal Services Internet Connector License (TSICL), 70–71
terminal services licensing server, **134**
Terminal Services Licensing tool, 50, *50*, **114–119**, *115*, *117*, *119*
Terminal Services Manager object, 404
Terminal Services Manager tool, **49**, *50*
    for sending messages, 248–249
    for terminating applications, 251
    for user and process information, **245–246**, *245*
    for user sessions, **253**, *253*, 259
Terminal Services Profile and Home Directory setting, 234
Terminal Services Profile tab, 53, 224
Terminal Services Session object, 404
Terminal Services Setup screen, 112, *112*
terminal sessions. *See* sessions
[TerminalServices] section
    in ristndrd.sif, 154
    for terminal servers, 130, 134
terminating
    applications, **251–252**
    RDP sessions, 202
TermSrvr.mst file, 272
thin client computing, 1, 3
ThinWire performance enhancements, 16
threads, **32–34**, 79–80
thresholds for load balancing rules, 310–311
/TIME filtering switch, 382–384
time logged on, filtering audit information by, 383–384
time-out settings, **220–222**, *221*
times in VBScript, 427
TIMEZONE variable, 148
TMP files, deleting on exit, 229
Total Bytes counter, 404
Total Compressed Bytes counter, 405
Total Cost of Ownership (TCO), 26
Total Protocol Cache Hit Ratio counter, 405
touch screen settings, 214
Trace logs, 407
training, **106–107**
transferring RDP connection settings, 193
trees, **95–96**
troubleshooting
    client connections, **203–205**
    installation jobs, 337, *338*
True Color
    in ICA connections, 211
    support for, 9
trust-based routing, 96
trust query cycles, 96

TSAC (Terminal Server Advanced Client) package, 7
TSCALs (Terminal Server Client Access Licenses), 61, 66–70, 74, 114–116
tscon tool, 52
tsdiscon tool, 52, 260
TSE (Terminal Server Edition), 4–5, 109
    for DOS applications, 289
    tsprof with, 225
TSICL (Terminal Services Internet Connector License), 70–71
tskill tool, 52, 252
tsmkudir.cmd script, 282
tsmkufil.cmd script, 282
tsprof tool, 52, **224–226**
tsshutdn tool, 52, 262
.TSV (tab-delimited) log files, 409, 412
tuning
    installed applications, **272**
        benefits of, **273–277**, *275*
        compatibility scripts for, **278–283**
        editing manually, **277–278**
        Registry settings for, **283–290**, *286*, *288–289*
    shadowing permissions, **256–259**, *257–258*
twconfig tool, 63
txtsetup.sif file, 138
type variants, 427

U

UDFs (uniqueness database files), 128, **134–136**
unattend.txt file, 162–168
unattended installations. *See also* automatically deploying terminal services
    MetaFrame, **161–162**
        prep work for, **162–163**
        scripting for, **162–168**
        packaging in, **325–327**, *326*
Unattended Program package, 319
[Unattended] section
    in answer files, 127
    in ristndrd.sif, 140, 152
    for terminal servers, 131
UNC names, 332–333, *332*
uninstalling printer drivers, **356**, *357*
[UniqueIDs] section, 135
Uniqueness Database Files (UDFs), 128, **134–136**
universal printer drivers (UPDs), 12, **348–350**, *350*, 360
[Update ICA Clients] section, 167
updates
    client display protocols, **217**
    for MetaFrame installation, **160–161**

to profile information, **224–226**
system files, **121–122**
UPDs (universal printer drivers), 12, 349–350, *350*, 360
[Upgrade Settings] section, 168
upgrading in MetaFrame installation, **170–174**
UPN (User Principal Name) support, 95–96
% Usage counter, 400, 419
Usage Peak counter, 400
Usage Reports tab, 303–304, *303*
Use Connection Settings For Each Server option, 367
Use Default option, 208, 211
Use Default NT Authentication option, 394
Use Remote Control With the Following Settings option, 256
Use Standard Windows Authentication option, 231
Use Temporary Folders Per Session setting, 48
user applications, **390–391**
User Authentication Module, 33
user collaboration, 17
[User Data] section, 127
user global objects, 277
user interface, **24**
User Logon Settings, 235
user logon time, 246
USER NAME variable, 148
User object, 434
user policies, 18
User Policies task, 243
User Principal Name (UPN) support, 95–96
user sessions, **252**
    command-line tools for, **255–256**
    ending and preventing, **259–261**, *261*
    graphical tools for, **253–255**, *253–255*
    ids for, 246
    shadowing permissions for, **256–259**, *257–258*
[UserData] section
    in ristndrd.sif, 140, 152
    for terminal servers, 132
USERDOMAIN variable, 148
UserName key, 165
usernames
    with processes, 246
    referencing, **290**
users and user accounts
    auditing access by. *See* auditlog utility
    for client printer usage, **369–373**, *369–373*
    connections for, **262–264**, *263–264*
    information for, 5, **244–248**, *245*
    load balancing in, **96**
    for published applications, **297–298**, *297–298*
    Registry entries for, 273

Users tab – working sets   **457**

in shared environments, **269**
training, **106–107**
Users tab, 245–246, 249, 253
usrlogn1.cmd file, 281
usrlogn2.cmd file, 281
usrlogon.cmd file, 280–281

V

values
  in answer files, 126
  in Registry, 284
variables, 427, **429–430**
VBScript, 425–426
  data types in, **427–428**
  objects, properties, and methods in, **428–429**
  operators in, **428**
  procedures in, **428**
  statements in, **429–431**
VDMs (Virtual DOS Machines), 28, 267
video cards, **93**
video output in shared environments, **266**
Virtual Bytes counter, 405
Virtual Channel object, 434
Virtual DOS Machines (VDMs), 28, 267
virtual memory, **34–36**
Virtual Memory Manager (VMM), 34–35, 38
virtual printer ports, 346
virtual storage areas, 80
Visio application, 280
Visual Studio application, 279
VMM (Virtual Memory Manager), 34–35, 38

W

wait states, 82
warehouses, 25
WBTs (Windows-based terminals), 66, 101–102
Web Console, 12
web services for MetaFrame installation, **159**
wfcname.ini file, 169
WFS files, 317
Win16 client, **203**
Win32 Subsystem, 33
Win32K.SYS file, 39
WinChat application, 290
Window Manager, 39
window size
  for ICA, 211–212, *212*
  for published applications, 294

Windows 2000 Server, 5–7
  access licensing in, **66–70**
    application licensing, **75**
    Internet connector licenses, **70–71**
    MetaFrame licensing, **71–74**
  auditing. *See* auditlog utility
  installing terminal services on, **110–119**, *111–113, 115, 117, 119*
  management tools for, **46–47**
    command-line utilities, **50–52**
    Terminal Services Client Configuration, **47**, *47*
    Terminal Services Configuration, **47–49**, *49*
    Terminal Services enhancements, **52–55**, *53–54*
    Terminal Services Licensing, **50**, *50*
    Terminal Services Manager, **49**, *50*
  printing in, 341
    drivers for, 342, **357–358**
    GDI for, **342**
    mapping to sessions in, **371–372**
    monitors for, **344**
    process, **345–348**, *346–347*
    processors for, **343–344**
    providers for, **343**
    routers for, 343
    spoolers for, **342–343**
  System Monitor for. *See* System Monitor
Windows-based terminals (WBTs), 66, 101–102
Windows Components Wizard, **110–113**, *111–112*
Windows Management Instrumentation (WMI), 428
Windows .NET server, **7–9**
Windows operating systems
  application demands in, **286–289**, *286, 288–289*
  CE, 103
  load balancing in, **21**
Windows Script Host (WSH), 426, **430–431**
Windows Setup
  for RIS installation, 139
  for Terminal Services Licensing, 114
Windows Task Manager, 53
Windows terminals
  client connections on, **212–215**
  as client types, **101–102**
  support for, 25, 66
WinInstall, **122–125**
WinLogon process, 38–40
WINSPOOL.DRV file, 343
WMI (Windows Management Instrumentation), 428
Word application, 279–280
Working Set counter, 402, 405
working sets, 35, 80

/WRITE filtering switch, 383, 386
WSH (Windows Script Host), 426, 430–431

X

X Window system, 3

Y

"You do not have access to this session" message, 203

"Your interactive logon privilege has been disabled" message, 204

Z

Zone object, 434
ZoneName key, 164
zones, **42–44**
    in cloning servers, 169
    names for, 156

The Mark Minasi Windows® Administrator Series

The Essential Resource for Windows Administrators

- Written by leading authorities and reviewed by series editor **Mark Minasi**, author of the best-selling *Mastering Windows 2000 Server*

- Concise, focused material based upon real-world implementation of Windows

Windows 2000 Group Policy, Profiles, and IntelliMirror
Windows 2000 Group Policy has one goal: to make your administrative life easier. This book will help you understand what Group Policies are, how they're created, applied, and modified.

By Jeremy Moskowitz
0-7821-2881-5 • $49.99

Windows 2000 Automated Deployment and Remote Administration
If you're frustrated with the time required to perform simple tasks in Windows, then this book is for you. It is for experienced administrators who want to learn how to automate tasks they've been doing by hand.

By Christa Anderson
0-7821-2885-8 • $49.99

Windows 2000 Enterprise Storage Solutions
This book offers real-world coverage and examples of Windows 2000 storage enhancements, Storage Area Networks (SANs), cluster technology, file system backup/recovery, and SCSI (Small Computer Systems Integration) solutions.

By J. Peter Bruzzese and Chris Wolf
0-7821-2883-1 • $49.99

Windows Terminal Services
If you're a Windows administrator needing to provide remote employees and local clients access to applications installed on the server, then this is book you can't afford to be without. It addresses every issue Windows administrators need to know about to install, configure, and maintain Terminal Services from the ground up.

By Christa Anderson
0-7821-2895-5 • $49.99
Available October 2002

Linux for Windows Administrators
For Windows administrators or consultants who recognize the growing need for Linux skills, this book provides practical information on integrating Linux and Windows. Using familiar Windows terminology, the authors explain all of Linux's essentials, dispel its myths, and show how to use Linux in enterprise networks alongside Windows.

By Mark Minasi and Dan York
0-7821-4119-6 • $49.99
Available November 2002

SYBEX®
www.sybex.com

The Craig Hunt Linux Library

- Series content provides in-depth advanced coverage of key Linux topics that Linux professionals need to know

- Written or meticulously reviewed by Craig Hunt—best-selling author, renowned speaker, and Linux guru—along with top Linux authors

- Specifically written for networking professionals and systems administrators

Linux Journal Readers' Choice Award one of the **"Most Indispensible Linux Books"**

Linux System Administration, Second Edition
Vicki Stanfield, Roderick W. Smith
0-7821-4138-2 • $49.99

Named one of the **Top Five Linux Books** by Linux Online

Linux Apache Web Server Administration, Second Edition
0-7821-4137-4 • $49.99

Linux Samba Server Administration
Roderick W. Smith
0-7821-2740-1 • $39.99

Linux Network Servers
0-7821-4123-4 • $49.99

Linux Sendmail Administration
Roderick W. Smith
0-7821-2737-1 • $39.99

Linux DNS Server Administration
Craig Hunt
0-7821-2736-3 • $39.99

Linux Security
Ramón J. Hontañón
0-7821-2741-X • $49.99

Linux NFS and Automounter Administration
Erez Zadok
0-7821-2739-8 • $39.99

Written for Professionals, by Professionals

SYBEX®
www.sybex.com

The PC Problem-Solving Wonder!

Using easy-to-follow language, this book shows you how to prevent disasters, fix the ones that occur, and maximize your PC's power and longevity. Based on author Mark Minasi's popular $800 seminars, it is an unbelievable value.

ISBN: 0-7821-4075-0
$59.99 US

Updated to Cover Recent PC Advances

Over 1.5 Million copies sold!

Major Coverage of the 2003 Edition includes:

- QuickSteps Section
- Distinct Troubleshooting Sections
- Exclusive Mark Minasi Video
- Visual Guides to Nine Essential Upgrades
- New Section on Scanners
- Building the Ultimate Computer
- Rejuvenating Your Old Computer
- Buyers Guide
- Notebook Computers
- Flash Memory Cards

www.sybex.com   SYBEX®

TELL US WHAT YOU THINK!

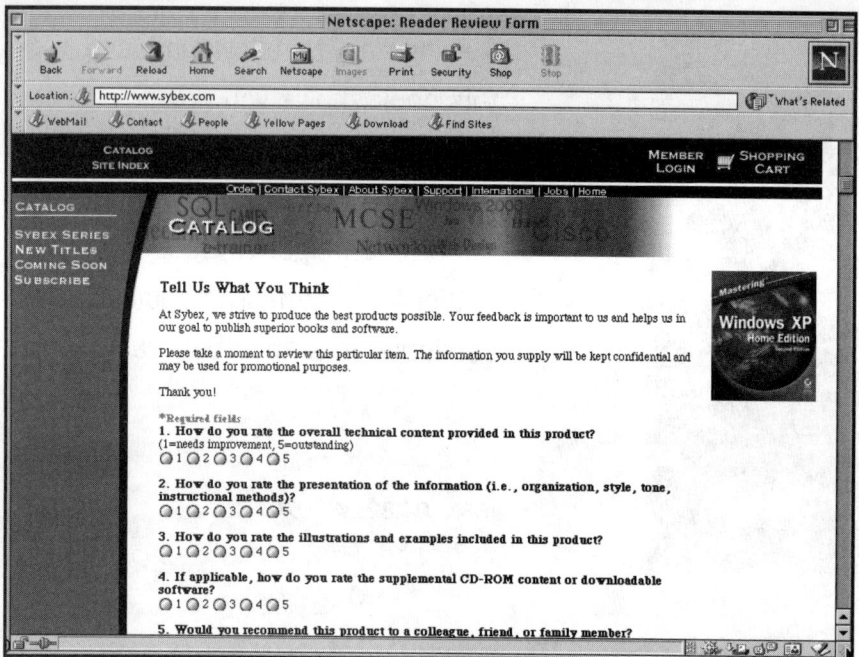

Your feedback is critical to our efforts to provide you with the best books and software on the market. Tell us what you think about the products you've purchased. It's simple:

1. Go to the Sybex website.
2. Find your book by typing the ISBN number or title into the Search field.
3. Click on the book title when it appears.
4. Click **Submit a Review**.
5. Fill out the questionnaire and comments.
6. Click **Submit**.

With your feedback, we can continue to publish the highest quality computer books and software products that today's busy IT professionals deserve.

www.sybex.com

SYBEX Inc. • 1151 Marina Village Parkway, Alameda, CA 94501 • 510-523-8233